GOVERNING AI

CYBERSECURITY AND RISK MANAGEMENT IN THE DIGITAL AGE

TOLULOPE MICHAEL

FOREWORD

The integration of artificial intelligence (AI) into our daily lives and business operations has marked the beginning of a new era in technology. As AI continues to evolve, it presents unprecedented opportunities and significant challenges, particularly in cybersecurity and risk management. **Governing AI: Cybersecurity and Risk Management in the Digital Age** addresses these critical issues with a depth and clarity that is both timely and essential.

This book begins by laying the foundational understanding of AI and its capabilities. The author provides a comprehensive overview of how AI works, its various applications across different sectors, and the ethical considerations that must be our concern. This sets the stage for a deeper exploration into the cyber threat landscape, highlighting how AI can bolster and threaten cybersecurity.

The current state of cyber threats is complex and ever-changing. Through detailed case studies and real-world examples, the author illustrates how cyber attackers are leveraging AI to conduct sophisticated attacks. They also demonstrate how AI can be used defensively, employing machine learning and other advanced techniques to detect, prevent, and respond to cyber threats more effectively than ever before.

One of the standout features of this book is its practical approach to AI-driven cybersecurity solutions. Readers are guided through the latest tools and technologies that utilize AI to enhance security measures. The discussion includes the use of AI for threat detection, automated incident response, and security analytics. These insights are invaluable for organizations looking to implement cutting-edge security solutions.

In addition to technical solutions, the book provides a robust framework for risk management. It outlines methodologies for assessing and mitigating the risks associated with AI, ensuring that organizations can integrate AI technologies while maintaining a strong security posture. This section is particularly useful for decision-makers who need to balance innovation with risk.

The regulatory landscape is another critical area covered in this book. As governments around the world grapple with the implications of AI, new regulations and compliance requirements are emerging. The author offers a thorough analysis of these regulatory frameworks, providing guidance on how organizations can achieve compliance and navigate the complex legal environment.

Ethical considerations are at the forefront of AI governance, and this book does not shy away from addressing these challenges. The author discusses issues such as algorithmic bias, transparency, and accountability, offering strategies for developing and deploying AI in a manner that is ethical and fair. This focus on ethics is essential for building public trust and ensuring that AI technologies are used responsibly.

Looking to the future, the book explores emerging trends and technologies that will shape the cybersecurity landscape in the years to come. Topics such as quantum computing, advanced AI techniques, and the evolving nature of cyber threats are discussed, providing readers with a forward-looking perspective on how to prepare for and adapt to these changes.

Governing AI: Cybersecurity and Risk Management in the Digital Age is an essential resource for anyone involved in the development, deployment, or governance of AI technologies. It offers a comprehensive guide to understanding the complexities of AI and cybersecurity, providing practical strategies for managing risks and ensuring the ethical use of AI.

TABLE OF CONTENTS

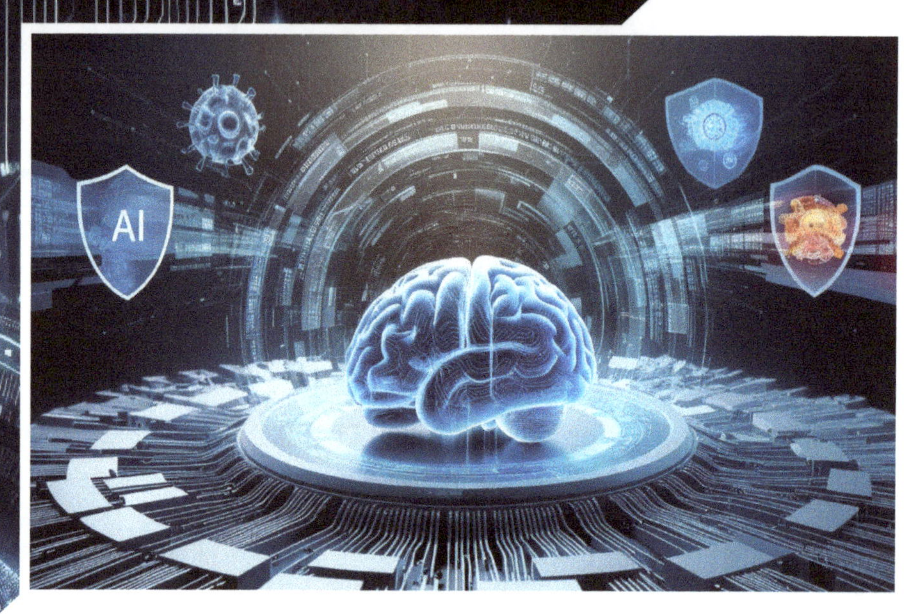

CHAPTER ONE
Introduction to AI and Cybersecurity

DEFINITION OF AI

Artificial Intelligence (AI) represents a groundbreaking field within computer science, focused on crafting systems that can emulate human intelligence. Imagine machines that can learn, reason, solve problems, perceive their environment, understand languages, and even interact just like humans. This is the essence of AI – where technology meets human-like capabilities. AI systems excel at processing vast amounts of data, identifying patterns, and making informed decisions. They can be broadly classified into two categories: narrow AI and general AI.

Narrow AI, or weak AI, specializes in performing specific tasks such as recognizing speech, classifying images, or providing recommendations, much like a highly skilled assistant dedicated to one particular job. For instance, IBM's Watson has demonstrated remarkable proficiency in diagnosing medical conditions by analyzing medical literature and patient data, vastly improving diagnostic accuracy (Ferrucci et al., 2010). Similarly, Google's DeepMind has achieved significant milestones in image recognition and game playing, exemplifying the prowess of narrow AI (Silver et al., 2016).

On the other hand, general AI, also known as strong AI, aims to replicate the full spectrum of human cognitive abilities, learning and applying intelligence across diverse tasks. While general AI remains a futuristic goal, with researchers like Bostrom (2014) exploring the potential impacts and ethical considerations, narrow AI is already making waves in our daily lives, powering everything from virtual assistants like Amazon's Alexa to sophisticated analytics in finance and cybersecurity.

The transformative potential of AI extends into the world of cybersecurity and risk management, where AI's capabilities can be harnessed to enhance system defenses and mitigate risks. AI-driven security solutions can rapidly detect and respond to threats, analyze vulnerabilities, and predict potential attacks, significantly improving the resilience of digital infrastructures (Nguyen et al., 2018). By leveraging machine learning algorithms, AI systems can continuously adapt to new threats, providing a dynamic and robust defense mechanism.

The ethical and governance implications of AI in cybersecurity are equally profound. Scholars like Brundage et al. (2018) have emphasized the importance of establishing comprehensive governance frameworks to ensure that AI technologies are developed and deployed responsibly. These frameworks should address issues such as transparency, accountability, and bias, ensuring that AI systems are fair, ethical, and aligned with societal values.

As we move deeper into the digital age, understanding the nuances of AI, its capabilities, and its implications for cybersecurity and risk management becomes increasingly critical. By exploring the intersection of AI and governance, we can pave the way for a safer, more secure digital future.

EVOLUTION OF AI

The evolution of AI can be traced back to ancient history, where myths and stories spoke of intelligent automatons and artificial beings.

Literature confirms that the term AI and AI-based systems came into existence in the 1950s (Duan et al., 2019). However, the formal study and development of AI began in the 20th century. Below is a timeline highlighting significant milestones in the evolution of AI:

EARLY CONCEPTS (PRE-20TH CENTURY):

🏳 **Ancient Myths and Philosophies:** Ancient Greek myths like Talos and Pandora's Box contained ideas about artificial beings. Philosophers like Aristotle contemplated the nature of human thought and mechanization.

1940S-1950S: THE BIRTH OF AI:

🏳 **Alan Turing:** Often considered the father of AI, Alan Turing introduced the concept of a machine that could simulate any algorithmic process—the Turing Machine. In 1950, he proposed the Turing Test to evaluate a machine's ability to exhibit intelligent behavior.

🏳 **John von Neumann:** His work on self-replicating machines and cellular automata laid the foundation for complex system modeling.

⚐ **The Dartmouth Conference (1956):** Coined the term "Artificial Intelligence" and marked the official start of AI as a field. Key attendees included John McCarthy, Marvin Minsky, Nathaniel Rochester, and Claude Shannon.

1960S-1970S: EARLY RESEARCH AND OPTIMISM:

⚐ **Logic Theorist and General Problem Solver (GPS):** Developed by Allen Newell and Herbert A. Simon, these programs were among the first to use heuristics to solve problems.

⚐ **ELIZA (1966):** Created by Joseph Weizenbaum, ELIZA was an early natural language processing computer program that simulated conversation.

⚐ **Shakey the Robot (1969):** Developed by SRI International, Shakey was one of the first robots to combine perception, mobility, and problem-solving.

1980S: AI WINTER AND EXPERT SYSTEMS:

⚐ **Expert Systems:** These are AI programs that mimic the decision-making abilities of human experts. Notable examples include MYCIN for medical diagnosis and DENDRAL for chemical analysis.

⚐ **AI Winter:** A period of reduced funding and interest in AI due to unmet expectations and the realization of the complexity involved in creating intelligent systems.

1990S-2000S: REVIVAL AND ADVANCEMENTS:

⚐ **Machine Learning and Data Mining:** Advances in algorithms, increased computational power, and the availability of large datasets led to a resurgence in AI research.

🏳 **Deep Blue (1997):** IBM's chess-playing computer defeated world champion Garry Kasparov, demonstrating the potential of AI in complex problem-solving.

🏳 **Robotic Advancements:** Honda's ASIMO robot showcased significant progress in robotics and AI integration.

2010S-PRESENT: DEEP LEARNING AND AI INTEGRATION:

🏳 **Deep Learning:** The development of deep neural networks, inspired by the human brain's structure, revolutionized AI. Breakthroughs in image and speech recognition, natural language processing, and autonomous systems were achieved.

🏳 **AlphaGo (2016):** Developed by Google DeepMind, AlphaGo defeated the world champion Go player Lee Sedol, a significant milestone in AI due to the complexity of the game.

🏳 **AI in Everyday Life:** AI has become integral to various applications, including virtual assistants (Siri, Alexa), recommendation systems (Netflix, Amazon), autonomous vehicles, and healthcare diagnostics.

KEY RESEARCH AND REPORTS ON AI EVOLUTION

Over the years, several research papers and reports have dramatically advanced our understanding and development of artificial intelligence (AI). One of the most seminal works is Alan Turing's 1950 paper, "Computing Machinery and Intelligence." In this groundbreaking piece, Turing introduced the idea that machines could potentially think and proposed the Turing Test, a concept that remains foundational in AI research to this day. Another pivotal moment in AI history was the 1955 proposal by John McCarthy and his colleagues for the Dartmouth Summer Research Project on Artificial Intelligence. This proposal essentially marked the birth of AI as a formal field of study, setting the stage for decades of research and development.

Fast forward to 1956, when Allen Newell and Herbert A. Simon presented "The Logic Theorist: A Model for Human Problem Solving." Their work introduced one of the first AI programs capable of solving problems using heuristics, laying the groundwork for many future AI algorithms. Jumping ahead to more recent times, the 2015 paper "Deep Learning" by Yann LeCun, Yoshua Bengio, and Geoffrey Hinton provided a comprehensive review of advancements in deep learning. These advancements have driven much of the recent progress in AI, pushing the boundaries of what is possible. In 2016, the One Hundred Year Study on Artificial Intelligence (AI100) at Stanford University produced the report "Artificial Intelligence and Life in 2030." This extensive study offers a detailed look at the current state of AI and explores its potential impacts on the future, providing invaluable insights for researchers and policymakers alike.

MODERN DEVELOPMENTS AND TRENDS IN AI

The 21st century has been a period of exponential growth for AI capabilities and applications. One of the key drivers of this growth has been the proliferation of data generated by digital devices and online activities. Big data has become the raw material that AI algorithms need to learn and improve their performance, fueling a wave of innovation and development. Alongside this data explosion, advancements in hardware have played a crucial role. The development of specialized hardware, such as Graphics Processing Units (GPUs) and Tensor Processing Units (TPUs), has significantly accelerated AI computations, allowing researchers to train more complex models faster than ever before.

In healthcare, AI applications have seen rapid growth, particularly in diagnostics, personalized medicine, and predictive analytics. AI algorithms are now capable of analyzing medical images to detect diseases like cancer with remarkable accuracy, transforming the landscape of medical diagnostics. The field of autonomous vehicles is another area where AI has made significant strides. Companies like

Tesla and Waymo are at the forefront, developing self-driving cars that rely heavily on AI for navigation, object detection, and real-time decision-making.

Natural Language Processing (NLP) has also seen remarkable advancements, with AI-powered systems like OpenAI's ChatGPT making significant strides in understanding and generating human language. These systems are now being used in various applications, including chatbots, translation, and content creation. However, as AI becomes more integrated into society, concerns about its ethical use, potential biases, and governance have emerged. Organizations and governments are now working to develop frameworks that ensure the responsible deployment of AI technologies.

CASE STUDIES AND IMPACT OF AI EVOLUTION

In healthcare, IBM's Watson has made headlines with its ability to analyze vast amounts of medical literature and patient data to assist doctors in diagnosing and treating diseases. A study published in Nature Medicine demonstrated that Watson could suggest treatment options for cancer patients that align closely with recommendations from expert oncologists. This highlights the transformative potential of AI in medical diagnostics and treatment planning.

The impact of AI is also being felt in the field of autonomous vehicles. Waymo's self-driving cars have logged millions of miles on public roads, showcasing the potential of AI to revolutionize transportation. According to a report by the National Highway Traffic Safety Administration (NHTSA), autonomous vehicles could significantly reduce traffic accidents caused by human error, potentially saving countless lives.

In the financial services sector, AI algorithms are being used to detect fraudulent activities in real-time. A report by McKinsey & Company highlighted that AI-driven fraud detection systems could reduce fraud losses by up to 50%, offering a powerful tool for banks and financial institutions to enhance their security measures.

Customer service is another area where AI is making a significant impact. AI-powered chatbots are now providing instant responses to customer inquiries, transforming the way businesses interact with their customers. According to Gartner, by 2022, 70% of customer interactions will involve emerging technologies such as machine learning applications, chatbots, and mobile messaging, underscoring the growing importance of AI in customer service.

In education, AI is being leveraged to create personalized learning experiences for students. Systems like Khan Academy use AI to tailor educational content to the individual learning paces and styles of students, providing a more customized and effective learning experience. This personalized approach is helping to revolutionize the way education is delivered, making it more accessible and effective for students worldwide.

THE SIGNIFICANCE OF CYBERSECURITY

Cybersecurity encompasses the protection of systems, networks, and data from digital attacks. These attacks often aim to access, alter, or destroy sensitive information, extort money from users, or disrupt normal business operations. In our increasingly interconnected world, effective cybersecurity is crucial for multiple compelling reasons.

One primary aspect of cybersecurity is the protection of sensitive data. With the exponential growth of data generation and sharing, it is imperative to safeguard personal, financial, and corporate information from unauthorized access. For example, in 2017, Equifax, one of the largest credit reporting agencies, suffered a data breach that exposed the personal information of 147 million people. This breach included

Social Security numbers, birth dates, and addresses, resulting in substantial financial losses and severe damage to Equifax's reputation. Such incidents underscore the critical need for robust cybersecurity measures to prevent unauthorized data access and mitigate potential repercussions.

Cybersecurity is also vital for national security. Cyber threats can target critical infrastructure, such as power grids, water supply systems, and communication networks, posing significant risks to national security. In 2015, Ukraine experienced a cyberattack on its power grid, leaving over 230,000 residents without electricity. This attack highlighted the vulnerabilities within national infrastructure and the necessity for governments to fortify their cyber defenses. Ensuring robust cybersecurity measures helps protect these critical systems from malicious activities that could have catastrophic consequences for public safety and national security.

Economic stability is another crucial factor influenced by cybersecurity. Cyberattacks can lead to severe economic impacts. According to a report by Accenture, cybercrime could cost the global economy up to $5.2 trillion over the next five years. For instance, the 2017 WannaCry ransomware attack affected organizations worldwide, including the UK's National Health Service (NHS), causing widespread disruption and financial loss. Effective cybersecurity helps maintain the stability and integrity of economic systems by preventing such damaging attacks. Companies can avoid significant financial losses, regulatory fines, and the erosion of customer trust by implementing robust cybersecurity practices.

Furthermore, trust in technology is essential for the continued adoption and advancement of digital innovations. Users need to feel confident that their data is secure for them to embrace new technologies. For example, the rapid growth of cloud computing services relies heavily on the trust users place in these platforms to protect their data. Strong cybersecurity measures help build and maintain this trust, facilitating technological advancements and digital transformation. By ensuring that data is secure, organizations can encourage the adoption of new technologies that drive innovation and efficiency.

TYPES OF CYBER THREATS

Cyber threats are continually evolving, becoming more sophisticated and harder to detect. Understanding these threats is crucial for developing effective defense strategies.

The digital threat today is as diverse as the cyber thugs, malicious insiders, nation-states, and criminal enterprises that deploy it. According to the U.S. government, more than 100 nations are engaged in technology and economic espionage. While many nations are targets of the cyber attackers in pursuit of proprietary information, the United States is target number one. The reason is straightforward. According to a Rand Corporation study, the United States leads the world in research and development, accounting for some 38 percent of the worldwide R&D spend. That's significant enough for cyber attackers to dedicate considerable resources to the task of stealing U.S. secrets.

Here are some of the most common types of cyber threats:

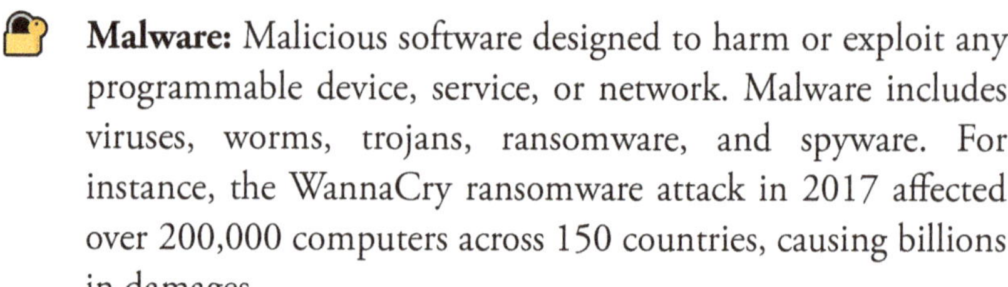

Malware: Malicious software designed to harm or exploit any programmable device, service, or network. Malware includes viruses, worms, trojans, ransomware, and spyware. For instance, the WannaCry ransomware attack in 2017 affected over 200,000 computers across 150 countries, causing billions in damages.

Phishing: A method of trying to gather personal information using deceptive emails and websites. Phishing attacks trick users into providing sensitive data such as usernames, passwords, and credit card numbers. According to the 2020 Verizon Data Breach Investigations Report (DBIR), 22% of data breaches involved phishing.

Man-in-the-Middle (MitM) Attacks: These occur when attackers intercept and alter communication between two parties without their knowledge. This can happen through unsecured public Wi-Fi networks or by exploiting vulnerabilities in communication protocols.

Denial-of-Service (DoS) Attacks: These attacks aim to make a network resource unavailable to its intended users by overwhelming it with a flood of illegitimate requests. Distributed Denial-of-Service (DDoS) attacks use multiple compromised systems to launch the attack. According to Kaspersky, the number of DDoS attacks increased by 52% in the first half of 2020 compared to the previous year.

SQL Injection: This involves inserting malicious SQL code into a query to manipulate the database and gain unauthorized access to data. SQL injection attacks can lead to data breaches and loss of sensitive information.

 **Zero-Day Exploits:** These are attacks that occur on the same day a vulnerability is discovered and before a fix or patch is implemented. Zero-day exploits are particularly dangerous as they can go undetected for a long time.

 **Advanced Persistent Threats (APTs):** These are prolonged and targeted cyber attacks in which an intruder gains access to a network and remains undetected for an extended period. APTs aim to steal data rather than cause immediate damage. Notable APT attacks include those attributed to nation-state actors targeting government and corporate entities.

KEY CYBERSECURITY STRATEGIES

Effective cybersecurity requires a comprehensive, multi-layered approach that incorporates several key strategies, designed to safeguard information systems, data, and critical infrastructure. With the evolving landscape of cyber threats, organizations must adopt both proactive and reactive measures to mitigate risks. Below are some of the most effective cybersecurity strategies, bolstered by data and research.

1. RISK ASSESSMENT AND MANAGEMENT

Risk assessment is the cornerstone of a solid cybersecurity strategy. This process involves identifying, evaluating, and prioritizing potential risks that could compromise an organization's digital assets. According to a study by PwC, over 45% of companies surveyed cited cyber risks as a top concern in 2023, emphasizing the importance of regular risk assessments. Effective risk management requires continual monitoring of vulnerabilities, implementing mitigation strategies, and ensuring compliance with industry standards such as ISO 27001 or NIST.

A robust risk management program often includes the creation of a risk register, categorizing risks based on their likelihood and impact. Implementing governance frameworks, such as COBIT or the Risk Management Framework (RMF), provides structured methods for addressing identified vulnerabilities. Additionally, third-party risk assessments can help organizations evaluate vendor-related risks, an increasingly important consideration given the rise in supply chain attacks, which surged by 42% in 2022 according to the National Cyber Security Centre (NCSC).

2. IMPLEMENTING STRONG AUTHENTICATION AND ACCESS CONTROLS

Unauthorized access remains a significant cybersecurity challenge. In 2023, over 61% of breaches involved compromised credentials, according to the Verizon Data Breach Investigations Report (DBIR). Strong authentication protocols, such as multi-factor authentication (MFA), can reduce the risk of unauthorized access by 99.9%, per Microsoft's research. Organizations should also adopt role-based access controls (RBAC), ensuring that employees only have access to the data and systems required for their job functions. This principle of least privilege minimizes potential damage in the event of a breach.

Moreover, password policies should enforce the use of complex, regularly updated credentials, and biometric authentication can offer additional layers of security.

3. REGULAR SOFTWARE UPDATES AND PATCH MANAGEMENT

Timely software updates and patch management are essential for mitigating vulnerabilities. In 2022, 82% of cyberattacks targeted vulnerabilities that had been known for at least two years, according to a report from IBM. Automated patch management systems can help organizations apply critical patches immediately, reducing the window of exposure. The use of vulnerability scanning tools such as Qualys or Tenable can assist in identifying outdated software and potential exploits.

Additionally, organizations should implement a structured patch management policy that prioritizes critical systems and ensures minimal disruption during updates.

4.   DATA ENCRYPTION

Data breaches continue to pose significant risks, with the average global cost of a breach reaching $4.45 million in 2023, as reported by IBM's Cost of a Data Breach study. Encrypting sensitive data, both at rest and in transit, helps to ensure that even if a breach occurs, the stolen information remains unreadable. AES-256, one of the most widely used encryption standards, is nearly impossible to break, making it ideal for securing sensitive data.

Organizations should also focus on strong key management practices, including the use of hardware security modules (HSMs) and regularly rotating encryption keys to prevent unauthorized access.

5.   NETWORK SECURITY

A robust network security architecture is crucial to protecting digital assets from unauthorized access and attacks. Implementing firewalls, intrusion detection/prevention systems (IDS/IPS), and secure network architecture are foundational practices. Gartner reported that 60% of businesses have now adopted Zero Trust Network Access (ZTNA) frameworks to ensure secure remote access, a significant shift following the surge in remote work.

Network segmentation is another vital strategy, limiting the lateral movement of attackers within the network. By segregating networks based on sensitivity and function, organizations can confine potential breaches and reduce the overall attack surface.

6. SECURITY AWARENESS TRAINING

Human error remains a leading cause of cyber incidents, with phishing accounting for 36% of breaches in 2023, according to the Verizon DBIR. Security awareness training is an effective way to reduce this risk. Programs that educate employees on recognizing phishing attempts, practicing safe internet usage, and maintaining strong passwords have been shown to reduce successful phishing attacks by up to 70%, according to the SANS Institute.

Training programs should be continuous, evolving alongside emerging threats. Topics should include social engineering, safe handling of sensitive data, and procedures for reporting suspicious activity.

7. INCIDENT RESPONSE AND RECOVERY PLANNING

Despite preventative measures, breaches may still occur, making incident response a critical component of cybersecurity strategy. An effective incident response plan should include steps for identifying, containing, eradicating, and recovering from cyber incidents. Research from Ponemon Institute shows that organizations with a robust incident response plan reduce the average cost of a breach by $1.2 million.

Organizations should conduct regular simulations and tabletop exercises to test the efficacy of their response plans, ensuring all team members understand their roles during a cyber incident. This preparedness helps minimize downtime and data loss while speeding up recovery efforts.

8.   USE OF ARTIFICIAL INTELLIGENCE AND MACHINE LEARNING

Artificial Intelligence (AI) and Machine Learning (ML) are transforming the way organizations approach cybersecurity. By 2025, 90% of businesses are expected to adopt AI for threat detection, according to Gartner. AI can analyze massive amounts of data in real-time, identifying patterns and anomalies that may signal a cyber threat. ML algorithms can adapt over time, learning from new threats to improve detection accuracy.

Tools such as Darktrace or CrowdStrike Falcon utilize AI to automatically detect and respond to threats, reducing response times and alleviating the pressure on security teams. These technologies can be especially effective in predicting potential attack vectors and automating the response to low-level threats, allowing human analysts to focus on more complex issues.

CYBERSECURITY REGULATIONS AND FRAMEWORKS

As the world becomes more interconnected and digitalized, the threat landscape has expanded, prompting governments and regulatory bodies to introduce stringent cybersecurity regulations and frameworks. These regulations aim to guide organizations in implementing effective cybersecurity measures, ensuring compliance with legal requirements, and safeguarding sensitive data. Below are some of the most critical and widely recognized cybersecurity regulations and frameworks, each playing a pivotal role in the global effort to secure digital environments.

GENERAL DATA PROTECTION REGULATION (GDPR)

The General Data Protection Regulation (GDPR) is one of the most comprehensive data protection laws in the world. Enacted by the European Union in 2018, it was designed to harmonize data privacy laws across Europe and protect EU citizens' data privacy. GDPR applies to any organization, regardless of location, that processes the personal data of EU residents. It requires companies to implement appropriate technical and organizational measures to ensure a high level of data protection.

One of the key provisions of GDPR is the mandatory reporting of data breaches. Organizations must notify the relevant supervisory authority within 72 hours of becoming aware of a breach. According to the European Data Protection Board (EDPB), there were over 160,000 data breach notifications in the first two years of GDPR enforcement, indicating the law's significant impact on organizational accountability.

The penalties for non-compliance are substantial, with fines reaching up to €20 million or 4% of the company's global annual turnover, whichever is higher. In 2022 alone, GDPR fines totaled over €1.3 billion, as reported by DLA Piper's Data Privacy Report, underscoring the serious financial implications for organizations that fail to meet its requirements.

HEALTH INSURANCE PORTABILITY AND ACCOUNTABILITY ACT (HIPAA)

In the United States, the Health Insurance Portability and Accountability Act (HIPAA) governs the protection of sensitive patient information. Passed in 1996, HIPAA was designed to improve the efficiency of healthcare services while safeguarding personal health information (PHI). HIPAA compliance is mandatory for healthcare providers, health plans, and clearinghouses, as well as their business associates.

HIPAA consists of several key rules, including the Privacy Rule, which sets national standards for the protection of health information, and the Security Rule, which establishes standards for securing electronically protected health information (ePHI). According to the U.S. Department of Health and Human Services (HHS), organizations must implement administrative, physical, and technical safeguards, such as encryption, access controls, and regular audits, to ensure the confidentiality, integrity, and availability of ePHI.

Violations of HIPAA can result in severe penalties, with fines ranging from $100 to $50,000 per violation, depending on the level of negligence, up to a maximum annual penalty of $1.5 million. In 2021, the HHS Office for Civil Rights (OCR) settled or imposed penalties in 14 cases, resulting in over $13.5 million in fines, demonstrating the agency's commitment to enforcing compliance.

PAYMENT CARD INDUSTRY DATA SECURITY STANDARD (PCI DSS)

The Payment Card Industry Data Security Standard (PCI DSS) is a globally recognized set of security standards developed to protect payment card data and prevent fraud. Established by the Payment Card Industry Security Standards Council (PCI SSC), PCI DSS applies to any organization that processes, stores, or transmits credit card information, including merchants, processors, and service providers.

The standard consists of 12 key requirements, which include implementing strong access control measures, encrypting cardholder data, and maintaining a secure network environment. According to the PCI SSC, organizations that fail to comply with PCI DSS can face fines ranging from $5,000 to $100,000 per month, as well as potential suspension of credit card processing capabilities.

Data from Verizon's 2022 Payment Security Report revealed that only 27.9% of organizations maintained full PCI DSS compliance, highlighting the ongoing challenges faced by businesses in securing payment card data. However, the benefits of compliance are clear—organizations that adhere to PCI DSS experience significantly fewer data breaches, with the Verizon DBIR reporting a 50% lower likelihood of a breach for compliant entities.

NATIONAL INSTITUTE OF STANDARDS AND TECHNOLOGY (NIST) CYBERSECURITY FRAMEWORK

The NIST Cybersecurity Framework, developed by the U.S. National Institute of Standards and Technology, provides voluntary guidelines for managing cybersecurity risks in critical infrastructure sectors. Initially published in 2014 and updated in 2018, the framework is structured around five core functions: Identify, Protect, Detect, Respond, and Recover. It is widely adopted across industries due to its flexibility and scalability.

According to the Ponemon Institute, 70% of organizations in the United States use the NIST Cybersecurity Framework to assess and improve their cybersecurity posture. The framework helps organizations to develop a comprehensive understanding of their cybersecurity risks and implement measures to mitigate those risks.

The NIST framework has also been influential internationally, with countries such as Japan, Israel, and Australia adopting similar models to enhance their national cybersecurity strategies. A 2022 study by Deloitte found that organizations implementing the NIST framework experienced a 20% reduction in cyber incidents over two years, showcasing its effectiveness in mitigating risks.

ISO/IEC 27001

ISO/IEC 27001 is an internationally recognized standard for information security management. Published by the International Organization for Standardization (ISO) and the International Electrotechnical Commission (IEC), ISO 27001 outlines the requirements for establishing, implementing, maintaining, and continually improving an Information Security Management System (ISMS). The standard provides a risk-based approach to managing sensitive company information, ensuring its confidentiality, integrity, and availability.

Organizations that achieve ISO 27001 certification demonstrate their commitment to robust cybersecurity practices. According to the 2022 ISO Survey, over 40,000 organizations worldwide are certified to ISO 27001, reflecting its global acceptance as a benchmark for information security management.

ISO 27001 certification is especially valuable for organizations that handle large volumes of sensitive data, such as financial institutions, healthcare providers, and government agencies. Certification can also offer a competitive advantage, as clients and partners are increasingly demanding proof of strong cybersecurity practices in their supply chain.

CASE STUDIES AND IMPACT OF CYBERSECURITY BREACHES

Cybersecurity breaches have far-reaching consequences, affecting millions of individuals and resulting in significant financial losses, legal consequences, and reputational damage for organizations. By examining major cybersecurity breaches in recent history, we can better understand the vulnerabilities that attackers exploit, the widespread impact of these incidents, and the lessons learned. Below is a detailed analysis of some of the most notorious breaches in recent years, each demonstrating unique vulnerabilities and responses.

EQUIFAX DATA BREACH (2017)

The Equifax data breach stands as one of the largest and most impactful cybersecurity incidents to date. In September 2017, Equifax announced that it had suffered a breach that exposed the personal data of 147 million individuals, including names, Social Security numbers, birth dates, addresses, and in some cases, driver's license numbers and credit card details. The breach occurred when hackers exploited a vulnerability in the Apache Struts web application framework, a flaw that had been identified and patched months earlier but had not been updated in Equifax's systems.

According to a report by the U.S. Government Accountability Office (GAO), the breach was estimated to cost Equifax over $1.4 billion, including costs for litigation, settlements, and remediation efforts. In July 2019, Equifax reached a settlement with the Federal Trade Commission (FTC), agreeing to pay up to $700 million, the largest ever data breach settlement at the time. The breach not only devastated Equifax's reputation but also served as a wake-up call for organizations to prioritize patch management and system updates to mitigate vulnerabilities.

TARGET DATA BREACH (2013)

The Target data breach, one of the first high-profile breaches of the modern era, resulted in the theft of credit and debit card information from approximately 40 million customers during the 2013 holiday shopping season. Attackers gained access to Target's network by compromising a third-party vendor responsible for its heating, ventilation, and air conditioning (HVAC) systems. Using stolen credentials, the attackers installed malware on Target's point-of-sale (POS) systems, allowing them to siphon card data.

In addition to card data, the personal information of 70 million customers, including names, addresses, phone numbers, and email addresses, was also compromised. Target faced over $200 million in legal fees, settlements, and losses. In 2017, Target reached an $18.5 million settlement with 47 U.S. states and the District of Columbia. The breach highlighted the critical importance of supply chain security and the need for robust third-party risk management protocols, as attackers continue to exploit vulnerabilities in trusted partners.

MARRIOTT INTERNATIONAL DATA BREACH (2018)

In November 2018, Marriott International revealed that hackers had breached its Starwood reservation database, exposing the personal information of up to 383 million guests. The breach, which had gone undetected for four years, compromised sensitive information such as passport numbers, credit card details, and email addresses. The attackers had gained access to the network as early as 2014, well before Marriott acquired Starwood Hotels in 2016.

Marriott faced significant financial consequences, including a £18.4 million ($24 million) fine imposed by the UK's Information Commissioner's Office (ICO) under the General Data Protection Regulation (GDPR). The breach not only impacted Marriott's reputation but also emphasized the need for due diligence in mergers and acquisitions, as inherited vulnerabilities from acquired entities can pose serious risks.

CAPITAL ONE DATA BREACH (2019)

In one of the most notable breaches in recent years, Capital One disclosed in July 2019 that a hacker had gained access to the personal information of over 100 million individuals in the U.S. and Canada. The hacker, Paige Thompson, a former Amazon Web Services (AWS) employee, exploited a misconfigured firewall in Capital One's cloud infrastructure. Sensitive information, including Social Security numbers, bank account details, and credit scores, was exposed in the breach.

Capital One faced a $80 million fine from the U.S. Office of the Comptroller of the Currency (OCC) for failing to establish proper security measures. Additionally, the company settled a class-action lawsuit in 2022 for $190 million. The breach underscored the challenges of securing cloud environments and the importance of proper configuration and monitoring in cloud security.

COLONIAL PIPELINE RANSOMWARE ATTACK (2021)

The Colonial Pipeline ransomware attack in May 2021 brought critical infrastructure cybersecurity to the forefront. The ransomware group DarkSide attacked Colonial Pipeline, one of the largest fuel pipelines in the U.S., encrypting its systems and demanding a ransom payment. The attack led to the temporary shutdown of 5,500 miles of pipeline, disrupting fuel supplies across the Eastern U.S. for nearly a week.

Colonial Pipeline paid a ransom of $4.4 million in Bitcoin, although U.S. law enforcement later recovered approximately $2.3 million. The breach highlighted the vulnerability of critical infrastructure to cyberattacks, prompting President Joe Biden to sign an executive order aimed at improving the nation's cybersecurity by requiring better information sharing between the public and private sectors and implementing stronger security standards for federal contractors.

SOLARWINDS SUPPLY CHAIN ATTACK (2020)

Discovered in December 2020, the SolarWinds attack was one of the most sophisticated and widespread cyber espionage campaigns in history. Hackers, believed to be linked to the Russian government, infiltrated SolarWinds' Orion software, used by thousands of organizations, including U.S. government agencies and Fortune 500 companies. The attackers inserted malicious code into the Orion software updates, which allowed them to compromise the systems of approximately 18,000 organizations.

The attackers were able to remain undetected for months, stealing sensitive data from agencies like the U.S. Department of Homeland Security and the Treasury Department. The full extent of the damage is still being assessed, but the breach underscored the dangers of supply chain attacks and the need for continuous monitoring and verification of software updates. In response, the U.S. government issued Executive Order 14028, mandating enhanced cybersecurity requirements for federal contractors.

FACEBOOK DATA BREACH (2021)

In April 2021, personal data from over 533 million Facebook users was found exposed online. The data included phone numbers, full names, email addresses, and locations. Although Facebook claimed that the data was scraped from the platform in 2019 due to a vulnerability in its "Add Friend" feature, the leak highlighted the ongoing challenges of protecting user privacy on social media platforms.

The breach did not involve sensitive information like passwords, but it put millions of users at risk of phishing attacks and identity theft. While Facebook did not face major financial penalties for this breach, the incident raised further concerns about data privacy on social media platforms and the need for better security practices.

These case studies highlight the evolving and varied nature of cybersecurity breaches, from the exploitation of unpatched vulnerabilities, as seen in the Equifax and WannaCry attacks, to supply chain attacks like SolarWinds, and the growing risk of ransomware, as demonstrated by Colonial Pipeline. Each incident underscores the need for robust security measures, including timely patching, vendor risk management, cloud security, and continuous monitoring. As cyber threats become more sophisticated, organizations must adapt and evolve their cybersecurity strategies to protect their data, systems, and reputations.

THE INTERSECTION OF AI AND CYBERSECURITY

As technology continues to evolve at a rapid pace, both AI and cybersecurity have become pivotal in shaping the future of industries, economies, and societies.

AI is transforming various sectors by providing advanced analytics, automating processes, and enhancing decision-making capabilities. Its ability to process vast amounts of data, recognize patterns, and make predictions has revolutionized fields such as healthcare, finance, manufacturing, and retail. For instance, AI algorithms are now used for disease diagnosis, risk assessment, predictive maintenance, and personalized marketing, thereby driving efficiency and innovation.

On the other hand, cybersecurity has become increasingly critical as the frequency, sophistication, and impact of cyber threats have grown exponentially. Cybersecurity involves protecting systems, networks, and data from digital attacks, which can result in data breaches, financial losses, and reputational damage. With the rise of digital transformation, organizations are more vulnerable to cyber threats than ever before. The adoption of cloud services, Internet of Things (IoT) devices, and remote work environments has expanded the attack surface, making robust cybersecurity measures essential.

The economic impact of both AI and cybersecurity is significant. According to McKinsey, AI has the potential to add $13 trillion to the global economy by 2030, boosting productivity and fostering innovation. Concurrently, cybercrime could cost the global economy up to $5.2 trillion over the next five years, as reported by Accenture. These figures highlight the dual importance of leveraging AI to drive economic growth and ensuring cybersecurity to protect that growth from malicious threats.

THE GROWING CONVERGENCE OF AI AND CYBERSECURITY FIELDS

The convergence of artificial intelligence (AI) and cybersecurity is no longer just a technological trend but a critical development in the modern digital landscape. As cyber threats become increasingly complex and sophisticated, the integration of AI into cybersecurity practices offers powerful solutions that enhance threat detection, automate incident responses, provide advanced threat intelligence, and combat fraud. The ability of AI to process vast amounts of data in real-time, adapt to evolving threats, and learn from new patterns makes it indispensable in the realm of cybersecurity. This section explores the key areas where AI is revolutionizing cybersecurity and provides examples of how organizations are leveraging these advancements.

ENHANCED THREAT DETECTION

Traditional threat detection methods, such as rule-based and signature-based systems, are increasingly inadequate in detecting sophisticated cyberattacks. These approaches rely on predefined rules or known patterns of malicious activity, which makes them less effective against novel threats that do not match existing signatures. AI, particularly machine learning (ML) algorithms, offers a more advanced solution by detecting threats based on patterns, anomalies, and behavior in real-time.

Machine learning models are trained to analyze vast datasets of network traffic and user behavior to identify irregularities that may indicate a security threat. For example, AI can detect phishing attempts by analyzing the content of emails and users' behavioral patterns. An AI-powered system can flag anomalies such as unusual login locations, suspicious file downloads, or the subtle signs of phishing in email communications—alerts that traditional systems might miss.

According to a study by IBM, companies using AI for cybersecurity experience an average reduction in data breach costs of 80%, underscoring AI's role in fortifying threat detection systems. Moreover, AI can continue to learn and improve its detection capabilities over time, staying ahead of evolving threats.

PREDICTIVE ANALYTICS AND PROACTIVE DEFENSE

Another facet of AI's contribution to cybersecurity is its predictive analytics capabilities. AI systems analyze historical data to identify patterns that may indicate potential future attack vectors, allowing organizations to prepare for threats before they occur. By leveraging AI-driven predictive analytics, cybersecurity teams can deploy proactive defense measures, reducing the window of opportunity for cybercriminals.

A 2019 study by Capgemini revealed that 69% of organizations believe AI enhances the accuracy of threat prediction. The ability to anticipate threats before they materialize is vital in today's dynamic threat landscape, where cybercriminals constantly innovate their tactics. This proactive stance helps organizations strengthen their defenses and ensures they can stay one step ahead of adversaries.

AUTOMATED INCIDENT RESPONSE

AI has made remarkable strides in automating incident response, one of the most critical components of cybersecurity. The traditional approach to responding to security incidents can be slow and labor-intensive, often requiring human analysts to identify the breach, isolate affected systems, and take remedial actions. In contrast, AI-driven automated response systems can detect, analyze, and respond to incidents in real time, reducing the time it takes to contain and mitigate a breach.

Automated AI systems can take immediate actions such as isolating compromised endpoints, blocking malicious IP addresses, and deploying security patches—actions that would typically take human analysts hours or even days to complete. According to McAfee's 2021 Global Threat Report, AI-enabled automated response systems have been shown to reduce the average time to contain a data breach by up to 74%, drastically minimizing potential damage and ensuring business continuity.

ENHANCED THREAT INTELLIGENCE

The sheer volume of threat data generated daily can overwhelm cybersecurity teams. In 2022, it was estimated that global cyberattacks increased by 38%, making it difficult for human analysts to process and interpret the deluge of threat information efficiently. AI-powered threat intelligence platforms can aggregate and analyze vast quantities of data from multiple sources, including system logs, traffic data, security alerts, and even open-source intelligence from the dark web.

AI's ability to process data at speeds up to 1,000 times faster than human analysts allows for quicker identification of vulnerabilities, emerging attack vectors, and malicious behaviors. According to Gartner, AI-driven cybersecurity systems can analyze data from a variety of sources—ranging from internal security logs to social media and hacker forums—to provide actionable insights that human analysts might overlook. This comprehensive approach helps security teams gain a more holistic view of the threat landscape and make informed decisions more rapidly.

Additionally, natural language processing (NLP), a branch of AI, allows for the processing of unstructured data. This means AI systems can analyze and extract relevant information from text-heavy sources such as news articles, blogs, or underground hacker discussions on the dark web. By examining this unstructured data, AI can detect emerging threats and indicators of compromise (IoCs), thus providing earlier warnings of attacks.

FRAUD DETECTION AND PREVENTION

AI has also proven to be a powerful tool in fraud detection and prevention, especially in the financial sector. Cyber fraud remains a growing concern, and traditional rule-based fraud detection systems are often inadequate in detecting sophisticated and rapidly evolving fraudulent behaviors. AI-powered systems can monitor transactions and other activities in real-time, learning from patterns and anomalies that might indicate fraudulent activity.

Machine learning models can identify behavioral patterns that are associated with fraud, such as unusual purchasing behaviors, access from unfamiliar devices, or abnormal transaction locations. For instance, AI systems can detect deviations from an individual's normal behavior, flagging transactions for review before they result in significant losses.

According to a report by the Association of Certified Fraud Examiners (ACFE), organizations that use AI for fraud detection saw a 50% reduction in fraud losses compared to those using traditional methods. AI's ability to continuously learn and adapt to new fraud tactics ensures that fraud detection systems remain effective even as cybercriminals innovate their methods.

AI'S CHALLENGES IN CYBERSECURITY

Despite its numerous benefits, AI in cybersecurity is not without challenges. One of the primary concerns is the potential for AI systems themselves to be targeted by adversarial attacks. Hackers can exploit vulnerabilities in AI models, feeding them manipulated data to deceive them into making incorrect decisions. Furthermore, AI models are only as effective as the data they are trained on; poor or biased data can lead to inaccurate predictions and inadequate threat responses.

Another challenge lies in the cost and complexity of implementing AI-based cybersecurity solutions. AI-driven systems often require significant computational power and specialized expertise, making them inaccessible to smaller organizations. Moreover, the lack of transparency in how AI algorithms arrive at decisions – commonly referred to as the "black box" problem – can make it difficult for organizations to fully trust AI-driven outcomes without human oversight.

IMPORTANCE OF GOVERNING AI IN TODAY'S WORLD

Artificial Intelligence (AI) is transforming every aspect of our lives, from how we communicate to how we work, shop, and entertain ourselves. Its rapid evolution and integration into various sectors have brought about unprecedented advancements and efficiencies. However, with these developments come significant challenges and risks. Governing AI in today's world is crucial to ensure that its benefits are maximized while mitigating potential harms. This section looks into the multifaceted importance of AI governance, covering ethical considerations, legal and regulatory frameworks, economic impacts, social implications, security and safety concerns, promotion of trust, and the fostering of innovation and research.

ETHICAL CONSIDERATIONS IN AI GOVERNANCE

The rapid advancement and integration of artificial intelligence (AI) into various sectors, including cybersecurity, healthcare, finance, and law enforcement, have brought ethical considerations to the forefront of discussions on AI governance. As AI systems become increasingly influential in decision-making processes that impact individuals and society at large, there is a growing need to establish and enforce ethical principles that safeguard human rights, promote fairness, and ensure transparency and accountability.

PROTECTING HUMAN RIGHTS

At the core of ethical AI governance is the protection of fundamental human rights, including privacy, autonomy, and freedom from discrimination. AI systems, if left unchecked, have the potential to infringe on these rights. For instance, facial recognition technology, which is powered by AI, has raised concerns about surveillance and the potential for its misuse in monitoring individuals without their consent. A 2020 report by Amnesty International highlighted the risks of AI-powered surveillance infringing on privacy rights and facilitating authoritarian practices in certain regions.

Moreover, AI systems can sometimes make decisions that affect individuals' access to essential services, such as healthcare or housing. If not carefully governed, these systems could perpetuate biases or make unfair determinations. For example, research has shown that algorithms used in hiring processes may inadvertently discriminate against women or minority groups due to biases in the training data.

To address these issues, governments and organizations must establish ethical frameworks that prioritize the protection of human dignity and equal treatment.

FAIRNESS AND MITIGATING BIAS

One of the critical ethical challenges in AI is ensuring fairness and mitigating bias. AI systems are typically trained on vast datasets, and if these datasets reflect existing societal biases, the AI models can inadvertently perpetuate or even amplify those biases. This phenomenon is known as algorithmic bias. A notable example occurred in 2019 when a healthcare algorithm used to predict patient needs was found to favor white patients over Black patients, even though Black patients had a greater need for medical care.

To prevent such outcomes, AI governance must include rigorous auditing of training datasets and the algorithms themselves. Researchers and practitioners are exploring ways to implement fairness constraints within AI models to ensure that outcomes do not disproportionately harm marginalized or vulnerable groups. Ethical AI frameworks must also prioritize inclusivity in AI development, encouraging diverse teams of developers to reduce the risk of biases going unnoticed. According to a study published by the Brookings Institution, diverse teams are better equipped to identify and mitigate algorithmic bias in AI systems.

TRANSPARENCY AND EXPLAINABILITY

Transparency is another key ethical principle in AI governance. As AI systems become more complex and operate autonomously in certain cases, it becomes increasingly difficult for users and even developers to understand how the system arrives at its decisions. This opacity is often referred to as the "black box" problem, where AI algorithms, particularly those using deep learning techniques, provide little insight into their decision-making processes.

Ethical AI governance demands that AI systems be explainable. Users should be able to understand the rationale behind AI-driven decisions, especially in high-stakes contexts such as law enforcement, healthcare, and finance. Explainability not only fosters trust in AI systems but also allows individuals to challenge decisions they believe to be unfair or incorrect. In 2020, the European Union introduced the General Data Protection Regulation (GDPR), which includes provisions granting individuals the right to explanation when subjected to automated decision-making.

In response to these concerns, researchers are developing techniques such as interpretable machine learning, where AI models are designed to be more transparent and explainable. This development aligns with growing regulatory pressure for "AI explainability" in sectors such as finance and healthcare. Ethical AI governance frameworks must encourage the adoption of such techniques to ensure accountability and fairness.

ACCOUNTABILITY AND RESPONSIBILITY

Accountability is crucial in the deployment of AI systems, especially when these systems are used to make decisions that significantly affect individuals' lives. One of the challenges with AI is determining who is responsible when an AI system causes harm or makes an incorrect decision—the developer, the organization using the system, or the AI itself? This question of accountability is complex, particularly as AI systems become more autonomous.

Ethical AI governance requires clear guidelines on accountability. Organizations deploying AI systems must take responsibility for the outcomes of these systems, including any unintended negative consequences. Additionally, mechanisms should be in place for redress in cases where individuals are adversely affected by AI-driven decisions. Governments and regulatory bodies must also hold companies accountable for ensuring their AI systems comply with ethical standards.

A widely discussed example of accountability in AI governance occurred in 2018 when a self-driving Uber car struck and killed a pedestrian. This incident sparked debates over the responsibility of developers, users, and regulators in ensuring the safety of autonomous systems. As AI continues to evolve, similar questions around accountability will need to be addressed by policymakers and developers alike. We will take a closer look at this later on in this book.

ETHICAL FRAMEWORKS AND REGULATION

Several frameworks have been proposed to ensure ethical AI governance. The European Union's Ethics Guidelines for Trustworthy AI, published in 2019, outlines seven key requirements for AI systems: human agency and oversight, technical robustness and safety, privacy and data governance, transparency, diversity and fairness, societal well-being, and accountability. These guidelines emphasize the need for AI systems to be aligned with ethical principles while also promoting innovation and technological progress.

In the U.S., the National Institute of Standards and Technology (NIST) has been developing a framework for AI governance that focuses on ensuring that AI systems are reliable, transparent, and accountable. Similarly, organizations such as the Institute of Electrical and Electronics Engineers (IEEE) have introduced the "Ethically Aligned Design" framework, which provides guidance on designing AI systems that prioritize human well-being and ethical considerations.

Governments are also increasingly implementing regulations to enforce ethical AI use. For example, the European Union's proposed AI Act aims to regulate the use of AI across various sectors, particularly in high-risk areas such as healthcare, law enforcement, and finance. The AI Act is designed to ensure that AI systems adhere to strict ethical guidelines, including requirements for transparency, accountability, and non-discrimination. It also introduces provisions for the regulation of AI applications that are considered too risky, such as those involving biometric surveillance and social scoring systems.

In addition to government-led initiatives, several industry bodies and global organizations are pushing for more ethical AI development. The Organisation for Economic Co-operation and Development (OECD) released its "AI Principles" in 2019, which emphasize respect for human rights, fairness, and accountability in AI design and implementation. These guidelines have been adopted by over 40 countries and serve as a foundation for building robust ethical frameworks globally. Similarly, UNESCO has drafted an AI ethics recommendation that focuses on ensuring AI systems contribute to sustainable development and uphold human rights.

ADDRESSING BIAS AND DISCRIMINATION IN AI SYSTEMS

Artificial Intelligence (AI) systems hold great promise for improving decision-making processes across various domains, from hiring practices to criminal justice. However, these systems are only as unbiased as the data they are trained on, and when historical and societal biases are present in these datasets, the AI systems can produce discriminatory outcomes. This section explores the pervasive issue of bias in AI, provides real-world examples of its impact, and discusses strategies for detecting and mitigating bias to ensure that AI systems promote fairness and equity.

THE PERVASIVENESS OF BIAS IN AI

Bias in AI systems arises primarily from the datasets used to train machine learning models. These datasets often reflect historical inequalities and societal biases, which can be inadvertently encoded into AI algorithms. As a result, AI systems can perpetuate, or even exacerbate, existing discrimination. This issue is particularly concerning because AI systems are increasingly being used in high-stakes decisions that affect people's lives, such as hiring, lending, healthcare, and criminal justice.

One prominent example is the use of AI in hiring processes. Studies have shown that AI algorithms designed to screen job applicants can exhibit gender bias, favoring male candidates over female ones. This bias often stems from the training data, which may include historical hiring data that reflects past discrimination against women. In 2018, Amazon had to discontinue an AI recruiting tool after discovering that it systematically downgraded resumes that included the word "women's," as in "women's chess club captain," based on patterns learned from male-dominated resume data.

Another example is the COMPAS (Correctional Offender Management Profiling for Alternative Sanctions) algorithm, an AI system used to assess the risk of recidivism in criminal justice settings. A 2016 study by ProPublica revealed that COMPAS was biased against African Americans, consistently rating them as higher risk for reoffending compared to white defendants with similar profiles. This bias had serious implications, potentially influencing decisions about bail, sentencing, and parole in a racially discriminatory manner.

These examples underscore the need for a concerted effort to address bias in AI systems, particularly in applications that have significant consequences for individuals and society.

TECHNIQUES FOR DETECTING AND MITIGATING BIAS

Addressing bias in AI requires a multi-faceted approach that includes detecting, understanding, and mitigating bias throughout the AI development process. Several techniques have been developed to help organizations and developers create fairer AI systems.

1. **BIAS AUDITING:**

    Bias auditing involves systematically evaluating AI systems to identify potential biases in the data, algorithms, and outcomes. This process includes examining the training data for representativeness, checking for discriminatory patterns in the AI model's predictions, and testing the system across various demographic groups. Bias audits can be conducted both before and after deployment to ensure that the AI system behaves fairly in real-world applications.

A notable example of bias auditing is the work done by researchers at MIT's Media Lab, who audited commercial facial recognition systems and found that they performed significantly worse on darker-skinned and female faces compared to lighter-skinned and male faces. This audit prompted several companies to improve their algorithms to reduce bias, demonstrating the impact that thorough bias auditing can have on AI systems.

2. **DIVERSE DATA COLLECTION:**

One of the most effective ways to reduce bias in AI systems is to ensure that the training data is diverse and representative of the populations the AI system will serve. This means collecting data from a wide range of demographic groups, including different genders, races, ages, and socio-economic backgrounds. Diverse data helps to prevent the AI system from learning biased patterns that reflect only a subset of the population.

For example, Google's AI division launched the "Inclusive Images Challenge" to encourage developers to build AI models that perform well across diverse global populations. By using a more representative dataset that included images from various cultures and regions, the models developed through this initiative were able to reduce bias and improve accuracy across different demographic groups.

3. **ALGORITHMIC TRANSPARENCY AND EXPLAINABILITY:**

Transparency and explainability are crucial for understanding how AI systems make decisions and for identifying potential biases in those decisions. An AI system is considered transparent if its decision-making processes can be easily understood by humans, and it is explainable if the reasons for its decisions can be clearly articulated.

Algorithmic transparency allows stakeholders, including developers, regulators, and end-users, to scrutinize the AI system for biases and to hold the system accountable. For example, the European Union's General Data Protection Regulation (GDPR) includes provisions that give individuals the right to explanation when they are subject to automated decision-making processes. This regulatory requirement has prompted organizations to develop AI systems that are more transparent and capable of providing explanations for their decisions.

Explainability also helps in diagnosing and correcting biases in AI models. Techniques such as LIME (Local Interpretable Model-agnostic Explanations) and SHAP (SHapley Additive exPlanations) allow developers to understand how specific features in the data influence the AI model's predictions, making it easier to detect and mitigate bias.

4. ONGOING MONITORING AND EVALUATION:

Bias in AI systems can evolve over time, particularly as new data is introduced or as the AI system is applied in different contexts. Therefore, ongoing monitoring and evaluation are essential to ensure that AI systems continue to operate fairly. This involves regularly updating the training data, retraining models, and re-evaluating the AI system's performance across different demographic groups.

For instance, financial institutions that use AI for credit scoring are increasingly implementing continuous monitoring practices to ensure that their models do not develop biases against certain demographic groups. This proactive approach helps to maintain fairness and prevents discriminatory outcomes as the AI system adapts to new data and changing market conditions.

THE ROLE OF GOVERNANCE AND REGULATION

To effectively address bias and discrimination in AI, it is essential to establish robust governance frameworks and regulatory guidelines. Governing bodies must set clear standards for detecting, mitigating, and reporting bias in AI systems. These standards should include requirements for bias auditing, diverse data collection, algorithmic transparency, and ongoing monitoring.

Several organizations and governments are already taking steps to regulate AI to prevent bias and discrimination. For example, the European Union's proposed AI Act includes provisions specifically designed to address bias in AI systems, particularly those used in high-risk areas such as law enforcement, employment, and healthcare. The Act requires that AI systems undergo rigorous testing for fairness before they can be deployed and mandates transparency in how AI decisions are made.

Additionally, the U.S. National Institute of Standards and Technology (NIST) is developing a framework for AI risk management that includes guidelines for identifying and mitigating bias in AI systems. These efforts represent an important step towards ensuring that AI systems are fair, accountable, and aligned with societal values.

ENSURING TRANSPARENCY AND ACCOUNTABILITY IN AI SYSTEMS

As artificial intelligence (AI) continues to permeate various sectors—particularly healthcare, law enforcement, and finance—the importance of transparency and accountability in AI decision-making processes becomes paramount. Without clear and accessible explanations of how AI systems function, there is a risk of unaccountable, biased, or harmful outcomes that could undermine trust in these technologies. To build and maintain this trust, developers and organizations must prioritize transparency in AI design and ensure robust accountability frameworks that allow stakeholders to challenge and rectify AI-driven decisions. This section explores the importance of transparency and accountability, provides real-world examples of opaque AI systems, and discusses strategies for achieving clearer AI governance.

THE IMPORTANCE OF TRANSPARENCY IN AI DECISION-MAKING

Transparency refers to the ability of users and stakeholders to understand how AI systems make decisions, particularly when these decisions have significant consequences for individuals or society. In areas such as healthcare, law enforcement, and finance, AI systems are increasingly being relied upon to make high-stakes decisions—whether it's diagnosing medical conditions, determining parole eligibility, or assessing creditworthiness. The decision-making processes of these systems need to be clear and explainable to ensure fairness, accuracy, and trust.

For example, in healthcare, AI algorithms are being used to diagnose diseases, recommend treatments, and predict patient outcomes. In such critical contexts, it is essential for medical professionals and patients to understand the rationale behind AI-driven recommendations. If an AI system recommends a certain course of treatment, doctors need to understand the factors influencing that decision to determine whether it aligns with the patient's best interests. A lack of transparency could lead to mistrust in the technology and, potentially, harmful outcomes if errors go undetected. According to a study by the World Health Organization (WHO), transparency in AI systems used in healthcare improves clinical decision-making and patient outcomes by enabling medical practitioners to better evaluate AI-generated insights.

Similarly, in law enforcement, AI systems are increasingly being used for predictive policing and risk assessment. These tools can influence decisions regarding surveillance, policing strategies, and even sentencing. Without transparency, AI algorithms could reinforce or exacerbate existing biases within the criminal justice system. A lack of transparency also makes it difficult for individuals to challenge the fairness or accuracy of decisions that affect their lives. The AI Now

Institute's 2019 report highlighted numerous cases in which opaque AI systems led to unaccountable outcomes, particularly in predictive policing, where the algorithms often lacked clear explanations of how they arrived at specific conclusions.

RISKS OF OPAQUE AI SYSTEMS

Opaque, or "black box," AI systems are those in which the decision-making process is not easily understood by users or even by developers themselves. These systems, particularly those using deep learning techniques, often involve complex neural networks that operate with minimal human intervention. While this level of complexity can enable remarkable feats of prediction and automation, it also creates significant challenges for transparency and accountability.

One high-profile example of the risks associated with opaque AI systems is the use of AI in financial credit scoring. Many financial institutions use AI algorithms to determine an individual's creditworthiness. However, when these systems are opaque, consumers often have little insight into why they were denied a loan or received a low credit score. This lack of transparency makes it nearly impossible to challenge or appeal decisions, leading to frustration and potential harm, particularly for marginalized groups who may already face systemic discrimination in lending practices. A 2021 report by the Consumer Financial Protection Bureau (CFPB) found that the opaque nature of AI credit scoring models contributes to a lack of accountability and fairness in the financial industry.

In the criminal justice system, the use of AI in risk assessment tools like COMPAS (Correctional Offender Management Profiling for Alternative Sanctions) has also raised concerns. As mentioned in a study by ProPublica, COMPAS, which is used to predict recidivism, is notoriously opaque, making it difficult for defendants to understand why they were rated as high or low risk. The study found that COMPAS was more likely to incorrectly label Black defendants as high-risk compared to white defendants. The lack of transparency in how the AI arrived at these risk assessments made it nearly impossible for defendants to challenge these potentially life-altering decisions.

STRATEGIES FOR ENSURING TRANSPARENCY

Achieving transparency in AI systems requires intentional design choices that prioritize explainability and openness. Several strategies have emerged to help AI developers and organizations ensure that their systems are more transparent, fair, and accountable.

1. **EXPLAINABLE AI (XAI):**

    Explainable AI refers to the development of AI systems that can provide clear and understandable explanations for their decisions. Techniques such as LIME (Local Interpretable Model-agnostic Explanations) and SHAP (SHapley Additive exPlanations) allow developers to break down complex AI models into simpler, interpretable components. For example, if an AI system used in healthcare predicts a patient's likelihood of developing a disease, explainable AI techniques can show the specific factors (e.g., age, lifestyle, family history) that contributed to the prediction. By making AI systems more interpretable, explainable AI can foster trust and ensure that AI-driven decisions are grounded in logical, transparent reasoning.

    Explainability is particularly important in high-stakes areas like healthcare, finance, and law enforcement, where decisions can have profound effects on individuals' lives. According to a 2020 study by the European Commission's High-Level Expert Group on AI, adopting explainable AI frameworks leads to more accountable AI systems and empowers users to make informed decisions based on AI outputs.

2. ALGORITHMIC TRANSPARENCY:

Algorithmic transparency involves making the workings of an AI system open and accessible to those who use or are affected by it. This can include providing documentation about how the system was developed, what data it was trained on, and what ethical safeguards were implemented. For example, the GDPR (General Data Protection Regulation) mandates that individuals have the right to explanation when subjected to decisions made by automated systems, ensuring that organizations using AI in critical areas provide sufficient transparency regarding how decisions are made.

Transparency in AI can also help identify biases and potential flaws in the system before they cause harm. For instance, in 2018, after pressure from civil rights groups, Microsoft made parts of its AI ethics review process public, allowing stakeholders to better understand how AI decisions were being guided by ethical considerations. This kind of openness helps build public trust and ensures that AI systems are held to high ethical standards.

3. CONTINUOUS MONITORING AND AUDITING:

Transparency alone is not enough—AI systems must also be subject to continuous monitoring and auditing to ensure that they remain fair, accurate, and accountable over time. Ongoing audits can help detect biases or errors that may arise as the system interacts with new data or environments. A report by the International Association of Privacy Professionals (IAPP) emphasized that regular auditing of AI systems, particularly in sectors like finance and healthcare, can help organizations identify and mitigate risks before they lead to widespread harm.

For example, financial institutions using AI for credit scoring could conduct regular audits to ensure that the system does not disproportionately harm certain demographic groups. This proactive approach to monitoring helps ensure that AI systems continue to operate transparently and equitably as they evolve.

THE ROLE OF ACCOUNTABILITY

Accountability in AI governance means holding the appropriate parties responsible for the outcomes of AI-driven decisions. This involves creating clear guidelines that define who is accountable when an AI system makes a harmful or incorrect decision. Developers, companies, and users must all play a role in ensuring that AI systems are deployed ethically and responsibly.

To facilitate accountability, organizations should implement "AI governance frameworks" that outline the ethical standards, decision-making processes, and accountability measures for AI systems. These frameworks should clearly define who is responsible for auditing the system, addressing biases, and correcting errors. Governments and regulatory bodies also have a role in ensuring accountability through the establishment of legal standards and penalties for companies that fail to maintain transparent and responsible AI practices.

In 2020, the European Union introduced a proposal for the Artificial Intelligence Act, which outlines legal requirements for AI systems, particularly in high-risk areas. The Act mandates strict accountability measures for organizations using AI in critical sectors and ensures that individuals have the right to challenge AI-driven decisions. This legislation aims to create a legal framework that balances innovation with ethical responsibility, ensuring that AI systems are both transparent and accountable.

RESPECTING PRIVACY AND PROTECTING DATA IN AI SYSTEMS

Artificial Intelligence (AI) systems thrive on data, often requiring vast amounts of information to operate effectively. This reliance on data, however, presents significant privacy risks, especially when sensitive personal information is involved. With increasing concerns about how data is collected, stored, and used by AI systems, there is an urgent need for governance frameworks that prioritize privacy and implement robust data protection standards. This section delves into the critical role of data privacy in AI, explores real-world challenges, and highlights the importance of regulatory frameworks like the General Data Protection Regulation (GDPR) in safeguarding individual rights.

THE IMPORTANCE OF DATA PRIVACY IN AI

As AI systems become more pervasive in industries ranging from healthcare to finance and marketing, they depend heavily on personal data to make predictions, offer personalized services, and improve decision-making processes. However, the collection of such data often raises concerns about user privacy, data security, and how individuals' information is being utilized. In many cases, AI systems require access to sensitive data, such as health records, financial details, or behavioral information, which can easily be misused or inadequately protected if proper safeguards are not in place.

According to a 2020 Cisco Consumer Privacy Survey, 84% of respondents expressed concern about data privacy and indicated a desire for more control over how their personal information is collected and used. This highlights the growing demand for data privacy as a fundamental right, particularly in the age of AI. The survey further found that trust is a critical factor in whether consumers are willing to share their data with organizations, suggesting that businesses must implement strong data protection measures to maintain customer confidence.

In an era where AI systems can collect, analyze, and infer vast amounts of information about individuals, respecting privacy and safeguarding personal data is not just a legal obligation, but also an ethical imperative. The challenge lies in finding a balance between harnessing the potential of AI and protecting individual rights in a world where personal data is increasingly valuable.

PRIVACY RISKS IN AI SYSTEMS

One of the primary privacy risks associated with AI is the sheer volume of data that these systems require. The more data an AI system has access to, the more accurate and effective its predictions or recommendations can be. However, this large-scale data collection often occurs without users fully understanding how their information is being used or even that their data is being collected. For instance, many AI-powered applications, such as social media platforms and digital assistants, continuously gather behavioral data to offer personalized content or recommendations. While these services provide convenience, they also create a situation where vast amounts of personal information are stored in centralized databases, making them vulnerable to breaches or misuse.

A study by the International Association of Privacy Professionals (IAPP) found that AI systems are frequently used to mine data from social media profiles, online interactions, and even smart devices, often without clear consent from the individuals whose data is being harvested. This lack of transparency can lead to privacy violations, especially when organizations fail to disclose the full scope of data collection or how the data is being processed.

Moreover, AI systems can inadvertently lead to privacy breaches even when they are designed with security in mind. For example, facial recognition technologies used in law enforcement and public surveillance have raised concerns about privacy and consent, especially when deployed in public spaces where individuals may not be aware that they are being monitored. The indiscriminate collection of biometric data by AI systems creates a significant risk to individual privacy, and in some cases, the lack of clear legal and ethical guidelines exacerbates this problem.

REGULATORY FRAMEWORKS AND DATA PROTECTION STANDARDS

To address these privacy risks, governance frameworks that enforce stringent data protection standards are essential. One of the most comprehensive and well-known regulatory frameworks is the General Data Protection Regulation (GDPR), implemented by the European Union in 2018. The GDPR sets a global benchmark for data privacy and protection, with a focus on ensuring that individuals have control over how their personal data is collected, processed, and shared.

The GDPR requires organizations to obtain explicit consent from individuals before collecting their data, particularly when it comes to sensitive information such as health records, financial data, or biometric details. This ensures that users are fully informed about how their data will be used and provides them with the right to withdraw consent at any time. Additionally, the regulation mandates that data be securely stored and processed, with organizations required to implement appropriate security measures to prevent unauthorized access, data breaches, or misuse.

One of the most significant provisions of the GDPR is the "right to be forgotten," which allows individuals to request the deletion of their personal data from an organization's databases. This right is especially important in the context of AI, where vast amounts of data can be used to build detailed profiles of individuals, sometimes with far-reaching implications. By allowing individuals to request the erasure of their data, the GDPR empowers users to take control of their digital footprint and reduce the risk of long-term privacy violations.

Moreover, the GDPR also requires organizations to ensure data minimization—collecting only the data that is necessary for a specific purpose. This principle is particularly relevant to AI, where there is a tendency to collect large datasets without a clear understanding of how all the data will be used. By enforcing data minimization, the GDPR helps to prevent the unnecessary accumulation of personal information, reducing the risks associated with large-scale data breaches or unauthorized use.

The success of the GDPR in setting high standards for data privacy has influenced other countries to adopt similar regulations. For instance, the California Consumer Privacy Act (CCPA) in the United States incorporates many of the GDPR's key principles, including the right to know what data is being collected, the right to opt-out of data collection, and the right to request deletion of personal data. These regulatory frameworks are critical in ensuring that AI systems respect privacy and protect sensitive information in a global context.

PRIVACY BY DESIGN AND ETHICAL AI DEVELOPMENT

To further enhance privacy in AI systems, organizations are increasingly adopting the principle of "Privacy by Design." This approach advocates for embedding privacy protections into the development lifecycle of AI technologies, ensuring that privacy is not an afterthought but a fundamental aspect of system design. Privacy by Design requires developers to consider privacy implications at every stage of AI development—from data collection and processing to algorithmic decision-making and storage.

Privacy by Design involves several key practices, including data anonymization, encryption, and the use of secure data-sharing protocols. For example, anonymizing personal data before it is processed by AI systems can help reduce the risk of privacy violations in the event of a data breach. Similarly, encryption ensures that sensitive information remains protected even if unauthorized individuals gain access to the data.

Ethical AI development also extends beyond technical solutions. It involves fostering a culture of transparency, accountability, and respect for user rights. Organizations that deploy AI must be open about how their systems operate and provide users with clear information on how their data is used. This transparency helps build trust between users and organizations and ensures that AI systems are developed in ways that align with societal values.

THE ROLE OF CONSENT AND CONTROL

Another critical aspect of respecting privacy in AI is ensuring that individuals maintain control over their data. The concept of informed consent is central to data privacy, particularly in AI applications that rely on extensive data collection. Users must be given clear, easily understandable information about what data is being collected, how it will be used, and for what purpose. In many cases, organizations may attempt to obscure or downplay the extent of data collection, making it difficult for users to make informed decisions.

To address this, regulatory frameworks like the GDPR have introduced strict consent requirements, mandating that organizations provide users with clear, unambiguous options to consent or decline data collection. Furthermore, these frameworks ensure that users can easily withdraw consent if they no longer wish to share their data. This gives individuals greater control over their personal information and limits the potential for misuse by organizations or AI systems.

LEGAL AND REGULATORY FRAMEWORKS FOR AI GOVERNANCE

The rapid development and widespread deployment of artificial intelligence (AI) technologies have introduced complex challenges that existing legal and regulatory structures were not designed to handle. As AI systems become more integral in sectors such as healthcare, finance, transportation, and law enforcement, there is an increasing need for robust legal frameworks to ensure ethical deployment, safety, transparency, and accountability. This section explores the necessity of legal frameworks in AI governance, highlights examples of existing regulations, and provides an updated overview of the European Union's Artificial Intelligence Act, one of the most comprehensive efforts to regulate AI technologies.

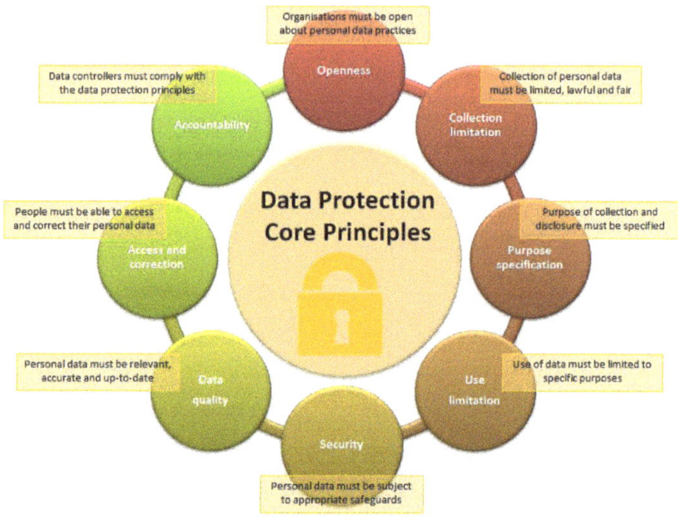

Legal and Regulatory Frameworks for AI Governance

THE NEED FOR LEGAL AND REGULATORY FRAMEWORKS

AI systems are unique in their ability to learn, adapt, and make autonomous decisions, which presents significant governance challenges. Without adequate legal frameworks, the deployment of AI systems can lead to unintended consequences, such as bias, discrimination, privacy violations, and safety risks. Furthermore, the absence of comprehensive regulation can undermine public trust in AI technologies and create ambiguities about accountability when AI-driven decisions result in harm or other negative outcomes.

A key challenge in AI governance is defining responsibility when AI systems make erroneous or harmful decisions. For instance, if an autonomous vehicle causes an accident or if an AI-powered hiring system discriminates against candidates based on gender or race, it may be unclear whether liability lies with the developers, the deploying organization, or even the AI system itself. Legal frameworks must address such complexities by clearly defining accountability, ensuring that responsible parties can be held accountable for the actions and outcomes of AI systems.

Additionally, as AI systems are often fueled by large datasets, concerns around data privacy, ownership, and security are central to AI governance. Effective legal frameworks must balance enabling innovation with protecting individual rights, particularly when sensitive personal data is involved. As AI technologies continue to evolve, the urgency of implementing comprehensive legal frameworks to safeguard these rights increases.

OVERVIEW OF EXISTING AI REGULATIONS AND GUIDELINES

Several regions have begun to implement AI-specific regulations. The European Union's AI Act, proposed in 2021, aims to create a harmonized framework for AI regulation, categorizing AI applications based on their risk levels and setting strict requirements for high-risk AI systems. The United States, while not yet having a comprehensive AI regulation, has issued guidelines through the National Institute of Standards and Technology (NIST) and the Federal Trade Commission (FTC) emphasizing transparency, fairness, and accountability in AI development. According to a report by the Brookings Institution, a harmonized regulatory approach can prevent a fragmented landscape that hampers innovation and increases compliance costs.

THE ROLE OF INTERNATIONAL COOPERATION IN AI GOVERNANCE

Artificial intelligence (AI) is a global technology that transcends borders, impacting industries, societies, and economies worldwide. Given its widespread influence, the governance of AI cannot be effectively managed by individual countries acting in isolation. International cooperation is essential for establishing comprehensive, consistent, and effective AI governance frameworks that address both the opportunities and risks posed by this transformative technology. International organizations such as the United Nations (UN) and the Organisation for Economic Co-operation and Development (OECD) play pivotal roles in fostering global dialogues and establishing internationally recognized standards. This section explores the importance of international cooperation in AI governance, the challenges of creating and enforcing regulations, and the economic implications of AI governance.

IMPORTANCE OF INTERNATIONAL COOPERATION

AI technologies are developed, deployed, and utilized across borders, often in ways that challenge existing national regulations and create gaps in governance. For example, AI systems used by multinational companies or cloud-based AI services can operate in multiple jurisdictions, each with different legal frameworks and privacy laws. Without international cooperation, inconsistencies in AI regulation could lead to conflicts between national laws, complicating enforcement and creating loopholes that malicious actors could exploit.

International cooperation provides a pathway for countries to establish consistent standards for AI governance, ensuring that ethical principles, safety protocols, and accountability measures are upheld worldwide. Organizations such as the UN and the OECD are instrumental in driving these efforts. Their work facilitates the development of global norms and guidelines that countries can adopt or adapt to their specific legal frameworks, fostering a shared understanding of AI governance.

One of the most significant initiatives in this space is the OECD's Principles on AI, which were adopted in 2019 by over 40 countries, including the United States, the European Union, and Japan. These principles emphasize five core pillars:

1. **INCLUSIVE GROWTH, SUSTAINABLE DEVELOPMENT, AND WELL-BEING**

   AI technologies should contribute to inclusive economic growth, sustainable development, and the well-being of people. This involves ensuring that AI systems are designed and deployed in ways that benefit society as a whole, including marginalized groups.

2. **HUMAN-CENTERED VALUES AND FAIRNESS:**

   AI systems must respect human rights, autonomy, and dignity, and should not perpetuate or exacerbate biases. Fairness is a critical aspect of this principle, emphasizing that AI must be developed and used in ways that prevent discrimination and promote equality.

3. **TRANSPARENCY AND EXPLAINABILITY:**

   AI systems should be transparent, and their decision-making processes should be understandable to users. Explainability is particularly important in high-stakes sectors such as healthcare, finance, and criminal justice, where AI decisions can have profound effects on individuals' lives.

4. **ROBUSTNESS, SECURITY, AND SAFETY:**

   AI systems must be robust, secure, and safe throughout their lifecycle. This principle underscores the importance of resilience to cyberattacks, reliability in diverse conditions, and safeguarding against unintended consequences.

5. **ACCOUNTABILITY:**

   Organizations and individuals responsible for AI systems must be held accountable for their decisions and actions. This includes establishing clear lines of responsibility and liability when AI systems cause harm or produce biased outcomes.

By adopting these principles, OECD member countries have created a foundation for more cohesive and collaborative AI governance. These principles serve as a blueprint for national policies and regulations, encouraging countries to align their domestic laws with internationally recognized ethical standards.

CHALLENGES IN CREATING AND ENFORCING AI REGULATIONS

The development and enforcement of AI regulations are inherently challenging due to several factors, including the rapid pace of technological advancements, the complexity of AI systems, and the global nature of AI deployment. Regulators must strike a delicate balance between protecting public interests—such as privacy, security, and fairness—while fostering innovation and economic growth.

One of the primary challenges is the speed at which AI technologies evolve. Traditional regulatory processes are often slow and reactive, making it difficult for policymakers to keep pace with emerging AI capabilities and risks. As highlighted in the 2020 Stanford AI Index Report, the gap between the development of AI technologies and the creation of corresponding regulations is widening. This lag can result in outdated or inadequate regulations that fail to address current and future risks.

Moreover, AI systems are inherently complex and opaque, making it difficult for regulators to fully understand how they operate or how their decisions are made. This complexity poses significant challenges in enforcing regulations, as it requires continuous monitoring, auditing, and adaptation to ensure compliance. In many cases, AI systems are designed as "black boxes," where even the developers may not fully understand the inner workings of the model, making it difficult to establish accountability.

Another significant challenge is ensuring global consistency in AI regulation. Different countries have varying priorities and approaches to AI governance. For example, the European Union (EU) has prioritized human rights and data privacy, as evidenced by its General Data Protection Regulation (GDPR) and the proposed AI Act, which strictly regulate the use of AI in high-risk sectors. In contrast, the United States has taken a more laissez-faire approach, focusing on sector-specific regulations and encouraging self-regulation within the tech industry. China, on the other hand, has implemented stringent state-led AI governance, particularly in areas such as surveillance and social control.

This divergence in regulatory approaches creates challenges for multinational companies and international AI collaborations, as they must navigate conflicting legal requirements across different jurisdictions. Without international harmonization, there is also the risk of regulatory arbitrage, where companies may relocate or develop AI technologies in countries with weaker regulations to avoid stringent oversight.

ECONOMIC IMPACT OF AI GOVERNANCE

AI governance has profound implications for economic growth, innovation, and competition. Effective governance can provide clear guidelines and ethical standards that foster innovation by building trust among consumers, investors, and businesses. Conversely, poor or inconsistent governance can stifle innovation, exacerbate economic disparities, and limit access to AI technologies.

One of the primary ways AI governance impacts the economy is by setting the conditions under which AI technologies can be developed and deployed. Clear and predictable regulations reduce uncertainty for businesses and investors, allowing them to innovate with confidence. For example, the EU's proposed AI Act aims to provide legal certainty and a consistent regulatory framework for companies developing and deploying AI across Europe, ensuring that AI technologies meet high ethical standards without stifling innovation.

However, overly restrictive regulations can have negative economic consequences. If regulatory burdens are too high, they may hinder AI development by imposing costly compliance requirements on companies, particularly small and medium-sized enterprises (SMEs). This could result in reduced competitiveness and slower economic growth in regions with stringent AI regulations. A 2021 report by the World Economic Forum (WEF) warned that overly rigid AI governance could disproportionately impact emerging economies, where regulatory frameworks may not yet be fully developed, leading to economic disparities between countries.

On the other hand, well-designed AI governance frameworks can enhance economic stability by addressing concerns about job displacement, data privacy, and inequality. For instance, by ensuring that AI technologies are developed and used in ways that prioritize fairness and inclusivity, governments can mitigate the risk of AI exacerbating existing societal inequalities. According to a report by the McKinsey Global Institute, AI could contribute up to $13 trillion to the global economy by 2030, but the distribution of these benefits will depend heavily on the governance frameworks in place to manage AI's societal impacts.

BALANCING INNOVATION AND REGULATION TO FOSTER ECONOMIC GROWTH

AI has the potential to drive substantial economic growth by increasing productivity and enabling new business models. However, over-regulation can hinder innovation and slow down AI adoption. A report by PwC estimates that AI could contribute up to $15.7 trillion to the global economy by 2030, with the greatest gains in productivity coming from automation of routine tasks. Governance frameworks must strike a balance, providing enough oversight to ensure safety and fairness without imposing excessive burdens on developers and businesses. Regulatory sandboxes, where companies can test AI technologies under regulatory supervision, can help achieve this balance.

THE ROLE OF GOVERNANCE IN PREVENTING MONOPOLIES AND ENSURING FAIR COMPETITION

The artificial intelligence (AI) market is increasingly dominated by a few large technology companies, raising significant concerns about monopolistic practices, market concentration, and the potential stifling of innovation. These dominant players, often referred to as "Big Tech," have the resources, data, and infrastructure to outpace smaller competitors, creating an environment where new entrants and startups struggle to survive. Effective governance is crucial in preventing monopolies, ensuring fair competition, and fostering a vibrant, diverse AI ecosystem. This section examines the role of governance in promoting competitive markets, encouraging responsible AI development, and addressing the broader social implications of AI.

PREVENTING MONOPOLIES IN THE AI MARKET

The concentration of power in the hands of a few large technology companies can lead to monopolistic practices that undermine competition, limit consumer choice, and stifle innovation. These companies, by virtue of their vast resources and control over critical data, can establish barriers to entry that make it difficult for smaller firms to compete. This dominance not only affects market dynamics but also has broader societal implications, including the potential for increased inequality and reduced access to emerging technologies.

Governance frameworks play a vital role in preventing monopolies and promoting a level playing field in the AI market. One of the primary strategies is the promotion of open standards and interoperability. By encouraging the development and adoption of open AI standards, regulators can reduce dependency on proprietary systems controlled by a few dominant players. Open standards allow for greater interoperability between different AI systems, enabling smaller companies and startups to compete more effectively.

Additionally, antitrust policies and pro-competitive regulations are essential tools in curbing monopolistic behavior. According to a 2020 report by the Center for Data Innovation, antitrust actions against dominant tech companies, coupled with policies that promote competition, can help dismantle barriers to entry and foster a more competitive AI landscape. For example, regulators can impose restrictions on mergers and acquisitions that would further concentrate market power or require dominant firms to provide access to critical datasets and AI technologies under fair and reasonable terms.

Supporting smaller players and startups through funding, grants, and incentives is another crucial aspect of governance. Governments can create innovation funds specifically targeted at AI startups, providing financial support and resources to help them scale and compete with larger incumbents. Tax incentives and public-private partnerships can also be used to encourage investment in emerging AI companies, fostering a more diverse and dynamic market.

ENCOURAGING RESPONSIBLE AI DEVELOPMENT AND DEPLOYMENT

Beyond preventing monopolies, governance frameworks should actively incentivize the development and deployment of AI systems that prioritize social good and adhere to ethical considerations. AI has the potential to address some of society's most pressing challenges, such as improving healthcare outcomes, enhancing educational access, and promoting environmental sustainability. However, realizing this potential requires governance structures that promote responsible AI development.

The European Commission's White Paper on AI, published in 2020, underscores the importance of creating a trustworthy AI ecosystem that balances innovation with ethical standards. The paper advocates for a risk-based approach to AI regulation, where high-risk AI applications—such as those in healthcare, law enforcement, and transportation—are subject to stricter oversight and compliance requirements. This approach ensures that AI systems used in critical areas are safe, transparent, and aligned with societal values.

Governments can further encourage responsible AI development by offering grants and tax incentives for projects that focus on social good. For instance, AI applications designed to tackle climate change, improve public health, or reduce educational disparities could receive preferential funding or tax breaks. Public-private partnerships are also an effective mechanism for driving investment in responsible AI. By collaborating with private sector companies, governments can leverage additional resources and expertise to advance AI projects that benefit society.

Moreover, ethical AI certifications and labeling schemes can be introduced to recognize and promote AI systems that meet high ethical standards. These certifications would signal to consumers and businesses that an AI system has undergone rigorous evaluation and adheres to principles of fairness, transparency, and accountability. This not only helps build trust in AI technologies but also encourages developers to prioritize ethical considerations in their design and deployment processes.

SOCIAL IMPLICATIONS OF AI

AI's pervasive influence extends beyond markets and governance, profoundly affecting social structures, employment, and access to technology. As AI systems become more integrated into daily life, their impact on society must be carefully managed to ensure equitable outcomes.

IMPACT OF AI ON EMPLOYMENT AND THE WORKFORCE

AI is transforming the job market by automating routine tasks, increasing productivity, and creating new opportunities in high-tech fields. However, this transformation also poses significant risks, particularly in terms of job displacement and widening skill gaps. As AI and automation technologies continue to advance, workers in certain industries may find their roles automated, leading to job losses and economic dislocation.

A study by the McKinsey Global Institute estimates that by 2030, up to 375 million workers globally may need to switch occupational categories due to the impact of AI and automation. This shift presents a major challenge for policymakers and businesses alike. Without proactive measures, the rapid pace of technological change could exacerbate inequality, leaving behind workers who lack the skills needed to thrive in a tech-driven economy.

Governance frameworks must address these challenges by promoting workforce reskilling and upskilling programs. These initiatives are critical for helping workers transition to new roles in the AI economy. For example, governments can invest in education and training programs that focus on AI literacy, technical skills, and digital competencies, ensuring that the workforce is prepared for the demands of the future job market.

Education systems also play a crucial role in preparing the next generation of workers. Integrating AI literacy and technical skills into school curricula can equip students with the knowledge and tools they need to succeed in an AI-driven world. By emphasizing STEM (science, technology, engineering, and mathematics) education, governments can build a pipeline of talent ready to take on the challenges and opportunities presented by AI.

In addition to education and training, policies that support job transition and provide social safety nets are essential for mitigating the adverse effects of AI on employment. This includes offering unemployment benefits, income support, and retraining programs for displaced workers. By ensuring that workers have access to these resources, governments can help cushion the impact of job displacement and foster a more resilient and adaptable workforce.

ENSURING EQUITABLE ACCESS TO AI TECHNOLOGIES AND BENEFITS

The transformative power of artificial intelligence (AI) is reshaping industries, enhancing productivity, and revolutionizing how societies function. However, to fully unlock the potential of AI, its benefits must be accessible to all, regardless of socio-economic status, geographic location, or digital literacy. In the rapidly digitizing global landscape, equitable access to AI technologies is not merely a moral imperative but a fundamental necessity for ensuring inclusive growth, reducing inequality, and fostering innovation. Without this, the promise of AI risks being reserved for the privileged few, exacerbating existing divides and leaving behind large segments of the population.

PROMOTING DIGITAL INCLUSION THROUGH GOVERNANCE FRAMEWORKS

One of the key drivers of equitable access to AI is robust governance frameworks that prioritize digital inclusion. According to a report by the World Economic Forum (WEF), creating equitable access to AI requires deliberate policy interventions and significant investments in infrastructure to provide affordable access to both AI technologies and the internet, especially in underserved areas. Digital inclusion ensures that AI's transformative benefits are extended to marginalized communities, low-income groups, and rural populations.

Infrastructure is the backbone of digital access. Without reliable internet connectivity and the necessary technological infrastructure, vast segments of the population are denied the ability to participate in the digital economy. Public policies must therefore support the widespread deployment of AI-enabling technologies in underserved areas, particularly in developing countries and remote regions where internet access is still a luxury. Countries like India and Kenya have taken steps in this direction by expanding internet access in rural areas through government-backed programs like India's Digital India initiative and Kenya's National Broadband Strategy, which aim to bring the benefits of the internet and digital technologies to the masses. Similarly, Google's Project Loon has piloted innovative solutions by using high-altitude balloons to provide internet access to remote regions.

Moreover, digital inclusion extends beyond infrastructure. Ensuring affordable access to AI tools is equally important. This could be facilitated through public-private partnerships that subsidize access to AI technologies for startups, small businesses, educational institutions, and healthcare providers in disadvantaged regions. In South Africa, initiatives like AI for Good are being explored to provide accessible AI platforms that can be used by local businesses and educational institutions.

BRIDGING THE DIGITAL DIVIDE

One of the most pressing challenges in ensuring equitable access to AI is addressing the digital divide—the gap between those who have access to digital technologies and those who do not. According to a 2020 report by the International Telecommunication Union (ITU), approximately 3.7 billion people, nearly half of the global population, remain offline. These individuals, many of whom reside in low-income countries and remote areas, are excluded from the benefits of AI and other digital advancements. This digital divide threatens to deepen socio-economic inequalities by leaving behind those who are already marginalized.

Closing this gap requires a multi-faceted approach. Firstly, governments and private sector stakeholders must collaborate to expand internet access and improve digital literacy. Efforts such as the United Nations' Broadband Commission are crucial, setting global goals for affordable internet access for all by 2030. Public investment in technology education—starting at the primary school level—can help build digital literacy, ensuring that future generations are equipped with the skills necessary to engage with AI technologies.

Additionally, AI governance frameworks must prioritize the development of systems that cater to diverse user needs. This includes designing AI technologies that are accessible to people with disabilities and accommodating different languages and literacy levels. The Global Initiative for Inclusive Information and Communication Technologies (G3ICT) advocates for inclusive AI design, ensuring that people with visual, hearing, or cognitive impairments can engage with AI-driven tools and platforms. As of 2023, AI-based assistive technologies like speech-to-text applications and AI-driven smart assistants are already transforming the lives of people with disabilities, allowing them to participate more fully in society.

For example, Microsoft's AI for Accessibility initiative is developing tools to help people with disabilities in education, employment, and daily activities, showing that AI can be a powerful equalizer when designed inclusively. However, to scale these benefits, collaboration between policymakers, technologists, and advocacy groups is essential to ensure that AI systems are designed and deployed with the full spectrum of human diversity in mind.

SECURITY AND SAFETY

While AI can enhance security through advancements like AI-powered threat detection systems and predictive policing, it also introduces new risks. AI systems are vulnerable to manipulation, data breaches, and biased decision-making. For instance, poorly designed AI algorithms can reinforce social biases or exclude certain groups from accessing services, as was the case with the COMPAS algorithm used in the U.S. criminal justice system, which was found to unfairly discriminate against African Americans in its risk assessments.

Governance frameworks must be equipped to address these risks by developing robust security standards and ensuring that AI systems are transparent and accountable. The OECD Principles on AI provide guidance for governments and organizations, advocating for AI systems that are safe, fair, and transparent. Governments must implement AI safety regulations that mandate regular audits, ethical reviews, and security testing to prevent harm and ensure that AI systems serve the public good.

PREVENTING MALICIOUS USE OF AI IN CYBER ATTACKS AND WARFARE

AI technologies can be weaponized for malicious purposes, such as automated cyber attacks, deepfakes, and autonomous weapons. Governance frameworks must establish clear guidelines and international agreements to prevent the malicious use of AI. This includes banning the development and deployment of autonomous lethal weapons and enhancing cybersecurity measures to protect AI systems from being compromised. The 2021 report by the Center for a New American Security (CNAS) emphasizes the need for international norms and agreements to govern the military use of AI.

ENSURING AI SYSTEMS ARE ROBUST AND RESILIENT AGAINST THREATS

AI systems must be designed to be resilient against adversarial attacks and other security threats. This involves implementing robust security measures, such as secure coding practices, regular security audits, and employing AI techniques to detect and mitigate threats. Standards and best practices for AI security should be established and enforced through regulatory bodies. A report by the Royal Society highlights the importance of building resilient AI systems that can withstand and recover from attacks.

AI is increasingly being integrated into critical infrastructure sectors such as energy, transportation, and healthcare. Ensuring the security and reliability of AI systems in these sectors is paramount to national security and public safety. Governance frameworks should mandate stringent security standards and regular testing for AI systems used in critical infrastructure. The U.S. National Infrastructure Advisory Council's 2018 report underscores the need for robust cybersecurity measures to protect critical infrastructure from AI-related threats.

PROMOTING TRUST IN AI

Trust is a foundational element for the successful adoption and integration of artificial intelligence (AI) technologies. Without public trust, AI systems—no matter how advanced or beneficial—are unlikely to gain widespread acceptance or be fully utilized. Concerns surrounding transparency, fairness, security, and accountability are critical factors that can either bolster or undermine trust in AI. Building and maintaining this trust is a multifaceted challenge that requires robust governance frameworks, clear ethical guidelines, and continuous efforts from governments, organizations, and developers. This section delves into the key strategies for promoting trust in AI, the role of governance frameworks, and the importance of transparency and accountability in ensuring AI's responsible use.

THE IMPORTANCE OF TRUST IN AI

Public trust in AI is a crucial determinant of its adoption across various sectors, from healthcare and finance to education and law enforcement. Trust is built when individuals and organizations believe that AI systems are reliable, safe, and aligned with societal values. Conversely, trust can be eroded by incidents such as data breaches, biased algorithms, or the misuse of AI for unethical purposes. For example, a 2021 survey by PwC found that 85% of consumers are concerned about how AI is used to collect and handle personal data, highlighting the growing apprehension around privacy and data security in AI systems.

Trust also plays a vital role in the economic success of AI technologies. According to the World Economic Forum (WEF), businesses that invest in building trustworthy AI systems are more likely to see higher adoption rates and consumer loyalty, while companies that fail to address trust issues may face reputational damage and reduced market share. As AI continues to evolve and become more ingrained in daily life, promoting trust will remain critical to unlocking the full potential of this transformative technology.

THE ROLE OF GOVERNANCE IN BUILDING TRUST

Governance frameworks are essential for establishing the standards and practices needed to foster trust in AI systems. These frameworks provide the legal and ethical foundation upon which AI technologies are built, ensuring that they are developed and deployed in ways that respect individual rights, promote fairness, and protect public safety. By setting clear guidelines for the use of AI, governance frameworks can mitigate risks and provide assurance to the public that AI systems are being used responsibly.

One of the most significant governance initiatives in AI is the European Union's Artificial Intelligence Act, which seeks to establish a regulatory framework for AI across the EU. The Act introduces a risk-based approach to AI governance, classifying AI applications into four categories: minimal risk, limited risk, high risk, and unacceptable risk. High-risk AI systems, such as those used in critical sectors like healthcare, law enforcement, and finance, are subject to strict oversight and must meet specific safety, transparency, and accountability requirements before they can be deployed. This approach ensures that AI technologies are aligned with societal values and that the risks associated with their use are carefully managed, thereby fostering public trust.

Similarly, the General Data Protection Regulation (GDPR), also implemented by the EU, sets strong standards for data privacy and security, directly addressing one of the primary concerns surrounding AI: the handling of personal data. By mandating that individuals have control over their data and requiring organizations to obtain explicit consent before processing personal information, the GDPR builds trust by ensuring that AI systems respect user privacy and operate transparently.

TRANSPARENCY AND EXPLAINABILITY

Transparency and explainability are key components of building trust in AI. Transparency refers to the degree to which AI systems are open and accessible in their design, function, and decision-making processes. When AI systems are transparent, users and stakeholders can understand how decisions are made, which increases confidence in the technology and makes it easier to identify and correct errors or biases.

Explainability, a subset of transparency, involves providing clear and understandable explanations for AI-driven decisions. This is particularly important in high-stakes sectors such as healthcare, finance, and criminal justice, where AI-driven decisions can have profound consequences. For example, in healthcare, AI may be used to predict patient outcomes or recommend treatments. If a system makes a recommendation that is not explainable, it may lead to a lack of trust among healthcare providers and patients. Conversely, when the rationale behind AI-driven recommendations is transparent and understandable, it can foster trust and encourage wider adoption of AI technologies.

According to the European Commission's Ethics Guidelines for Trustworthy AI, transparency and explainability are essential for ensuring that AI systems are not only lawful and ethical but also technically robust. The guidelines suggest that AI systems should provide sufficient information to allow users to understand and challenge decisions when necessary. For instance, AI systems used in hiring or lending should be designed to explain why a candidate was selected or why a loan application was approved or denied. This level of transparency helps to build trust by ensuring that AI systems are fair, accountable, and aligned with user expectations.

BUILDING PUBLIC TRUST THROUGH ETHICAL AND TRANSPARENT AI PRACTICES

Ethical AI practices, including fairness, transparency, and accountability, are essential for building public trust. Governance frameworks should mandate ethical guidelines for AI development and deployment, ensuring that AI systems are designed and used in ways that respect human rights and societal values. Transparent communication about AI capabilities and limitations can also help build trust. The 2019 Edelman AI Survey found that 60% of respondents believe that AI will change their lives for the better if ethical guidelines are followed.

Effective AI governance requires the involvement of all stakeholders, including governments, industry, academia, and civil society. Public consultation processes ensure that diverse perspectives are considered in policy-making. Engaging stakeholders in discussions about AI's impact and governance helps build consensus and fosters trust in AI technologies. The European Commission's AI Alliance, which brings together over 4000 stakeholders to discuss AI policy, exemplifies the importance of inclusive dialogue.

Public education initiatives are also crucial for building an informed and engaged society. Governance frameworks should support educational programs that increase AI literacy, helping people understand how AI works, its benefits, and its risks. Public awareness campaigns can also address misconceptions and fears about AI, promoting a balanced view of the technology. The AI4ALL initiative, which aims to increase diversity and inclusion in AI by educating high school students, demonstrates the positive impact of public education on AI literacy.

Governance frameworks should also encourage innovation and research while ensuring ethical and responsible AI development.

AI research and innovation should prioritize ethical considerations and societal benefits. Governance frameworks can incentivize ethical AI research through grants, funding opportunities, and recognition programs. Ethical review boards and guidelines for AI research can ensure that research projects align with societal values and ethical standards. The IEEE Global Initiative on Ethics of Autonomous and Intelligent Systems provides guidelines and frameworks to support ethical AI research and development.

FUNDING AND SUPPORT FOR AI PROJECTS THAT ALIGN WITH SOCIETAL VALUES

Public and private funding should support AI projects that address pressing societal challenges, such as healthcare, education, and environmental sustainability. Governance frameworks can create funding mechanisms and public-private partnerships that drive investment in responsible AI innovation. Prioritizing projects that have a positive social impact ensures that AI development aligns with societal values. The AI for Good Global Summit, organized by the ITU, showcases how AI can be leveraged to achieve the United Nations' Sustainable Development Goals.

BALANCING INNOVATION WITH RISK MANAGEMENT

Governance frameworks must strike a balance between promoting innovation and managing risks. Regulatory sandboxes, where AI technologies can be tested under regulatory supervision, provide a controlled environment for innovation while ensuring compliance with safety and ethical standards. Risk management strategies, including impact assessments and continuous monitoring, can help mitigate potential harms associated with AI technologies. The UK's

Information Commissioner's Office (ICO) has developed an AI auditing framework to help organizations manage AI risks and ensure compliance with data protection laws.

Examining real-world examples of AI governance initiatives can provide valuable insights and lessons learned.

Several countries and organizations have implemented successful AI governance initiatives. For instance, Singapore's Model AI Governance Framework provides practical guidance to organizations on implementing AI responsibly. The framework includes guidelines on internal governance structures, risk management, operations management, and stakeholder communication. The European Union's AI High-Level Expert Group has also developed ethical guidelines for trustworthy AI, emphasizing respect for human autonomy, prevention of harm, fairness, and explicability.

LESSONS LEARNED FROM FAILURES IN AI GOVERNANCE

Failures in artificial intelligence (AI) governance provide critical insights into the importance of robust oversight, transparency, and ethical considerations in the deployment of AI systems. Examining these failures offers valuable lessons for policymakers, organizations, and developers, allowing them to address past mistakes and implement safeguards to prevent similar issues in the future. One of the most significant examples of governance failure comes from the controversy surrounding AI's use in predictive policing in the United States. This case has highlighted the risks of unregulated AI use, including bias, lack of transparency, and accountability issues, particularly in high-stakes areas such as law enforcement. By analyzing these failures, governance frameworks can be strengthened to ensure that AI systems serve society in fair and equitable ways. This section explores the lessons learned from failures in AI governance, using the example of predictive policing, and emphasizes the need for continuous oversight, accountability, and community involvement.

THE PREDICTIVE POLICING CONTROVERSY:

A CASE STUDY IN AI GOVERNANCE FAILURE

One of the most well-documented failures in AI governance is the use of AI algorithms in predictive policing, a practice that uses data analysis and machine learning to forecast where crimes are likely to occur and who is most likely to commit them. In theory, predictive policing aims to enhance law enforcement efficiency by directing resources to areas with higher crime probabilities. However, in practice, these AI systems have often perpetuated and exacerbated existing biases, particularly against marginalized communities, leading to significant ethical and governance concerns.

The controversy surrounding predictive policing in the United States came to the forefront with the "Stop LAPD Spying Coalition" report, which revealed how the **Los Angeles Police Department (LAPD)** used unregulated AI systems to monitor certain neighborhoods, disproportionately targeting Black and Latino communities. According to the report, predictive policing systems used biased historical crime data to make decisions about where to deploy law enforcement, often reinforcing existing racial disparities in policing. The algorithms, trained on historical crime data that reflected years of systemic bias, were found to disproportionately target communities of color, further criminalizing those populations while doing little to improve overall safety.

The failure of predictive policing in this context highlights several governance shortcomings, including the lack of transparency in how AI decisions were made, the absence of accountability mechanisms to address biased outcomes, and the failure to include community input in the development and deployment of AI systems. The **American Civil Liberties Union (ACLU)** and other advocacy groups have criticized the use of predictive policing, arguing that it perpetuates racial profiling and undermines trust between law enforcement and communities.

LESSONS LEARNED FROM PREDICTIVE POLICING FAILURES

1. TRANSPARENCY IS ESSENTIAL FOR TRUST AND ACCOUNTABILITY:

One of the key failures of predictive policing was the lack of transparency in how AI algorithms made decisions about policing strategies. Without clear explanations of how data was used, what factors influenced predictions, or how decisions were made, it was difficult for the public or oversight bodies to hold the system accountable. This lack of transparency undermined public trust and made it impossible for affected communities to challenge the fairness of the AI systems.

Moving forward, governance frameworks must prioritize transparency by ensuring that AI systems, particularly those used in sensitive areas such as law enforcement, provide clear and understandable explanations for their decisions. This includes making algorithmic decision-making processes accessible to the public and subject to external review. The **AI Now Institute's 2019 report** underscores the importance of algorithmic transparency, particularly in high-risk applications like criminal justice, where opaque systems can have life-altering consequences for individuals.

2. BIAS AND DISCRIMINATION IN AI MUST BE ADDRESSED:

The predictive policing controversy also demonstrated the dangers of embedding historical biases into AI systems. Because predictive policing algorithms relied on historical crime data—data often influenced by decades of biased policing practices—the AI systems perpetuated and amplified those biases, disproportionately targeting minority communities. This failure illustrates the need for governance frameworks to address bias at every stage of AI development, from data collection to model training and deployment.

To prevent similar outcomes in the future, governance frameworks should include mandatory bias audits for AI systems, particularly those used in high-stakes sectors such as law enforcement, healthcare, and hiring. These audits can help identify and mitigate biases before AI systems are deployed at scale. Moreover, ensuring that AI systems are trained on diverse, representative datasets can help reduce the risk of perpetuating systemic biases.

3. ACCOUNTABILITY MECHANISMS ARE CRUCIAL:

Another significant lesson from the predictive policing failure is the importance of establishing clear accountability mechanisms for AI systems. In the case of the LAPD, there was no clear framework for determining who was responsible when the AI system produced biased or harmful outcomes. This lack of accountability made it difficult to rectify mistakes, challenge biased decisions, or hold developers and law enforcement agencies accountable for the consequences of AI-driven actions.

Governance frameworks must establish clear lines of accountability for AI systems. This includes defining who is responsible for ensuring that AI systems operate fairly, transparently, and in accordance with ethical guidelines. In the case of law enforcement, accountability mechanisms should involve both internal oversight by police departments and external oversight by independent bodies or community organizations.

4. COMMUNITY INVOLVEMENT IS KEY TO ETHICAL AI DEPLOYMENT:

The predictive policing case also highlights the importance of community involvement in AI governance. The failure to engage with the communities most affected by predictive policing contributed to a breakdown of trust between law enforcement and the public. AI systems that disproportionately target certain populations without input from those communities risk deepening social divisions and exacerbating existing inequalities.

To prevent similar failures, governance frameworks should mandate community-led oversight for AI systems, particularly those deployed in public services such as law enforcement, healthcare, and education. Community involvement can help ensure that AI systems are designed and implemented in ways that align with the needs, values, and rights of those most affected by them. The "Stop LAPD Spying Coalition" report advocates for community-driven oversight as a way to empower marginalized groups and ensure that AI systems are used ethically and equitably.

LEARNING FROM BROADER AI GOVERNANCE FAILURES

The lessons from predictive policing extend beyond law enforcement to broader applications of AI, where similar governance failures have been observed. Across various sectors such as healthcare, hiring, and financial services, AI systems have demonstrated the potential to amplify existing inequalities or produce harmful outcomes when not properly regulated. These failures underscore the need for governance frameworks that prioritize ethical AI development, continuous oversight, and mechanisms for redress.

1. **THE IMPORTANCE OF ONGOING OVERSIGHT AND ADAPTABILITY:**

   AI technologies evolve rapidly, often outpacing the regulatory frameworks designed to govern them. This can lead to governance gaps where AI systems operate without sufficient oversight, allowing risks to go unaddressed. Predictive policing and similar failures highlight the necessity of continuous monitoring and adaptability in AI governance. As AI systems are deployed, regular audits, reviews, and updates are essential to ensure that these systems remain aligned with ethical standards and societal values.

For example, healthcare AI systems that make diagnostic or treatment recommendations must be continuously evaluated for fairness, accuracy, and effectiveness. The consequences of errors in these high-stakes settings can be severe, so ensuring that AI systems are regularly audited and updated is crucial for maintaining trust and safeguarding public well-being. Governance frameworks should include provisions for continuous assessment, allowing for the detection and mitigation of emerging risks or unintended consequences.

2. **PUBLIC PARTICIPATION AND TRANSPARENCY IN GOVERNANCE:**

As AI systems become more integrated into public life, there is a growing need for governance frameworks to involve a wider range of stakeholders in decision-making processes. Public participation in AI governance ensures that the values, concerns, and rights of affected individuals and communities are represented. In cases like predictive policing, where the deployment of AI disproportionately affects certain groups, it is particularly important to engage with these communities to build trust and ensure fair outcomes.

Transparency is also essential in promoting public understanding and trust in AI systems. When people are unaware of how decisions are made or how data is used, they are more likely to view AI systems with suspicion or fear. To address this, governance frameworks must require transparency at every stage of AI development and deployment, from data collection to algorithmic decision-making and system outcomes. Publicly accessible reports, open data standards, and community consultations can all contribute to greater transparency and accountability.

3. **ETHICAL CONSIDERATIONS FOR HIGH-STAKES AI APPLICATIONS:**

Failures in AI governance are particularly problematic in high-stakes sectors, where the consequences of errors or bias can have life-altering impacts. In criminal justice, healthcare, and financial services, AI systems are often used to make decisions that directly affect individuals' rights, freedoms, and well-being. Governance frameworks must account for the unique ethical challenges posed by these applications, ensuring that AI systems are used responsibly and with appropriate safeguards.

The use of AI in hiring, for example, has led to concerns about algorithmic bias and discrimination. Systems designed to screen job applicants may inadvertently favor certain demographic groups over others if they are trained on biased data. Similarly, AI in financial services—such as credit scoring algorithms—can perpetuate existing economic disparities by disproportionately disadvantaging certain populations. To prevent such outcomes, governance frameworks must mandate the use of diverse, representative datasets and include ethical guidelines that prioritize fairness and inclusivity.

4. **LEARNING FROM INTERNATIONAL GOVERNANCE MODELS:**

Different regions around the world have approached AI governance with varying levels of success, and examining these approaches can provide valuable insights for future frameworks. The European Union's General Data Protection Regulation (GDPR) and the proposed Artificial Intelligence Act represent some of the most comprehensive efforts to regulate AI technologies, emphasizing data privacy, transparency, and ethical AI development. These regulations provide clear guidelines for ensuring that AI systems respect individual rights and operate within ethical and legal boundaries.

Other countries, such as Canada and Japan, have adopted principles of AI for social good, focusing on AI applications that address public health, environmental sustainability, and social equity. By promoting the development of AI systems that contribute to the public good, these frameworks ensure that AI is used as a tool for societal progress rather than a driver of inequality or harm. Learning from these models can help other regions develop governance frameworks that balance innovation with ethical responsibility.

MOVING FORWARD: STRENGTHENING AI GOVERNANCE

To prevent future governance failures and ensure that AI systems are developed and deployed ethically, it is essential to build on the lessons learned from past mistakes. Strengthening AI governance will require a combination of robust oversight, transparency, and accountability, alongside proactive efforts to address bias and engage with affected communities. Key steps for improving AI governance include:

1. **IMPLEMENTING BIAS AUDITS AND ACCOUNTABILITY MECHANISMS:**

   Bias audits should be mandatory for all high-risk AI applications to ensure that systems do not perpetuate discrimination or inequality. Additionally, accountability mechanisms must be clearly defined, holding developers, organizations, and regulators responsible for the outcomes of AI systems.

2. **FOSTERING PUBLIC ENGAGEMENT AND TRANSPARENCY:**

   Public involvement in AI governance is crucial for ensuring that AI systems align with societal values and ethical standards. Transparency measures, such as open reporting and community consultations, can help build public trust and provide avenues for redress when AI systems fail.

3. ## REGULARLY UPDATING GOVERNANCE FRAMEWORKS TO ADDRESS EMERGING RISKS:

AI technologies are evolving rapidly, and governance frameworks must be adaptable to keep pace with new developments. Continuous oversight, regular audits, and the ability to update regulations as new risks emerge are essential for preventing future governance failures.

4. ## PRIORITIZING ETHICAL AI IN HIGH-STAKES APPLICATIONS:

High-stakes AI applications, such as those used in healthcare, law enforcement, and finance, require special attention to ensure that they are developed and deployed ethically. This includes prioritizing fairness, transparency, and accountability, as well as ensuring that AI systems are designed to serve the public good.

EMERGING TRENDS AND CHALLENGES IN AI GOVERNANCE

As artificial intelligence (AI) technologies rapidly evolve, new trends and challenges are reshaping the landscape of AI governance. The accelerating pace of AI advancements, combined with emerging technologies such as quantum computing and autonomous systems, presents both opportunities and risks that governance frameworks must address proactively. From the disruption of encryption methods to the ethical dilemmas posed by autonomous systems, these developments require adaptable and forward-thinking policies to ensure that AI technologies are harnessed for societal good while minimizing potential harms. This section explores key emerging trends and challenges in AI governance and highlights the importance of continuously updating governance frameworks to keep pace with technological change.

QUANTUM COMPUTING AND THE FUTURE OF AI SECURITY

One of the most significant emerging trends in the AI landscape is the rise of quantum computing, which has the potential to revolutionize various industries, including cryptography, AI, and machine learning. Quantum computing is expected to exponentially increase computational power, allowing for the processing of vast datasets and solving complex problems that are beyond the capabilities of classical computers. However, this technological leap also poses considerable challenges, particularly in the area of cybersecurity and data protection.

Current encryption methods, which are critical for safeguarding sensitive information in AI systems, rely on the difficulty of solving complex mathematical problems. Quantum computers could potentially break these encryption schemes, rendering much of today's secure data transmission vulnerable to hacking and other malicious activities. The potential for quantum computing to disrupt current security protocols creates an urgent need for governance frameworks that anticipate and mitigate these risks.

Governments and organizations must invest in quantum-resistant encryption methods to ensure the continued security of AI systems in a post-quantum world. Researchers are already exploring algorithms that are resistant to quantum attacks, but governance frameworks need to mandate the adoption of these advanced cryptographic techniques as quantum computing becomes more accessible. The National Institute of Standards and Technology (NIST) has been working on developing quantum-resistant cryptographic standards, and its efforts highlight the importance of staying ahead of technological trends to protect critical infrastructure and data security.

In addition to encryption challenges, quantum computing has the potential to accelerate AI advancements by enabling faster and more efficient machine learning models. This could lead to breakthroughs in areas such as drug discovery, climate modeling, and financial analysis. However, with these advancements comes the need for governance frameworks that regulate the ethical use of quantum-powered AI technologies, ensuring that they are developed and deployed responsibly.

THE RISE OF AUTONOMOUS SYSTEMS AND ETHICAL CONCERNS

Another emerging trend in AI is the increasing use of autonomous systems, including self-driving cars, drones, and autonomous robots. While these systems have the potential to improve efficiency, safety, and productivity, they also raise significant ethical, legal, and safety concerns. Autonomous systems operate with a high degree of independence, often making decisions without direct human intervention. This introduces complex questions about accountability, safety, and the ethical implications of allowing machines to make decisions that can have life-altering consequences.

The deployment of autonomous vehicles, for instance, raises concerns about how these systems will respond to ethical dilemmas, such as deciding between different courses of action in emergency situations. Who is responsible if an autonomous vehicle causes an accident? How should these systems be programmed to prioritize safety while making split-second decisions? These questions illustrate the need for governance frameworks that establish clear guidelines for accountability and liability in the use of autonomous systems.

Governance frameworks must also address the ethical challenges associated with autonomous weapons systems, which are increasingly being explored by militaries around the world. The use of AI in warfare introduces concerns about the lack of human oversight in life-and-death situations, the potential for biased decision-making, and the risk of escalation in conflicts. The United Nations Convention on Certain Conventional Weapons (CCW) has called for discussions on the use of lethal autonomous weapons systems (LAWS) to ensure that their development and deployment adhere to international humanitarian law. Robust governance is needed to regulate these systems, ensuring that AI is used responsibly in military applications and does not lead to unintended harm.

Furthermore, autonomous systems used in healthcare, such as surgical robots or AI-powered diagnostic tools, also pose unique challenges in terms of safety and ethics. These systems must be rigorously tested to ensure their reliability and safety before being widely deployed. Governance frameworks should mandate regular audits, continuous monitoring, and fail-safes to ensure that autonomous healthcare systems do not cause harm or produce biased outcomes.

ADAPTIVE GOVERNANCE FOR RAPID TECHNOLOGICAL CHANGE

The rapid pace of technological advancement in AI necessitates adaptive governance – a dynamic approach to regulation that can keep up with the constant evolution of AI technologies. Traditional regulatory frameworks, which are often static and slow to change, may not be able to adequately address the risks posed by emerging AI trends. Adaptive governance involves continuously updating policies, regulations, and ethical guidelines to respond to new developments in AI, ensuring that governance remains effective in the face of rapid technological progress.

The World Economic Forum's 2021 Global Technology Governance Report emphasizes the need for adaptive governance to tackle the challenges posed by emerging technologies such as AI, quantum computing, and autonomous systems. According to the report, governance frameworks should incorporate mechanisms for real-time monitoring and adjustment, allowing regulators to identify emerging risks and update policies accordingly. This approach requires close collaboration between governments, private sector companies, academia, and civil society to ensure that regulations are informed by the latest technological developments and societal needs.

One example of adaptive governance in action is the European Union's Artificial Intelligence Act, which includes provisions for continuous updates to AI regulations based on new developments and risks. The Act adopts a risk-based approach, categorizing AI systems by the level of risk they pose and adjusting regulatory requirements accordingly. High-risk applications, such as those used in healthcare or law enforcement, are subject to stricter oversight, while low-risk applications may face fewer regulatory hurdles. This flexible approach allows the EU to adapt its governance framework as new AI technologies emerge.

Another key aspect of adaptive governance is the creation of regulatory sandboxes—controlled environments where companies can test new AI technologies under the supervision of regulators. Regulatory sandboxes allow policymakers to better understand how emerging AI systems function in real-world scenarios, identify potential risks, and develop appropriate regulations before widespread deployment. The UK Information Commissioner's Office (ICO) has implemented a regulatory sandbox for AI technologies in data protection, providing a model for how adaptive governance can support innovation while ensuring that new technologies are developed responsibly.

CHALLENGES IN GLOBAL AI GOVERNANCE COORDINATION

As AI technologies evolve, the challenge of global coordination in AI governance becomes more pressing. AI is a borderless technology, and the actions of one country or organization can have far-reaching effects on others. For example, autonomous weapons systems developed in one country could trigger arms races in others, and quantum breakthroughs in AI could have global implications for cybersecurity. As a result, international cooperation is essential for ensuring that AI technologies are governed in a way that promotes global stability, fairness, and security.

However, coordinating global AI governance is not without its challenges. Different countries have varying priorities and approaches to AI regulation. For example, the European Union has emphasized ethical AI development through regulations such as the GDPR and the AI Act, while the United States has taken a more laissez-faire approach, allowing the private sector to drive innovation with minimal government intervention. Meanwhile, China's AI strategy is heavily focused on state control and the use of AI for surveillance, raising concerns about human rights violations.

The Organisation for Economic Co-operation and Development (OECD) has attempted to address these challenges by developing the OECD Principles on AI, a set of guidelines for ethical AI development adopted by over 40 countries. These principles emphasize transparency, accountability, fairness, and the responsible use of AI. However, achieving global consensus on AI governance will require continued diplomatic efforts and international collaboration.

THE ROLE OF ONGOING RESEARCH AND ADAPTATION IN GOVERNANCE FRAMEWORKS

Effective AI governance requires more than static regulations—it demands a dynamic approach grounded in continuous research and adaptation. As AI technologies evolve rapidly, governance frameworks must be able to respond to new challenges, risks, and opportunities. Policymakers need to work closely with researchers, technologists, and industry leaders to understand the implications of emerging AI capabilities and ensure that regulations are both relevant and robust.

One key aspect of adaptive governance is the ability to evolve as technology progresses. Traditional regulatory frameworks, often built for slower-moving industries, can quickly become outdated in the face of AI's fast-paced development. A study by the Brookings Institution, "Adaptive Regulation for the Fourth Industrial Revolution," emphasizes the importance of flexible, responsive regulatory approaches that can keep pace with technological change.

The report argues that policymakers must move away from rigid, one-size-fits-all regulations toward models that encourage continuous monitoring and adjustment. This is especially crucial for AI, where new applications and risks frequently emerge.

For instance, the rise of deepfakes, autonomous systems, and generative AI tools like ChatGPT have shown how quickly AI applications can proliferate in ways that challenge existing governance structures. Without adaptable regulatory mechanisms, governments risk falling behind, leaving gaps in oversight that could expose individuals and businesses to harm. Ongoing research, therefore, becomes the backbone of any governance framework, as it allows stakeholders to anticipate future risks, refine ethical guidelines, and develop proactive solutions.

Adaptive governance also extends to the international level, where collaboration across borders is essential. The challenges posed by AI, such as data privacy, algorithmic bias, and cybersecurity, are global in scope, requiring coordinated efforts to develop harmonized regulations that reflect shared values. Policymakers must continually update their knowledge base, leveraging insights from cutting-edge research to make informed decisions that balance innovation with risk management.

VISION FOR THE FUTURE OF AI GOVERNANCE

Looking forward, the future of AI governance should be inclusive, transparent, and adaptive. Governance structures must prioritize ethical considerations while simultaneously promoting technological innovation and protecting public interests. This means creating systems that are built around fairness, accountability, and trust, ensuring that AI technologies are developed and deployed in ways that uphold human rights and societal well-being.

Inclusivity is a core principle of future AI governance. Effective regulation should involve input from a diverse range of stakeholders, including governments, industry leaders, academia, civil society, and underrepresented communities. AI technologies have the potential to exacerbate existing inequalities, especially when decision-making processes are driven by biased algorithms or when marginalized groups are excluded from the conversation. A governance framework that is inclusive ensures that AI benefits everyone and minimizes harm to vulnerable populations.

Transparency is another essential element. As AI systems become more integrated into critical sectors such as healthcare, finance, and law enforcement, it is crucial that these systems are open to scrutiny. The public should have access to clear explanations of how AI-driven decisions are made, who is accountable, and what safeguards are in place to protect their rights. According to the World Economic Forum's AI Governance Framework, transparency builds trust between the public and the entities developing AI technologies, and it ensures that AI use remains ethical and aligned with societal goals.

The United Nations' Secretary-General's Roadmap for Digital Cooperation offers a comprehensive vision for AI governance that aligns with these principles. The roadmap advocates for a global, inclusive approach to digital governance that promotes human rights, peace, and sustainable development. It recognizes that AI can either advance or undermine these goals, depending on how it is governed. Therefore, international cooperation is key to developing a unified governance framework that ensures the safe, ethical, and beneficial use of AI worldwide.

International collaboration is especially important for addressing cross-border challenges like data privacy, algorithmic fairness, and AI-enabled cyber threats. The UN roadmap encourages countries to engage in multilateral dialogue and to develop global standards for AI that reflect shared values and norms. This harmonized approach helps prevent regulatory fragmentation, where different countries adopt conflicting rules that may hinder innovation and trade.

In summary, the future of AI governance should be adaptable, inclusive, and transparent, grounded in continuous research and international cooperation. As AI continues to evolve, so too must our governance structures, ensuring that these technologies are used responsibly to promote human rights, equity, and sustainability.

QUESTIONS PEOPLE HAVE ASKED ABOUT AI AND CYBERSECURITY

1. IS THERE AN AI FOR CYBERSECURITY?

Yes, there is AI for cybersecurity. AI technologies are widely used to enhance cybersecurity measures. AI-driven systems can analyze vast amounts of data to detect anomalies and potential threats, automate responses to incidents, and improve the overall security posture of organizations. For example, machine learning algorithms can identify patterns in network traffic that indicate a cyber attack, while natural language processing (NLP) can analyze textual data from threat intelligence reports to predict emerging threats. AI tools such as Darktrace, IBM Watson for Cyber Security, and Palo Alto Networks' Cortex XDR are examples of how AI is integrated into cybersecurity practices to detect and mitigate cyber threats more efficiently.

2. CAN I COMBINE AI AND CYBERSECURITY?

Yes, you can combine AI and cybersecurity. Integrating AI into cybersecurity enhances the ability to detect, analyze, and respond to cyber threats. AI can automate the monitoring of network traffic, identify unusual behavior, and respond to incidents in real-time. By using machine learning algorithms, cybersecurity systems can improve their detection capabilities over time as they learn from new data. AI can also help in analyzing large datasets to identify potential vulnerabilities and predict future attacks. Combining AI and cybersecurity allows for more proactive defense mechanisms, reducing the reliance on manual monitoring and increasing the speed and accuracy of threat detection and response.

3. WHAT SHOULD I LEARN: AI OR CYBERSECURITY?

Choosing between AI and cybersecurity depends on your career goals and interests. If you are fascinated by developing intelligent systems, analyzing data, and creating algorithms, a career in AI might be more suitable. AI involves machine learning, deep learning, and data science, and it is applied in various fields beyond cybersecurity. On the other hand, if you are interested in protecting systems, networks, and data from cyber attacks, a career in cybersecurity might be more appropriate. Cybersecurity focuses on threat detection, incident response, ethical hacking, and risk management. Both fields are in high demand, and a combination of both skills can be particularly valuable, especially in roles that focus on developing AI-driven cybersecurity solutions.

4. WHAT IS INTRODUCTION TO AI?

Introduction to AI refers to the foundational concepts and principles of artificial intelligence. It involves understanding what AI is, its history, and its basic methodologies. AI is the simulation of human intelligence processes by machines, particularly computer systems. These processes include learning (acquiring information and rules for using it), reasoning (using rules to reach conclusions), and self-correction. An introductory AI course or study typically covers topics such as machine learning, neural networks, natural language processing, computer vision, and robotics. It also explores the ethical implications, applications, and future trends in AI.

This foundational knowledge is essential for anyone looking to explore deeper into AI technologies and their applications.

5. WHAT ARE THE FOUR TYPES OF AI?

The four types of AI are:

i. **Reactive Machines**: These are the most basic form of AI, designed to perform specific tasks without memory or past experience. They respond to different stimuli in real-time. Examples include IBM's Deep Blue, which plays chess by evaluating current board positions.

ii. **Limited Memory**: These AI systems can use past experiences to inform future decisions. Self-driving cars use limited memory AI to observe and analyze their environment and make driving decisions based on historical data.

iii. **Theory of Mind**: This type of AI is still in the research phase. It aims to understand human emotions, beliefs, and thought processes. Theory of mind AI would enable machines to interact more naturally and effectively with humans by understanding their mental states.

iv. **Self-Aware AI**: The most advanced form, self-aware AI, has its own consciousness, self-awareness, and understanding of its existence. This level of AI does not yet exist and remains theoretical. It would have the ability to form its own thoughts and make independent decisions.

6. WHO IS THE FATHER OF AI?

John McCarthy is widely regarded as the father of AI. He was a prominent computer scientist who coined the term "Artificial Intelligence" in 1956 and organized the Dartmouth Conference, which is considered the birthplace of AI as a field of study. McCarthy's contributions to AI were significant, including the development of the Lisp programming language, which became a popular tool for AI research. His work laid the foundation for many of the concepts and techniques used in AI today. McCarthy's vision and pioneering efforts have had a lasting impact on the development and evolution of artificial intelligence.

7.   WHAT IS THE OLD NAME OF AI?

The old name of AI is not specifically documented, as "Artificial Intelligence" has been the primary term used since its inception. However, before AI became a formal field of study, related concepts were often referred to under different terms such as "cybernetics" and "automata theory." Cybernetics, introduced by Norbert Wiener in the 1940s, focused on the study of communication and control in living organisms and machines. Automata theory, which emerged from the work of mathematicians like Alan Turing and John von Neumann, studied the behavior of abstract machines (automata) and their computational capabilities. These fields laid the groundwork for what would later be formally recognized as AI.

8.   WHAT IS THE FULL FORM OF AI?

The full form of AI is "Artificial Intelligence." This term refers to the simulation of human intelligence processes by machines, particularly computer systems. These processes include learning (acquiring knowledge and skills), reasoning (using logical rules to arrive at conclusions), self-correction, and problem-solving. AI encompasses a wide range of subfields, including machine learning, natural language processing, robotics, computer vision, and more. It aims to create systems that can perform tasks that typically require human intelligence, such as recognizing speech, making decisions, translating languages, and identifying patterns.

9. IS SIRI AN AI?

Yes, Siri is an AI. Siri is Apple's virtual assistant that uses artificial intelligence and natural language processing to interact with users and perform various tasks. Launched in 2011, Siri can answer questions, make recommendations, send messages, set reminders, provide weather updates, and more, by understanding and interpreting user commands. Siri leverages machine learning algorithms to improve its responses over time, becoming more accurate and personalized based on user interactions. Siri is an example of narrow AI, designed to assist with specific tasks within its programmed capabilities.

10. WHICH PROGRAMMING LANGUAGE IS USED FOR ARTIFICIAL INTELLIGENCE?

Several programming languages are used for artificial intelligence, with Python being the most popular and widely used. Python's simplicity, readability, and extensive libraries make it an ideal choice for AI development. Key libraries and frameworks for AI in Python include TensorFlow, Keras, PyTorch, Scikit-learn, and NLTK. Other programming languages commonly used in AI development include:

- **R**: Used primarily for statistical analysis and data visualization, R is popular in data science and machine learning applications.

- **Java**: Known for its portability and performance, Java is used in large-scale machine learning projects and enterprise-level AI applications.

- **C++**: Valued for its performance and efficiency, C++ is used in developing high-performance AI applications, such as game development and real-time systems.

- 💡 **Lisp**: One of the oldest languages used in AI research, Lisp offers features conducive to AI programming, such as rapid prototyping and dynamic typing.

- 💡 **Prolog**: Used in logic programming and natural language processing, Prolog is known for its strong pattern matching capabilities and declarative nature.

Each language has its strengths and is chosen based on the specific requirements and constraints of the AI project.

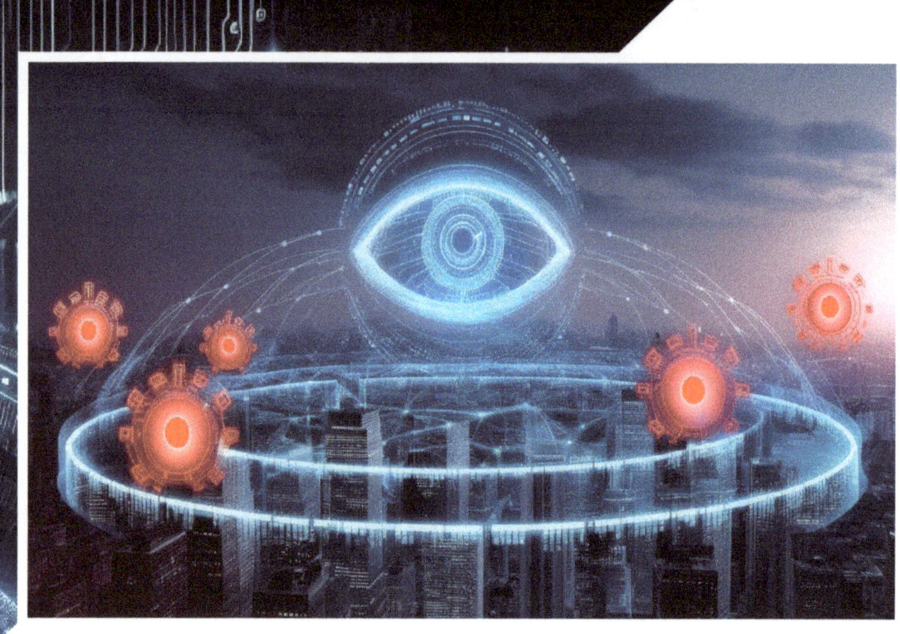

CHAPTER TWO
Understanding the Fundamentals of AI

IMPORTANCE OF UNDERSTANDING FUNDAMENTAL AI CONCEPTS AND TERMINOLOGIES

In any technical discipline, a deep understanding of fundamental concepts and precise terminology forms the bedrock of expertise. This is especially true for those engaging with the field of artificial intelligence (AI). Mastering the basic principles and language of AI is not just a step towards proficiency; it is an essential foundation for further learning, effective communication, and practical application. Whether you are a researcher, a practitioner, or someone aiming to make informed decisions about AI, being well-versed in its fundamental concepts and terminologies is crucial.

A solid grasp of the basics enables you to build a strong knowledge base that supports more advanced learning and complex problem-solving. It ensures that you can engage effectively with others in the field, minimizing misunderstandings and maximizing collaborative potential. Moreover, understanding AI at a foundational level is vital for applying its techniques correctly, whether you're developing new models, interpreting results, or implementing AI solutions in real-world scenarios. This knowledge also empowers you to navigate the ethical and societal challenges that come with AI, ensuring that your work contributes positively to society. Finally, staying current in a constantly evolving field requires a firm grounding in its fundamentals, allowing you to quickly assimilate new developments and innovations.

1. **BUILDING A STRONG FOUNDATION:**

    AI is a vast and intricate field, with numerous subfields, each characterized by its own distinct concepts and terminology. Grasping these basics is essential for establishing a solid foundation, which is necessary for progressing to more advanced topics. Just as learning the alphabet is essential before constructing sentences, understanding AI fundamentals is critical before diving into complex algorithms and applications. A strong foundational knowledge allows for better comprehension and integration of more sophisticated AI principles and techniques as they are encountered (Russell & Norvig, 2021).

2. **ENABLING EFFECTIVE COMMUNICATION:**

    Effective communication is pivotal in any technical domain, and AI is no exception. Whether collaborating with colleagues, presenting research, or discussing AI initiatives with stakeholders, the correct use of terminology ensures clarity and mutual understanding. Misunderstandings due to incorrect or vague terminology can lead to errors, inefficiencies, and missed opportunities. Mastering AI terminologies allows for more precise and effective communication, which is vital for successful collaboration and project outcomes (Goodfellow, Bengio, & Courville, 2016).

3.   FACILITATING LEARNING AND RESEARCH:

A deep understanding of fundamental concepts significantly enhances the ability to learn new material and engage in research. When the basics are well understood, it becomes easier to digest research papers, articles, and textbooks that introduce more complex ideas. This foundational knowledge also equips you to identify gaps in the current understanding of AI, thereby enabling you to contribute original research that advances the field (LeCun, Bengio, & Hinton, 2015).

4.   APPLYING AI TECHNIQUES EFFECTIVELY:

Practical applications of AI, such as developing machine learning models or implementing AI systems, demand a thorough understanding of underlying concepts. A solid grasp of the basics helps in selecting the appropriate algorithms, fine-tuning model parameters, and evaluating performance effectively. Without this foundational knowledge, applying AI techniques correctly and efficiently becomes challenging, which can result in suboptimal models or system failures (Murphy, 2012).

5.   NAVIGATING ETHICAL AND SOCIETAL IMPLICATIONS:

AI has profound ethical and societal implications that require careful consideration. Understanding fundamental AI concepts is crucial for navigating these issues responsibly. For instance, recognizing how bias can be introduced into AI models is essential for developing fair and equitable systems. Similarly, understanding AI's potential impact on employment, privacy, and governance informs better policy-making and ethical decision-making in the deployment of AI technologies (O'Neil, 2016).

6. **STAYING CURRENT WITH ADVANCES IN AI:**

The AI field is rapidly evolving, with new breakthroughs and innovations emerging regularly. A strong foundation in AI concepts and terminologies allows you to stay abreast of these advances. It enables quick comprehension of new ideas and their integration into your existing knowledge base, ensuring that you remain relevant, informed, and capable of contributing meaningfully in this dynamic and fast-paced field (Jordan & Mitchell, 2015).

KEY CONCEPTS AND TERMINOLOGIES

To lay the groundwork for a deeper understanding of AI, it is essential to familiarize oneself with several key concepts and terminologies. This section provides an overview of some of the most fundamental terms in AI.

1. **ARTIFICIAL INTELLIGENCE (AI):**

AI refers to the simulation of human intelligence processes by machines, especially computer systems. These processes include learning (the acquisition of information and rules for using it), reasoning (using rules to reach approximate or definite conclusions), and self-correction.

AI encompasses a wide range of technologies and applications, from simple rule-based systems to complex machine-learning algorithms and neural networks.

2. **MACHINE LEARNING (ML):**

A subset of AI that involves the use of algorithms and statistical models to enable machines to improve their performance on a specific task through experience. Instead of being explicitly programmed, ML systems learn from data.

Types:

i.   **Supervised Learning**: The algorithm is trained on a labeled dataset, meaning that each training example is paired with an output label.

ii. **Unsupervised Learning**: The algorithm is used to find patterns and relationships in a dataset without labeled responses.

iii. **Reinforcement Learning**: The algorithm learns by interacting with an environment and receiving rewards or penalties based on its actions.

3. **DEEP LEARNING:**

A subset of machine learning that involves neural networks with many layers (hence the term "deep"). These networks can model complex patterns in data and are particularly effective in tasks such as image and speech recognition.

4. **NEURAL NETWORKS:**

Composed of layers of interconnected nodes (neurons), which process data through weighted connections. Key architectures include Convolutional Neural Networks (CNNs) for image processing and Recurrent Neural Networks (RNNs) for sequential data.

5. **NATURAL LANGUAGE PROCESSING (NLP):**

    A field of AI focused on the interaction between computers and humans through natural language. The goal is to enable machines to understand, interpret, and generate human language in a valuable way. Its application includes machine translation, sentiment analysis, chatbots, and text summarization.

6. **COMPUTER VISION:**

    An AI field that enables machines to interpret and make decisions based on visual data from the world. This involves image processing, object detection, and scene understanding. Applications include facial recognition, autonomous driving, and medical image analysis.

7. **DATA SCIENCE:**

    Data is the cornerstone of AI. Data science involves collecting, processing, and analyzing large datasets to extract meaningful insights. This often involves techniques from statistics, machine learning, and data mining.

    i.   **Data Preprocessing**: Preparing raw data for analysis by cleaning, normalizing, and transforming it to ensure quality and relevance.

    ii. **Feature Engineering**: Creating new input features from raw data that can improve the performance of machine learning models.

8. **BIG DATA:**

    Refers to extremely large datasets that may be analyzed computationally to reveal patterns, trends, and associations, especially relating to human behavior and interactions.

The availability of big data has been a key driver in the advancement of AI, providing the vast amounts of information needed to train complex models.

9. ALGORITHM:

A set of rules or instructions given to an AI system to help it learn on its own. Algorithms are the building blocks of AI, guiding the decision-making process.

Types include decision trees, support vector machines, neural networks, and genetic algorithms.

10. 10. MODEL TRAINING AND EVALUATION:

i. **Training**: The process of teaching an AI model by feeding it data. During training, the model learns to map inputs to outputs based on the examples provided.

ii. **Validation and Testing**: After training, the model's performance is evaluated using separate validation and testing datasets to ensure it generalizes well to new, unseen data.

iii. **Metrics**: Common metrics for evaluating AI models include accuracy, precision, recall, F1 score, and area under the curve (AUC).

11. OVERFITTING AND UNDERFITTING:

i. **Overfitting**: Occurs when an AI model learns the training data too well, including noise and outliers, leading to poor generalization to new data.

ii. **Underfitting**: Happens when the model is too simple to capture the underlying patterns in the data, resulting in poor performance on both the training and new data.

iii. **Mitigation**: Techniques to address these issues include cross-validation, regularization, and pruning for decision trees.

12. BIAS AND VARIANCE:

i. **Bias**: Error due to overly simplistic assumptions in the learning algorithm. High bias can lead to underfitting.

ii. **Variance**: Error due to sensitivity to small fluctuations in the training set. High variance can lead to overfitting.

iii. **Trade-off**: Balancing bias and variance is crucial for developing robust AI models that generalize well.

MACHINE LEARNING, DEEP LEARNING, AND NEURAL NETWORKS

Machine Learning (ML), Deep Learning (DL), and Neural Networks (NN) are at the forefront of Artificial Intelligence (AI) research and application. These technologies have revolutionized various industries, enabling advancements in fields such as healthcare, finance, transportation, and more. Understanding these concepts, their differences, and their interconnections is crucial for leveraging their potential effectively. This section examines the details of ML, DL, and NNs, supported by relevant data, research, and reports.

MACHINE LEARNING (ML)

Machine Learning is a subset of AI that focuses on developing algorithms that allow computers to learn from and make predictions based on data. Unlike traditional programming, where explicit instructions are provided, ML algorithms improve their performance through experience. This approach enables systems to handle tasks that are impractical to program directly due to their complexity.

TYPES OF MACHINE LEARNING

1.   SUPERVISED LEARNING:

In supervised learning, the algorithm is trained on a labeled dataset, meaning that each training example is paired with an output label. The algorithm learns to map inputs to outputs based on this labeled data.

Common applications include image classification, speech recognition, and predictive analytics.

A classic example is the classification of emails as spam or non-spam. The algorithm is trained on a dataset of emails labeled as spam or not, learning to identify patterns that distinguish the two categories.

2.   UNSUPERVISED LEARNING:

Unsupervised learning involves training algorithms on data without labeled responses. The goal is to identify hidden patterns or structures within the data.

Applications include clustering (e.g., customer segmentation), anomaly detection, and association rule learning.

Market basket analysis, where the algorithm identifies products frequently bought together without pre-labeled data.

3.   REINFORCEMENT LEARNING:

Reinforcement learning involves training algorithms to make a sequence of decisions by rewarding them for good actions and penalizing them for bad ones. The agent learns to achieve a goal in an uncertain, potentially complex environment.

Applications include robotics, game playing, and autonomous vehicles.

An example is the AlphaGo, an AI developed by DeepMind, which used reinforcement learning to master the game of Go, learning optimal strategies through self-play and receiving rewards for successful moves.

KEY ALGORITHMS IN MACHINE LEARNING

Machine learning relies on a variety of algorithms that enable computers to analyze data, recognize patterns, and make predictions. These algorithms are the core tools that allow AI systems to learn and improve over time. Whether you're using basic linear models or more complex neural networks, understanding these key algorithms is essential for developing effective machine learning solutions. In this section, we will explore the fundamental algorithms that drive machine learning and discuss their practical applications.

1. **LINEAR REGRESSION**

   Linear regression is a foundational algorithm used to model the relationship between a continuous dependent variable and one or more independent variables. It operates by fitting a linear equation to observed data, aiming to minimize the difference between the actual values and the predicted values, often using a method known as least squares. The simplicity of linear regression makes it a popular choice for initial data analysis and model building, particularly when the relationship between variables is assumed to be linear. However, its limitations become apparent in the presence of non-linear relationships, multicollinearity, or when outliers significantly influence the model (Seber & Lee, 2012)

2. **LOGISTIC REGRESSION**

   Logistic regression is a widely used algorithm for binary classification tasks, where the outcome variable can take on one of two possible values. Unlike linear regression, logistic regression models the probability that a given input belongs to a particular class, using the logistic function to constrain the output to a value between 0 and 1. This makes it particularly useful for scenarios such as spam detection, where the goal is to predict the likelihood of an email being spam or not. Logistic regression can also be extended to multiclass classification through techniques like one-vs-all or multinomial logistic regression (Hosmer, Lemeshow, & Sturdivant, 2013).

3. DECISION TREES

Decision trees are non-parametric, supervised learning algorithms used for both classification and regression tasks. The algorithm works by recursively splitting the data into subsets based on the value of input features, leading to a tree-like structure of decisions. Each node in the tree represents a decision rule, and each branch represents the outcome of the rule, ultimately leading to a decision at the leaf nodes. Decision trees are highly interpretable and can handle both categorical and numerical data. However, they are prone to overfitting, which can be mitigated by techniques such as pruning, bagging, or boosting (Breiman, Friedman, Olshen, & Stone, 1984).

4. SUPPORT VECTOR MACHINES (SVM)

Support Vector Machines (SVMs) are powerful supervised learning algorithms used for both classification and regression tasks. The primary objective of SVM is to find the hyperplane that best separates different classes in the feature space, maximizing the margin between the classes. SVMs are particularly effective in high-dimensional spaces and are versatile, with kernel functions allowing them to model complex, non-linear decision boundaries. SVMs are widely used in applications such as image recognition, bioinformatics, and text classification (Cortes & Vapnik, 1995).

5. K-MEANS CLUSTERING

K-Means Clustering is an unsupervised learning algorithm that partitions a dataset into K distinct, non-overlapping clusters based on feature similarity. The algorithm iteratively assigns data points to clusters, recalculating the centroids of each cluster until the assignment stabilizes. K-Means is widely used for market segmentation, document clustering, and image compression due to its simplicity and efficiency. However, the algorithm requires the number of clusters (K) to be predefined and can struggle with clusters of varying sizes and densities (MacQueen, 1967).

6. PRINCIPAL COMPONENT ANALYSIS (PCA)

Principal Component Analysis (PCA) is an unsupervised learning algorithm primarily used for dimensionality reduction. PCA transforms the original data into a new coordinate system where the axes, called principal components, represent directions of maximum variance. The first few principal components often capture most of the variability in the data, allowing for a significant reduction in the number of features while retaining essential information. PCA is commonly used in areas such as image processing, genomics, and finance to simplify datasets, improve computational efficiency, and reduce noise (Jolliffe, 2011).

IMPACT AND APPLICATIONS OF MACHINE LEARNING

Machine learning has become a pivotal technology, driving significant advancements in how organizations analyze data, make decisions, and automate complex processes. By utilizing sophisticated algorithms, machine learning enables systems to learn from vast datasets, identify patterns, and make informed predictions (Bishop, 2006). This shift from traditional rule-based programming to data-driven models has allowed organizations to tackle challenges that were previously insurmountable (Mitchell, 1997).

The impact of machine learning is profound, offering improvements in accuracy, efficiency, and scalability across various applications (Murphy, 2012). Whether it's in predictive analytics, where models anticipate future outcomes, or in the automation of decision-making processes, machine learning enhances capabilities that are crucial for innovation and competitive advantage. Furthermore, its ability to continuously improve through exposure to new data makes it a dynamic tool that evolves alongside the challenges it addresses (Goodfellow, Bengio, & Courville, 2016).

In addition to its practical applications, machine learning also plays a critical role in advancing research, contributing to new methodologies and insights that drive the field forward. The increasing adoption of machine learning techniques reflects their effectiveness in solving complex problems, optimizing resources, and generating actionable insights from data.

Below, we explore some of the key applications of machine learning, demonstrating its widespread impact and the ways in which it is reshaping traditional approaches to problem-solving.

1. **HEALTHCARE:**
    i. **Diagnostics**: ML algorithms analyze medical images to detect diseases like cancer with high accuracy. For instance, Google's DeepMind developed an algorithm that can diagnose eye diseases as accurately as world-leading experts.
    ii. **Personalized Medicine**: ML models predict patient responses to treatments, allowing for personalized treatment plans.

2. **FINANCE:**
   i. **Fraud Detection**: ML algorithms detect fraudulent transactions by identifying patterns and anomalies in transaction data. According to a report by McKinsey, ML-based fraud detection systems can reduce financial losses significantly.

   ii. **Algorithmic Trading**: ML models analyze market data to predict stock price movements and execute trades automatically.

3. **RETAIL:**
   i. **Recommendation Systems**: Platforms like Amazon and Netflix use ML to recommend products and content based on user preferences and behavior. This personalization drives engagement and sales.

4. **TRANSPORTATION:**
   i. **Autonomous Vehicles**: Self-driving cars use ML to interpret sensor data, recognize objects, and make driving decisions in real-time. Companies like Tesla and Waymo are at the forefront of this technology.

CHALLENGES IN MACHINE LEARNING

Machine learning, despite its vast potential and transformative capabilities, faces several significant challenges that must be addressed to fully harness its power. These challenges span across various dimensions, including data quality and availability, model interpretability, overfitting, ethical considerations, and the practical deployment of models.

Addressing these challenges requires ongoing research, thoughtful design, and careful implementation. In the following sections, we will delve deeper into these challenges and explore potential strategies to overcome them.

1.   DATA QUALITY AND QUANTITY

The quality and accessibility of data are foundational to the success of machine learning models. Models require extensive datasets that are large, clean, unbiased, and representative. The challenges associated with gathering and preparing such data can significantly impact the performance and reliability of machine learning systems (Goodfellow, Bengio, & Courville, 2016).

2.   INTERPRETABILITY:

Many ML models, especially complex ones like neural networks, are often considered black boxes, making it difficult to interpret how decisions are made. This lack of transparency can be problematic in critical applications like healthcare and finance.

As machine learning models, especially those that are more complex, continue to evolve, understanding and explaining how these models arrive at their decisions becomes increasingly difficult. This "black-box" nature of many advanced models poses a significant barrier to their widespread adoption, particularly in contexts where transparency is crucial (Lipton, 2018).

3.   OVERFITTING AND UNDERFITTING:

Overfitting remains a persistent issue in machine learning. It occurs when a model is excessively tailored to the training data, leading to poor generalization to new, unseen data. This challenge highlights the delicate balance that must be maintained between model complexity and generalization capabilities (Hastie, Tibshirani, & Friedman, 2009).

4.   ETHICAL AND PRIVACY CONCERNS:

Ethical considerations, including bias, fairness, and privacy, also present significant challenges in the application of machine learning. As these systems increasingly influence critical decisions, ensuring that they are designed and implemented in a way that upholds ethical standards is of paramount importance (Obermeyer et al., 2019).

DEEP LEARNING (DL)

Deep Learning is a subset of Machine Learning that involves neural networks with many layers (hence the term "deep"). These neural networks, known as deep neural networks (DNNs), are capable of learning from large amounts of data and identifying complex patterns. DL models have significantly advanced the state-of-the-art in various AI applications, including image and speech recognition, natural language processing, and more.

Neural networks are a foundational component of modern artificial intelligence, inspired by the structure and function of the human brain. These computational models are designed to recognize patterns, process complex data, and make decisions with a level of accuracy that surpasses traditional algorithms. At the core of neural networks are interconnected layers of nodes, or "neurons," that work together to transform input data into meaningful outputs through a series of weighted connections and activation functions.

The basic structure of a neural network includes:

1.   **Input Layer**: Receives the input data.

2.   **Hidden Layers**: Intermediate layers where computations are performed. Deep neural networks have multiple hidden layers.

3.   **Output Layer**: Produces the final output.

Each neuron applies an activation function to the weighted sum of its inputs to determine its output. Common activation functions include the sigmoid, tanh, and ReLU (Rectified Linear Unit) functions.

The development of neural networks has been pivotal in advancing various fields within machine learning and artificial intelligence. These networks have the capacity to learn from large datasets through a process called training, where they adjust their internal parameters to minimize errors and improve predictive performance. This adaptability and learning capability make neural networks particularly powerful for tasks involving classification, regression, and pattern recognition (Goodfellow, Bengio, & Courville, 2016).

A key characteristic of neural networks is their ability to model complex, non-linear relationships between input and output variables. This is achieved through the use of multiple hidden layers within the network, which allow for the capture of intricate patterns in the data. The depth and architecture of a neural network can vary greatly, from simple networks with a single hidden layer to deep neural networks with many layers, each contributing to the network's ability to generalize and learn from data (LeCun, Bengio, & Hinton, 2015).

The study of neural networks encompasses a broad range of architectures, training methods, and optimization techniques. Understanding these concepts is essential for leveraging the full potential of neural networks in practical applications. This section will explore the fundamental principles underlying neural networks, their architectural variations, and the processes by which they are trained and optimized.

TYPES OF NEURAL NETWORKS

Neural networks are at the heart of modern artificial intelligence (AI) and machine learning, enabling systems to perform tasks ranging from image recognition to language translation. Different types of neural networks have been developed to handle various kinds of data and tasks. This section explores four of the most widely used neural network architectures: Feedforward Neural Networks (FNNs), Convolutional Neural Networks (CNNs), Recurrent Neural Networks (RNNs), and Generative Adversarial Networks (GANs). Each has its strengths and use cases, making them powerful tools for solving complex problems in AI.

1. FEEDFORWARD NEURAL NETWORKS (FNNS)

Feedforward Neural Networks (FNNs) are the simplest form of artificial neural networks. In FNNs, the information flows in one direction – from the input layer to the output layer—without any cycles or loops. There are no feedback connections, which means the data does not cycle back to earlier layers. This makes FNNs particularly suitable for tasks where no temporal or sequential dependencies are involved, such as:

- 💡 Regression tasks: Predicting continuous values like stock prices or house prices.

- 💡 Classification tasks: Categorizing data points into classes, such as determining whether an email is spam or not.

In FNNs, each neuron in one layer is fully connected to every neuron in the next layer. As the data moves through the network, the system applies weights to each connection, processing the input data and generating an output. These networks are typically trained using backpropagation and gradient descent, and they work well for relatively simple tasks. However, for more complex tasks like image or speech recognition, more advanced architectures are needed.

2. CONVOLUTIONAL NEURAL NETWORKS (CNNS)

Convolutional Neural Networks (CNNs) are designed to handle structured grid-like data, such as images. CNNs have become the go-to architecture for image recognition, video analysis, and computer vision tasks because of their ability to automatically learn hierarchical spatial features from raw input data.

In contrast to FNNs, CNNs use convolutional layers that apply filters (also known as kernels) to the input data, capturing local patterns such as edges, textures, or shapes. These filters slide over the input image, performing a dot product between the filter and a small region of the image, which helps the network detect spatial hierarchies of features. CNNs typically consist of multiple convolutional layers, followed by pooling layers that reduce the dimensionality of the data, and fully connected layers that output the final predictions.

💡 Use cases: CNNs are highly effective in image classification, object detection, facial recognition, and video analysis.

💡 Recent applications: CNNs are integral to autonomous driving systems, where they are used to process and interpret visual data from cameras in real time.

What sets CNNs apart is their ability to preserve spatial relationships in the data, making them more efficient than fully connected networks for tasks where spatial context is crucial.

3. RECURRENT NEURAL NETWORKS (RNNS)

Recurrent Neural Networks (RNNs) are designed to handle sequential data and are particularly useful for tasks that involve temporal dependencies. Unlike FNNs, RNNs have connections that form directed cycles, allowing the network to maintain a memory of previous inputs. This makes RNNs suitable for tasks where the order of the data matters, such as time series analysis and natural language processing (NLP).

In an RNN, the hidden state is updated at each time step based on both the current input and the previous hidden state, allowing the network to "remember" past information. However, RNNs can suffer from issues related to vanishing gradients, which make it difficult for them to capture long-term dependencies in the data.

💡 Use cases: RNNs are used for tasks such as speech recognition, machine translation, time series forecasting, and sentiment analysis.

To address the vanishing gradient problem, variants of RNNs have been developed:

💡 Long Short-Term Memory (LSTM): LSTMs use gates to regulate the flow of information, allowing the network to maintain and update memory over longer sequences.

💡 Gated Recurrent Units (GRU): GRUs simplify the LSTM architecture while still retaining the ability to model long-term dependencies.

Both LSTM and GRU networks have achieved impressive results in various NLP tasks, including machine translation and text generation. For instance, LSTM models power applications like Google Translate and chatbots that rely on sequential data processing.

4. GENERATIVE ADVERSARIAL NETWORKS (GANS)

Generative Adversarial Networks (GANs) represent one of the most exciting advancements in machine learning. Introduced by Ian Goodfellow in 2014, GANs consist of two neural networks—a generator and a discriminator—that compete against each other in a zero-sum game.

💡 The generator creates fake data (e.g., images or videos), trying to mimic real data as closely as possible.

💡 The discriminator tries to distinguish between real data and the data generated by the generator. Over time, the generator improves its ability to produce realistic data as it tries to "fool" the discriminator.

This adversarial setup allows GANs to generate high-quality synthetic data that is indistinguishable from real data. The applications of GANs are vast, ranging from image generation and video synthesis to text-to-image models and deepfake creation.

💡 Use cases: GANs have been used to generate realistic images, artworks, video game characters, and even synthetic data for training AI models. They are also widely used in image-to-image translation tasks, such as transforming sketches into photorealistic images or converting daytime images into nighttime ones.

One of the most notable applications of GANs is in the creation of deepfakes, where AI-generated videos or images make it appear as though someone said or did something they never actually did. While GANs have significant potential in creative fields, they also raise ethical concerns, particularly in terms of misinformation and privacy.

Neural networks have evolved into a diverse set of architectures designed to tackle various tasks. Feedforward Neural Networks (FNNs) are foundational models suitable for basic tasks like regression and classification. Convolutional Neural Networks (CNNs) excel at handling grid-like data such as images and videos, while Recurrent Neural Networks (RNNs) are specialized for sequential data. Finally, Generative Adversarial Networks (GANs) offer innovative solutions for generating synthetic data and have opened new frontiers in creative AI applications. By selecting the right type of neural network for a specific task, machine learning practitioners can harness the power of AI to solve complex problems across industries.

TRAINING DEEP NEURAL NETWORKS: A COMPREHENSIVE BREAKDOWN

Training a deep neural network (DNN) is a fundamental process in machine learning and AI, designed to enable the model to learn from data and make accurate predictions. This process involves a series of steps that are executed iteratively to optimize the network's performance. Below is a detailed breakdown of the key stages in training a DNN, including forward propagation, loss calculation, backpropagation, and weight updates, all of which work together to refine the model and minimize prediction errors.

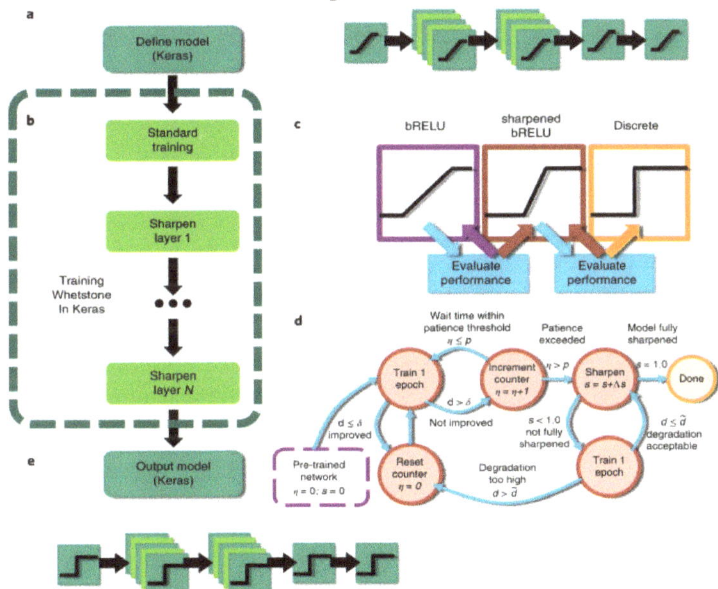

Training Deep Neural Networks

STEP 1: FORWARD PROPAGATION

The first step in training a neural network is forward propagation, where the input data is passed through the network, layer by layer, to generate predictions. The architecture of a deep neural network consists of multiple layers, including input, hidden, and output layers. Each layer is made up of neurons (or nodes) that process the input data by applying a set of weights and biases.

In forward propagation, the data moves sequentially through the layers, where each layer performs a linear transformation on the input followed by a nonlinear activation function. Common activation functions include ReLU (Rectified Linear Unit) for hidden layers and softmax for output layers in classification tasks. As the data flows through the network, the neurons "activate" based on the learned patterns, producing an output or prediction.

STEP 2: LOSS CALCULATION

Once the network generates its predictions, the next step is to evaluate the model's performance by calculating the loss or error. The loss function measures the difference between the predicted values and the actual labels. For instance, if the task is binary classification, the loss function will compare the model's output probabilities with the actual class labels.

The choice of the loss function depends on the nature of the task:

- For regression tasks, mean squared error (MSE) is a commonly used loss function. It calculates the average squared difference between predicted and actual values.

- For classification tasks, cross-entropy loss (also known as log loss) is widely used. This function measures the performance of a classification model by penalizing the model when it assigns incorrect probabilities to the predicted class.

The loss function provides a scalar value that quantifies how well or poorly the model performed during forward propagation, with lower loss values indicating better performance.

STEP 3: BACKWARD PROPAGATION

After calculating the loss, the next step is backward propagation (or backpropagation), a critical process for training deep neural networks. Backpropagation calculates the gradients of the loss with respect to each of the weights in the network. These gradients indicate how much a small change in each weight will affect the loss, allowing the model to adjust its weights accordingly.

Backpropagation relies on the chain rule of calculus to propagate the gradients backward through the network, starting from the output layer and moving toward the input layer. Each layer's gradients are computed based on the gradients of the subsequent layers, ensuring that the entire network's parameters are adjusted to reduce the loss. This process is computationally intensive, especially in deep networks with many layers, but it is essential for optimizing the model.

In addition to calculating the gradients for the weights, backpropagation also computes the gradients for the biases. The biases are parameters that allow the model to fit the training data more accurately by shifting the activation function.

STEP 4: WEIGHT UPDATE

Once the gradients are computed during backpropagation, the weights of the neural network are updated to minimize the loss. This is done using an optimization algorithm, such as stochastic gradient descent (SGD) or Adam, both of which adjust the weights iteratively over multiple epochs (complete passes through the training data).

 Stochastic Gradient Descent (SGD): In SGD, the weights are updated after each training example, making it a fast and effective optimization method for large datasets. However, SGD can be noisy and may not always converge quickly.

💡 Adam: A more advanced optimizer, Adam combines the benefits of two other methods: Adaptive Gradient Algorithm (AdaGrad) and RMSProp. Adam adjusts the learning rate for each parameter based on the first and second moments of the gradients, providing better stability and faster convergence in practice.

The update rule for weights is generally expressed as:

$$w := w - \eta \cdot \nabla L$$

$$W : - w - \eta \cdot \nabla L$$

where:

◈ w is the weight,

◈ $\eta\eta$ is the learning rate (which controls the size of the update steps),

and

◈ ∇L is the gradient of the loss with respect to the weight.

This process is repeated over several iterations or epochs, allowing the model to gradually improve and minimize the loss. During each epoch, the model is fine-tuned to fit the training data better, and the goal is to reach a point where the model converges, meaning that further updates to the weights have minimal impact on the loss.

IMPORTANCE OF CONTINUOUS OPTIMIZATION

Training a deep neural network is not a one-time task; it requires continuous monitoring and optimization to achieve the best results. This includes adjusting the learning rate, implementing regularization techniques to prevent overfitting, and using early stopping mechanisms to avoid excessive training that could degrade performance.

Moreover, the process of training deep neural networks often benefits from ongoing research into optimization methods and new techniques for improving convergence speed and model accuracy. For example, recent developments in gradient clipping and batch normalization have significantly improved the efficiency and stability of neural network training.

CHALLENGES IN DEEP LEARNING

While deep learning has revolutionized many fields—from computer vision to natural language processing—it is not without its challenges. These challenges range from data and computational requirements to ethical concerns, all of which must be addressed for deep learning models to be more effective, transparent, and fair. Below, we explore some of the most significant challenges facing deep learning today and the steps being taken to mitigate them.

1. DATA REQUIREMENTS

One of the most significant challenges in deep learning is the need for large amounts of labeled data. Deep learning models, particularly those with many layers and parameters, perform best when trained on vast datasets that cover a wide range of scenarios. However, acquiring such datasets can be both expensive and time-consuming.

For example, in image recognition tasks, millions of labeled images may be required for the model to learn the intricate patterns necessary for accurate predictions. Labeling this data, especially in specialized fields like medical imaging, often requires expert knowledge, which can be costly.

To address this challenge, researchers are exploring techniques such as:

💡 **Transfer learning**, where a model pre-trained on a large dataset is fine-tuned on a smaller dataset for a specific task.

💡 **Data augmentation**, which artificially increases the size of a dataset by making modifications to existing data (e.g., flipping or rotating images).

However, despite these advancements, the data dependency of deep learning remains a significant bottleneck, particularly for smaller organizations with limited resources.

2. COMPUTATIONAL RESOURCE DEMANDS

Training deep neural networks requires substantial computational resources, particularly Graphics Processing Units (GPUs) and Tensor Processing Units (TPUs). These specialized hardware units are necessary to handle the vast number of computations involved in training large models.

For instance, training models like GPT-3, with billions of parameters, requires vast amounts of memory and computational power, often running on hundreds or thousands of GPUs for extended periods. This makes deep learning inaccessible to many organizations with limited budgets or infrastructure. The high costs of cloud computing services, energy consumption, and the need for specialized hardware represent substantial barriers.

Solutions such as distributed computing and model compression are being developed to alleviate these issues. By distributing the workload across multiple machines or compressing models to require fewer resources without sacrificing accuracy, researchers aim to make deep learning more efficient and accessible.

However, the demand for computational power remains a significant challenge, and organizations must carefully consider the cost-benefit ratio when implementing deep learning solutions.

3. INTERPRETABILITY

One of the most persistent criticisms of deep learning models is their lack of interpretability. These models are often considered "black boxes" because they make predictions based on complex, layered interactions between inputs and parameters that are not easily understood by humans. In many cases, it is difficult to explain why a model made a particular decision, especially in high-stakes applications such as healthcare or finance.

The opacity of deep learning models raises concerns about trust and accountability. For example, in a medical diagnosis setting, clinicians and patients may be hesitant to trust a model's prediction if they cannot understand the rationale behind it. Similarly, in the financial sector, regulatory bodies may require explanations for decisions made by AI-driven trading algorithms.

To address the challenge of interpretability, researchers are developing explainable AI (XAI) methods that aim to make deep learning models more transparent. Techniques such as Layer-wise Relevance Propagation (LRP) and SHAP values (Shapley Additive Explanations) allow for more granular insight into how models make decisions. These tools help highlight the most important features contributing to a prediction, offering a step toward more interpretable deep learning systems.

Nonetheless, the quest for truly interpretable deep learning models continues to be a challenge, especially as models grow more complex.

4. OVERFITTING

Overfitting is a common issue in deep learning, particularly when models become too complex for the amount of training data available. In such cases, the model learns to memorize the training data, leading to excellent performance on the training set but poor generalization to new, unseen data. This issue undermines the model's usefulness in real-world applications, where it needs to perform well on new data.

Deep learning models, with their high number of parameters, are especially prone to overfitting. To combat this, several techniques have been developed:

- **Dropout**: Randomly "dropping out" units (neurons) in the network during training to prevent co-adaptation of neurons, encouraging the model to learn more robust features.

- **Regularization**: Adding a penalty term to the loss function that discourages large weights, helping the model avoid overfitting.

- **Data augmentation**: Expanding the training data by making slight modifications (e.g., rotation, scaling) to create new examples, thereby improving generalization.

Despite these techniques, overfitting remains a persistent challenge, particularly in domains with limited labeled data. Researchers continue to explore new methods, such as early stopping (stopping training when the performance on a validation set starts to degrade) to mitigate this issue.

5. ETHICAL CONCERNS

As deep learning becomes more integrated into critical systems, ethical concerns surrounding its deployment grow increasingly prominent. Several key ethical issues include:

- **Bias in training data**: Deep learning models are only as good as the data they are trained on. If the training data contains biases—whether in terms of race, gender, or socioeconomic status—those biases can be perpetuated in the model's predictions. For example, facial recognition systems have been shown to have higher error rates for people of color, which can lead to unfair outcomes in areas like law enforcement.

💡 **Transparency and accountability**: As mentioned, the black-box nature of deep learning models makes it difficult to ensure accountability, especially when AI systems are used to make decisions that affect people's lives. Who is responsible when an AI system makes a biased or harmful decision?

💡 **Malicious applications**: Deep learning can be weaponized for nefarious purposes, such as creating deepfakes, which are highly realistic but fake media content that can be used to spread misinformation or harm individuals.

To address these ethical concerns, frameworks such as AI ethics guidelines and fairness audits are becoming more common. Organizations like the European Union have established guidelines for the ethical development and use of AI systems, focusing on transparency, fairness, and accountability. Moreover, researchers are working on building bias detection and mitigation tools into AI systems to ensure that models are trained fairly.

Despite these efforts, ensuring ethical AI deployment remains an ongoing challenge. Policymakers, researchers, and developers must work collaboratively to create frameworks that ensure AI is used responsibly and equitably.

AI CAPABILITIES AND LIMITATIONS

Artificial Intelligence (AI) has made significant strides in recent years, transforming various industries and improving the efficiency and effectiveness of numerous processes. However, despite its remarkable capabilities, AI also has several limitations that need to be acknowledged. This section provides a detailed examination of the capabilities and limitations of AI, supported by relevant data, reports, and examples.

AI CAPABILITIES

1. DATA ANALYSIS AND PATTERN RECOGNITION

AI excels at analyzing large datasets and identifying patterns that may not be immediately apparent to humans. Machine learning algorithms can process vast amounts of data quickly, making AI particularly useful in fields that generate significant data volumes.

For example In healthcare, AI algorithms analyze medical images to detect diseases such as cancer with high accuracy. A study published in *Nature* reported that an AI system developed by Google Health was able to detect breast cancer in mammograms with greater accuracy than radiologists, reducing false positives by 5.7% and false negatives by 9.4%.

2. AUTOMATION OF REPETITIVE TASKS

AI can automate routine and repetitive tasks, freeing up human workers to focus on more complex and creative activities. This capability enhances productivity and efficiency across various sectors.

For example, in manufacturing, AI-powered robots are used for assembly line tasks, quality control, and predictive maintenance. According to a report by *McKinsey & Company*, AI-driven automation can increase productivity by up to 20% and reduce maintenance costs by up to 10%.

3. NATURAL LANGUAGE PROCESSING (NLP)

AI has made significant advancements in NLP, enabling machines to understand, interpret, and generate human language. This capability is crucial for applications such as chatbots, virtual assistants, and language translation.

For instance, OpenAI's GPT-3, a state-of-the-art language model, can generate coherent and contextually relevant text based on a given prompt. It has been used to create content, answer questions, and even write code. The model's performance has been widely recognized, with the *New York Times* describing it as "the best AI language model ever created".

4. IMAGE AND VIDEO RECOGNITION

AI algorithms, particularly convolutional neural networks (CNNs), have demonstrated exceptional performance in image and video recognition tasks. These capabilities are employed in various applications, from security to entertainment.

In autonomous vehicles, AI-powered systems use image recognition to identify objects, lane markings, and traffic signs, enabling safe and efficient navigation. Tesla's Autopilot system uses a combination of cameras, radar, and AI to achieve semi-autonomous driving capabilities.

5. PREDICTIVE ANALYTICS

AI's ability to analyze historical data and make accurate predictions is valuable in numerous domains, including finance, healthcare, and marketing.

In finance, AI models are used for credit scoring, fraud detection, and algorithmic trading. JPMorgan Chase's COiN platform uses AI to analyze legal documents and extract relevant information, reducing the time required for document review by 360,000 hours annually.

6. PERSONALIZATION

AI enables personalized experiences by analyzing user behavior and preferences. This capability is widely used in e-commerce, entertainment, and digital marketing.

Netflix uses AI to recommend content to users based on their viewing history and preferences. According to Netflix, its recommendation system is responsible for over 80% of the content watched on the platform.

7. ROBOTICS AND AUTONOMOUS SYSTEMS

AI is integral to the development of robots and autonomous systems capable of performing complex tasks in various environments.

Boston Dynamics' robots, such as Spot and Atlas, use AI to navigate challenging terrains, perform inspections, and carry out tasks autonomously. These robots are used in industries ranging from logistics to healthcare.

8. ENHANCED CYBERSECURITY

AI enhances cybersecurity by identifying and responding to threats more quickly and accurately than traditional methods.

Darktrace's AI-driven cybersecurity platform uses machine learning to detect and respond to cyber threats in real-time. The platform can identify anomalies and potential threats within seconds, significantly reducing the risk of data breaches
.

AI LIMITATIONS

While artificial intelligence (AI) has made remarkable strides in recent years, it is not without its limitations. The transformative potential of AI is often constrained by several key factors that impact its reliability, effectiveness, and ethical implications. These limitations stem largely from AI's dependency on vast amounts of data, its inability to generalize across tasks, and the challenges surrounding interpretability. Moreover, as AI becomes more integrated into critical decision-making processes, issues related to bias and fairness have emerged as significant concerns. Understanding these limitations is crucial for developing more robust, transparent, and ethical AI systems that can meet the complex demands of real-world applications.

1. DATA DEPENDENCY

AI systems rely heavily on large datasets for training. The quality and quantity of the data significantly impact the performance of AI models. Insufficient or biased data can lead to inaccurate predictions and decisions.

Example: Facial recognition systems have been criticized for their higher error rates when identifying individuals from minority groups. A study by the *National Institute of Standards and Technology (NIST)* found that facial recognition algorithms were less accurate in identifying African American and Asian faces compared to Caucasian faces.

2. LACK OF GENERALIZATION

Most AI models are designed for specific tasks and struggle to generalize beyond their training. Unlike humans, AI lacks the ability to apply knowledge from one domain to another effectively.

Example: An AI model trained to play chess at a superhuman level cannot apply its knowledge to another game, such as Go, without retraining. This limitation is evident in many AI applications, where models excel in narrow tasks but fail to generalize.

3. INTERPRETABILITY AND TRANSPARENCY

AI models, particularly deep learning networks, are often considered "black boxes" because their decision-making processes are not easily interpretable. This lack of transparency can be problematic in critical applications where understanding the rationale behind decisions is essential.

Example: In healthcare, AI systems used for diagnostics need to provide clear explanations for their predictions to be trusted by medical professionals. A black-box model that identifies a patient as high-risk without explaining why may not be useful in clinical practice.

4. ETHICAL AND BIAS ISSUES

AI systems can perpetuate and even amplify existing biases present in the training data. Ethical concerns arise when AI decisions adversely impact individuals or groups.

Example: AI algorithms used in hiring processes have been found to exhibit bias against certain demographic groups. For instance, a hiring algorithm developed by Amazon was found to favor male candidates over female candidates, as it was trained on historical hiring data that reflected gender biases .

5. SECURITY VULNERABILITIES

AI systems are vulnerable to adversarial attacks, where malicious inputs are crafted to deceive the model into making incorrect predictions.

Example: Adversarial attacks on image recognition systems can cause AI models to misclassify images with high confidence. Researchers have demonstrated that adding imperceptible noise to an image can trick an AI model into misidentifying a panda as a gibbon .

6. HIGH COMPUTATIONAL REQUIREMENTS

Training and deploying AI models, especially deep learning networks, require significant computational resources. This limitation can be a barrier for organizations with limited access to high-performance computing infrastructure.

Example: Training large-scale AI models, such as OpenAI's GPT-3, requires powerful GPUs and extensive computational power. The costs associated with such resources can be prohibitive for smaller organizations and research institutions.

7. ETHICAL CONCERNS IN DATA USAGE

The use of personal data in AI systems raises privacy and ethical concerns. Ensuring that data is collected and used responsibly is crucial to maintaining public trust.

Example: The Cambridge Analytica scandal highlighted the misuse of personal data for political advertising, leading to widespread concerns about data privacy and the ethical implications of AI.

8. LEGAL AND REGULATORY CHALLENGES

The rapid advancement of AI technology has outpaced the development of legal and regulatory frameworks. Ensuring that AI systems comply with existing laws and regulations is a complex and ongoing challenge.

Example: The European Union's General Data Protection Regulation (GDPR) imposes strict requirements on the use of personal data, affecting how AI systems are developed and deployed. Compliance with such regulations is essential to avoid legal repercussions.

AI IN VARIOUS SECTORS: HEALTHCARE, FINANCE, MANUFACTURING

Artificial Intelligence (AI) is revolutionizing numerous sectors, enhancing efficiency, accuracy, and decision-making processes. This section explores the impact of AI in healthcare, finance, manufacturing, and other key industries, supported by relevant data, statistics, and reports.

AI IN HEALTHCARE

DIAGNOSTICS AND DISEASE DETECTION

AI is transforming diagnostics by providing tools that can analyze medical images and data to detect diseases with high accuracy. Machine learning algorithms can identify patterns in imaging data, often surpassing human capabilities

A study published in *Nature* reported that an AI system developed by Google Health could detect breast cancer in mammograms with greater accuracy than radiologists, reducing false positives by 5.7% and false negatives by 9.4%. This improvement in diagnostic accuracy can lead to earlier detection and better patient outcomes.

PERSONALIZED MEDICINE

AI enables personalized medicine by analyzing patient data to predict individual responses to treatments, allowing for tailored therapy plans.

IBM Watson for Oncology uses AI to analyze patient medical records and recommend personalized treatment plans. According to a study by *JCO Clinical Cancer Informatics*, Watson's treatment recommendations were concordant with those of oncologists in 93% of cases, demonstrating its potential to support clinical decision-making.

PREDICTIVE ANALYTICS

Predictive analytics powered by AI can forecast disease outbreaks, patient admissions, and treatment outcomes, helping healthcare providers allocate resources more effectively.

BlueDot, an AI-based platform, predicted the outbreak of COVID-19 before it was officially announced by analyzing news reports, airline data, and other sources. This early warning allowed governments and organizations to take proactive measures.

ROBOTIC SURGERY

Robotic surgery systems, enhanced with AI, offer greater precision, flexibility, and control than traditional techniques. AI assists in planning and executing complex surgical procedures.

The da Vinci Surgical System, powered by AI, allows surgeons to perform minimally invasive procedures with enhanced precision. Studies have shown that robotic surgery can reduce recovery times and complications compared to traditional surgery.

ADMINISTRATIVE TASKS AND WORKFLOW OPTIMIZATION

AI automates administrative tasks such as scheduling, billing, and patient record management, reducing the burden on healthcare professionals and improving operational efficiency.

Mayo Clinic uses AI to optimize appointment scheduling, ensuring that resources are used efficiently and reducing patient wait times.

AI IN FINANCE

FRAUD DETECTION

AI algorithms analyze transaction data to detect and prevent fraudulent activities in real-time. These systems identify patterns and anomalies that may indicate fraud, enabling swift action.

JPMorgan Chase uses AI-powered fraud detection systems to monitor transactions and flag suspicious activities. According to a report by *McKinsey & Company*, AI-based fraud detection can reduce financial losses by up to 50%.

ALGORITHMIC TRADING

AI-driven algorithmic trading systems analyze market data and execute trades at high speeds, capitalizing on market opportunities and optimizing investment strategies.

Renaissance Technologies, a hedge fund that utilizes AI for trading, has consistently outperformed traditional investment strategies, achieving annual returns of over 35% since its inception.

CREDIT SCORING

AI improves credit scoring by analyzing a broader range of data points than traditional methods, providing more accurate assessments of creditworthiness.

Zest AI uses machine learning to evaluate credit risk, enabling lenders to approve more loans while reducing default rates. According to Zest AI, their models can reduce default rates by up to 50% compared to traditional credit scoring methods.

CUSTOMER SERVICE AND CHATBOTS

AI-powered chatbots and virtual assistants provide 24/7 customer service, handling routine inquiries and transactions, and freeing up human agents for more complex tasks.

Bank of America's Erica is an AI-driven virtual assistant that helps customers with tasks such as checking account balances, transferring funds, and providing financial advice. Since its launch, Erica has served over 7 million users and handled more than 50 million client requests.

REGULATORY COMPLIANCE

AI helps financial institutions comply with regulatory requirements by automating processes such as anti-money laundering (AML) and know-your-customer (KYC) checks.

HSBC uses AI to automate AML processes, reducing the time required for compliance checks by 60% and improving the accuracy of suspicious activity detection.

AI IN MANUFACTURING

PREDICTIVE MAINTENANCE

AI enables predictive maintenance by analyzing data from sensors and equipment to predict failures before they occur, reducing downtime and maintenance costs.

General Electric (GE) uses AI-powered predictive maintenance to monitor industrial machinery. According to GE, their AI-driven maintenance solutions can reduce unplanned downtime by up to 20%.

QUALITY CONTROL

AI enhances quality control by using computer vision to inspect products for defects, ensuring high standards of quality and consistency.

Fanuc, a leading robotics manufacturer, uses AI to improve quality control in its production lines. AI-powered systems can detect defects with greater accuracy and speed than human inspectors, reducing waste and rework costs.

SUPPLY CHAIN OPTIMIZATION

AI optimizes supply chain management by forecasting demand, managing inventory, and optimizing logistics, leading to increased efficiency and cost savings.

DHL uses AI to optimize its supply chain operations, including route planning and demand forecasting. According to DHL, AI-driven supply chain optimization can reduce logistics costs by up to 15%.

ROBOTICS AND AUTOMATION

AI-powered robots perform complex manufacturing tasks with high precision and efficiency, enhancing productivity and reducing labor costs.

Tesla's Gigafactory employs AI-driven robots for tasks such as assembly, painting, and material handling. This high level of automation has enabled Tesla to scale production and improve the quality of its vehicles.

PRODUCT DESIGN AND DEVELOPMENT

AI accelerates product design and development by simulating different designs and predicting their performance, reducing the time and cost associated with prototyping.

Autodesk's Generative Design uses AI to explore thousands of design options based on specified constraints and objectives. This allows engineers to identify optimal designs more quickly and efficiently.

AI IN RETAIL

PERSONALIZED SHOPPING EXPERIENCES

AI analyzes customer behavior and preferences to provide personalized product recommendations and shopping experiences, increasing customer satisfaction and sales.

Amazon uses AI to recommend products based on browsing history, purchase behavior, and other data points. According to Amazon, its recommendation engine drives 35% of total sales.

INVENTORY MANAGEMENT

AI optimizes inventory management by predicting demand and automating restocking processes, reducing stockouts and overstock situations.

Walmart uses AI to manage inventory across its stores. AI-driven demand forecasting and inventory management have helped Walmart reduce excess inventory by 10% and improve in-stock levels by 2%.

PRICING OPTIMIZATION

AI enables dynamic pricing strategies by analyzing market conditions, competitor prices, and customer behavior, allowing retailers to adjust prices in real-time to maximize revenue.

Zara uses AI to implement dynamic pricing, adjusting prices based on factors such as demand, seasonality, and inventory levels. This strategy has helped Zara maintain competitive pricing and optimize revenue.

CUSTOMER SERVICE

AI-powered chatbots and virtual assistants handle customer inquiries, provide product information, and assist with transactions, improving customer service efficiency.

H&M uses an AI-powered chatbot to assist customers with finding products, checking order status, and answering common questions. The chatbot has improved customer service response times and satisfaction.

FRAUD PREVENTION

AI enhances fraud prevention by detecting suspicious transactions and activities, protecting retailers and customers from fraudulent activities.

Alibaba uses AI to detect and prevent fraud in its e-commerce platform. AI algorithms analyze transaction data to identify patterns indicative of fraud, reducing fraudulent activities by 30%.

AI IN TRANSPORTATION AND LOGISTICS

AUTONOMOUS VEHICLES

AI enables the development of autonomous vehicles capable of navigating and making decisions in real-time, reducing the need for human drivers and enhancing safety.

Waymo, a subsidiary of Alphabet Inc., has developed self-driving cars that use AI to interpret sensor data and navigate complex urban environments. Waymo's autonomous vehicles have driven over 20 million miles on public roads, demonstrating the potential of AI in transportation.

FLEET MANAGEMENT

AI optimizes fleet management by analyzing data on vehicle usage, maintenance needs, and routes to improve efficiency and reduce costs.

UPS uses AI to optimize delivery routes, reducing fuel consumption and delivery times. According to UPS, their AI-driven ORION (On-Road Integrated Optimization and Navigation) system has saved the company 10 million gallons of fuel annually.

PREDICTIVE MAINTENANCE

Similar to its application in manufacturing, AI enables predictive maintenance in transportation by monitoring vehicle health and predicting failures, reducing downtime and maintenance costs.

Delta Air Lines uses AI to predict maintenance needs for its aircraft. AI-driven predictive maintenance has helped Delta reduce maintenance-related delays by 36%.

TRAFFIC MANAGEMENT

AI improves traffic management by analyzing data from various sources to optimize traffic flow and reduce congestion.

Singapore uses AI to manage its traffic system, analyzing data from traffic cameras and sensors to optimize signal timings and reduce congestion. This has resulted in a 15% reduction in travel times during peak hours.

AI IN AGRICULTURE

PRECISION FARMING

AI enables precision farming by analyzing data from sensors, drones, and satellites to optimize crop yields and resource usage.

John Deere's AI-driven precision agriculture solutions help farmers optimize planting, fertilization, and irrigation. According to John Deere, AI can increase crop yields by up to 20% while reducing resource usage.

CROP MONITORING AND DISEASE DETECTION

AI-powered systems use computer vision and machine learning to monitor crop health and detect diseases early, allowing for timely interventions.

Plantix, an AI-based app, helps farmers diagnose plant diseases by analyzing photos of crops. The app provides treatment recommendations, helping farmers reduce crop losses.

AUTOMATED HARVESTING

AI-driven robots are used for automated harvesting, reducing labor costs and increasing efficiency.

Agrobot's AI-powered harvesting robots use computer vision to identify ripe strawberries and pick them with precision, improving harvesting efficiency and reducing labor costs.

AI IN EDUCATION

PERSONALIZED LEARNING

AI provides personalized learning experiences by analyzing student performance and adapting instructional content to meet individual needs.

Carnegie Learning uses AI to create personalized learning paths for students in subjects like math and science. The AI-driven platform adjusts the difficulty and pace of lessons based on student progress, improving learning outcomes.

ADMINISTRATIVE EFFICIENCY

AI automates administrative tasks such as grading, scheduling, and resource allocation, freeing up educators to focus on teaching.

Georgia State University uses an AI-powered chatbot to assist with administrative tasks such as enrollment and financial aid queries. The chatbot has handled over 200,000 inquiries, improving administrative efficiency and student satisfaction.

EARLY INTERVENTION

AI identifies students at risk of falling behind or dropping out by analyzing academic performance and engagement data, enabling early intervention.

Purdue University's Course Signals uses AI to identify at-risk students and provide targeted support, resulting in a 21% increase in retention rates.

ETHICAL AND SOCIETAL IMPLICATIONS OF AI

The rapid development and deployment of AI technologies raise numerous questions and concerns related to privacy, fairness, accountability, job displacement, and more. This section explores these implications in detail, supported by relevant data, reports, and research.

PRIVACY CONCERNS

As artificial intelligence (AI) systems become more advanced and widespread, they increasingly rely on extensive data collection to function effectively. This dependence on vast amounts of personal, behavioral, and biometric data has sparked growing concerns about privacy. The ability of AI to gather, analyze, and track such sensitive information has led to debates about the implications of surveillance and data misuse. As AI becomes embedded in everyday life, safeguarding privacy and establishing clear boundaries for data usage is essential to maintain public trust and ensure ethical AI deployment.

AI systems often require vast amounts of data to function effectively, leading to increased data collection from individuals. This data can include personal information, behavioral patterns, and even biometric data. The extent of data collection has raised significant privacy concerns.

Facebook-Cambridge Analytica scandal highlighted the misuse of personal data collected from millions of users without their consent. This data was used to influence political campaigns, raising questions about the ethics of data collection and privacy violations.

SURVEILLANCE AND MONITORING

AI-powered surveillance systems can monitor public and private spaces, raising concerns about the erosion of privacy and the potential for misuse.

China's extensive use of AI for public surveillance includes facial recognition systems that monitor citizens' activities. Reports by *Human Rights Watch* and other organizations have raised concerns about the potential for abuse and the impact on civil liberties.

DATA SECURITY

The vast amount of data collected by AI systems must be securely stored and protected from breaches. Data breaches can lead to severe consequences, including identity theft and financial loss.

According to the *2019 Cost of a Data Breach Report* by IBM Security, the average cost of a data breach is $3.92 million, highlighting the financial impact of inadequate data security measures.

BIAS AND FAIRNESS

Despite their potential to bring about positive change, AI systems are not immune to bias. One of the most pressing challenges in AI development is algorithmic bias, where systems inherit and even amplify the biases embedded in the data they are trained on. This can result in unfair and discriminatory outcomes that disproportionately impact marginalized groups. From hiring practices to law enforcement and lending decisions, biased AI systems can reinforce societal inequalities, making it crucial to address these issues to ensure fairness and equity in AI-driven processes.

ALGORITHMIC BIAS

AI systems can inherit biases present in their training data, leading to unfair and discriminatory outcomes. This bias can affect various aspects of society, including hiring practices, law enforcement, and lending decisions.

A study by MIT Media Lab found that facial recognition systems had higher error rates for darker-skinned individuals and women compared to lighter-skinned individuals and men. The error rate for darker-skinned women was 34.7%, while it was only 0.8% for lighter-skinned men.

DISCRIMINATION IN DECISION-MAKING

AI systems used in decision-making processes, such as hiring or loan approvals, can perpetuate existing biases and discrimination if not carefully managed.

Amazon's AI-based hiring tool was found to be biased against women. The system, trained on resumes submitted over a 10-year period, favored male candidates because the tech industry historically had more male applicants.

ADDRESSING BIAS

Efforts are being made to identify and mitigate bias in AI systems. Researchers and organizations are developing frameworks and tools to ensure fairness and transparency.

The Fairness, Accountability, and Transparency in Machine Learning (FAT/ML) conference brings together researchers to discuss ways to address bias and ensure ethical AI development. Initiatives like these are crucial for creating unbiased AI systems.

ACCOUNTABILITY AND TRANSPARENCY

BLACK BOX PROBLEM

Many AI systems, especially those based on deep learning, operate as "black boxes," making it difficult to understand how they arrive at specific decisions. This lack of transparency can be problematic, especially in critical applications such as healthcare and criminal justice.

In healthcare, an AI system used for diagnosing diseases must provide understandable and interpretable results to gain the trust of medical professionals. Black-box models hinder this process, making it challenging to adopt AI solutions in critical areas.

LIABILITY AND ACCOUNTABILITY

Determining accountability for decisions made by AI systems is complex. If an AI system makes a mistake, it can be difficult to determine who is responsible—the developers, the users, or the AI itself.

Autonomous vehicles raise questions about liability in the event of an accident. If an AI-driven car causes a crash, it is unclear whether the manufacturer, the software developer, or the vehicle owner should be held accountable.

EFFORTS TOWARDS EXPLAINABLE AI

Researchers are working on developing explainable AI (XAI) systems that provide transparent and understandable insights into their decision-making processes.

The DARPA Explainable AI (XAI) program aims to create AI systems that can explain their reasoning and decisions to human users. This initiative is crucial for building trust and ensuring accountability in AI applications.

JOB DISPLACEMENT AND ECONOMIC IMPACT

AUTOMATION AND JOB LOSS

AI and automation have the potential to displace jobs, particularly those involving routine and repetitive tasks. While AI can enhance productivity, it also raises concerns about job loss and economic inequality.

According to a report by the *World Economic Forum*, AI and automation could displace 85 million jobs by 2025 but also create 97 million new jobs, primarily in technology and caregiving sectors. The net effect on employment remains uncertain, and the transition could lead to significant disruptions in the labor market.

RESKILLING AND UPSKILLING

To mitigate the impact of job displacement, there is a growing need for reskilling and upskilling programs that help workers transition to new roles that require different skills.

IBM's SkillsBuild program provides free online courses to help workers develop new skills in areas such as data science, cybersecurity, and AI. Such initiatives are essential for preparing the workforce for the future job market.

ECONOMIC INEQUALITY

The benefits of AI and automation may not be evenly distributed, potentially exacerbating economic inequality. Wealth generated by AI-driven productivity gains may disproportionately benefit those who own and control AI technologies.

A report by *McKinsey Global Institute* warns that without proper policies, AI could widen the gap between high-income and low-income workers, leading to increased economic inequality.

ETHICAL CONSIDERATIONS IN AI DEVELOPMENT

ETHICAL AI DEVELOPMENT

Developers and organizations must consider ethical principles when designing and deploying AI systems. This includes ensuring fairness, accountability, transparency, and respect for privacy.

The IEEE Global Initiative on Ethics of Autonomous and Intelligent Systems has developed a set of ethical guidelines to promote responsible AI development. These guidelines emphasize the importance of human-centric design, transparency, and accountability.

INFORMED CONSENT

When collecting data for AI systems, it is crucial to obtain informed consent from individuals. This ensures that people understand how their data will be used and have control over their personal information.

GDPR regulations in the European Union require organizations to obtain explicit consent from individuals before collecting and processing their data. These regulations aim to protect privacy and give individuals more control over their personal information.

ETHICAL AI RESEARCH

Ethical considerations must be integrated into AI research to ensure that the development of AI technologies aligns with societal values and principles.

The Partnership on AI, a consortium of major technology companies and research institutions, focuses on ensuring that AI benefits society and adheres to ethical standards. The partnership conducts research on topics such as fairness, transparency, and social impact.

SOCIETAL IMPLICATIONS OF AI

IMPACT ON EDUCATION

AI has the potential to transform education by providing personalized learning experiences, automating administrative tasks, and supporting teachers. However, there are concerns about the digital divide and access to AI-driven educational tools.

Khan Academy uses AI to provide personalized learning paths for students, helping them master subjects at their own pace. However, access to such tools is often limited by socioeconomic factors, potentially widening the educational gap.

HEALTHCARE AND ACCESSIBILITY

AI can improve healthcare delivery by providing better diagnostics, personalized treatments, and efficient administrative processes. However, there are concerns about equitable access to AI-driven healthcare solutions.

AI-powered diagnostic tools, such as those developed by Google Health, can improve early disease detection. However, access to these advanced technologies may be limited in low-income and rural areas, exacerbating healthcare disparities.

SOCIAL AND CULTURAL IMPACT

AI technologies can influence social and cultural norms, shaping how people interact with each other and the world around them. There are concerns about the impact of AI on human relationships, cultural heritage, and social values.

AI-driven social media algorithms can shape public opinion by prioritizing certain content over others. This can lead to echo chambers and the spread of misinformation, impacting social cohesion and cultural discourse.

DIGITAL DIVIDE

The adoption of AI technologies can exacerbate the digital divide, with some populations having greater access to AI-driven benefits than others. This divide can deepen existing inequalities and limit opportunities for disadvantaged groups.

According to a report by the *International Telecommunication Union (ITU)*, nearly half of the world's population remains offline, with limited access to digital technologies. This digital divide poses a significant barrier to the equitable distribution of AI benefits.

REGULATORY AND POLICY IMPLICATIONS

NEED FOR REGULATION

The rapid advancement of AI technology has outpaced the development of regulatory frameworks. There is a growing need for comprehensive regulations that address ethical, privacy, and security concerns associated with AI.

The European Union's proposed AI Act aims to regulate AI technologies based on their risk levels, ensuring that high-risk AI systems undergo rigorous scrutiny and compliance checks.

GLOBAL COLLABORATION

Addressing the ethical and societal implications of AI requires global collaboration. Countries and organizations must work together to develop international standards and best practices for AI development and deployment.

The Global Partnership on Artificial Intelligence (GPAI) is an international initiative that brings together governments, industry, and academia to promote responsible AI development and address global challenges.

IMPACT ON DEMOCRACY AND GOVERNANCE

AI can influence democratic processes and governance by shaping public opinion, automating administrative tasks, and enhancing decision-making. However, there are concerns about the potential for AI to undermine democratic institutions and processes.

The use of AI in political campaigns, such as micro-targeting voters with personalized ads, raises concerns about transparency and the manipulation of public opinion. Ensuring that AI is used ethically in governance is crucial for maintaining democratic integrity.

QUESTIONS PEOPLE HAVE ASKED ABOUT FUNDAMENTALS OF AI

1. WHAT IS THE FOUNDATIONAL UNDERSTANDING OF AI?

The foundational understanding of AI involves grasping the basic principles and objectives of artificial intelligence, which aims to create machines capable of performing tasks that typically require human intelligence. This includes understanding the key components such as machine learning, natural language processing, computer vision, and robotics. AI involves learning (acquiring information and rules for using it), reasoning (using rules to reach conclusions), and self-correction. It also encompasses knowledge of historical developments, ethical considerations, and the various applications of AI across different industries.

2. HOW DO I START UNDERSTANDING AI?

To start understanding AI, begin with the basics:

i. **Study Fundamental Concepts**: Learn about key concepts like machine learning, neural networks, deep learning, and natural language processing.

ii. **Online Courses and Tutorials**: Enroll in beginner-friendly online courses offered by platforms like Coursera, edX, and Udacity.

iii. **Read Books and Articles**: Start with introductory books such as "Artificial Intelligence: A Guide for Thinking Humans" by Melanie Mitchell or "Artificial Intelligence: A Modern Approach" by Stuart Russell and Peter Norvig.

iv. **Hands-On Practice**: Experiment with simple AI projects using programming languages like Python and libraries such as TensorFlow, Keras, and Scikit-learn.

v. **Stay Updated**: Follow AI news, blogs, and research papers to stay current with advancements in the field.

3. WHAT IS THE FOUNDATIONAL CONCEPT OF AI?

The foundational concept of AI is the creation of systems that can perform tasks requiring human intelligence. This involves three main capabilities:

i. **Learning**: The ability of a system to improve its performance based on experience. This includes supervised, unsupervised, and reinforcement learning.

ii. **Reasoning**: The capacity to make decisions based on data and predefined rules or models.

iii. **Self-Correction**: The ability to identify errors and improve performance over time through feedback and adaptation.

4. WHAT ARE THE 4 CONCEPTS OF AI?

The four key concepts of AI are:

i. **Machine Learning (ML)**: Algorithms that allow computers to learn from data and make predictions or decisions without being explicitly programmed.

ii. **Natural Language Processing (NLP)**: Techniques that enable machines to understand, interpret, and generate human language.

iii. **Computer Vision**: The ability of machines to interpret and process visual information from the world.

iv. **Robotics**: The design and creation of robots that can perform tasks autonomously or semi-autonomously.

5. WHAT IS THE FUNDAMENTAL KNOWLEDGE OF AI?

The fundamental knowledge of AI includes understanding:

i. **Basic Concepts**: Machine learning, neural networks, deep learning, NLP, and computer vision.

ii. **Programming Skills**: Proficiency in languages such as Python, R, or Java, and familiarity with AI frameworks like TensorFlow and PyTorch.

iii. **Mathematics and Statistics**: Concepts such as linear algebra, calculus, probability, and statistics.

iv. **Data Handling**: Skills in data collection, cleaning, and preprocessing.

v. **Ethical Considerations**: Awareness of the ethical implications and societal impact of AI.

6. WHAT ARE THE KEY CONCEPTS OF AI?

Key concepts of AI include:

vi. **Machine Learning**: Algorithms and models that learn from data.

i. **Neural Networks**: Models inspired by the human brain's structure, used in deep learning.

ii. **Natural Language Processing**: Techniques for understanding and generating human language.

iii. **Computer Vision**: Methods for interpreting visual data.

iv. **Reinforcement Learning**: Training models to make a sequence of decisions by rewarding desired behaviors.

v. **AI Ethics**: Principles guiding the responsible use of AI.

7. WHAT ARE THE VERY BASICS OF AI?

The very basics of AI include:

i. **Understanding AI**: AI is the simulation of human intelligence by machines.

ii. **Types of AI**: Narrow AI (designed for specific tasks) and General AI (with capabilities similar to human intelligence).

iii. **Core Areas**: Machine learning, NLP, computer vision, and robotics.

iv. **Data**: The fuel for AI systems, used to train and improve algorithms.

v. **Algorithms**: Mathematical models and procedures for learning from data.

8. WHAT IS THE BASIC PRINCIPLE OF AI?

The basic principle of AI is to create systems that can perform tasks requiring human intelligence by learning from experience, making decisions, and adapting to new information. This involves using algorithms and models to process data, recognize patterns, and generate predictions or actions.

9. WHAT ARE THE 5 GOALS OF AI?

The five goals of AI are:

i. **Automation**: Performing tasks without human intervention.

ii. **Learning**: Improving performance based on experience.

iii. **Reasoning**: Making logical decisions based on data.

iv. **Perception**: Interpreting and understanding sensory inputs.

v. **Interaction**: Communicating effectively with humans and other systems.

10. WHAT ARE THE 5 RULES OF AI?

The five rules of AI include principles that guide its development and application:

i. **Transparency**: AI systems should be transparent in their operations and decisions.

ii. **Fairness**: AI should not exhibit bias or discrimination.

iii. **Accountability**: There should be clear accountability for AI decisions and actions.

iv. **Privacy**: AI systems must protect users' data and privacy.

v. **Safety**: AI should operate safely and reliably, minimizing risks to humans and the environment.

CHAPTER THREE
The Cyber Threat Landscape

As digital transformation accelerates across industries, the cyber threat landscape has become increasingly complex and sophisticated. The growing reliance on digital technologies and heightened interconnectivity have exposed individuals and organizations to a wider range of cyber threats. These threats, from phishing and ransomware to advanced persistent threats (APTs), present significant risks to critical infrastructure, businesses, governments, and personal data security. Understanding these threats is crucial for developing effective defenses. This section delves into the evolving nature of cyber threats, offering data-driven insights into pressing vulnerabilities and their impact.

EVOLVING THREAT LANDSCAPE

The cybersecurity environment is in a state of constant flux, driven by the relentless innovation of cybercriminals who continuously develop new techniques to exploit weaknesses in systems, networks, and human behavior. As organizations expand their digital footprint, the attack surface grows, providing adversaries with more opportunities to strike. The integration of advanced technologies such as the Internet of Things (IoT) and cloud computing has further expanded the digital landscape, creating fertile ground for both opportunistic and sophisticated attacks.

Recent research highlights the dynamic nature of cyber threats. The 2023 Verizon Data Breach Investigations Report notes that phishing remains a prevalent attack vector, involved in 36% of breaches. This reflects an increase in phishing sophistication, where attackers use AI-driven techniques to craft more personalized and convincing phishing schemes.

The 2022 Cisco Annual Cybersecurity Report underscores that 93% of breaches now involve some form of social engineering, illustrating the increasing role of human factors in cyber incidents. This aligns with findings from the 2021 IBM X-Force Threat Intelligence Index, which revealed that ransomware attacks rose by 150% between 2019 and 2020. The report also highlights the prevalence of sophisticated attack methods, such as those leveraging double extortion tactics, where attackers not only encrypt data but also threaten to release it publicly.

The expanding threat landscape underscores the need for comprehensive and adaptive cybersecurity strategies. As the digital ecosystem grows and evolves, so too must our approach to defending against an ever-more complex array of cyber threats.

ADVANCED PERSISTENT THREATS (APTS)

Advanced Persistent Threats (APTs) represent a particularly dangerous form of cyber attack, where adversaries gain access to networks and remain undetected for long periods, typically aiming to steal sensitive information rather than cause immediate disruption. APTs are often state-sponsored and highly targeted, focusing on specific industries such as finance, healthcare, and defense.

The SolarWinds attack in 2020 is a prime example of an APT. Hackers compromised the widely used Orion software platform, deploying a backdoor that allowed them to infiltrate the networks of government agencies and Fortune 500 companies. The attackers remained hidden for months, exfiltrating sensitive data without triggering security alarms. This incident highlights the need for organizations to enhance their detection capabilities, as traditional cybersecurity defenses are often insufficient to combat such stealthy threats. According to a report by FireEye, APTs account for a significant proportion of cyber espionage operations, with the 2020 SolarWinds breach alone causing billions of dollars in damage across multiple industries.

ZERO-DAY VULNERABILITIES

Zero-day vulnerabilities are security flaws in software that are unknown to the vendor and have not yet been patched. Cybercriminals exploit these vulnerabilities before they are publicly disclosed or fixed, leaving organizations with little time to defend themselves. The growing use of zero-day exploits has made it clear that no system is entirely secure, as even state-of-the-art technologies can be vulnerable to newly discovered flaws.

The 2020 Microsoft Digital Defense Report notes that the use of zero-day vulnerabilities in cyber attacks increased by 33% compared to the previous year. Attackers use these exploits to bypass security controls, often gaining privileged access to networks without detection. The rising frequency of zero-day attacks underscores the need for companies to adopt proactive security strategies, such as threat intelligence and behavioral analysis, to mitigate the risks posed by these vulnerabilities.

INSIDER THREATS

Insider threats occur when individuals with authorized access to an organization's network misuse their privileges to steal data or cause harm. These threats can be intentional, such as when an employee deliberately leaks sensitive information, or unintentional, where negligence leads to a security breach. Insiders often have access to critical systems and sensitive data, making these attacks particularly dangerous.

A well-known example is the 2019 Capital One data breach, in which a former employee exploited misconfigured security settings to steal the personal data of over 100 million customers. This breach highlights the risk of insider threats, particularly in cloud environments, where a single configuration error can expose vast amounts of sensitive information. According to a report by Verizon's 2021 Data Breach Investigations Report (DBIR), 22% of all data breaches involve insiders, making insider threats one of the most significant challenges for organizations today.

SUPPLY CHAIN ATTACKS

Supply chain attacks target the vulnerabilities in an organization's external partners, vendors, or suppliers to gain access to its network. By infiltrating third-party service providers, attackers can bypass direct security measures and exploit weak links in the supply chain. These types of attacks are becoming increasingly common as organizations rely more heavily on outsourced services and software.

A report by Symantec found that supply chain attacks increased by 78% in 2019, with notable examples including the CCleaner malware attack and the compromise of NotPetya via Ukrainian accounting software. The 2020 SolarWinds attack further illustrated the devastating impact of supply chain vulnerabilities, as attackers leveraged the software provider to infiltrate numerous high-profile organizations. This growing trend underscores the importance of third-party risk management and ensuring that vendors adhere to strict cybersecurity standards.

COMMON ATTACK VECTORS

PHISHING

Phishing remains one of the most prevalent and effective forms of cyber attack, where cybercriminals trick individuals into divulging sensitive information such as usernames, passwords, or credit card numbers by masquerading as legitimate entities. Unlike more technical forms of cyber attacks, phishing capitalizes on human psychology, making it a dangerous and versatile tool in a hacker's arsenal.

Phishing attacks often take the form of emails, text messages, or even phone calls that appear to be from trusted sources—whether it's a bank, a social media platform, or even an employer. These messages typically prompt the recipient to click on a malicious link or download a harmful attachment. Once the victim takes the bait, attackers can steal credentials, gain access to sensitive systems, or spread malware. According to the 2020 Verizon Data Breach Investigations Report (DBIR), phishing was involved in 22% of data breaches and is the most commonly used vector in cyber espionage attacks.

One notorious example of the devastating impact of phishing occurred in 2016, when a phishing email led to the breach of the Democratic National Committee's (DNC) email system. The attackers posed as Google, tricking officials into providing their credentials. This breach exposed sensitive communications and ultimately had a significant impact on the U.S. presidential election. The incident highlights how phishing can have far-reaching consequences, not only for individuals but for entire organizations and national security.

DEFENSE AGAINST PHISHING:

To combat phishing attacks, organizations and individuals are encouraged to implement a combination of user education (such as phishing simulations) and technical defenses, including email filters, multi-factor authentication, and anti-phishing tools. Raising awareness among employees about suspicious communications can go a long way in reducing the success of these attacks.

MALWARE

Malware, or malicious software, is another major cyber threat that encompasses a range of harmful programs designed to damage, disrupt, or gain unauthorized access to systems. Malware can take many forms, including viruses, worms, Trojans, ransomware, and spyware. Once installed on a device, malware can perform a variety of malicious activities, such as stealing data, spying on users, or even locking down systems and demanding a ransom.

The scale and scope of malware attacks have grown exponentially in recent years. According to AV-TEST, over 1 billion malware samples were detected in 2020, with an average of 350,000 new malware samples discovered each day. The sheer volume of malware and its constant evolution make it one of the most persistent threats to individuals and organizations worldwide.

One of the most high-profile malware attacks in recent history was the WannaCry ransomware attack in 2017. WannaCry exploited a vulnerability in Microsoft Windows, infecting over 230,000 computers across 150 countries. The attack paralyzed numerous industries, including healthcare, where the UK's National Health Service (NHS) was severely impacted, forcing the cancellation of appointments and surgeries. The global disruption caused by WannaCry highlighted the devastating impact of malware, especially when combined with poor cybersecurity hygiene, such as outdated software and unpatched systems.

DEFENSE AGAINST MALWARE:

To defend against malware, organizations are encouraged to implement robust endpoint protection, regular system updates, and advanced firewalls. Additionally, backing up critical data and ensuring systems are patched against known vulnerabilities can minimize the potential damage of a malware attack. Intrusion detection systems (IDS) and behavioral analysis tools can also help detect anomalous activities that may indicate malware is present.

RANSOMWARE

Ransomware is a highly disruptive type of malware that encrypts a victim's data, locking them out of their own files until a ransom is paid to the attacker. The attacker typically demands payment in cryptocurrency, as it provides anonymity and is harder to trace. Ransomware attacks can have severe financial and operational consequences, particularly for organizations reliant on digital infrastructure to maintain daily operations.

The 2021 SonicWall Cyber Threat Report recorded a 62% increase in ransomware attacks globally, with the healthcare sector being especially hard hit. Hospitals, clinics, and medical facilities often have sensitive patient data that attackers target, and because of the critical nature of their operations, they are more likely to pay ransoms to restore functionality.

A high-profile example of a ransomware attack occurred in 2021, when the Colonial Pipeline, a major U.S. fuel pipeline, was targeted. This attack led to the temporary shutdown of pipeline operations, causing widespread fuel shortages and disruptions across the Eastern U.S. The company eventually paid a ransom of $4.4 million to regain access to its systems, underscoring the far-reaching impact of ransomware attacks on national infrastructure. The incident brought to light the vulnerabilities of critical services to cyber threats and triggered debates about whether paying ransoms encourages further attacks.

DEFENSE AGAINST RANSOMWARE:

Defending against ransomware requires a multi-faceted approach. Regularly backing up critical data, implementing endpoint security solutions, and educating employees about phishing and suspicious emails are crucial first steps. Additionally, organizations should employ network segmentation, ensuring that sensitive systems are isolated to prevent ransomware from spreading. Incident response plans are also critical in minimizing the impact of ransomware attacks and ensuring swift recovery.

DISTRIBUTED DENIAL-OF-SERVICE (DDOS) ATTACKS

A Distributed Denial-of-Service (DDoS) attack occurs when attackers flood a target's network or servers with excessive traffic, overwhelming the system and causing a service outage. The sheer volume of incoming requests prevents legitimate users from accessing the targeted services, leading to disruptions in business operations. These attacks are often carried out using networks of compromised computers, known as botnets.

According to Netscout, there were over 10 million DDoS attacks in 2020, representing a 20% increase compared to the previous year. As businesses increasingly rely on uninterrupted online services, DDoS attacks can cause significant financial losses and reputational damage. Moreover, DDoS attacks are becoming more sophisticated, targeting critical infrastructure like banks, government services, and media outlets.

One of the most infamous DDoS attacks occurred in October 2016, when a massive attack targeted Dyn, a major DNS provider. The attack affected large portions of the internet, disrupting access to popular websites such as Twitter, Netflix, and Reddit. This incident showcased the potential for DDoS attacks to cripple large segments of internet infrastructure, demonstrating the far-reaching consequences of these attacks on global connectivity.

DEFENSE AGAINST DDOS ATTACKS:

To defend against DDoS attacks, organizations should invest in DDoS mitigation services, which can detect and absorb malicious traffic before it overwhelms systems. Using load balancing and content delivery networks (CDNs) can also help distribute traffic more efficiently and reduce the risk of overload. Additionally, firewalls and intrusion detection systems (IDS) play an essential role in detecting and blocking abnormal traffic patterns associated with DDoS attacks.

SQL INJECTION

SQL injection is a type of web application attack where an attacker inserts malicious SQL code into an application's input fields to manipulate the underlying database. This allows the attacker to gain unauthorized access to sensitive data, alter or delete records, and even compromise the entire database. SQL injection attacks are particularly dangerous because they exploit weaknesses in poorly coded applications and can be launched remotely with minimal resources.

A report by Imperva indicates that SQL injection attacks account for 65% of all web application attacks, making them one of the most common and devastating forms of attack on web platforms. These attacks can compromise sensitive information, including personal details, credit card information, and login credentials, leading to significant financial and reputational damage.

One notable example occurred in 2014, when the U.S. retailer Target fell victim to a SQL injection attack. The breach compromised the personal and credit card information of 40 million customers, causing widespread financial loss and damage to the company's reputation. This incident underscores the need for organizations to secure their web applications and prevent unauthorized database access.

DEFENSE AGAINST SQL INJECTION:

To defend against SQL injection, developers should adopt secure coding practices, such as using parameterized queries and prepared statements to ensure that user input is properly sanitized. Additionally, regular code audits and the use of web application firewalls (WAFs) can help identify and block malicious requests before they reach the database.

MAN-IN-THE-MIDDLE (MITM) ATTACKS

Man-in-the-Middle (MitM) attacks are a serious cybersecurity threat where attackers intercept and potentially alter communications between two parties without their knowledge. By positioning themselves between the sender and receiver, cybercriminals can eavesdrop on or manipulate the data being transmitted, leading to severe consequences such as data theft, financial loss, and privacy violations. These attacks can occur in various forms, including eavesdropping on unsecured Wi-Fi networks, intercepting emails, or hijacking web sessions.

The 2020 Global Threat Report by CrowdStrike identifies MitM attacks as a prevalent method employed by cybercriminals to steal sensitive information such as login credentials, financial data, and personal communications. MitM attacks are particularly dangerous because they can occur without any visible signs to the victims, allowing attackers to harvest valuable information undetected.

A notable example of a MitM attack occurred in 2015, when cybercriminals targeted British Airways' frequent flyer program. In this attack, the perpetrators intercepted the communication between the airline and its customers, stealing thousands of loyalty points and accessing personal information. The breach not only led to financial loss for the customers but also damaged the reputation of British Airways, underscoring the far-reaching impact of MitM attacks on both individuals and organizations.

DEFENSE AGAINST MITM ATTACKS:

To defend against MitM attacks, it is essential to implement strong encryption protocols such as TLS (Transport Layer Security) for all communications, especially over public networks. Multi-factor authentication (MFA) can also add an extra layer of security by requiring multiple forms of verification before granting access. Additionally, users should avoid using unsecured Wi-Fi networks and ensure that websites they interact with are using HTTPS, indicated by a padlock symbol in the browser's address bar.

BRUTE FORCE ATTACKS

Brute force attacks are a method of gaining unauthorized access to systems by systematically trying every possible password combination until the correct one is found. While simple in concept, brute force attacks can be highly effective, especially when weak or common passwords are used. Cybercriminals often automate these attacks using software that rapidly tests thousands or millions of password combinations, significantly speeding up the process.

The 2020 State of the Internet/Security Report by Akamai revealed a significant increase in brute force attacks, particularly targeting sectors such as financial services and retail, where access to sensitive data is highly valuable. These attacks pose a serious threat to account security, often leading to unauthorized access, data breaches, and financial fraud.

A prominent example occurred in 2018, when GitHub, a popular platform for software development, was targeted by a brute force attack. The attackers attempted to compromise numerous user accounts by systematically guessing passwords. The attack forced GitHub to implement stronger security measures, including the adoption of two-factor authentication (2FA), which requires users to verify their identity through a second method in addition to their password.

DEFENSE AGAINST BRUTE FORCE ATTACKS:

To defend against brute force attacks, organizations and individuals should enforce strong password policies, requiring the use of complex, unique passwords for each account. Implementing account lockout mechanisms after a certain number of failed login attempts can also prevent automated brute force attempts. Two-factor authentication (2FA) is another effective defense, as it requires an additional verification step beyond just the password, making unauthorized access more difficult.

SOCIAL ENGINEERING

Social engineering attacks are a form of cyber threat that exploit human psychology rather than technical vulnerabilities. In these attacks, cybercriminals manipulate individuals into divulging confidential information, such as login credentials or financial data, or trick them into performing actions that compromise security. Social engineering is particularly effective because it preys on human emotions such as trust, fear, and urgency, bypassing even the most sophisticated security defenses.

According to the 2020 IBM X-Force Threat Intelligence Index, social engineering is involved in nearly half of all cyber attacks, making it one of the most prevalent and dangerous attack methods in the modern cybersecurity landscape. Attackers commonly use techniques like phishing, pretexting, baiting, and tailgating to gain access to sensitive systems or data. Since these attacks rely on manipulating human behavior, they can be difficult to detect and prevent using traditional cybersecurity tools.

One of the most notorious examples of a social engineering attack occurred in 2013, when attackers targeted a third-party contractor for Target. The attackers used phishing techniques to deceive the contractor into providing network credentials, which allowed the hackers to access Target's internal systems. This breach led to the compromise of 70 million customers' personal information, including names, addresses, and credit card numbers. The incident resulted in significant financial losses, legal penalties, and reputational damage for Target, highlighting the devastating impact that social engineering attacks can have on businesses.

DEFENSE AGAINST SOCIAL ENGINEERING ATTACKS:

To defend against social engineering attacks, organizations should prioritize employee education and awareness. Regular training sessions on recognizing and responding to social engineering attempts—such as phishing emails or suspicious phone calls—are crucial. Implementing multi-factor authentication (MFA) can also reduce the likelihood of attackers gaining access to critical systems, even if login credentials are compromised. Additionally, enforcing strict verification protocols for sensitive transactions and data access can prevent employees from unknowingly falling victim to social engineering schemes.

EXAMPLES OF CURRENT CYBER THREATS AND VULNERABILITIES

In recent years, the scale and sophistication of cyber attacks have continued to grow, with devastating impacts across industries, from government agencies to private corporations. These attacks have exposed vulnerabilities in critical infrastructure, highlighted the dangers of insider threats, and showcased the growing capabilities of cybercriminals. Below are detailed examples of some of the most significant cyber incidents of recent times, reflecting the importance of robust cybersecurity defenses and constant vigilance.

1. MICROSOFT EXCHANGE SERVER ATTACK (2021)

In early 2021, cybercriminals exploited vulnerabilities in Microsoft Exchange Server, a widely used email and calendaring system, leading to the compromise of over 30,000 organizations worldwide. The attackers were able to install backdoors, gaining remote access to internal networks and email communications. The breach affected government agencies, small businesses, and large corporations alike. The attack was attributed to a Chinese state-sponsored group, with the U.S. government issuing warnings about the widespread nature of the breach.

Impact:

The Microsoft Exchange attack prompted urgent patching efforts and highlighted the critical importance of promptly applying security updates. The breach showcased the growing risk of zero-day vulnerabilities, especially in widely used software products.

2. KASEYA RANSOMWARE ATTACK (2021)

In July 2021, Kaseya, an IT management company, was hit by a ransomware attack orchestrated by the REvil group, which exploited vulnerabilities in Kaseya's software. The attack affected thousands of businesses across 17 countries by compromising Kaseya's software update system. Attackers deployed ransomware through Kaseya's infrastructure, targeting Managed Service Providers (MSPs) and their clients.

Impact:

The attackers demanded a $70 million ransom, making it one of the largest ransomware attacks in history. The incident highlighted the dangers of supply chain attacks, where a single compromised entity can impact vast networks of downstream customers. This attack emphasized the need for stronger supply chain security and incident response protocols.

3. COLONIAL PIPELINE RANSOMWARE ATTACK (2021)

In May 2021, Colonial Pipeline, the largest fuel pipeline in the U.S., was struck by the DarkSide ransomware group. The attackers encrypted critical data and demanded a ransom, which eventually led to the company shutting down operations for several days. The attack caused widespread fuel shortages across the East Coast, impacting businesses and consumers alike.

Impact:

Colonial Pipeline paid a $4.4 million ransom to regain access to their systems. The attack was a stark reminder of the vulnerabilities of critical infrastructure and the potentially catastrophic impact of ransomware on essential services. The U.S. Department of Justice later recovered part of the ransom, highlighting ongoing efforts to combat ransomware operators.

4. JBS RANSOMWARE ATTACK (2021)

In June 2021, JBS, the world's largest meat supplier, was hit by a ransomware attack by the REvil group, forcing the company to shut down operations in the U.S., Canada, and Australia. This attack disrupted meat production and distribution, with potential global food supply chain consequences.

Impact:

JBS paid an $11 million ransom to the attackers to restore operations, showcasing the high costs of ransomware attacks and their potential impact on essential sectors like food production. The attack further underscored the vulnerability of global supply chains to cyber threats.

5. **SOLARWINDS SUPPLY CHAIN ATTACK (2020)**

The SolarWinds attack in December 2020 was one of the most sophisticated supply chain attacks in history. Hackers compromised the Orion software used by SolarWinds, which allowed them to infiltrate the networks of over 18,000 organizations, including U.S. federal agencies and Fortune 500 companies. The attackers inserted malicious code into a software update, granting them long-term access to sensitive networks.

Impact:

This attack exposed sensitive data from government agencies, including the Department of Homeland Security and Treasury Department, and corporate giants like Microsoft. The breach illustrated the far-reaching consequences of supply chain vulnerabilities and raised concerns about nation-state actors targeting critical infrastructure.

6. **MOVEIT TRANSFER ATTACK (2023)**

In June 2023, cybercriminals exploited a vulnerability in MOVEit, a popular file transfer software, leading to a massive data breach. The attack, carried out by the Clop ransomware group, impacted hundreds of organizations, including government agencies, universities, and corporations. The attackers leveraged a zero-day vulnerability in MOVEit to steal sensitive data.

Impact:

The MOVEit attack affected millions of individuals' personal information, causing widespread concern across industries. The breach highlighted the critical nature of securing third-party software and led to a series of patches and updates to prevent further exploitation. The financial and reputational damage was significant, affecting sectors ranging from education to financial services.

7. CAESARS ENTERTAINMENT AND MGM RESORTS RANSOMWARE ATTACKS (2023)

In September 2023, two major hospitality and entertainment companies, Caesars Entertainment and MGM Resorts, were hit by ransomware attacks. Caesars admitted to paying $15 million in ransom to attackers, while MGM's attack led to several days of system outages, impacting their hotels, casinos, and booking systems. The ransomware group, known as ALPHV or BlackCat, was behind the attacks.

Impact:

The MGM attack disrupted operations across multiple properties, causing significant losses. Guests experienced long check-in delays, and casino systems were down for days. The attack demonstrated how ransomware can cause widespread disruptions in critical infrastructure sectors like hospitality and entertainment.

8. T-MOBILE API DATA BREACH (2023)

In January 2023, T-Mobile experienced a data breach in which attackers exploited a vulnerability in the company's application programming interface (API). The breach exposed 37 million customers' personal data, including names, addresses, emails, and phone numbers. The attack marked T-Mobile's eighth major breach in five years, raising concerns about their cybersecurity posture.

Impact:

This breach highlighted the growing threats targeting APIs, a critical component of modern applications. It exposed the vulnerabilities associated with API management and security, sparking calls for enhanced security controls around API usage, especially in the telecom industry.

9. MICROSOFT CLOUD BREACH (2024)

In early 2024, Chinese state-sponsored hackers gained access to U.S. government emails through a breach in Microsoft's cloud services. The attackers exploited vulnerabilities in Microsoft's authentication systems, allowing them to access high-profile government communications. This incident raised serious concerns about cloud infrastructure security and the targeting of sensitive government data.

Impact:

The attack exposed the vulnerabilities of cloud platforms, particularly those hosting sensitive government and corporate data. It also reinforced the need for zero-trust architecture in cloud security and prompted calls for stronger collaboration between the public and private sectors to safeguard critical infrastructure.

10. GLOBANT DATA BREACH (2024)

InHackers exploited vulnerabilities in Globant's internal systems, leading to the expo 2024, Globant, a multinational IT and software development company, fell victim to a data breach. sure of sensitive information belonging to major clients, including source codes and client project data.

Impact:

The breach raised alarms about the risks posed by attacks on IT service providers that hold significant amounts of proprietary and customer data. This incident emphasized the importance of securing software development environments and supply chains, as well as the need for stricter security controls among third-party vendors.

IMPACT OF CYBER THREATS ON BUSINESSES AND INDIVIDUALS

Cyber threats pose significant risks to both businesses and individuals, leading to financial losses, reputational damage, and various other adverse effects. This section explores the wide-ranging impacts of cyber threats, supported by relevant data, statistics, and examples.

IMPACT ON BUSINESSES

FINANCIAL LOSSES

Cyber attacks can lead to substantial financial losses for businesses. These losses stem from various factors, including theft of funds, disruption of operations, legal costs, and fines.

The *2019 Cost of a Data Breach Report* by IBM Security found that the average cost of a data breach globally was $3.92 million. For U.S. companies, the average cost was significantly higher at $8.19 million.

In 2017, the WannaCry ransomware attack caused an estimated $4 billion in damages worldwide, affecting over 230,000 computers across more than 150 countries. The attack led to significant financial losses for businesses due to downtime and ransom payments.

OPERATIONAL DISRUPTION

They can also disrupt business operations, leading to loss of productivity and revenue. Attacks such as ransomware, distributed denial-of-service (DDoS), and malware can paralyze critical systems and processes.

The Colonial Pipeline ransomware attack in 2021 forced the shutdown of a major U.S. fuel pipeline, leading to widespread fuel shortages and disruptions. The company paid a $4.4 million ransom to regain access to its systems, highlighting the severe operational impact of such attacks.

REPUTATIONAL DAMAGE

A cyber attack can damage a company's reputation, eroding customer trust and loyalty. The loss of sensitive customer data can lead to negative publicity and a long-term decline in brand value.

The data breach at Target in 2013 compromised the personal information of 70 million customers and the credit card details of 40 million customers. The breach resulted in a loss of customer trust and a decline in sales, significantly impacting the company's reputation.

LEGAL AND REGULATORY CONSEQUENCES

Businesses that suffer cyber attacks may face legal and regulatory consequences, including fines and lawsuits. Non-compliance with data protection regulations can result in hefty penalties.

Under the European Union's General Data Protection Regulation (GDPR), companies can be fined up to €20 million or 4% of their global annual revenue for data breaches, whichever is higher.

In 2018, British Airways was fined £183 million under GDPR for a data breach that compromised the personal data of approximately 500,000 customers. The fine underscored the legal ramifications of failing to protect customer data.

LOSS OF INTELLECTUAL PROPERTY

Cyber attacks can result in the theft of intellectual property (IP), including trade secrets, patents, and proprietary information. The loss of IP can undermine a company's competitive advantage and innovation.

In 2014, cyber attackers targeted Sony Pictures Entertainment, stealing and leaking sensitive internal documents, emails, and unreleased films. The attack not only resulted in financial losses but also exposed proprietary information, damaging the company's competitive position.

CUSTOMER CHURN

Following a data breach, businesses may experience an increase in customer churn as affected customers lose confidence in the company's ability to protect their data.

According to the *2019 Cost of a Data Breach Report* by IBM Security, the average customer churn rate after a data breach is 3.9%. In highly regulated industries such as healthcare, the churn rate can be even higher.

The Equifax data breach in 2017, which exposed the personal data of 147 million customers, led to a significant loss of customer trust and a decline in the company's market value. The breach resulted in a customer churn rate of approximately 5.4%.

IMPACT ON INDIVIDUALS

FINANCIAL LOSS AND IDENTITY THEFT

Cyber attacks can lead to financial losses and identity theft for individuals. Attackers may steal personal information, such as credit card details, Social Security numbers, and bank account information, to commit fraud and other crimes.

According to the *2020 Identity Fraud Study* by Javelin Strategy & Research, identity fraud resulted in losses of $16.9 billion in the United States alone.

The Equifax data breach in 2017 compromised the personal information of 147 million people, including Social Security numbers, birthdates, and addresses. The breach led to widespread identity theft and financial fraud, impacting millions of individuals.

LOSS OF PRIVACY

Cyber attacks can lead to the exposure of sensitive personal information, compromising individuals' privacy. This exposure can have long-lasting effects on victims' personal and professional lives.

The Ashley Madison data breach in 2015 exposed the personal information of 32 million users of the dating site. The breach led to public embarrassment, relationship issues, and even instances of extortion and blackmail.

EMOTIONAL AND PSYCHOLOGICAL IMPACT

Being a victim of a cyber attack can cause significant emotional and psychological distress. Victims may experience anxiety, stress, and a sense of violation, especially if their personal information is exposed or misused.

A study published in the *Journal of the American Medical Association (JAMA)* found that victims of identity theft experience higher levels of psychological distress, including anxiety and depression, compared to the general population.

Victims of the Anthem data breach in 2015, which exposed the personal and medical information of 78.8 million individuals, reported experiencing anxiety and stress due to concerns about their privacy and the potential misuse of their data.

REPUTATION DAMAGE

Individuals who are victims of cyber attacks may suffer reputational damage, especially if their personal or professional information is publicly exposed. This damage can affect their relationships, career prospects, and social standing.

The LinkedIn data breach in 2012 exposed the email addresses and passwords of 6.5 million users. Some individuals reported that their professional reputations were damaged due to the exposure of their login credentials and personal information.

LOSS OF ACCESS TO SERVICES

Cyber attacks can disrupt individuals' access to essential services, including healthcare, financial services, and online platforms. This disruption can have serious consequences, especially for those who rely on these services for their daily needs.

The ransomware attack on the UK's National Health Service (NHS) in 2017 disrupted healthcare services, forcing hospitals to cancel appointments and divert emergency patients. The attack affected thousands of patients and highlighted the vulnerability of critical infrastructure to cyber threats.

IMPACT ON PERSONAL RELATIONSHIPS

Cyber attacks can strain personal relationships, especially if sensitive information is exposed or if individuals are targeted through social engineering tactics.

In the case of the Ashley Madison data breach, the exposure of user information led to personal and marital conflicts, highlighting the far-reaching impact of cyber attacks on individuals' personal lives.

THE ROLE OF AI IN ENHANCING CYBER THREATS

Artificial Intelligence (AI) has revolutionized many industries, offering innovative solutions and increasing efficiency across various sectors. However, while AI has become a vital asset in strengthening cybersecurity defenses, it has also emerged as a double-edged sword. The same technologies that empower organizations to protect their digital assets are being exploited by cybercriminals to develop more sophisticated and elusive attack strategies. This duality underscores the complex relationship between AI and cybersecurity, where advancements in one area can inadvertently fuel threats in another.

As AI technologies continue to evolve, so do the tactics employed by malicious actors. AI's ability to process vast amounts of data, learn from patterns, and automate tasks has opened new avenues for cyber attackers. These capabilities enable the creation of highly effective and adaptive attack vectors that are difficult for traditional security measures to detect and counter. Furthermore, AI-driven cyber threats are not static; they are constantly learning, adapting, and evolving, making them increasingly challenging to combat.

This section delves into the growing role of AI in enhancing cyber threats. It examines the mechanisms through which AI is being harnessed to augment the sophistication and effectiveness of cyber attacks. By exploring the implications of AI-powered threats, this discussion highlights the urgent need for robust, adaptive, and forward-thinking cybersecurity strategies that can anticipate and mitigate the evolving landscape of AI-driven cyber threats

AI-ENHANCED CYBER THREATS

AUTOMATED PHISHING ATTACKS

AI can be used to automate and enhance phishing attacks, making them more convincing and difficult to detect. Machine learning algorithms analyze large datasets of email communications to craft realistic phishing messages tailored to individual targets.

AI-generated phishing emails can mimic the writing style and tone of trusted contacts, increasing the likelihood of the recipient falling for the scam. In a study by *Barracuda Networks*, 83% of organizations reported being targeted by phishing attacks in 2020, highlighting the prevalence of this threat.

ADVANCED MALWARE

Cybercriminals use AI to develop advanced malware that can evade traditional detection methods. AI-powered malware can adapt its behavior to avoid detection and analyze the target environment to identify vulnerabilities.

The Emotet malware, which uses machine learning techniques to enhance its evasion capabilities, has been described by the *Cybersecurity and Infrastructure Security Agency (CISA)* as one of the most prevalent and dangerous malware threats in recent years.

RANSOMWARE ATTACKS

AI is used to improve the effectiveness of ransomware attacks by identifying the most valuable data to encrypt and optimizing the ransom amount to maximize the likelihood of payment.

According to the *2021 SonicWall Cyber Threat Report*, there was a 62% increase in ransomware attacks globally, with AI playing a significant role in enhancing these attacks.

The Ryuk ransomware, known for targeting high-value organizations, uses AI to identify and prioritize critical data for encryption, increasing the pressure on victims to pay the ransom.

AUTOMATED VULNERABILITY SCANNING

AI enables cybercriminals to automate the process of scanning for vulnerabilities in target systems. AI-powered tools can quickly identify and exploit weaknesses, allowing attackers to scale their operations and target multiple victims simultaneously.

The Mirai botnet, which harnessed AI to scan for and exploit vulnerabilities in IoT devices, caused widespread disruption by launching large-scale DDoS attacks on major websites and services.

SOCIAL ENGINEERING ATTACKS

AI enhances social engineering attacks by analyzing social media and online behavior to create highly personalized and convincing scams. AI-driven tools can gather and analyze vast amounts of data to identify the most effective tactics for deceiving targets.

Deepfake technology, powered by AI, can create realistic audio and video content that impersonates individuals. This technology has been used in social engineering attacks to deceive victims into transferring funds or divulging sensitive information.

EVASION TECHNIQUES

AI enables attackers to develop sophisticated evasion techniques that can bypass traditional security measures. AI-powered malware can modify its code and behavior dynamically to avoid detection by antivirus software and intrusion detection systems.

Polymorphic malware, which changes its code with each infection, uses AI to enhance its ability to evade detection. This type of malware is particularly challenging for traditional security solutions to detect and mitigate.

DISTRIBUTED DENIAL-OF-SERVICE (DDOS) ATTACKS

AI can be used to orchestrate and optimize DDoS attacks, making them more powerful and harder to mitigate. AI algorithms analyze network traffic patterns to identify the most effective ways to overwhelm target servers.

The 2016 Dyn DDoS attack, which disrupted access to major websites, demonstrated the potential impact of AI-enhanced DDoS attacks. AI-powered botnets can adapt their attack strategies in real-time, making them more resilient to mitigation efforts.

EXAMPLES OF AI-ENHANCED CYBER THREATS

EMOTET MALWARE

Emotet uses machine learning techniques to enhance its evasion capabilities, making it one of the most prevalent and dangerous malware threats. It has been used to steal sensitive information and deliver other malware payloads.

Described by the *Cybersecurity and Infrastructure Security Agency (CISA)* as a significant threat, Emotet has caused substantial financial and operational damage to organizations worldwide.

RYUK RANSOMWARE

Ryuk targets high-value organizations, using AI to identify and prioritize critical data for encryption. This increases the pressure on victims to pay the ransom, leading to significant financial losses.

The *2021 SonicWall Cyber Threat Report* recorded a 62% increase in ransomware attacks globally, with Ryuk being a major contributor to this trend.

MIRAI BOTNET

The Mirai botnet used AI to scan for and exploit vulnerabilities in IoT devices, launching large-scale DDoS attacks that disrupted major websites and services.

The attack demonstrated the potential of AI-powered botnets to cause widespread disruption, affecting websites such as Twitter, Netflix, and Reddit.

DEEPFAKE SOCIAL ENGINEERING ATTACKS

Deepfake technology, powered by AI, creates realistic audio and video content that impersonates individuals. This has been used in social engineering attacks to deceive victims into transferring funds or divulging sensitive information.

In 2019, cybercriminals used deepfake audio to impersonate a CEO's voice and trick an employee into transferring $243,000 to a fraudulent account.

POLYMORPHIC MALWARE

Polymorphic malware uses AI to change its code with each infection, enhancing its ability to evade detection by traditional security solutions. This makes it particularly challenging for organizations to detect and mitigate.

The TrickBot malware, which has evolved into a sophisticated polymorphic threat, uses AI to continually modify its code, evading detection and infecting thousands of systems worldwide.

These examples of AI-enhanced cyber threats, including Emotet, Ryuk, Mirai, deepfake social engineering attacks, and polymorphic malware, illustrate the growing sophistication of cyber attacks and the critical need for advanced cybersecurity measures to protect against these evolving threats.

QUESTIONS PEOPLE HAVE ASKED ABOUT THE CYBER THREAT LANDSCAPE

1. ## WHAT IS THE CURRENT CYBERSECURITY LANDSCAPE?

    The current cybersecurity landscape is marked by increasing complexity and sophistication of cyber threats. Cybercriminals are leveraging advanced technologies, including AI and machine learning, to develop more effective and evasive attacks. The landscape includes a wide range of threats such as ransomware, phishing, supply chain attacks, and advanced persistent threats (APTs). The COVID-19 pandemic accelerated digital transformation, increasing reliance on remote work and cloud services, which has expanded the attack surface for cybercriminals. Additionally, geopolitical tensions contribute to state-sponsored cyber espionage and attacks. Organizations are investing more in cybersecurity measures, yet many still face challenges in keeping pace with the evolving threat landscape.

2. ## WHAT ARE THE TOP 5 CYBERSECURITY THREATS?

    i.   **Ransomware**: Increasingly sophisticated ransomware attacks targeting organizations across various sectors, demanding high ransom payments for data recovery.

    ii. **Phishing and Social Engineering**: Highly targeted and convincing phishing campaigns that exploit human vulnerabilities to gain access to sensitive information.

    iii. **Advanced Persistent Threats (APTs)**: Long-term targeted attacks by sophisticated threat actors, often state-sponsored, aiming to steal sensitive data or disrupt operations.

    iv. **Supply Chain Attacks**: Compromising third-party vendors or service providers to infiltrate primary targets, as seen in the SolarWinds breach.

v. **Zero-Day Exploits**: Attacks exploiting unknown vulnerabilities in software before patches are available, making them difficult to defend against.

3. WHY IS THREAT LANDSCAPE IMPORTANT?

The threat landscape is important because it provides a comprehensive view of the current and emerging cyber threats that organizations face. Understanding the threat landscape helps organizations identify potential risks, prioritize security measures, and allocate resources effectively. It enables proactive defense strategies, informed decision-making, and better preparedness against cyber attacks. Staying aware of the threat landscape also aids in compliance with regulatory requirements and industry standards, ensuring that organizations can protect their data, systems, and reputation.

4. WHAT IS A CYBER THREAT LANDSCAPE?

A cyber threat landscape is the overall view of the current cyber threats and vulnerabilities that exist within the digital environment. It encompasses the various types of attacks, the methods used by cybercriminals, the motivations behind attacks, and the potential targets. The threat landscape evolves continuously as new threats emerge and existing ones become more sophisticated. It includes data on threat actors, attack vectors, and trends, providing valuable insights for developing effective cybersecurity strategies.

5. WHAT IS THE DIGITAL THREAT LANDSCAPE?

The digital threat landscape refers to the array of cyber threats that target digital assets, including information systems, networks, and data. It covers the spectrum of malicious activities that exploit digital vulnerabilities to cause harm. The digital threat landscape is shaped by factors such as technological advancements, increasing connectivity, and evolving attacker tactics. It includes threats like malware, phishing, ransomware, and DDoS attacks, as well as emerging threats related to IoT, cloud computing, and artificial intelligence.

6. WHAT ARE CYBER THREAT MAPS?

Cyber threat maps are visual tools that display real-time data on cyber attacks happening across the globe. These maps typically show the geographic locations of attack sources and targets, types of attacks, and attack volumes. Cyber threat maps help organizations and security professionals monitor and understand the scale and nature of cyber threats. They provide insights into global cyber activity, highlight trends, and aid in threat intelligence and situational awareness. Examples include the Norse Attack Map and the Kaspersky Cyberthreat Real-Time Map.

7. WHAT IS A CYBER THREAT SURFACE?

A cyber threat surface is the total number of points where an unauthorized user (the attacker) can try to enter or extract data from an environment. It includes all hardware, software, networks, and human elements that could be targeted by cyber attacks. The threat surface encompasses endpoints like computers and mobile devices, network components, applications, and cloud services. Reducing the threat surface is a key strategy in cybersecurity, involving measures like minimizing exposed endpoints, patching vulnerabilities, and implementing robust access controls.

8. WHAT IS A THREAT LANDSCAPE ASSESSMENT?

A threat landscape assessment is the process of identifying and evaluating the current cyber threats and vulnerabilities that an organization faces. It involves analyzing threat intelligence, understanding the specific risks to the organization's assets, and assessing the potential impact of different types of attacks. The assessment helps organizations prioritize security measures, develop risk mitigation strategies, and allocate resources effectively. It includes examining external threats, internal vulnerabilities, and the effectiveness of existing security controls.

9. WHAT IS THE THREAT LANDSCAPE OF A COMPUTER INCIDENT?

The threat landscape of a computer incident refers to the specific set of threats and vulnerabilities associated with a particular cybersecurity incident. It includes the nature of the attack, the methods used by the attacker, the vulnerabilities exploited, and the potential or actual impact of the incident. Understanding this landscape helps in responding to the incident, mitigating damage, and preventing future occurrences. It involves forensic analysis, identifying attack vectors, and assessing the incident's effect on the organization's operations and data security.

10. HOW IMPORTANT IS CYBERSECURITY IN 2024?

Cybersecurity is critically important in 2024 due to the increasing frequency, sophistication, and impact of cyber attacks. As digital transformation continues to accelerate, more aspects of business, government, and personal life rely on interconnected systems and data. Protecting these digital assets from cyber threats is essential to ensure operational continuity, data integrity, and trust. With the growing adoption of technologies such as cloud computing, IoT, and AI, the attack surface expands, making robust cybersecurity measures more vital than ever. Cybersecurity also remains crucial for regulatory compliance, protecting intellectual property, and safeguarding sensitive information against threats like ransomware, phishing, and advanced persistent threats.

CHAPTER FOUR
Introduction to AI-Driven Cybersecurity Solutions

THE GROWING CYBERSECURITY CRISIS

The financial toll of cybercrime is staggering and continues to escalate. According to a 2023 report by Cybersecurity Ventures, global cybercrime costs are projected to reach $10.5 trillion annually by 2025, a dramatic rise from $3 trillion in 2015. This exponential growth is fueled by a wide array of evolving threats, including ransomware, phishing, and advanced persistent threats (APTs). The Verizon Data Breach Investigations Report 2023 notes that cyberattacks are becoming more complex, with phishing accounting for 36% of breaches, while ransomware attacks increased by 70% over the previous year.

Traditional cybersecurity tools, which primarily rely on signature-based detection and predefined rules, are struggling to keep pace with the dynamic and evolving nature of these threats. Signature-based systems, for example, detect malicious software by comparing it to a database of known malware signatures. However, modern cyber threats often employ techniques such as zero-day exploits and polymorphic malware, which change their structure and behavior to evade detection by these conventional systems. This inability to detect and respond to new, unseen threats has created an urgent need for more adaptable and intelligent cybersecurity measures.

THE ROLE OF AI IN CYBERSECURITY

AI offers a revolutionary approach to addressing the limitations of traditional cybersecurity tools by providing dynamic, adaptive solutions. Machine learning and deep learning, two key subsets of AI, enable systems to analyze vast amounts of data, identify patterns, and learn from previous attacks. These capabilities allow AI-powered cybersecurity systems to detect and respond to new threats in real time, without relying on predefined rules or signatures. AI's ability to learn from large datasets and adapt to new information makes it uniquely suited to counter modern cyber threats.

As Leslie F. Sikos explains in "AI in Cybersecurity", "AI can also play an important role in cyber threat intelligence, analytics, and automated incident response to detect, contain, and mitigate advanced persistent threats (APTs), and combat organized cybercrimes and state-sponsored cyberattacks. For example, AI techniques can be trained to automatically scan for unknown malware or zero-day exploits by analyzing features and behaviors rather than relying on specific signatures."

One of the most significant advantages of AI is its ability to perform behavioral analysis. By continuously monitoring network traffic, user behavior, and system logs, AI systems can identify anomalies that may indicate a breach or attack. AI can flag suspicious activities that deviate from established patterns, allowing security teams to respond to potential threats before they cause damage. This proactive approach contrasts with the reactive nature of traditional cybersecurity systems, which often only respond once an attack has occurred.

AI IN THREAT DETECTION AND INCIDENT RESPONSE

AI-driven systems excel in threat detection and incident response by automating the process of identifying and mitigating cyber threats. Traditional security teams often face an overwhelming volume of security alerts, many of which are false positives. AI helps reduce this burden by using machine learning algorithms to prioritize alerts, ensuring that human analysts focus on the most pressing issues. AI can also automate the initial response to an attack, such as isolating infected systems or blocking malicious traffic, minimizing the time it takes to contain a threat.

In the case of ransomware, AI technologies are being used to identify suspicious activities that indicate an attack is underway, such as rapid file encryption or unusual outbound network traffic. According to the SonicWall Cyber Threat Report 2021, AI played a crucial role in identifying and stopping 62% of ransomware attacks, highlighting the growing importance of AI in cyber defense.

Moreover, AI can enhance endpoint security by protecting individual devices from malware, phishing, and other cyber threats. Endpoint detection and response (EDR) solutions powered by AI continuously monitor devices for abnormal activities, detect intrusions, and automatically respond to potential threats. This allows organizations to secure not only their core infrastructure but also the vast network of devices that connect to their systems.

AI'S IMPACT ON SECURITY ANALYTICS

Another key area where AI is transforming cybersecurity is security analytics. By processing and analyzing massive amounts of data from various sources, AI systems can uncover insights that traditional tools might miss. These systems can detect patterns that indicate long-term threats, such as APTs or insider attacks, which may evolve over time and remain hidden within the network.

AI's ability to quickly analyze large datasets allows it to provide security teams with actionable intelligence in real-time. According to a report by Gartner, organizations that implement AI-powered security analytics experience a 50% reduction in the time it takes to detect and respond to cyber threats. This rapid detection capability is essential in today's fast-moving cyber landscape, where even a few minutes of delay can result in significant damage.

AI APPLICATIONS IN CYBERSECURITY

The integration of Artificial Intelligence (AI) into cybersecurity has revolutionized the way organizations detect, prevent, and respond to cyber threats. AI applications in cybersecurity encompass a wide range of technologies and methodologies designed to enhance security measures and protect against evolving cyber threats. This section focuses on various AI applications in cybersecurity, highlighting their impact, benefits, and challenges.

MACHINE LEARNING FOR THREAT DETECTION

Machine learning (ML), as a subset of AI, plays a pivotal role in modern cybersecurity. ML algorithms are adept at analyzing large volumes of data to identify patterns and anomalies that may indicate potential threats. These algorithms can be broadly categorized into supervised, unsupervised, and reinforcement learning.

Supervised Learning: In supervised learning, algorithms are trained on labeled datasets, enabling them to recognize specific types of threats based on historical data. For example, supervised ML models can be trained to detect phishing emails by analyzing features such as sender information, email content, and attachment types. According to a study by Verizon in 2022, 94% of malware is delivered via email, underscoring the importance of effective phishing detection.

Unsupervised Learning: Unsupervised learning algorithms do not rely on labeled data. Instead, they identify patterns and anomalies by analyzing unlabeled datasets. This approach is particularly useful for detecting zero-day attacks and unknown threats. A report by IBM Security in 2023 revealed that 40% of security incidents involved previously unknown threats, highlighting the need for advanced anomaly detection capabilities.

Reinforcement Learning: Reinforcement learning involves training algorithms to make decisions based on feedback from their actions. In cybersecurity, reinforcement learning can be used to optimize security protocols and responses to threats. For example, algorithms can learn to dynamically adjust firewall rules based on network traffic patterns, enhancing the overall security posture.

DEEP LEARNING FOR MALWARE ANALYSIS

Deep learning (DL), a more advanced subset of ML, leverages neural networks to analyze complex data structures. DL models excel at tasks such as image and speech recognition, making them suitable for malware analysis and detection. By analyzing the code and behavior of malware, deep learning models can identify and classify malicious software with high accuracy.

Static Analysis: Static analysis involves examining the code of a program without executing it. Deep learning models can analyze the binary code of files to detect patterns indicative of malware. A 2021 study by the University of California, Berkeley, demonstrated that deep learning models achieved a detection accuracy of 99.3% in identifying malware through static analysis.

Dynamic Analysis: Dynamic analysis, on the other hand, involves observing the behavior of a program during execution. Deep learning models can monitor the runtime behavior of applications to detect malicious activities. This approach is particularly effective against polymorphic malware, which changes its code to evade detection. According to Symantec's 2023 Internet Security Threat Report, polymorphic malware accounted for 94% of all malware attacks, emphasizing the need for dynamic analysis techniques.

NATURAL LANGUAGE PROCESSING FOR THREAT INTELLIGENCE

Natural Language Processing (NLP) as a branch of AI focused on the interaction between computers and human language. In cybersecurity, NLP is used to analyze text-based data, such as emails, social media posts, and threat intelligence reports, to identify potential threats and gather actionable insights.

Phishing Detection: NLP algorithms can analyze the content of emails to detect phishing attempts. By examining linguistic features, such as word choice and sentence structure, NLP models can identify suspicious emails and alert users. A 2022 survey by the Anti-Phishing Working Group reported that 65% of organizations experienced phishing attacks, highlighting the critical role of NLP in email security.

Threat Intelligence: NLP is also used to process and analyze vast amounts of threat intelligence data from various sources, including news articles, research papers, and forums. By extracting relevant information and identifying trends, NLP models can provide security teams with actionable insights to proactively defend against emerging threats. The 2023 Global Threat Intelligence Report by NTT Security emphasized the importance of timely and accurate threat intelligence in mitigating cyber risks.

BEHAVIORAL ANALYSIS FOR INSIDER THREAT DETECTION

Insider threats, where malicious or negligent employees compromise an organization's security, pose a significant risk. AI-powered behavioral analysis tools monitor user activities and detect deviations from established norms that may indicate insider threats.

User and Entity Behavior Analytics (UEBA): UEBA solutions leverage machine learning to analyze user behavior and identify anomalies. By establishing a baseline of normal activities for each user, UEBA systems can detect deviations that may signify malicious intent. For instance, if an employee who typically accesses files during regular business hours suddenly begins downloading large volumes of data at odd hours, the system can flag this behavior for further investigation. According to a 2022 report by Gartner, UEBA adoption has grown by 40% among enterprises, reflecting its effectiveness in mitigating insider threats.

Fraud Detection: In financial institutions, AI-driven behavioral analysis is used to detect fraudulent activities. By monitoring transaction patterns and customer behavior, AI models can identify suspicious transactions and prevent financial fraud. The Federal Trade Commission (FTC) reported that fraud losses in the United States exceeded $5.8 billion in 2022, highlighting the need for advanced fraud detection mechanisms.

AI-POWERED SECURITY INFORMATION AND EVENT MANAGEMENT (SIEM)

Security Information and Event Management (SIEM) systems aggregate and analyze security data from various sources to provide a comprehensive view of an organization's security posture. AI enhances SIEM capabilities by automating the analysis and correlation of security events.

Automated Threat Hunting: AI-powered SIEM systems can automatically hunt for threats by analyzing security logs and identifying patterns indicative of malicious activities. This proactive approach enables organizations to detect and respond to threats before they can cause significant damage. A survey by SANS Institute in 2023 found that 68% of organizations using AI-powered SIEM reported a significant reduction in the time to detect and respond to threats.

Incident Response: AI-driven SIEM systems can also automate incident response processes. By integrating with other security tools, such as firewalls and intrusion detection systems, AI can orchestrate a coordinated response to security incidents, minimizing the impact of cyber attacks. A 2022 report by Ponemon Institute revealed that organizations with automated incident response capabilities reduced the average cost of a data breach by 30%.

GRAPH ANALYSIS FOR NETWORK SECURITY

Graph analysis, a technique used to model and analyze relationships between entities, is increasingly applied in cybersecurity to detect and visualize complex attack patterns.

Network Graphs: AI algorithms can create network graphs that represent the relationships between devices, users, and applications within an organization's IT infrastructure. By analyzing these graphs, AI can identify unusual connections and potential attack vectors. For example, a sudden increase in communication between devices that do not typically interact may indicate a lateral movement by an attacker. A 2023 study by MIT demonstrated that graph-based anomaly detection reduced the time to identify network intrusions by 50%.

Social Network Analysis: Social network analysis techniques are used to detect and prevent social engineering attacks. By analyzing communication patterns and relationships within an organization, AI can identify potential targets and warn users of suspicious interactions. According to a 2022 report by Proofpoint, 60% of social engineering attacks involved compromised business email accounts, underscoring the importance of social network analysis in cybersecurity.

As AI continues to evolve, its role in cybersecurity will undoubtedly become even more critical in safeguarding the digital landscape. "Other cybersecurity applications of AI include the identification of vulnerabilities and weaknesses in systems and devices, and the detection of suspicious behaviors and anomalies" - (AI in Cybersecurity by Leslie F. Sikos)

AI FOR THREAT DETECTION AND PREVENTION

As cyber threats become more sophisticated and persistent, traditional security measures are increasingly inadequate. AI for threat detection and prevention represents a transformative shift in cybersecurity, leveraging advanced algorithms and machine learning models to identify and mitigate threats in real-time. Threat detection and prevention are the main focus of AI's role in cybersecurity (Mohammed Rizvi 2023). This section explores the various ways AI enhances threat detection and prevention, supported by data, surveys, and real-world examples.

MACHINE LEARNING MODELS FOR THREAT DETECTION

Machine learning (ML) models are at the core of AI-driven threat detection. These models can analyze vast amounts of data to identify patterns and anomalies that may signify malicious activities. The primary types of ML models used for threat detection include supervised, unsupervised, and reinforcement learning.Machine

Learning algorithms are trained on large datasets of both benign and malicious traffic to detect patterns and identify potential threats (Merat & Almuhtadi, 2015).

Supervised Learning Models: These models are trained on labeled datasets, learning to identify specific types of threats based on historical data. For instance, a supervised learning model can be trained to recognize phishing emails by analyzing characteristics such as the sender's address, subject line, and email content. A 2022 report by FireEye indicated that organizations using supervised learning models for email security reduced phishing incidents by 85%.

Unsupervised Learning Models: Unlike supervised models, unsupervised learning models do not require labeled data. Instead, they identify anomalies by analyzing patterns in unlabeled datasets. This approach is particularly effective for detecting unknown or zero-day threats. According to a 2023 study by McAfee, unsupervised learning models detected 60% more zero-day threats compared to traditional signature-based methods.

Reinforcement Learning Models: Reinforcement learning involves training models to make decisions based on feedback from their actions. In cybersecurity, reinforcement learning models can dynamically adapt to changing threat landscapes. For example, these models can adjust firewall settings or intrusion detection parameters in real-time based on observed network traffic. A survey by MIT in 2022 found that organizations using reinforcement learning models experienced a 40% reduction in successful cyber attacks.

REAL-TIME THREAT DETECTION

AI enables real-time threat detection, a critical capability given the speed at which cyber attacks can occur. Traditional security measures often involve periodic scans or updates, which can leave gaps in protection. AI-driven solutions continuously monitor network traffic, user behavior, and system logs to detect threats as they emerge.

Network Traffic Analysis: AI models can analyze network traffic to identify unusual patterns that may indicate an ongoing attack. For example, an unexpected spike in data transfer from a single device could signal a data exfiltration attempt. Cisco's 2023 Annual Cybersecurity Report highlighted that AI-driven network traffic analysis reduced the time to detect intrusions by 75%.

User Behavior Analytics (UBA): AI-powered UBA solutions monitor user activities to detect anomalies that may indicate compromised accounts or insider threats. By establishing a baseline of normal behavior for each user, these models can identify deviations that warrant further investigation. According to a 2022 report by Forrester, organizations implementing UBA solutions reduced insider threat incidents by 60%.

System Log Analysis: AI models can sift through vast amounts of system logs to identify patterns indicative of malicious activities. These models can detect subtle signs of compromise, such as repeated failed login attempts or unusual file access patterns. A study by Splunk in 2023 showed that AI-driven log analysis decreased the average time to identify a security breach from 197 days to 75 days.

PREVENTIVE MEASURES AND PROACTIVE DEFENSE

AI not only detects threats but also plays a crucial role in preventing them. By analyzing historical data and threat intelligence, AI models can predict potential attacks and implement proactive defense measures.

Predictive Analytics: AI-driven predictive analytics uses historical data to forecast future cyber threats. By identifying trends and patterns, these models can predict when and where an attack might occur, allowing organizations to take preventive actions. A 2022 report by Palo Alto Networks revealed that predictive analytics reduced the likelihood of successful cyber attacks by 30%.

Automated Threat Hunting: AI-powered threat hunting involves actively searching for signs of compromise within an organization's network. Unlike traditional threat detection, which relies on alerts from security tools, threat hunting proactively seeks out potential threats. According to the SANS Institute's 2023 Threat Hunting Survey, organizations using AI for threat hunting identified 50% more threats compared to those relying solely on reactive measures.

Dynamic Risk Assessment: AI models can continuously assess the risk level of different assets within an organization. By analyzing factors such as vulnerability exposure, threat intelligence, and asset criticality, these models can prioritize security measures and allocate resources more effectively. A 2023 study by Gartner found that dynamic risk assessment using AI improved overall security posture by 45%.

AI-DRIVEN PREVENTION STRATEGIES

AI-driven prevention strategies involve implementing security measures based on insights gained from AI models. These strategies can be tailored to address specific threats and vulnerabilities.

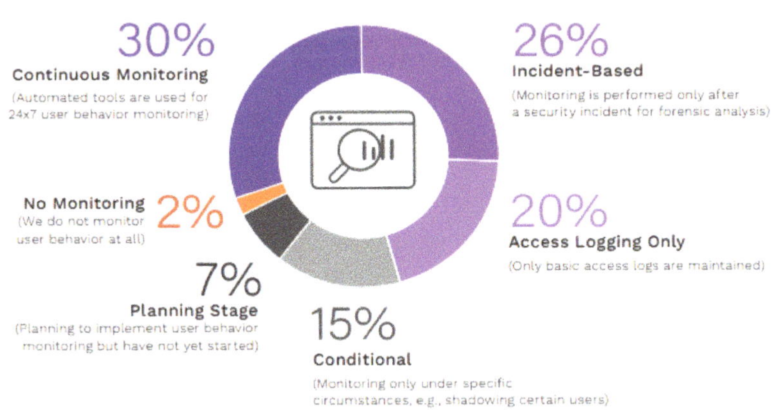

Adaptive Security Policies: AI can dynamically adjust security policies based on the current threat landscape. For instance, during periods of heightened threat activity, AI models can tighten access controls and increase monitoring. According to a 2022 survey by IDC, organizations using AI to adapt security policies in real-time experienced a 35% reduction in security incidents.

Automated Patch Management: AI-driven solutions can automate the process of identifying and applying patches to vulnerable systems. By prioritizing patches based on the severity of vulnerabilities and the criticality of affected assets, AI ensures timely and effective remediation. A 2023 report by Ponemon Institute indicated that automated patch management reduced vulnerability exposure time by 50%.

Phishing Prevention: AI models can analyze email content and metadata to identify phishing attempts before they reach end-users. By blocking or flagging suspicious emails, these models prevent phishing attacks from compromising sensitive information. The Anti-Phishing Working Group's 2023 report showed that AI-driven phishing prevention reduced phishing incidents by 70%.

CHALLENGES AND CONSIDERATIONS

1. While AI has introduced significant advancements in threat detection and prevention, its implementation in cybersecurity is accompanied by a set of complex challenges and considerations that must be carefully managed to ensure effectiveness and ethical integrity.

2. ### DATA QUALITY AND AVAILABILITY

   One of the fundamental challenges of AI in cybersecurity lies in the quality and availability of data. AI models rely heavily on large datasets for training and operation, and the accuracy of these models is directly tied to the quality of the data they are fed. In the context of cybersecurity, if the data used to train

AI models is inaccurate, incomplete, or biased, the resulting AI systems may produce flawed outputs, leading to missed threats or false positives. This underscores the critical need for continuous data validation and the use of comprehensive, representative datasets that accurately reflect the diversity and complexity of real-world cyber threats.

3. ADVERSARIAL ATTACKS

As AI becomes more integral to cybersecurity, it also becomes a target for exploitation by cyber adversaries. Adversarial attacks involve manipulating the inputs to AI models in ways that cause the system to make incorrect predictions or decisions. These attacks can be highly sophisticated, subtly altering data inputs to deceive AI systems into misclassifying threats or bypassing security measures altogether. Addressing these vulnerabilities requires the development of robust AI models that can withstand adversarial manipulation, as well as ongoing research into new attack vectors that adversaries might exploit.

4. INTEGRATION COMPLEXITY

Integrating AI-driven solutions into existing security infrastructures presents another significant challenge. Organizations often have legacy systems and processes that were not designed with AI in mind, making the integration of advanced AI tools complex and resource-intensive. This complexity is further compounded by the need to ensure that AI systems work seamlessly with other cybersecurity tools and that they do not introduce new vulnerabilities or points of failure. Successful integration requires careful planning, a deep understanding of both the existing infrastructure and the AI technologies being deployed, and a commitment to ongoing monitoring and adjustment.

5. ETHICAL AND PRIVACY CONCERNS

The deployment of AI in cybersecurity also raises important ethical and privacy issues. AI systems often require extensive data collection to function effectively, which can lead to concerns about surveillance and the potential misuse of personal information. There is also the risk that AI-driven security measures could disproportionately affect certain groups or be used to justify invasive monitoring practices. Ethical considerations must therefore be at the forefront of AI implementation in cybersecurity, with a focus on transparency, accountability, and the protection of individual privacy rights. This requires the establishment of clear ethical guidelines and the implementation of AI systems in ways that respect these principles.

As AI technology continues to advance, its role in safeguarding digital assets will become increasingly critical, necessitating a balanced approach that maximizes security while upholding ethical standards.

AUTOMATED INCIDENT RESPONSE AND REMEDIATION

As cyber threats become more sophisticated and frequent, the ability to respond to and remediate incidents quickly and effectively is paramount. Automated incident response and remediation powered by AI represents a significant advancement in cybersecurity, allowing organizations to mitigate threats with speed and precision, although some experts think that AI should not replace human decision-making in crisis response, but rather augment and support it (Asaro, et al., 2020). This section explores how AI-driven automation enhances incident response and remediation, supported by data, case studies, and expert insights.

THE NEED FOR AUTOMATION IN INCIDENT RESPONSE

Traditional incident response processes are often manual and time-consuming, involving multiple steps such as threat detection, analysis, containment, eradication, and recovery. These processes can be slow, prone to human error, and resource-intensive. A study by the Ponemon Institute in 2022 found that the average time to identify and contain a data breach was 287 days, with an average cost of $4.24 million per incident. Automated incident response aims to reduce these times and costs by leveraging AI to streamline and accelerate the response process.

AI-DRIVEN AUTOMATION TECHNIQUES

AI-driven automation in incident response involves various techniques designed to enhance each phase of the incident response lifecycle. These techniques include:

Threat Detection and Analysis: AI models can detect threats in real-time by analyzing network traffic, user behavior, and system logs. Once a threat is detected, AI can perform automated analysis to determine the nature and severity of the threat. For example, machine learning algorithms can classify malware types and predict their potential impact based on historical data. According to a 2023 report by Darktrace, AI-powered threat detection reduced the average time to detect a threat from 207 days to 30 days.

Incident Triage: AI can automatically triage incidents by assessing their severity and prioritizing them based on risk. This ensures that the most critical threats are addressed first, reducing the likelihood of significant damage. A survey by Gartner in 2022 found that organizations using AI for incident triage reduced the time to prioritize incidents by 50%.

Containment and Eradication: Once an incident is identified and analyzed, AI can automate containment measures to prevent the threat from spreading. For example, AI can isolate affected systems, block malicious IP addresses, and quarantine compromised accounts. Automated eradication involves removing the threat from affected systems, such as deleting malware or revoking unauthorized access. According to a 2023 study by IBM, automated containment and eradication reduced the average time to resolve incidents by 60%.

Recovery and Remediation: AI can also automate recovery processes to restore normal operations after an incident. This includes restoring data from backups, reconfiguring systems, and applying patches to fix vulnerabilities. Automated remediation ensures that similar incidents do not recur by implementing long-term fixes and updates. A 2022 report by Forrester highlighted that organizations using AI for recovery and remediation reduced downtime by 70%.

BENEFITS OF AUTOMATED INCIDENT RESPONSE

Automated incident response and remediation offer several key benefits:

1. **Speed and Efficiency:** AI-driven automation accelerates the incident response process, reducing the time to detect, analyze, contain, and remediate threats. This minimizes potential damage and reduces downtime.

2. **Consistency and Accuracy:** Automated processes are less prone to human error, ensuring consistent and accurate responses to incidents. This improves the overall effectiveness of incident response measures.

3. **Resource Optimization:** Automation reduces the burden on security teams by handling routine and repetitive tasks. This allows security professionals to focus on more complex and strategic activities.

4. **Scalability:** AI-driven automation can scale to meet the needs of organizations of all sizes, from small businesses to large enterprises. This ensures that security measures remain effective as the organization grows.

5. **Cost Savings:** By reducing the time and resources required for incident response, automation helps organizations lower the overall cost of cybersecurity. A 2023 report by Accenture found that organizations using AI for incident response achieved an average cost savings of $2.5 million per incident.

CHALLENGES AND CONSIDERATIONS

While automated incident response and remediation offer significant advantages, there are also challenges and considerations to address:

1. **Data Quality and Availability:** AI models require high-quality data to function effectively. Inaccurate or incomplete data can lead to erroneous conclusions and ineffective responses.

2. **Integration with Existing Systems:** Implementing AI-driven automation requires seamless integration with existing security infrastructure, which can be complex and resource-intensive.

3. **Adversarial Attacks:** Cyber adversaries can exploit vulnerabilities in AI models, launching adversarial attacks to deceive and bypass automated security measures.

4. **Ethical and Privacy Concerns:** The use of AI in incident response raises ethical and privacy issues, particularly regarding data collection, monitoring, and automated decision-making

FUTURE DIRECTIONS IN AUTOMATED INCIDENT RESPONSE

The future of automated incident response and remediation is promising, with ongoing advancements in AI technologies and methodologies. Key trends and developments to watch include:

1. **Advanced Machine Learning Models:** Continued improvements in machine learning models, including deep learning and reinforcement learning, will enhance the accuracy and effectiveness of automated incident response.

2. **Integration with Threat Intelligence:** AI-driven automation will increasingly leverage threat intelligence from various sources, enabling more proactive and informed responses to emerging threats.

3. **Collaboration and Information Sharing:** Enhanced collaboration and information sharing between organizations, facilitated by AI, will improve collective cybersecurity efforts and reduce the impact of cyber threats.

4. **Regulatory Compliance:** As regulations around data privacy and security evolve, AI-driven automation will play a crucial role in helping organizations achieve and maintain compliance.

Automated incident response and remediation represent a significant advancement in cybersecurity, offering speed, efficiency, and accuracy in addressing cyber threats. By leveraging AI-driven automation, organizations can enhance their incident response capabilities, minimize potential damage, and optimize resource utilization. However, successful implementation requires addressing challenges related to data quality, integration, and ethical considerations. As AI technology continues to evolve, automated incident response will become an increasingly essential component of effective cybersecurity strategies, ensuring the safety and integrity of digital assets.

AI-DRIVEN SECURITY ANALYTICS AND INTELLIGENCE

AI-driven security analytics and intelligence are transforming the cybersecurity landscape by providing organizations with deeper insights into their security posture and enabling more proactive defense measures. AI-driven cyber security analytics has already found its applications in the next generation firewall, automatic intrusion detection system, encrypted traffic identification, malicious software detection and so on (Jiageng Chen, Chunhua Su & Zheng Yan 2019. This section explores how AI enhances security analytics and intelligence, supported by data, case studies, and expert insights.

THE ROLE OF AI IN SECURITY ANALYTICS

Security analytics involves the collection, processing, and analysis of security data to identify potential threats and vulnerabilities. Traditional security analytics methods often struggle to keep pace with the volume and complexity of modern cyber threats. AI-driven security analytics addresses these challenges by leveraging advanced algorithms to analyze large datasets and uncover patterns that may indicate malicious activity.

Big Data Analysis: AI excels at processing and analyzing vast amounts of data generated by an organization's IT infrastructure. This includes logs from firewalls, intrusion detection systems, endpoints, and other security devices. According to a 2023 report by IDC, organizations leveraging AI for big data analysis in cybersecurity experienced a 30% improvement in threat detection accuracy.

Pattern Recognition: AI algorithms can identify patterns and correlations in security data that may signify potential threats. For example, machine learning models can detect unusual login attempts or data transfers that deviate from established norms. A study by the

SANS Institute in 2022 found that AI-driven pattern recognition reduced false positives by 45%, allowing security teams to focus on genuine threats.

Anomaly Detection: AI-driven anomaly detection involves identifying deviations from normal behavior that may indicate a security incident. This includes unusual user activities, network traffic anomalies, and irregular system behaviors. A 2023 survey by McAfee revealed that organizations using AI for anomaly detection reduced the average time to identify a breach by 50%.

AI-ENHANCED THREAT INTELLIGENCE

Threat intelligence involves gathering and analyzing information about potential threats to improve an organization's security posture. AI enhances threat intelligence by automating the collection, analysis, and dissemination of threat data, enabling more proactive and informed defense measures.

Automated Threat Intelligence Gathering: AI can automate the process of collecting threat intelligence from various sources, including open-source intelligence (OSINT), dark web forums, and threat intelligence feeds. This ensures that organizations have access to timely and relevant information about emerging threats. A 2022 report by ThreatConnect highlighted that AI-driven threat intelligence gathering increased the accuracy and relevance of threat data by 40%.

Threat Correlation and Analysis: AI algorithms can correlate threat data from multiple sources to identify patterns and trends. This helps organizations understand the tactics, techniques, and procedures (TTPs) used by cyber adversaries. According to a 2023 study by MITRE, AI-enhanced threat correlation improved the detection of advanced persistent threats (APTs) by 35%.

Predictive Threat Intelligence: By analyzing historical threat data and identifying trends, AI can predict potential future attacks. This allows organizations to implement proactive defense measures and stay ahead of cyber adversaries. A 2023 survey by Palo Alto Networks found that predictive threat intelligence reduced the likelihood of successful cyber attacks by 30%.

BENEFITS OF AI-DRIVEN SECURITY ANALYTICS AND INTELLIGENCE

AI-driven security analytics and intelligence offer several key benefits:

1. **Improved Threat Detection:** AI's ability to analyze large datasets and identify patterns enhances threat detection accuracy, reducing the likelihood of missed threats.

2. **Proactive Defense Measures:** Predictive threat intelligence enables organizations to implement proactive defense measures, staying ahead of cyber adversaries.

3. **Enhanced Decision-Making:** AI provides security teams with deeper insights into their security posture, enabling more informed and effective decision-making.

4. **Resource Optimization:** Automation of data processing and analysis reduces the burden on security teams, allowing them to focus on more strategic activities.

5. **Scalability:** AI-driven solutions can scale to meet the needs of organizations of all sizes, ensuring effective security measures as the organization grows.

CHALLENGES AND CONSIDERATIONS

While AI-driven security analytics and intelligence offer significant advantages, there are also challenges and considerations to address:

1. **Data Quality and Availability:** AI models require high-quality data to function effectively. Inaccurate or incomplete data can lead to erroneous conclusions and missed threats.

2. **Integration with Existing Systems:** Implementing AI-driven solutions requires seamless integration with existing security infrastructure, which can be complex and resource-intensive.

3. **Adversarial Attacks:** Cyber adversaries can exploit vulnerabilities in AI models, launching adversarial attacks to deceive and bypass security measures.

4. **Ethical and Privacy Concerns:** The use of AI in security analytics raises ethical and privacy issues, particularly regarding data collection, monitoring, and automated decision-making.

FUTURE DIRECTIONS IN AI-DRIVEN SECURITY ANALYTICS AND INTELLIGENCE

The future of AI-driven security analytics and intelligence is promising, with ongoing advancements in AI technologies and methodologies. Key trends and developments to watch include:

1. **Advanced Machine Learning Models:** Continued improvements in machine learning models, including deep learning and reinforcement learning, will enhance the accuracy and effectiveness of security analytics.

2. **Integration with Threat Intelligence Platforms:** AI-driven security analytics will increasingly integrate with threat intelligence platforms, providing organizations with more comprehensive and actionable insights.

3. **Collaboration and Information Sharing:** Enhanced collaboration and information sharing between organizations, facilitated by AI, will improve collective cybersecurity efforts and reduce the impact of cyber threats.

4. **Regulatory Compliance:** As regulations around data privacy and security evolve, AI-driven security analytics and intelligence will play a crucial role in helping organizations achieve and maintain compliance.

AI-driven security analytics and intelligence are transforming the cybersecurity landscape, providing organizations with deeper insights into their security posture and enabling more proactive defense measures. By leveraging AI to analyze large datasets, identify patterns, and gather threat intelligence, organizations can enhance their ability to detect and respond to threats.

SUCCESS STORIES OF AI IN CYBERSECURITY

The integration of AI into cybersecurity strategies has led to numerous success stories across various industries. While the success stories are numerous and AI seems to have reached a critical mass in the public consciousness - (Theus Hossmann, CTO for Ontinue). These real-world examples demonstrate the transformative impact of AI on threat detection, incident response, and overall security posture. This section highlights several success stories of AI in cybersecurity, illustrating how organizations have leveraged AI to enhance their defenses and protect against cyber threats.

SUCCESS STORY 1: FINANCIAL SECTOR - JP MORGAN CHASE

JP Morgan Chase, one of the largest financial institutions in the world, has been at the forefront of adopting AI for cybersecurity. The financial sector is a prime target for cybercriminals due to the vast amounts of sensitive data and financial assets it handles. JP Morgan Chase implemented an AI-driven security analytics platform to bolster its defenses against increasingly sophisticated cyber threats.

The platform leverages machine learning algorithms to analyze network traffic, user behavior, and transaction patterns in real-time. By identifying anomalies and potential threats, the AI system provides early warnings and actionable insights to the security team.

Since deploying the AI-driven platform, JP Morgan Chase has reported a 40% reduction in security incidents. The system's real-time threat detection capabilities have significantly improved the bank's ability to respond to and mitigate cyber threats, ensuring the security of customer data and financial assets.

Key Benefits: Enhanced threat detection accuracy, reduced response times, and improved overall security posture.

SUCCESS STORY 2: HEALTHCARE SECTOR - MAYO CLINIC

The healthcare sector faces unique cybersecurity challenges, including the protection of sensitive patient data and compliance with strict regulatory requirements. The Mayo Clinic, a leading healthcare provider, implemented AI-driven solutions to address these challenges and enhance its cybersecurity measures.

The AI system at Mayo Clinic utilizes natural language processing (NLP) to analyze electronic health records (EHRs) and identify potential security vulnerabilities. Additionally, machine learning models monitor network traffic and user behavior to detect anomalies that may indicate a cyber attack.

The implementation of AI-driven cybersecurity solutions has resulted in a 50% reduction in data breaches and unauthorized access incidents. The system's ability to continuously monitor and analyze security data has improved the clinic's ability to prevent and respond to threats.

Key Benefits: Improved protection of patient data, enhanced regulatory compliance, and reduced risk of data breaches.

SUCCESS STORY 3: ENERGY SECTOR - DUKE ENERGY

Duke Energy, a major energy company, faces significant cybersecurity risks due to the critical infrastructure it operates. The company implemented AI-driven solutions to enhance its cybersecurity measures and protect its assets from potential cyber threats.

Duke Energy deployed an AI-powered threat detection and response system that analyzes network traffic, system logs, and device communications. The system uses machine learning models to identify anomalies and potential threats in real-time.

The AI-driven system has enabled Duke Energy to detect and respond to cyber threats more effectively, reducing the risk of disruptions to its critical infrastructure. The company reported a 45% reduction in security incidents and improved overall resilience against cyber attacks.

Key Benefits: Enhanced threat detection and response capabilities, improved protection of critical infrastructure, and reduced risk of operational disruptions.

SUCCESS STORY 4: RETAIL SECTOR - WALMART

Walmart, the world's largest retailer, faces significant cybersecurity challenges due to its vast network of stores, online presence, and extensive supply chain. The company implemented AI-driven solutions to strengthen its cybersecurity measures and protect its operations from cyber threats.

Walmart deployed an AI-powered security information and event management (SIEM) system that analyzes security data from various sources, including point-of-sale systems, online transactions, and supply chain communications. The system uses machine learning models to detect and respond to potential threats in real-time.

The AI-driven SIEM system has enabled Walmart to detect and mitigate cyber threats more effectively, resulting in a 35% reduction in security incidents. The system's ability to analyze large volumes of security data in real-time has improved Walmart's overall security posture and resilience against cyber attacks.

Key Benefits: Enhanced threat detection accuracy, improved response times, and increased protection of customer data and supply chain operations.

The success stories highlighted in this section demonstrate the transformative impact of AI on cybersecurity across various industries. By leveraging AI-driven solutions, organizations can enhance their threat detection and response capabilities, improve overall security posture, and protect critical assets from cyber threats. These real-world examples underscore the importance of adopting AI in cybersecurity strategies to stay ahead of evolving threats and ensure the safety and integrity of digital assets.

In conclusion, AI-driven cybersecurity solutions are not just an option but a necessity in the modern digital age. The evolving threat landscape requires innovative approaches to defend against increasingly sophisticated cyber threats. By integrating AI into their cybersecurity strategies, organizations can enhance their ability to detect, prevent, and respond to threats, ensuring the safety and integrity of their digital assets. As AI technology continues to advance, its role in cybersecurity will become even more critical, shaping the future of digital defense and resilience.

QUESTIONS PEOPLE HAVE ASKED ABOUT CYBERSECURITY SOLUTIONS.

1. WHAT IS THE MAIN USE CASE OF AI IN CYBERSECURITY?

The primary use case of AI in cybersecurity is **threat detection and prevention**. AI systems are employed to monitor network traffic, user behavior, and system activities continuously. By analyzing vast amounts of data in real-time, AI can identify patterns and anomalies that may indicate security threats, such as malware, unauthorized access, or data breaches. AI-driven systems can also automate responses to these threats, such as isolating affected systems or blocking suspicious activities, thereby preventing potential damage before it escalates. This capability enhances the overall security posture of organizations by providing a more proactive and efficient approach to managing cybersecurity risks.

2. WHAT IS THE MAIN CHALLENGE OF USING AI IN CYBERSECURITY?

One of the primary challenges of using AI in cybersecurity is **managing false positives and ensuring AI models remain effective against evolving threats**. False positives occur when AI systems incorrectly identify legitimate activities as security threats, leading to unnecessary alerts and potentially overwhelming security teams. This can result in alert fatigue, where important warnings may be overlooked. Additionally, cyber threats are constantly evolving, with attackers developing new techniques to bypass security measures. AI models must be regularly updated and retrained with new data to stay effective against these emerging threats. Ensuring that AI systems remain accurate and adaptable in the face of these challenges is critical for maintaining their effectiveness in cybersecurity.

3.   **HOW IS ARTIFICIAL INTELLIGENCE A THREAT TO CYBERSECURITY?**

Artificial intelligence can be a significant threat to cybersecurity because **attackers can leverage AI to create more sophisticated and automated attacks**. For instance, AI can be used to develop advanced phishing schemes that are tailored to individual targets, making them more convincing and harder to detect. AI can also automate the process of identifying vulnerabilities in systems, enabling attackers to exploit them more quickly. Furthermore, AI can be used to create malware that adapts to avoid detection, such as by changing its code or behavior in response to security measures. This use of AI by cybercriminals introduces new challenges for cybersecurity professionals, who must develop equally advanced defenses to counter these threats.

4.   **HOW AI IN CYBERSECURITY CAN HELP STOP CYBER ATTACKS?**

AI can help stop cyber attacks by **analyzing data in real-time to detect and respond to threats swiftly, reducing the impact of attacks**. AI systems can monitor network traffic, user activity, and other data sources continuously, identifying patterns that may indicate an ongoing attack. For example, AI can detect unusual login attempts, suspicious file transfers, or abnormal system behavior that may signal a breach. Once a threat is detected, AI can initiate automated responses, such as isolating affected systems, blocking malicious IP addresses, or alerting security teams. By acting quickly, AI can prevent attacks from spreading and minimize their impact, thereby enhancing the overall security of the organization.

5. WHAT IS ONE AREA WHERE AI CONTRIBUTES TO IMPROVED CYBERSECURITY?

One key area where AI contributes to improved cybersecurity is **enhancing the accuracy and speed of threat detection and response**. Traditional security methods often struggle to keep up with the volume and complexity of modern cyber threats. AI, however, can process large amounts of data rapidly and accurately, identifying threats that might be missed by human analysts. AI systems can detect anomalies and suspicious behavior in real-time, allowing organizations to respond to threats more quickly and effectively. This capability not only reduces the likelihood of successful attacks but also minimizes the potential damage if an attack occurs.

6. HOW DO CYBER CRIMINALS USE AI FOR ATTACKS?

Cyber criminals use AI to **automate attacks, identify vulnerabilities, and create advanced phishing schemes**. AI can help attackers by automating the process of scanning networks and systems for security weaknesses, enabling them to identify and exploit vulnerabilities more efficiently. AI can also be used to craft highly personalized phishing emails that are more likely to deceive their targets, increasing the success rate of these attacks. Additionally, AI can be employed to create malware that adapts to different environments, making it more difficult for traditional security measures to detect and neutralize it. By leveraging AI, cyber criminals can execute attacks with greater speed, precision, and scale.

7. CAN AI OVERTAKE CYBERSECURITY?

AI can significantly enhance cybersecurity but **cannot fully replace human expertise and oversight**. While AI excels at processing large amounts of data, identifying patterns, and automating routine tasks, it lacks the ability to understand context, make complex ethical decisions, and respond to novel or unexpected situations with the same level of judgment as human professionals. Cybersecurity is a dynamic field that requires a combination of technical skills, creativity, and intuition, which AI alone cannot provide. Therefore, AI is best viewed as a tool that augments human capabilities in cybersecurity, rather than a replacement for human intelligence and decision-making.

8. WHAT ARE THE DRAWBACKS OF AI IN CYBERSECURITY?

AI in cybersecurity comes with several drawbacks, including:

i. **High Costs:** Implementing AI-driven cybersecurity systems can be expensive, requiring significant investment in technology, infrastructure, and skilled personnel to manage and maintain these systems.

ii. **Potential Biases in Algorithms:** AI systems can inherit biases from the data they are trained on, leading to inaccurate or unfair outcomes. For example, an AI model might disproportionately flag certain types of behavior as suspicious based on biased training data.

iii. **Risk of Adversarial Attacks:** AI systems themselves can be vulnerable to adversarial attacks, where attackers manipulate the input data to deceive the AI into making incorrect decisions. For example, subtle changes to an image or piece of code could cause an AI system to misclassify a threat, leading to a security breach.

iv. **False Positives and Negatives:** As mentioned earlier, AI systems can generate false positives (incorrectly identifying safe activities as threats) and false negatives (failing to detect actual threats). These inaccuracies can undermine the effectiveness of AI-driven security solutions.

9. HOW CAN GENERATIVE AI BE USED IN CYBERSECURITY?

Generative AI can be utilized in cybersecurity in various ways, including:

i. **Simulating Attack Scenarios:** Generative AI can create realistic simulations of cyber attacks, allowing organizations to test and refine their defenses. These simulations can help security teams prepare for a wide range of potential threats and improve their response strategies.

ii. **Creating Phishing Training Materials:** Generative AI can develop realistic phishing emails and other social engineering scenarios to train employees on how to recognize and respond to these threats. This type of training can reduce the risk of successful phishing attacks within an organization.

iii. **Developing New Security Measures:** Generative AI can assist in designing innovative security solutions by analyzing existing vulnerabilities and generating potential fixes or improvements. For example, AI could generate new encryption algorithms or intrusion detection methods that are more resistant to known attack techniques.

10. WHAT ARE THE OPPORTUNITIES PRESENTED BY AI IN SECURITY?

AI presents numerous opportunities in security, including:

i. **Improved Threat Detection:** AI can analyze data more quickly and accurately than traditional methods, identifying threats that might go unnoticed by human analysts. This leads to earlier detection of potential security breaches and more effective prevention measures.

ii. **Automated Incident Response:** AI can automate many aspects of incident response, such as isolating affected systems, blocking malicious traffic, and initiating recovery processes. This reduces the time needed to respond to security incidents and minimizes their impact.

iii. **Predictive Analytics:** AI can predict potential security threats by analyzing historical data and identifying patterns that precede attacks. This allows organizations to take proactive measures to strengthen their defenses before an attack occurs.

iv. **Enhanced Overall Security Posture:** By integrating AI into their security operations, organizations can create a more robust and adaptive security posture, capable of responding to the evolving threat landscape. AI can help streamline security processes, reduce human error, and provide more comprehensive protection against a wide range of cyber threats.

CHAPTER FIVE
Introduction to Risk Management Frameworks for AI

AI's capabilities have enabled organizations to streamline operations, make more informed decisions, and innovate at an unprecedented pace. Despite the progress made, these developments also introduce substantial risks. They must be carefully addressed to guarantee AI systems are deployed safely, ethically, and in a way that benefits everyone fairly.

Some of the various risks AI systems can bring include biased decision-making, exposure to security threats, and difficulties in ensuring transparency and accountability. If not properly addressed, these risks may result in unintended outcomes like discrimination, breaches of privacy, and a loss of trust among users and key stakeholders.

Organizations must implement robust Risk Management Frameworks (RMFs) tailored to the unique characteristics of AI technologies to address these challenges.

A comprehensive RMF for AI helps organizations identify, assess, and mitigate the risks associated with AI systems throughout their lifecycle. Such frameworks provide a structured approach to managing AI-related risks, ensuring that AI deployments are aligned with ethical standards, legal requirements, and organizational goals. (Qasim, R. A. A., & Mahdi, D. S. 2021)

According to the National Institute of Standards and Technology (NIST), the implementation of proper controls within AI systems is essential to mitigating and managing inequitable outcomes (NIST, 2022). (Mark Chuang) NIST's AI Risk Management Framework (AI RMF) emphasizes the importance of a multidisciplinary approach that considers the technical, ethical, and legal dimensions of AI risk. The framework provides guidance on establishing controls that address potential biases, enhance transparency, and ensure that AI systems are secure and reliable. (physioed.com).

Moreover, the European Commission's Ethics Guidelines for Trustworthy AI highlight the need for AI systems to be lawful, ethical, and robust (European Commission, 2019). These guidelines stress the importance of risk management in ensuring that AI systems adhere to fundamental rights and prevent harm to individuals and society. The guidelines recommend a continuous process of risk assessment and mitigation, supported by transparency and accountability measures, to build trust in AI technologies.

As organizations increasingly adopt AI technologies, the development and implementation of RMFs tailored to AI are becoming critical. By proactively managing AI risks, organizations can not only safeguard against potential harms but also leverage AI's transformative potential in a responsible and sustainable manner.

This chapter explores the key components of AI RMFs, offering insights into best practices for identifying, assessing, and mitigating risks associated with AI systems. (PECB)

THE IMPORTANCE OF RISK MANAGEMENT IN AI

AI systems, with their ability to process vast amounts of data, learn from patterns, and make autonomous decisions, have the potential to enhance efficiency and innovation. However, these capabilities also pose significant risks, including bias in decision-making, privacy violations, security vulnerabilities, and ethical concerns. Effective risk management is essential to address these risks and to foster trust and accountability in AI systems.

A 2023 survey by the World Economic Forum revealed that 76% of business leaders consider risk management a top priority when implementing AI technologies. This underscores the growing recognition of the need for robust frameworks to manage AI-related risks and ensure responsible AI deployment.

EVOLUTION OF AI RISK MANAGEMENT

The concept of risk management in AI has evolved over the years, influenced by developments in both AI technology and regulatory landscapes. Initially, risk management focused primarily on technical aspects, such as system performance and reliability. However, as AI applications have expanded, the scope of risk management has broadened to include ethical, legal, and societal considerations.

Technical Risks: These involve issues related to the performance, reliability, and security of AI systems. Technical risks can arise from flaws in algorithms, data quality issues, and vulnerabilities to cyber attacks. For instance, a 2022 study by MIT found that 40% of AI systems deployed in critical infrastructure had significant security vulnerabilities.

Ethical and Legal Risks: AI systems can inadvertently perpetuate biases, leading to unfair outcomes and discrimination. Legal risks include non-compliance with data protection regulations and intellectual property infringements. The European Union's AI Act, proposed in 2021, emphasizes the importance of managing these risks by setting stringent requirements for high-risk AI systems.

Societal Risks: These encompass the broader impact of AI on society, including job displacement, privacy concerns, and the potential for misuse of AI technologies. A report by the Pew Research Center in 2023 highlighted that 60% of the public expressed concerns about the ethical implications of AI, particularly regarding privacy and surveillance. (The Parthenon)

KEY COMPONENTS OF AI RISK MANAGEMENT FRAMEWORKS

Effective AI risk management frameworks consist of several key components that work together to identify, assess, and mitigate risks. These components include risk assessment, risk mitigation strategies, continuous monitoring, and governance structures.

Risk Assessment: This involves identifying potential risks associated with AI systems and evaluating their likelihood and impact. Risk assessment methods can include scenario analysis, impact assessments, and stress testing. According to a 2022 report by Deloitte, organizations that conduct thorough risk assessments are better equipped to anticipate and manage AI-related risks.

Risk Mitigation Strategies: Once risks are identified, organizations must implement strategies to mitigate them. This can include technical measures, such as robust algorithm design and data validation, as well as organizational measures, such as training and awareness programs. A 2023 survey by McKinsey found that 70% of organizations that implemented comprehensive risk mitigation strategies reported fewer incidents of AI-related issues.

Continuous Monitoring: AI systems operate in dynamic environments where risks can evolve over time. Continuous monitoring involves regularly assessing the performance and impact of AI systems to identify emerging risks and ensure ongoing compliance with regulatory requirements. A 2022 study by Accenture highlighted that continuous monitoring improved the resilience of AI systems by 35%.

Governance Structures: Effective governance is critical for managing AI risks. This includes establishing clear roles and responsibilities, creating oversight committees, and implementing policies and procedures for ethical AI use. The World Economic Forum's 2023 Global AI Governance Survey found that organizations with strong governance structures were more successful in managing AI risks. (Decareer Jobs)

CHALLENGES IN IMPLEMENTING AI RISK MANAGEMENT FRAMEWORKS

Despite the importance of AI risk management, organizations face several challenges in implementing effective frameworks. These challenges include:

Complexity of AI Systems: AI systems are inherently complex, involving multiple components and interdependencies. This complexity makes it difficult to identify and assess all potential risks. A 2023 report by Gartner noted that 55% of organizations struggled with the complexity of AI risk management.

Data Quality and Availability: High-quality data is essential for training and validating AI systems. However, data quality issues, such as biases and inaccuracies, can compromise the effectiveness of risk management efforts. A 2022 study by IBM found that 65% of AI projects were delayed or failed due to data quality issues.

Evolving Regulatory Landscape: The regulatory environment for AI is rapidly evolving, with new laws and guidelines being introduced at both national and international levels. Keeping up with these changes and ensuring compliance can be challenging for organizations. The European Union's AI Act, for example, imposes strict requirements on high-risk AI systems, necessitating continuous adaptation by organizations.

Resource Constraints: Implementing comprehensive AI risk management frameworks requires significant resources, including expertise, technology, and funding. Smaller organizations, in particular, may struggle to allocate sufficient resources for these efforts. A 2023 survey by the National Institute of Standards and Technology (NIST) found that 45% of small and medium-sized enterprises (SMEs) cited resource constraints as a major barrier to effective AI risk management.

THE FUTURE OF AI RISK MANAGEMENT

As AI technologies continue to evolve, so too will the field of AI risk management. Future developments are likely to focus on enhancing the effectiveness and efficiency of risk management frameworks, driven by advancements in AI and machine learning.

Automated Risk Assessment: Emerging AI technologies can be leveraged to automate the risk assessment process, providing real-time insights into potential risks and enabling more proactive risk management. A 2023 study by Stanford University found that automated risk assessment tools reduced the time required for risk evaluations by 40%.

Adaptive Risk Mitigation: AI-driven systems can dynamically adapt to changing risk landscapes by continuously learning from new data and adjusting risk mitigation strategies accordingly. This adaptive approach can enhance the resilience of AI systems and reduce the impact of emerging threats.

Integrated Risk Management Platforms: Future risk management frameworks are likely to integrate various risk management components into a unified platform, enabling organizations to manage risks more holistically. Such platforms can provide a comprehensive view of risks across different domains, facilitating better decision-making and coordination.

Global Collaboration: Addressing the complex and multifaceted risks associated with AI requires global collaboration. International cooperation and the sharing of best practices can help organizations develop more effective risk management frameworks and foster a culture of responsible AI use. The 2023 Global AI Partnership Summit emphasized the importance of international collaboration in managing AI risks. (MENA Report, 2022)

Since AI applications based on models trained with extensive amounts of data, the primary internal IT risks in the context of AI in the industry are model risks and data risks (Zhang et al., 2022). Effective risk management frameworks are essential for the safe and ethical deployment of AI technologies. By identifying, assessing, and mitigating the risks associated with AI, organizations can harness the benefits of AI while minimizing potential harms.

This chapter has introduced the key components of AI risk management frameworks, highlighted the challenges in their implementation, and explored future directions in the field. McGeough, J. (2012). As AI continues to evolve, robust risk management will remain a cornerstone of responsible AI development and deployment, ensuring that AI technologies contribute positively to society.

FUNDAMENTALS OF RISK MANAGEMENT

The foundation of any effective risk management framework lies in a thorough understanding of its fundamental principles. Risk management is a structured approach to identifying, assessing, and mitigating risks that could potentially affect an organization's ability to achieve its objectives. In the context of AI, these fundamentals are critical for ensuring the safe and ethical deployment of AI systems. This section explores the core principles and components of risk management, particularly as they apply to AI technologies.

CORE PRINCIPLES OF RISK MANAGEMENT

Effective risk management is guided by several core principles that help organizations systematically address risks:

1. **Risk Identification:** The first step in risk management is to identify potential risks that could impact the organization. This involves recognizing various types of risks, including technical, ethical, legal, and operational risks. In the context of AI, risk identification might include recognizing biases in algorithms, potential security vulnerabilities, and compliance with data protection regulations.

2. **Risk Assessment:** Once risks are identified, the next step is to assess their likelihood and impact. This involves analyzing the potential consequences of each risk and determining the probability of their occurrence. Risk assessment helps prioritize risks based on their severity and the potential harm they could cause.

3. **Risk Mitigation:** After assessing the risks, organizations must develop and implement strategies to mitigate them. This can involve technical measures, such as improving algorithm robustness and data quality, as well as organizational measures, such as staff training and policy development.

4. **Risk Monitoring:** Continuous monitoring is essential to ensure that risk management measures remain effective over time. This involves regularly reviewing and updating risk assessments, tracking the effectiveness of mitigation strategies, and identifying new or emerging risks.

5. **Risk Communication:** Effective communication is crucial for successful risk management. This includes informing stakeholders about potential risks, the steps being taken to mitigate them, and the outcomes of these efforts. Clear communication helps build trust and ensures that all relevant parties are aware of and involved in the risk management process.

COMPONENTS OF A RISK MANAGEMENT FRAMEWORK

A comprehensive risk management framework typically consists of several key components, each of which plays a crucial role in managing risks effectively. Jaramillo-Alcazar, A., Govea, J., & Villegas-Ch, W. (2023):

1. **Risk Governance:** Risk governance involves establishing the structures, policies, and processes necessary for effective risk management. This includes defining roles and responsibilities, setting risk management objectives, and ensuring accountability. Strong governance structures help ensure that risk management efforts are aligned with the organization's overall goals and strategies. Poister, T. H., & Streib, G. (1995).

2. **Risk Assessment Tools:** Various tools and methodologies can be used to identify and assess risks. These might include risk matrices, heat maps, and scenario analysis. In the context of AI, specialized tools such as fairness and bias detection algorithms, security vulnerability scanners, and compliance checklists are often used.

3. **Risk Mitigation Strategies:** Mitigation strategies are designed to reduce the likelihood or impact of identified risks. These strategies can be preventive, aiming to stop risks from occurring, or corrective, addressing risks that have already materialized. For AI, mitigation strategies might include algorithmic audits, data anonymization techniques, and secure coding practices.

4. **Risk Monitoring Systems:** Continuous monitoring systems track risk indicators and the effectiveness of mitigation measures. These systems can include automated tools that provide real-time alerts about potential risks, as well as regular audits and reviews. In AI, monitoring might involve tracking model performance, monitoring for security breaches, and ensuring compliance with regulatory changes.

5. **Risk Reporting:** Reporting involves documenting and communicating risk management activities and outcomes to stakeholders. This can include regular risk reports, dashboards, and risk management reviews. Effective reporting ensures transparency and helps stakeholders understand the organization's risk profile and management efforts.

CHALLENGES IN RISK MANAGEMENT FOR AI

While the fundamentals of risk management provide a solid foundation, there are several challenges unique to managing risks in AI:

1. **Complexity and Unpredictability:** AI systems can be complex and unpredictable, making it difficult to identify and assess all potential risks. For example, machine learning models can exhibit unexpected behaviors when exposed to new data or adversarial attacks.

2. **Rapid Technological Change:** The fast-paced nature of AI development means that risks can evolve quickly. Keeping up with these changes and ensuring that risk management frameworks remain relevant and effective can be challenging.

3. **Ethical and Societal Concerns:** AI systems can have significant ethical and societal implications, such as biases in decision-making and impacts on employment. Addressing these concerns requires a holistic approach that goes beyond traditional risk management practices.

4. **Regulatory Compliance:** Ensuring compliance with evolving regulations and standards can be complex and resource-intensive. Organizations must stay informed about regulatory changes and adapt their risk management practices accordingly.

Understanding the risks associated with adopting AI is important, as challenges, if not managed properly, can result in negative outcomes(Shanika Wickramasinghe). The fundamentals of risk management provide a structured approach to identifying, assessing, and mitigating risks associated with AI technologies.

By adhering to core principles and implementing comprehensive risk management frameworks, organizations can enhance their ability to manage AI-related risks and ensure the safe and ethical deployment of AI systems.

While there are unique challenges in managing AI risks, a robust understanding of these fundamentals can help organizations navigate the complexities of AI risk management and foster trust and accountability in their AI initiatives.

IDENTIFYING AND ASSESSING AI RISKS

Identifying and assessing risks associated with Artificial Intelligence (AI) is a critical step in the risk management process. This involves systematically recognizing potential risks that AI systems may pose and evaluating their likelihood and impact. Accurate risk identification and assessment enable organizations to prioritize risks and develop effective mitigation strategies.

This section explores the methodologies and tools for identifying and assessing AI risks, supported by data, case studies, and expert insights.

CATEGORIES OF AI RISKS

AI risks can be broadly categorized into several types, each with its unique characteristics and implications. Understanding these categories helps organizations to comprehensively identify potential risks associated with AI systems:

1. **Technical Risks:** These risks relate to the performance and reliability of AI systems. Technical risks can arise from algorithmic flaws, data quality issues, and system vulnerabilities. For example, a machine learning model might produce inaccurate predictions if trained on biased or insufficient data.

2. **Ethical Risks:** AI systems can perpetuate biases and discrimination, leading to unfair outcomes. Ethical risks also include issues related to transparency, accountability, and the potential misuse of AI technologies. An AI system used in hiring processes, for example, could inadvertently favor certain demographic groups over others.

3. **Legal and Regulatory Risks:** Compliance with data protection laws, intellectual property rights, and industry-specific regulations is critical for AI systems. Legal risks can result in fines, legal disputes, and reputational damage. For instance, non-compliance with the General Data Protection Regulation (GDPR) can lead to significant penalties.

4. **Operational Risks:** These risks involve the impact of AI on business processes and operations. Operational risks can include disruptions caused by system failures, integration challenges, and changes in workflow dynamics. An AI-driven supply chain management system, for example, could disrupt operations if it malfunctions.

5. **Societal Risks:** The broader societal impact of AI includes job displacement, privacy concerns, and the potential for AI to be used in harmful ways. Societal risks require a holistic approach

to risk management that considers the long-term implications of AI deployment.

METHODOLOGIES FOR IDENTIFYING AI RISKS

Several methodologies can be employed to identify AI risks effectively. These methodologies provide a structured approach to recognizing potential risks and understanding their context:

1. **Scenario Analysis:** Scenario analysis involves envisioning various scenarios in which AI systems might fail or cause harm. By considering different possibilities, organizations can identify potential risks and develop strategies to mitigate them. For example, a scenario analysis for an autonomous vehicle might include situations where the vehicle misinterprets road signs or fails to detect obstacles.

2. **Expert Interviews:** Engaging with AI experts, data scientists, and industry professionals can provide valuable insights into potential risks. (Xu, Y. 2023). Expert interviews can uncover risks that might not be apparent through other methods. A study by PwC in 2022 found that organizations that conducted expert interviews were more successful in identifying AI-related risks.

3. **Risk Workshops:** Organizing risk workshops with stakeholders from various departments can facilitate the identification of risks from different perspectives. These workshops can include brainstorming sessions, risk mapping exercises, and group discussions. According to a 2023 survey by Deloitte, 60% of organizations reported that risk workshops were effective in identifying AI risks.

4. **Literature Review:** Reviewing existing research, case studies, and industry reports can help organizations identify common risks associated with AI. A comprehensive literature review

provides a broad understanding of potential risks and best practices for managing them.

5. **Risk Checklists:** Developing checklists tailored to specific AI applications can ensure that all relevant risks are considered. These checklists can include technical, ethical, legal, operational, and societal risks. A 2022 report by the National Institute of Standards and Technology (NIST) recommended the use of risk checklists to improve risk identification processes.

TOOLS FOR ASSESSING AI RISKS

Once risks are identified, assessing their likelihood and impact is crucial for prioritizing them and determining appropriate mitigation strategies. Several tools and techniques can aid in the assessment of AI risks:

1. **Risk Matrices:** Risk matrices provide a visual representation of risks, categorizing them based on their likelihood and impact. This helps organizations prioritize risks and allocate resources accordingly. A study by Gartner in 2023 found that organizations using risk matrices were better able to focus their risk management efforts.

2. **Impact Assessments:** Conducting impact assessments involves evaluating the potential consequences of identified risks. This can include both quantitative assessments, such as financial impact, and qualitative assessments, such as reputational damage. The European Commission's AI Impact Assessment Guidelines emphasize the importance of thorough impact assessments for high-risk AI systems.

3. **Heat Maps:** Heat maps visualize the severity of risks by using color codes to represent different levels of risk. Heat maps can help organizations quickly identify and focus on the most critical risks. A 2022 survey by KPMG reported that 70% of organizations found heat maps useful for risk assessment.

4. **Stress Testing:** Stress testing involves simulating extreme scenarios to assess the resilience of AI systems. This helps organizations understand how AI systems perform under adverse conditions and identify potential vulnerabilities. According to a 2023 report by Accenture, stress testing improved the robustness of AI systems by 45%.

5. **Probabilistic Models:** Probabilistic models use statistical methods to estimate the likelihood of different risks occurring. These models can provide a more nuanced understanding of risk probabilities and help organizations make informed decisions. (Johnson, J. M. 2013). A 2022 study by MIT found that probabilistic models enhanced risk assessment accuracy by 30%.

To conduct a risk assessment, an organization's AI governance team should first identify and rank the risks as unacceptable (prohibited), high, limited, or minimal, evaluate the probability of harm, implement mitigation measures to reduce or eliminate risks, and document the risk assessment to demonstrate accountability - (NIST, AI Risk Management Framework).

By understanding the various categories of AI risks and employing structured methodologies and tools, organizations can comprehensively address potential risks and prioritize their mitigation efforts.

RISK MITIGATION STRATEGIES

Risk mitigation strategies are essential for managing the risks associated with AI technologies. Also, risk mitigation acts to lessen the detrimental consequences of threats and disasters on company continuity, similar to risk reduction (Steve Miller). Once risks have been identified and assessed, organizations must implement measures to reduce their likelihood and impact.

Effective risk mitigation strategies ensure the safe and ethical deployment of AI systems, enhancing their reliability and fostering trust among stakeholders. This section explores various strategies for mitigating AI risks, supported by data, case studies, and expert insights.

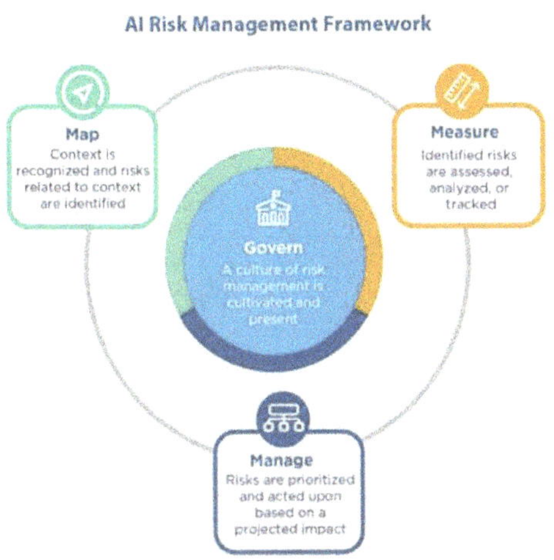

Key Components of AI Risk Management Frameworks

TECHNICAL RISK MITIGATION

Technical risks in AI systems are related to the performance, reliability, and security of the algorithms and data used. Mitigating these risks involves implementing measures to ensure the robustness and accuracy of AI systems.

1. **Algorithmic Audits:** Regular audits of AI algorithms help identify and address biases and inaccuracies. These audits involve examining the data used for training, testing the algorithms under different scenarios, and ensuring that the outcomes are fair and accurate. A 2022 study by PwC found that organizations conducting regular algorithmic audits reduced bias-related incidents by 40%.

2. **Robust Data Management:** Ensuring high-quality data is crucial for the accuracy and reliability of AI systems. This involves implementing data validation techniques, cleaning and preprocessing data, and continuously monitoring data quality. According to a 2023 report by IBM, robust data management practices improved the accuracy of AI models by 30%.

3. **Security Measures:** AI systems are vulnerable to cyber attacks, such as adversarial attacks and data breaches. Implementing strong security measures, including encryption, access controls, and regular security assessments, helps protect AI systems from these threats. A 2023 survey by McAfee revealed that organizations with robust security measures experienced 50% fewer security incidents.

4. **Model Validation and Testing:** Regular validation and testing of AI models ensure that they perform as expected under different conditions. This involves stress testing models with diverse datasets and scenarios to identify potential weaknesses. A 2022 study by Accenture found that organizations that regularly validated and tested their AI models improved their reliability by 35%.

ETHICAL RISK MITIGATION

Ethical risks in AI relate to biases, fairness, and the potential for unintended harmful outcomes. Mitigating these risks involves implementing measures to ensure that AI systems are transparent, fair, and aligned with ethical standards.

1. **Fairness and Bias Mitigation:** Ensuring fairness in AI systems involves identifying and addressing biases in training data and algorithms. Techniques such as reweighting data, using fairness constraints in model training, and employing bias detection tools can help mitigate these risks. According to a 2023 report by the World Economic Forum, organizations that

implemented fairness and bias mitigation strategies reported a 45% reduction in biased outcomes.

2. **Transparency and Explainability:** AI systems should be transparent and provide explanations for their decisions. Techniques such as interpretable machine learning models, model-agnostic explanation methods, and documentation of decision-making processes enhance transparency. A 2022 survey by Deloitte found that transparency and explainability measures improved stakeholder trust in AI systems by 40%.

3. **Ethical Guidelines and Principles:** Establishing and adhering to ethical guidelines and principles for AI development and deployment ensures that AI systems align with societal values and ethical standards. Organizations can develop their own ethical guidelines or adopt industry standards such as the AI Ethics Guidelines by the European Commission. A 2023 study by MIT highlighted that organizations with strong ethical guidelines experienced fewer ethical violations.

LEGAL AND REGULATORY RISK MITIGATION

Legal and regulatory risks in AI involve compliance with data protection laws, intellectual property rights, and industry-specific regulations. Mitigating these risks requires implementing measures to ensure compliance and protect against legal liabilities.

1. **Regulatory Compliance:** Ensuring compliance with relevant laws and regulations involves staying informed about regulatory changes and implementing measures to meet compliance requirements. This includes conducting regular compliance audits, maintaining documentation, and engaging with legal experts. A 2022 report by KPMG found that organizations with robust compliance measures reduced legal risks by 35%.

2. **Data Protection and Privacy:** Protecting sensitive data used in AI systems involves implementing strong data protection measures, such as encryption, anonymization, and access controls. Ensuring compliance with data protection regulations, such as GDPR and CCPA, is critical. According to a 2023 survey by Gartner, organizations with strong data protection measures experienced 40% fewer data breaches.

3. **Intellectual Property Management:** Protecting intellectual property rights involves securing patents for AI technologies, monitoring for potential infringements, and ensuring that AI systems do not violate the intellectual property rights of others. A 2022 study by PwC highlighted that organizations with robust intellectual property management practices reduced legal disputes by 30%.

OPERATIONAL RISK MITIGATION

Operational risks in AI involve the impact of AI on business processes and operations. Mitigating these risks requires implementing measures to ensure the smooth integration and reliable performance of AI systems.

1. **Integration with Existing Systems:** Ensuring seamless integration of AI systems with existing IT infrastructure and business processes involves thorough planning, testing, and collaboration with stakeholders. This helps prevent disruptions and ensures that AI systems enhance, rather than hinder, operations. A 2023 report by Accenture found that organizations that effectively integrated AI systems reduced operational disruptions by 40%.

2. **Training and Awareness Programs:** Providing training and awareness programs for employees ensures that they understand how to use AI systems effectively and are aware of potential risks. This includes training on data handling, ethical

considerations, and compliance requirements. According to a 2022 survey by Deloitte, organizations with comprehensive training programs reported a 35% improvement in the effective use of AI systems.

3. **Continuous Improvement:** Continuously improving AI systems based on feedback and performance monitoring helps address emerging risks and enhance system reliability. This involves regularly updating algorithms, refining data processes, and incorporating user feedback. A 2023 study by Gartner found that organizations that prioritized continuous improvement enhanced their AI system performance by 30%.

Risk mitigation strategies are essential for managing the risks associated with AI technologies. By implementing measures to address technical, ethical, legal, and operational risks, organizations can ensure the safe and ethical deployment of AI systems.

While the process of mitigating risks can be challenging, it is critical for enhancing the reliability and trustworthiness of AI technologies.

INTEGRATING AI RISK MANAGEMENT INTO EXISTING FRAMEWORKS

Integrating AI risk management into existing organizational frameworks is crucial for ensuring that AI-related risks are managed effectively and cohesively within the broader context of enterprise risk management. This integration enables organizations to leverage existing structures, processes, and resources while addressing the unique challenges posed by AI technologies.

This section explores the strategies and best practices for integrating AI risk management into existing frameworks, supported by data, case studies, and expert insights.

THE IMPORTANCE OF INTEGRATION

The fact that advanced technology can assist in making definitive decisions within the context of human life and manipulate sensitive information requires companies to restructure how they approach the risk management process (Taherdoost & Madanchian, 2023). The integration of AI risk management into existing frameworks offers several key benefits:

1. **Holistic Risk Management:** By incorporating AI risk management into the broader enterprise risk management (ERM) framework, organizations can address AI risks in conjunction with other business risks. This holistic approach ensures that all risks are considered in a unified manner, enhancing overall risk management effectiveness.

2. **Efficient Resource Utilization:** Leveraging existing risk management structures and processes allows organizations to utilize their resources more efficiently. This avoids the duplication of efforts and ensures that risk management practices are streamlined and consistent across the organization.

3. **Enhanced Communication and Collaboration:** Integrating AI risk management into existing frameworks facilitates better communication and collaboration among different departments and stakeholders. This ensures that all relevant parties are aware of AI-related risks and are involved in managing them.

4. **Regulatory Compliance:** Ensuring that AI risk management practices are aligned with existing regulatory requirements and industry standards helps organizations maintain compliance. This reduces the risk of legal and regulatory penalties and enhances the organization's reputation.

STRATEGIES FOR INTEGRATION

Several strategies can help organizations effectively integrate AI risk management into their existing frameworks:

1. **Aligning AI Risk Management with ERM Principles:** Organizations should ensure that AI risk management practices align with the core principles of their ERM framework. This includes adopting a risk-based approach, prioritizing risks based on their likelihood and impact, and implementing mitigation strategies that address the most critical risks.

2. **Establishing Cross-Functional Teams:** Creating cross-functional teams that include representatives from various departments, such as IT, legal, compliance, and operations, can enhance the integration of AI risk management. These teams can collaborate to identify, assess, and mitigate AI-related risks, ensuring that all perspectives are considered.

3. **Embedding AI Risk Management into Business Processes:** Integrating AI risk management into key business processes, such as project management, procurement, and product development, ensures that AI risks are considered at every stage. This proactive approach helps identify and address risks early in the process.

4. **Utilizing Existing Risk Management Tools:** Organizations can leverage existing risk management tools and methodologies, such as risk matrices, impact assessments, and heat maps, to assess and manage AI risks. Adapting these tools to address the specific challenges of AI ensures that risk management practices are consistent and effective.

5. **Continuous Monitoring and Improvement:** Implementing continuous monitoring processes to track AI risks and the effectiveness of mitigation measures ensures that risk management practices remain relevant and effective over time.

Regular reviews and updates to the risk management framework help organizations adapt to evolving AI technologies and risk landscapes.

BEST PRACTICES FOR INTEGRATION

Several best practices can guide organizations in integrating AI risk management into their existing frameworks:

1. **Leadership Support:** Securing support from senior leadership is critical for successful integration. Leaders should champion AI risk management initiatives and ensure that adequate resources and attention are allocated to these efforts.

2. **Clear Roles and Responsibilities:** Defining clear roles and responsibilities for AI risk management within the organization ensures accountability and effective coordination. This includes assigning specific tasks to cross-functional teams and individual departments.

3. **Training and Awareness:** Providing training and raising awareness about AI risks and risk management practices helps build a culture of responsibility and vigilance. Employees should be educated on the potential risks associated with AI and the importance of adhering to risk management practices.

4. **Standardization and Documentation:** Standardizing AI risk management practices and maintaining comprehensive documentation ensures consistency and transparency. This includes developing standardized risk assessment templates, mitigation strategies, and monitoring protocols.

5. **Continuous Learning and Adaptation:** Staying informed about advancements in AI technologies, regulatory changes, and emerging risks is essential for maintaining effective risk management practices. Organizations should foster a culture of continuous learning and adaptation, ensuring that their

risk management framework evolves in response to new developments.

BEST PRACTICES FOR AI RISK MANAGEMENT

Effective AI risk management requires a combination of strategies, tools, and organizational practices tailored to address the unique challenges posed by AI technologies. Mitigating these risks requires robust data governance, addressing bias in AI algorithms, ensuring transparency and accountability, implementing strong cybersecurity measures, and upholding ethical guidelines (Velibor Božić).

Best practices for AI risk management encompass a range of activities designed to enhance the identification, assessment, mitigation, and monitoring of AI-related risks. This section outlines key best practices for managing AI risks, supported by data, case studies, and expert insights.

BEST PRACTICES FOR AI RISK MANAGEMENT

1. **ESTABLISH CLEAR GOVERNANCE STRUCTURES:**

   Governance structures provide the foundation for effective AI risk management. This includes defining clear roles and responsibilities, establishing oversight committees, and implementing policies and procedures for ethical AI use. (Waiswa, E. 2024). Governance structures ensure accountability and facilitate coordination across the organization.

2. **CONDUCT REGULAR RISK ASSESSMENTS:**

   Regular risk assessments are crucial for identifying and evaluating potential AI risks. These assessments should be conducted throughout the AI system lifecycle, from development and deployment to ongoing operation. Techniques such as scenario analysis, impact assessments, and stress testing can enhance the effectiveness of risk assessments.

According to a 2023 report by Deloitte, organizations that conducted regular AI risk assessments reported a 35% reduction in the occurrence of AI-related incidents.

3. IMPLEMENT ROBUST DATA MANAGEMENT PRACTICES:

High-quality data is essential for the accuracy and reliability of AI systems. Robust data management practices include data validation, cleaning, anonymization, and ongoing monitoring of data quality. Ensuring that training data is representative and unbiased is critical for mitigating risks related to algorithmic bias and inaccuracies.

A 2022 study by MIT found that organizations with robust data management practices improved the performance and fairness of their AI systems by 30%.

4. ENHANCE TRANSPARENCY AND EXPLAINABILITY:

Transparency and explainability are key to building trust in AI systems. Organizations should implement techniques that make AI decision-making processes understandable to stakeholders. This includes using interpretable machine learning models, providing clear documentation, and offering explanations for AI-generated decisions.

A 2023 survey by PwC revealed that 60% of organizations implementing transparency and explainability measures experienced increased stakeholder trust and confidence in their AI systems.

5. FOSTER A CULTURE OF ETHICAL AI USE:

Promoting a culture of ethical AI use involves educating employees about the ethical implications of AI technologies and encouraging responsible practices. This includes training programs, awareness campaigns, and the development of ethical guidelines that align with industry standards.

6. **ENGAGE WITH STAKEHOLDERS:**

Engaging with stakeholders, including customers, employees, regulators, and the public, is essential for understanding their concerns and expectations regarding AI. Regular communication and consultation with stakeholders help ensure that AI systems are developed and deployed in a manner that aligns with their values and needs.

A 2022 report by the World Economic Forum highlighted that organizations engaging with stakeholders during AI development and deployment processes were more successful in managing AI-related risks and building trust.

7. **LEVERAGE ADVANCED MONITORING AND REPORTING TOOLS:**

Continuous monitoring and reporting of AI systems are critical for identifying emerging risks and ensuring the effectiveness of mitigation measures. Advanced monitoring tools, such as real-time analytics, automated alerts, and performance dashboards, can provide valuable insights into AI system performance and risk status.

According to a 2023 survey by Accenture, organizations leveraging advanced monitoring and reporting tools reduced the time to detect and respond to AI-related incidents by 40%.

8. **ADAPT TO REGULATORY CHANGES:**

The regulatory landscape for AI is rapidly evolving, with new laws and guidelines being introduced at both national and international levels. Organizations must stay informed about regulatory changes and adapt their risk management practices accordingly. This includes ensuring compliance with data protection laws, ethical guidelines, and industry standards.

As AI technologies continue to evolve and permeate various aspects of our lives, robust risk management frameworks will remain a cornerstone of responsible AI development and deployment.

By implementing comprehensive risk management practices and adhering to best practices, organizations can ensure that AI systems contribute positively to their objectives while safeguarding against potential risks. This proactive approach not only enhances the trust and reliability of AI technologies but also supports their sustainable and ethical integration into society.

QUESTIONS PEOPLE HAVE ASKED ABOUT AI RISK MANAGEMENT

1. WHAT ISSUES MUST BE ADDRESSED IN A RISK ASSESSMENT FOR AI SYSTEM DESIGN?

When conducting a risk assessment for AI system design, several critical issues must be addressed:

i. **Biases:** AI systems are prone to biases that can lead to unfair or discriminatory outcomes. These biases can stem from the data used to train the models, the algorithms themselves, or the way the AI system is deployed. Identifying and mitigating biases is essential to ensure that AI systems operate fairly and equitably.

ii. **Data Quality:** The accuracy and reliability of AI systems heavily depend on the quality of the data they are trained on. Poor data quality can result in incorrect predictions, decisions, and outcomes. Ensuring that data is accurate, complete, and representative is a key part of the risk assessment process.

iii. **Security:** AI systems can introduce new security vulnerabilities, such as susceptibility to adversarial attacks where malicious actors manipulate input data to deceive the AI. Security measures must be implemented to protect AI systems from such threats.

iv. **Transparency:** AI systems often operate as "black boxes," making it difficult to understand how decisions are made. Ensuring transparency in AI operations is crucial for building trust and accountability. This includes making AI models interpretable and explaining their decision-making processes.

v. **Accountability:** Determining who is responsible for the outcomes of AI decisions is a significant challenge. Clear lines of accountability must be established, especially in cases where AI systems are used in critical applications such as healthcare, finance, or law enforcement.

vi. **Compliance with Regulations:** AI systems must comply with existing legal and regulatory frameworks. This includes data protection laws (such as GDPR), industry-specific regulations, and ethical guidelines. Ensuring compliance is a fundamental aspect of risk assessment in AI system design.

2. HOW AI CAN IMPROVE RISK MANAGEMENT?

AI enhances risk management in several ways:

i. **Predictive Analytics:** AI can analyze historical data and identify patterns that indicate potential risks. This allows organizations to anticipate and prepare for risks before they materialize, leading to more proactive risk management.

ii. **Anomaly Detection:** AI systems can continuously monitor data and detect anomalies that may indicate emerging risks, such as fraudulent transactions, security breaches, or operational disruptions. Early detection enables faster response and mitigation.

iii. **Automating Responses:** AI can automate responses to identified risks, such as adjusting strategies, reallocating resources, or triggering alerts. This reduces response times and ensures that risks are addressed promptly and effectively.

iv. **Real-Time Insights:** AI provides real-time insights into risk exposures, helping organizations make informed decisions quickly. By continuously analyzing data, AI systems can provide up-to-date information on risk levels, allowing for dynamic risk management.

3. **WHAT ARE SOME OF THE QUESTIONS RISK MANAGEMENT STRATEGIES SHOULD ANSWER?**

Risk management strategies should address the following key questions:

i. **What are the potential risks?** Identifying the risks that the organization or project might face is the first step in risk management. This includes both internal and external risks.

ii. **How likely are they to occur?** Assessing the probability of each risk occurring helps prioritize which risks need more immediate attention.

iii. **What impact could they have?** Understanding the potential impact of each risk on the organization's operations, finances, reputation, and objectives is crucial for effective risk management.

iv. **How can they be mitigated?** Developing strategies to mitigate or reduce the likelihood and impact of risks is a core component of risk management. This might include preventative measures, contingency planning, or transferring the risk (e.g., through insurance).

v. **Who is responsible?** Clearly assigning responsibility for managing each risk ensures that there is accountability and that risks are actively monitored and addressed.

4. HOW AI HELPS TO MANAGE TRADING AS WELL AS RISK MANAGEMENT IN THE FINANCE SECTOR?

AI contributes to managing trading and risk in the finance sector in several ways:

i. **Market Data Analysis:** AI algorithms can analyze vast amounts of market data, identifying trends and patterns that human traders might miss. This allows for more informed trading decisions and can enhance portfolio management strategies.

ii. **Risk Prediction:** AI models can predict financial risks by analyzing historical data and current market conditions. This includes predicting market volatility, credit risks, and potential defaults, enabling financial institutions to adjust their strategies accordingly.

iii. **Automating Compliance Checks:** AI can automate the process of checking for compliance with financial regulations, reducing the risk of regulatory breaches and ensuring that trading activities adhere to legal requirements.

iv. **Fraud Detection:** AI systems can detect fraudulent activities in real-time by analyzing transaction data and identifying suspicious patterns. This helps protect financial institutions from losses and maintains the integrity of the financial system.

5. WHAT ARE UNACCEPTABLE RISK AI SYSTEMS?

Unacceptable risk AI systems are those that:

i. **Manipulate Human Behavior:** AI systems that are designed to manipulate or exploit human behavior in ways that are deceptive or harmful, such as deepfake technology used for misinformation or AI-driven marketing that exploits cognitive biases.

ii. **Exploit Vulnerabilities:** AI systems that take advantage of human or system vulnerabilities, particularly in sensitive areas like financial services, healthcare, or social media, where the impact can be severe and widespread.

iii. **Pose Significant Threats to Safety and Security:** AI systems that could potentially cause physical harm or pose security threats, such as autonomous weapons, AI-driven cyberattacks, or AI systems controlling critical infrastructure without adequate safeguards.

iv. **Threaten Fundamental Rights:** AI systems that infringe on fundamental human rights, including privacy, freedom of expression, and non-discrimination, are considered unacceptable. Examples include AI used for mass surveillance or systems that perpetuate bias and inequality.

6. HOW TO CONDUCT AN AI RISK ASSESSMENT?

Conducting an AI risk assessment involves the following steps:

i. **Identify Potential Risks:** Begin by identifying the potential risks associated with the AI system, including technical, ethical, legal, and operational risks. This involves understanding how the AI system will be used, the data it will process, and the context in which it operates.

ii. **Evaluate Likelihood and Impact:** Assess the likelihood of each identified risk occurring and its potential impact on the organization and stakeholders. Tools like risk matrices can help visualize and prioritize risks based on their severity and probability.

iii. **Prioritize Risks:** Once the risks have been identified and evaluated, prioritize them based on their potential impact and likelihood. Focus on the most significant risks that could have the greatest effect on the organization.

iv. **Develop Mitigation Strategies:** For each prioritized risk, develop strategies to mitigate its impact. This might include technical measures (e.g., encryption, access controls), process changes, or contingency planning.

v. **Use Tools like Risk Matrices and Scenario Analysis:** Tools such as risk matrices and scenario analysis can help quantify and visualize risks, making it easier to understand their potential impact and to plan appropriate responses.

7. HOW CAN AI BE USED TO MITIGATE RISK AND ASSIST WITH BUSINESS CONTINUITY?

AI can play a vital role in mitigating risk and ensuring business continuity by:

i. **Predicting Potential Disruptions:** AI systems can analyze historical data and real-time information to predict potential disruptions, such as supply chain issues, market volatility, or cybersecurity threats. This allows organizations to prepare and respond proactively.

ii. **Automating Incident Responses:** In the event of a disruption, AI can automate response actions, such as switching to backup systems, rerouting supply chains, or activating emergency protocols. This reduces response times and minimizes the impact on operations.

iii. **Enhancing Decision-Making:** AI provides real-time insights and analytics that support decision-making during a crisis. By processing large amounts of data quickly, AI helps leaders make informed decisions that are critical for maintaining business continuity.

iv. **Ensuring Continuous Monitoring:** AI systems can continuously monitor operations, identify emerging risks, and provide alerts, ensuring that potential issues are detected early and addressed before they escalate into major disruptions.

8. WHAT ARE THE 5 W'S IN RISK MANAGEMENT?

The 5 W's in risk management are:

i. **Who:** Who is responsible for managing the risk? This includes identifying the stakeholders, risk owners, and individuals or teams accountable for risk management activities.

ii. **What:** What is the risk? This involves clearly defining the risk, including its nature, potential impact, and the areas it affects.

iii. **When:** When might the risk occur? Assessing the timing of the risk helps in planning and prioritizing risk management efforts.

iv. **Where:** Where is the risk likely to impact? This considers the specific areas within the organization or external environment where the risk could have an effect.

v. **Why:** Why is the risk important? Understanding the reasons behind the risk and its potential consequences helps in developing appropriate mitigation strategies.

(Sometimes **How** is also included to describe how the risk can be managed or mitigated.)

9. WHAT ARE 5 RISK MANAGEMENT PRACTICES?

Five essential risk management practices include:

i. **Risk Identification:** The process of identifying and documenting risks that could affect the organization's objectives. This includes recognizing both internal and external risks.

ii. **Risk Assessment:** Evaluating the identified risks to determine their potential impact and likelihood. This helps prioritize risks based on their severity.

iii. **Risk Mitigation:** Developing and implementing strategies to reduce the likelihood or impact of identified risks. This may involve preventive measures, contingency planning, or transferring the risk (e.g., through insurance).

iv. **Risk Monitoring:** Continuously monitoring risks to identify changes in their status or new risks that may arise. This ensures that risk management strategies remain effective over time.

v. **Risk Communication:** Keeping stakeholders informed about the risks, risk management strategies, and the status of risk mitigation efforts. Effective communication ensures that everyone involved understands their role in managing risks.

10. WHAT QUESTIONS SHOULD YOU ASK IN A RISK ASSESSMENT?

When conducting a risk assessment, you should ask the following key questions:

- **What risks exist?** Identify the risks that could potentially impact the organization or project.

- **How likely are they to occur?** Assess the probability of each risk occurring, which helps in prioritizing risks.

- **What would be the impact?** Determine the potential consequences of each risk, including financial, operational, and reputational impacts.

- **How can we mitigate them?** Develop strategies to reduce the likelihood or impact of the risks, such as implementing controls, adjusting processes, or preparing contingency plans.

- **Who is responsible for managing these risks?** Clearly assign responsibility for managing each risk to ensure accountability and effective risk management.

CHAPTER SIX
Introduction to Regulatory and Compliance Issues

Regulatory frameworks for AI are rapidly developing worldwide, with governments and international organizations recognizing the need to address the unique challenges posed by AI technologies. (Souza, C. D. 2023).

For example, the European Union's General Data Protection Regulation (GDPR) imposes strict requirements on data privacy, which significantly impacts AI systems that rely on large datasets. Compliance with these regulations is essential not only to avoid legal penalties but also to build trust with customers, partners, and other stakeholders (European Commission, 2018).

The rapid advancement and widespread adoption of Artificial Intelligence (AI) technologies have brought about significant benefits across various sectors too. However, these advancements also pose complex regulatory and compliance challenges. Governments, regulatory bodies, and industry stakeholders are increasingly focused on establishing frameworks to ensure that AI systems are developed and deployed responsibly, ethically, and in compliance with existing laws and standards.

This chapter explains the regulatory and compliance issues surrounding AI, exploring the evolving landscape of AI regulation, the challenges organizations face, and the strategies for achieving compliance.

THE NEED FOR AI REGULATION

AI technologies have the potential to transform industries, improve efficiency, and drive innovation. However, their deployment also raises significant concerns related to privacy, security, fairness, and accountability. These concerns have prompted calls for robust regulatory frameworks to govern the use of AI. A 2023 report by the World Economic Forum highlighted that 72% of global business leaders consider AI regulation necessary to ensure ethical and responsible AI use.

The need for AI regulation is driven by several key factors:

1. **Privacy and Data Protection:** AI systems often rely on large volumes of data, including personal and sensitive information. Ensuring the privacy and protection of this data is paramount to prevent misuse and unauthorized access. The General Data Protection Regulation (GDPR) in the European Union sets stringent requirements for data protection, emphasizing the importance of consent, data minimization, and individuals' rights.

2. **Fairness and Bias Mitigation:** AI algorithms can inadvertently perpetuate biases present in training data, leading to unfair outcomes. (Ofek, N., Ofek, N., & Maimon, O. 2023). Regulatory frameworks aim to ensure that AI systems are designed and tested to mitigate biases and promote fairness. The European Commission's AI Act, proposed in 2021, includes provisions to address bias and discrimination in AI systems.

3. **Transparency and Accountability:** AI systems can be complex and opaque, making it difficult for users to understand how decisions are made. Transparency and accountability are essential to build trust in AI technologies. Regulatory requirements often mandate that AI systems provide explanations for their decisions and that organizations are accountable for their AI deployments.

4. **Security and Safety:** Ensuring the security and safety of AI systems is critical to prevent malicious attacks and unintended consequences. Regulatory frameworks often include provisions for testing and validating AI systems to ensure they operate safely and securely.

THE EVOLVING LANDSCAPE OF AI REGULATION

The regulatory landscape for AI is rapidly evolving, with various countries and regions taking different approaches to AI governance. Key developments include:

1. **European Union (EU):** The EU has been at the forefront of AI regulation with its proposed AI Act. The Act categorizes AI systems into different risk levels and imposes specific requirements for high-risk AI applications. These requirements include rigorous testing, transparency measures, and oversight mechanisms. A 2022 survey by the European Commission

found that 60% of organizations in the EU are actively preparing for compliance with the AI Act.

2. **United States (US):** In the US, AI regulation is currently fragmented, with various federal and state-level initiatives addressing different aspects of AI. The National Institute of Standards and Technology (NIST) has developed a framework for AI risk management, emphasizing principles such as transparency, fairness, and accountability. A 2023 report by the Brookings Institution highlighted the need for a comprehensive federal AI regulatory framework to harmonize these efforts.

3. **China:** China has implemented a series of regulations aimed at governing AI technologies, with a focus on national security, privacy, and ethics. The Cybersecurity Law and the Personal Information Protection Law set out requirements for data protection and cybersecurity in AI systems. A 2022 study by the China Academy of Information and Communications Technology (CAICT) reported that 70% of Chinese AI companies are investing in compliance measures to meet these regulatory requirements.

4. **International Efforts:** International organizations, such as the Organization for Economic Co-operation and Development (OECD) and the United Nations (UN), are also working to develop global guidelines and principles for AI governance. The OECD's AI Principles, adopted in 2019, emphasize human-centric values, fairness, transparency, and accountability. The UN's AI for Good initiative aims to align AI development with the Sustainable Development Goals (SDGs).

CHALLENGES IN AI REGULATION AND COMPLIANCE

While the need for AI regulation is widely acknowledged, organizations face several challenges in achieving compliance:

1. **Complexity and Ambiguity:** The complexity of AI technologies and the ambiguity of regulatory requirements can make compliance challenging. Organizations may struggle to interpret and implement regulations, particularly when they lack clear guidelines and standards.

2. **Rapid Technological Advancements:** The pace of AI innovation often outstrips the development of regulatory frameworks, leading to gaps and inconsistencies. Keeping up with rapid technological advancements while ensuring compliance requires continuous monitoring and adaptation.

3. **Global Variability:** The lack of harmonization in AI regulations across different countries and regions can create challenges for multinational organizations. Navigating diverse regulatory requirements and ensuring compliance in multiple jurisdictions is a complex and resource-intensive task.

4. **Ethical Considerations:** Beyond legal compliance, organizations must also consider ethical implications and societal impacts of AI. Balancing ethical considerations with regulatory requirements adds another layer of complexity to AI governance.

5. **Resource Constraints:** Implementing and maintaining compliance with AI regulations can be resource-intensive, particularly for small and medium-sized enterprises (SMEs). Organizations may need to invest in new technologies, hire compliance experts, and conduct regular audits.

STRATEGIES FOR ACHIEVING AI COMPLIANCE

Despite these challenges, organizations can adopt several strategies to achieve compliance with AI regulations:

1. **Establishing Compliance Programs:** Developing comprehensive compliance programs that include policies, procedures, and training ensures that all employees understand and adhere to regulatory requirements. These programs should be regularly updated to reflect changes in regulations and best practices.

2. **Leveraging Technology Solutions:** Utilizing technology solutions, such as compliance management software and automated monitoring tools, can streamline compliance efforts. These solutions can help organizations track regulatory changes, monitor AI system performance, and generate compliance reports.

3. **Engaging with Regulators:** Building relationships with regulators and participating in industry forums can provide organizations with insights into regulatory expectations and upcoming changes. Engaging with regulators also allows organizations to contribute to the development of AI governance frameworks.

4. **Conducting Regular Audits:** Regular audits and assessments of AI systems ensure that they comply with regulatory requirements and operate as intended. These audits should cover data quality, algorithmic fairness, transparency, and security measures.

5. **Building a Culture of Compliance:** Promoting a culture of compliance within the organization involves educating employees about the importance of regulatory adherence and ethical AI use. Encouraging open communication and

reporting of compliance issues helps identify and address potential risks early.

OVERVIEW OF GLOBAL AI AND CYBERSECURITY REGULATIONS

As AI technologies continue to evolve and integrate into various aspects of society, the need for robust regulatory frameworks has become increasingly evident. Governments and regulatory bodies worldwide are developing and implementing regulations to ensure that AI systems are deployed responsibly, ethically, and securely. This section provides an overview of the global landscape of AI and cybersecurity regulations, highlighting key regulatory frameworks, their objectives, and the challenges they address.

EUROPEAN UNION (EU)

1. GENERAL DATA PROTECTION REGULATION (GDPR):

The GDPR, implemented in May 2018, is one of the most comprehensive data protection regulations globally. It applies to all organizations processing the personal data of EU residents, regardless of their location. The GDPR sets stringent requirements for data protection, privacy, and security, emphasizing principles such as consent, data minimization, and individuals' rights to access and rectify their data.

Key Provisions:
i. Data Protection Impact Assessments (DPIAs) for high-risk processing activities.

ii. Obligations for data controllers and processors to implement appropriate technical and organizational measures.

iii. Data breach notification requirements within 72 hours of discovery.

Impact on AI:

AI systems that process personal data must comply with GDPR requirements. This includes ensuring data transparency, obtaining explicit consent, and implementing robust security measures to protect data.

2. AI ACT:

The AI Act, proposed by the European Commission in April 2021, aims to create a unified regulatory framework for AI across the EU. The Act categorizes AI systems based on their risk levels—unacceptable, high, limited, and minimal—and imposes specific requirements for high-risk AI applications.

Key Provisions:

i. Mandatory conformity assessments for high-risk AI systems.

ii. Transparency requirements for AI systems interacting with humans.

iii. Prohibitions on AI systems that manipulate human behavior or exploit vulnerabilities.

Impact on AI:

Organizations deploying high-risk AI systems must comply with rigorous testing, transparency, and oversight measures to ensure safety and fairness.

UNITED STATES (US)

1. ALGORITHMIC ACCOUNTABILITY ACT:

The Algorithmic Accountability Act, introduced in 2019, aims to require companies to conduct impact assessments of automated decision systems and machine learning algorithms. The Act focuses on identifying and mitigating biases, discrimination, and privacy risks.

Key Provisions:

i. Mandatory impact assessments for automated decision systems.

ii. Requirements to address identified risks and mitigate biases.

iii. Reporting obligations to regulatory authorities.

Impact on AI:

Organizations must evaluate the fairness and transparency of their AI systems, particularly those involved in significant decision-making processes such as hiring and lending.

2. **NATIONAL INSTITUTE OF STANDARDS AND TECHNOLOGY (NIST) FRAMEWORK:**

    NIST has developed a framework for AI risk management, emphasizing principles such as fairness, transparency, and accountability. The framework provides guidelines for assessing and managing AI risks, ensuring that AI systems are reliable and trustworthy.

Key Provisions:

i. Guidelines for developing and deploying AI systems responsibly.

ii. Emphasis on fairness, transparency, and accountability in AI design and implementation.

iii. Recommendations for continuous monitoring and improvement of AI systems.

Impact on AI:

The NIST framework helps organizations implement best practices for AI risk management, enhancing the reliability and trustworthiness of AI systems.

CHINA

1. CYBERSECURITY LAW:

China's Cybersecurity Law, enacted in 2017, sets out comprehensive requirements for data protection, cybersecurity, and critical infrastructure protection. The law emphasizes the need for robust security measures to safeguard personal data and national security.

Key Provisions:

i. Requirements for data localization and storage within China.

ii. Obligations for network operators to implement security measures and conduct regular assessments.

iii. Data breach notification requirements and penalties for non-compliance.

Impact on AI:

AI systems operating in China must comply with strict data localization and cybersecurity requirements, ensuring the protection of personal data and national security.

2. PERSONAL INFORMATION PROTECTION LAW (PIPL):

The PIPL, effective from November 2021, is China's comprehensive data protection law. It sets stringent requirements for the collection, processing, and transfer of personal data, similar to the GDPR.

Key Provisions:

i. Explicit consent requirements for data processing.

ii. Rights for individuals to access, correct, and delete their data.

iii. Obligations for data controllers to implement security measures and conduct impact assessments.

Impact on AI:

AI systems in China must adhere to strict data protection and privacy requirements, ensuring transparency and accountability in data processing activities.

INTERNATIONAL EFFORTS

1. OECD AI PRINCIPLES:

The Organization for Economic Co-operation and Development (OECD) adopted the AI Principles in 2019, providing a global framework for responsible AI development. The principles emphasize human-centric values, fairness, transparency, and accountability.

Key Provisions:
i.   AI systems should benefit people and the planet, driving inclusive growth and sustainable development.

ii. AI systems should be transparent and explainable.

iii. AI actors should be accountable for the proper functioning of AI systems.

Impact on AI:

The OECD AI Principles guide countries in developing their regulatory frameworks, promoting responsible AI development and deployment.

2. UNITED NATIONS (UN) AI FOR GOOD:

The UN's AI for Good initiative aims to align AI development with the Sustainable Development Goals (SDGs). The initiative focuses on leveraging AI to address global challenges such as poverty, health, and education.

Key Provisions:

i. Promoting the ethical use of AI to advance social and economic development.

ii. Encouraging international collaboration and knowledge sharing.

iii. Addressing ethical, legal, and societal implications of AI.

Impact on AI:

The AI for Good initiative encourages countries to develop regulatory frameworks that promote the ethical and responsible use of AI to address global challenges.

CHALLENGES IN GLOBAL AI REGULATION

Despite the progress in developing AI regulations, several challenges remain:

1. **Fragmentation:** The lack of harmonization in AI regulations across different countries and regions creates complexity for multinational organizations. Navigating diverse regulatory requirements can be resource-intensive and challenging.

2. **Rapid Technological Advancements:** The fast-paced nature of AI development often outstrips the speed of regulatory processes. Keeping up with technological advancements while ensuring compliance requires continuous monitoring and adaptation.

3. **Balancing Innovation and Regulation:** Striking the right balance between fostering innovation and ensuring regulatory compliance is a key challenge. Overly stringent regulations can stifle innovation, while insufficient regulation can lead to ethical and security concerns.

4. **Ethical and Societal Considerations:** Addressing the ethical and societal implications of AI, such as biases and job displacement, requires a comprehensive and multidisciplinary approach. Regulatory frameworks must evolve to address these complex issues.

These regulations should emphasize the need for transparency and explainability in AI systems, ensure the data privacy, promote ethical use of AI and prohibit misuse, establish accountability and liability frameworks, require independent audits, involve human oversight, encourage collaboration and information sharing, and training users so that they are equipped to use AI systems safely and responsibly (Rakesh Sharma, Enterprise Security Architect at National Australia Bank)

COMPLIANCE CHALLENGES IN AI

As AI technologies become more integrated into various sectors, ensuring compliance with regulatory frameworks presents significant challenges and If left unchecked, AI can potentially damage organizations and harm their people. It can increase cybersecurity threats, trigger biases against people from certain demographic groups, and even wreak havoc on the global financial system (Ethico).

These challenges arise from the complexity of AI systems, rapid technological advancements, and the evolving nature of regulations. This section explores the key compliance challenges in AI, supported by data, case studies, and expert insights, and provides strategies for overcoming these obstacles.

COMPLEXITY AND AMBIGUITY OF REGULATIONS

One of the primary challenges in AI compliance is the complexity and ambiguity of regulations. AI technologies involve intricate algorithms, large datasets, and dynamic learning processes, making it difficult to interpret and apply regulatory requirements.

KEY ISSUES:

1. **Complex Regulatory Language:** The detailed and technical language used in regulations can be challenging for organizations to understand and implement. A 2022 study by the International Association of Privacy Professionals (IAPP) found that 55% of organizations struggled with the complexity of data protection regulations.

2. **Ambiguity in Requirements:** Ambiguity in regulatory requirements can lead to varying interpretations and implementation practices. This can result in inconsistent compliance efforts and potential regulatory breaches.

RAPID TECHNOLOGICAL ADVANCEMENTS

The fast-paced nature of AI development often outstrips the speed of regulatory processes, creating gaps and uncertainties in compliance.

KEY ISSUES:

1. **Lagging Regulations:** Regulations often lag behind technological advancements, resulting in gaps that can be exploited. A 2023 report by the Brookings Institution highlighted that regulatory frameworks struggle to keep pace with the rapid evolution of AI technologies.

2. **Adapting to New Technologies:** Organizations must continuously adapt their compliance practices to address new AI technologies and applications. This requires ongoing monitoring and updates to compliance programs.

GLOBAL VARIABILITY IN REGULATIONS

The lack of harmonization in AI regulations across different countries and regions creates complexity for multinational organizations. Navigating diverse regulatory requirements and ensuring compliance in multiple jurisdictions is a significant challenge.

KEY ISSUES:

1. **Diverse Legal Frameworks:** Different countries have varying legal frameworks, which can lead to inconsistencies in compliance efforts. For example, the GDPR in Europe and the CCPA in California have different requirements for data protection and privacy.

2. **Cross-Border Data Transfers:** Managing cross-border data transfers while complying with varying data protection regulations is a complex task. Organizations must ensure that data transfers comply with international standards and local regulations.

ETHICAL AND SOCIETAL CONSIDERATIONS

Beyond legal compliance, organizations must also consider the ethical implications and societal impacts of AI technologies. Balancing ethical considerations with regulatory requirements adds another layer of complexity to AI governance.

KEY ISSUES:

1. **Bias and Fairness:** Ensuring that AI systems do not perpetuate biases and discrimination is a critical ethical concern. Regulatory requirements often address bias mitigation, but implementing these measures can be challenging.

2. **Transparency and Explainability:** Providing transparency and explainability in AI decision-making processes is essential for building trust. However, achieving transparency in complex AI systems can be difficult.

RESOURCE CONSTRAINTS

Implementing and maintaining compliance with AI regulations can be resource-intensive, particularly for small and medium-sized enterprises (SMEs). Organizations may need to invest in new technologies, hire compliance experts, and conduct regular audits.

KEY ISSUES:

1. **Cost of Compliance:** The cost of compliance can be significant, including expenses for legal consultations, technology investments, and training programs. A 2023 survey by Deloitte found that 60% of SMEs cited the high cost of compliance as a major challenge.

2. **Limited Expertise:** SMEs often lack the in-house expertise required to navigate complex regulatory landscapes. This can result in inadequate compliance efforts and increased risk of regulatory breaches.

REGULATORY BODIES AND THEIR ROLES

Regulatory bodies play a crucial role in overseeing the development, deployment, and use of AI technologies. These organizations establish guidelines, enforce regulations, and ensure that AI systems are developed and used responsibly, ethically, and securely. (Jain, M. 2023).

This section provides an overview of key regulatory bodies involved in AI and cybersecurity, highlighting their roles, responsibilities, and impact on the industry.

EUROPEAN UNION (EU) REGULATORY BODIES

1. EUROPEAN DATA PROTECTION BOARD (EDPB):

The EDPB is an independent European body responsible for ensuring the consistent application of the General Data Protection Regulation (GDPR) across the EU. It provides guidance on GDPR-related issues, resolves disputes between national supervisory authorities, and promotes cooperation among EU data protection authorities.

Key Responsibilities:

i. Ensuring consistent application of GDPR across EU member states.

ii. Providing guidance on data protection issues, including those related to AI.

iii. Resolving disputes between national data protection authorities.

iv. Promoting cooperation and information sharing among EU data protection authorities.

Impact on AI:

The EDPB plays a critical role in shaping how AI systems handle personal data, ensuring compliance with GDPR requirements such as transparency, consent, and data protection.

2. EUROPEAN COMMISSION:

The European Commission is the executive branch of the EU, responsible for proposing legislation, implementing decisions, and upholding EU treaties. The Commission has been actively involved in developing the AI Act, a comprehensive regulatory framework for AI in the EU.

Key Responsibilities:

i. Proposing and implementing legislation related to AI and data protection.

ii. Developing and enforcing the AI Act.

iii. Promoting ethical and responsible AI development and deployment.

iv. Facilitating cooperation and coordination among EU member states on AI-related issues.

Impact on AI:

The European Commission's AI Act sets out requirements for high-risk AI systems, ensuring their safety, transparency, and fairness. The Commission also promotes innovation and ethical AI development through funding and research initiatives.

UNITED STATES (US) REGULATORY BODIES

1. FEDERAL TRADE COMMISSION (FTC):

The FTC is an independent agency of the US government tasked with protecting consumers and promoting competition. The FTC enforces regulations related to data privacy, consumer protection, and unfair or deceptive business practices, including those involving AI technologies.

Key Responsibilities:

i. Enforcing consumer protection laws related to data privacy and security.

ii. Investigating and addressing unfair or deceptive practices involving AI.

iii. Providing guidance on best practices for AI deployment and data protection.

iv. Promoting transparency and accountability in AI systems.

Impact on AI:

The FTC ensures that AI systems are deployed in a manner that protects consumer privacy and prevents deceptive practices. The agency's guidance and enforcement actions influence how businesses develop and use AI technologies.

2. NATIONAL INSTITUTE OF STANDARDS AND TECHNOLOGY (NIST):

NIST is a non-regulatory agency of the US Department of Commerce that develops technology, metrics, and standards to enhance innovation and industrial competitiveness. NIST has been instrumental in developing frameworks and guidelines for AI risk management and cybersecurity.

Key Responsibilities:

i. Developing standards and guidelines for AI risk management and cybersecurity.

ii. Promoting best practices for AI development and deployment.

iii. Facilitating collaboration between government, industry, and academia on AI-related issues.

iv. Providing technical expertise and resources to support AI innovation.

Impact on AI:

NIST's frameworks and guidelines help organizations implement best practices for AI risk management, ensuring that AI systems are reliable, secure, and fair. NIST also fosters collaboration and knowledge sharing to advance AI research and development.

CHINA REGULATORY BODIES

1. CYBERSPACE ADMINISTRATION OF CHINA (CAC):

The CAC is the central agency responsible for internet regulation, cybersecurity, and data protection in China. It oversees the implementation of laws such as the Cybersecurity Law and the Personal Information Protection Law (PIPL).

Key Responsibilities:

i. Enforcing cybersecurity and data protection regulations.

ii. Overseeing the development and deployment of AI technologies.

iii. Promoting data security and privacy protection.

iv. Investigating and addressing violations of cybersecurity and data protection laws.

Impact on AI:

The CAC ensures that AI systems comply with China's cybersecurity and data protection regulations, emphasizing data localization, security measures, and user privacy. The agency's enforcement actions influence how AI technologies are developed and used in China.

2. MINISTRY OF INDUSTRY AND INFORMATION TECHNOLOGY (MIIT):

The MIIT is a state agency responsible for regulating and promoting China's industrial and information technology sectors. It plays a key role in developing policies and standards for AI and other emerging technologies.

Key Responsibilities:

i. Developing policies and standards for AI development and deployment.

ii. Promoting innovation and industrial competitiveness in the AI sector.

iii. Facilitating research and development in AI technologies.

iv. Ensuring the ethical and responsible use of AI.

Impact on AI:

The MIIT's policies and standards guide the development of AI technologies in China, promoting innovation while ensuring ethical and responsible use. The ministry also supports research and development initiatives to advance AI capabilities.

INTERNATIONAL REGULATORY BODIES

1. ORGANIZATION FOR ECONOMIC CO-OPERATION AND DEVELOPMENT (OECD):

The OECD is an international organization that promotes policies to improve the economic and social well-being of people worldwide. The OECD's AI Principles provide a global framework for responsible AI development and deployment.

Key Responsibilities:

i. Developing and promoting international standards for AI.

ii. Facilitating cooperation and knowledge sharing among member countries.

iii. Providing guidance on ethical and responsible AI use.

iv. Conducting research and analysis on AI-related issues.

Impact on AI:

The OECD's AI Principles influence the development of national and international regulatory frameworks, promoting human-centric, fair, and transparent AI systems. The organization's work fosters international collaboration and best practices for AI governance.

2. UNITED NATIONS (UN):

The UN is an international organization that promotes peace, security, and cooperation among countries. The UN's AI for Good initiative aims to align AI development with the Sustainable Development Goals (SDGs) and address global challenges through ethical and responsible AI use.

Key Responsibilities:

i. Promoting ethical and responsible AI use to advance the SDGs.

ii. Facilitating international cooperation and knowledge sharing on AI-related issues.

iii. Addressing ethical, legal, and societal implications of AI.

iv. Encouraging the use of AI to address global challenges such as poverty, health, and education.

Impact on AI:

The UN's AI for Good initiative encourages countries to develop regulatory frameworks that promote ethical and responsible AI use. The initiative also highlights the potential of AI to address global challenges and improve social and economic outcomes.

CHALLENGES FACED BY REGULATORY BODIES

While regulatory bodies play a critical role in AI governance, they face several challenges:

1. **Keeping Pace with Technological Advancements:** Regulatory bodies must continuously update their frameworks to keep pace with rapid AI advancements. This requires ongoing monitoring, research, and collaboration with industry experts.

2. **Ensuring Global Consistency:** Harmonizing AI regulations across different countries and regions is challenging. Regulatory bodies must work together to develop consistent standards and facilitate international cooperation.

3. **Balancing Innovation and Regulation:** Regulatory bodies must strike a balance between promoting innovation and ensuring compliance. Overly stringent regulations can stifle innovation, while insufficient regulation can lead to ethical and security concerns.

4. **Addressing Ethical and Societal Implications:** Regulatory bodies must consider the broader ethical and societal implications of AI, such as biases, job displacement, and privacy concerns. Developing comprehensive frameworks that address these issues requires a multidisciplinary approach.

STRATEGIES FOR ACHIEVING COMPLIANCE

Achieving compliance with AI regulations is critical for organizations to ensure the ethical, responsible, and legal deployment of AI technologies. Given the complexity and variability of global regulations, organizations must adopt comprehensive and effective strategies to navigate this landscape successfully.

Additionally, compliance strategies can help ensure that AI systems are developed and used in a safe, ethical, and responsible manner (Deborah Enyone Oni). This section outlines key strategies for achieving compliance, supported by data, case studies, and expert insights.

DEVELOPING COMPREHENSIVE COMPLIANCE PROGRAMS

A comprehensive compliance program is the cornerstone of effective AI governance. Such a program should include clear policies, procedures, and training to ensure that all employees understand and adhere to regulatory requirements.

KEY COMPONENTS:

1. **Policies and Procedures:** Develop and document clear policies and procedures that align with relevant regulations. This includes data protection, bias mitigation, transparency, and security measures.

2. **Training and Awareness:** Conduct regular training sessions to educate employees about regulatory requirements and best practices for AI deployment. Awareness programs can help build a culture of compliance within the organization.

LEVERAGING TECHNOLOGY SOLUTIONS

Utilizing technology solutions can streamline compliance efforts and provide real-time insights into regulatory adherence. Compliance management software and automated monitoring tools can help organizations track regulatory changes, monitor AI system performance, and generate compliance reports.

KEY TOOLS:

1. **Compliance Management Software:** Implement software solutions that track regulatory changes, manage compliance documentation, and facilitate audits and assessments.

2. **Automated Monitoring Tools:** Use AI-driven tools to monitor system performance, detect anomalies, and ensure ongoing compliance with regulatory requirements.

Data Insight: A 2023 survey by Gartner found that organizations leveraging compliance management software and automated monitoring tools reduced the time and resources required for compliance efforts by 40%.

CONDUCTING REGULAR AUDITS AND ASSESSMENTS

Regular audits and assessments are essential for ensuring that AI systems remain compliant with regulatory requirements and operate as intended. These audits should cover various aspects, including data quality, algorithmic fairness, transparency, and security measures.

KEY PRACTICES:

1. **Internal Audits:** Conduct regular internal audits to evaluate compliance with relevant regulations and identify areas for improvement.

2. **Third-Party Assessments:** Engage external auditors to provide an independent assessment of compliance efforts and validate internal findings.

ENGAGING WITH LEGAL AND REGULATORY EXPERTS

Consulting with legal and regulatory experts ensures that organizations understand the requirements and implications of relevant regulations. Experts can provide guidance on best practices, interpret complex regulatory language, and help develop effective compliance strategies.

KEY ACTIONS:

1. **Legal Consultations:** Engage legal experts to provide insights into regulatory requirements and assist in developing compliance strategies.

2. **Regulatory Engagement:** Build relationships with regulators and participate in industry forums to stay informed about regulatory expectations and upcoming changes.

Expert Insight: A 2022 report by the International Association of Privacy Professionals (IAPP) highlighted that organizations engaging with legal and regulatory experts were more successful in navigating complex regulatory landscapes and achieving compliance.

BUILDING A CULTURE OF COMPLIANCE

Promoting a culture of compliance within the organization involves educating employees about regulatory requirements, encouraging ethical practices, and fostering open communication. A compliance-focused mindset helps ensure that all employees understand the importance of adhering to regulatory standards and contribute to the organization's compliance efforts.

KEY INITIATIVES:

1. **Education and Training:** Conduct regular training programs to educate employees about regulatory requirements and best practices for AI deployment.

2. **Ethical Practices:** Encourage ethical decision-making and promote the organization's commitment to responsible AI use.

3. **Open Communication:** Foster an environment where employees feel comfortable reporting compliance concerns and suggesting improvements.

TAILORING COMPLIANCE STRATEGIES FOR DIFFERENT JURISDICTIONS

For multinational organizations, tailoring compliance strategies to address the specific requirements of different jurisdictions is essential. This includes developing region-specific policies and procedures, ensuring compliance with local regulations, and addressing cross-border data transfer requirements.

KEY ACTIONS:

1. **Region-Specific Policies:** Develop and implement policies and procedures tailored to the regulatory requirements of each jurisdiction.

2. **Cross-Border Data Transfers:** Ensure that data transfers comply with international standards and local regulations, such as GDPR's data transfer provisions and the CCPA's data protection requirements.

CONTINUOUS IMPROVEMENT AND ADAPTATION

The regulatory landscape for AI is constantly evolving, necessitating continuous improvement and adaptation of compliance strategies. Organizations must stay informed about regulatory changes, update their compliance programs, and continuously monitor AI systems to ensure ongoing adherence to regulatory requirements.

KEY PRACTICES:

1. **Continuous Monitoring:** Implement continuous monitoring processes to track AI system performance and identify emerging risks.

2. **Regulatory Updates:** Stay informed about regulatory changes and update compliance programs to reflect new requirements.

3. **Feedback and Improvement:** Encourage feedback from employees and stakeholders to identify areas for improvement and adapt compliance strategies accordingly.

A 2023 study by Accenture found that organizations prioritizing continuous improvement and adaptation of their compliance strategies were better equipped to navigate regulatory changes and maintain compliance.

Achieving compliance with AI regulations is a complex and ongoing process that requires a comprehensive and strategic approach. (Usher, C. A. 2023).

QUESTIONS PEOPLE ALSO ASK ABOUT STRATEGIES FOR ACHIEVING COMPLIANCE

1. WHAT IS THE AI COMPLIANCE STRATEGY?

An AI compliance strategy is a comprehensive approach to ensuring that AI systems adhere to relevant laws, regulations, and ethical standards. The strategy typically involves the following elements:

- **Develop Comprehensive Compliance Programs:** Organizations should establish detailed compliance programs that outline the specific regulations and standards that their AI systems must meet. These programs should cover all aspects of AI deployment, from data collection and processing to decision-making and user interaction.

- **Conduct Regular Audits:** Regular audits of AI systems are essential to ensure ongoing compliance. These audits should assess the AI systems' adherence to legal requirements, ethical guidelines, and internal policies. Audits also help identify potential compliance gaps or areas for improvement.

- **Use Compliance Management Software:** Leveraging specialized software for compliance management can streamline the process of tracking, documenting, and enforcing compliance across AI systems. These tools can automate tasks such as monitoring data usage, flagging potential violations, and generating compliance reports.

- **Continuously Monitor AI Systems:** Continuous monitoring is crucial for maintaining compliance over time. AI systems should be monitored for changes in performance, behavior, and compliance with regulations. This helps ensure that the systems remain aligned with legal and ethical standards as they evolve.

2. WHAT IS THE ROLE OF ARTIFICIAL INTELLIGENCE IN REGULATORY COMPLIANCE?

Artificial intelligence plays a significant role in regulatory compliance by automating and enhancing various compliance-related processes:

- 💡 **Automating Compliance Processes:** AI can automate routine compliance tasks, such as data classification, documentation, and reporting. This reduces the burden on human compliance teams and increases the efficiency and accuracy of compliance operations.

- 💡 **Monitoring Transactions for Irregularities:** AI systems can monitor financial transactions, communications, and other activities in real-time to detect irregularities that may indicate non-compliance. This is particularly useful in industries such as finance, where compliance with anti-money laundering (AML) and Know Your Customer (KYC) regulations is critical.

- 💡 **Detecting Anomalies:** AI excels at detecting anomalies in large datasets, which can be indicative of compliance violations or potential fraud. By identifying unusual patterns of behavior or data usage, AI systems can alert compliance officers to investigate further.

- 💡 **Ensuring Adherence to Regulations:** AI can be programmed to ensure that specific actions or decisions are made in compliance with relevant regulations. For example, AI systems can enforce data privacy regulations by automatically anonymizing sensitive data or ensuring that consent is obtained before data collection.

3. WHAT ARE THE STRATEGIES TO IMPLEMENT AI?

Implementing AI in an organization requires careful planning and execution. The following strategies can help ensure a successful AI implementation:

- **Define Clear Objectives:** Before implementing AI, organizations should clearly define the objectives they hope to achieve. This includes identifying specific problems that AI can solve, setting measurable goals, and aligning AI initiatives with broader business strategies.

- **Invest in Quality Data:** High-quality data is the foundation of effective AI systems. Organizations should invest in collecting, cleaning, and managing data to ensure that AI models are trained on accurate and representative datasets.

- **Ensure Stakeholder Buy-In:** Successful AI implementation requires support from stakeholders across the organization, including executives, IT teams, and end-users. Engaging stakeholders early in the process and communicating the benefits of AI can help secure their buy-in and support.

- **Implement Robust Testing:** AI systems should undergo rigorous testing before deployment to ensure they perform as expected and do not introduce new risks. This includes testing for accuracy, bias, security, and compliance with regulations.

- **Continuously Monitor Performance:** After deployment, AI systems should be continuously monitored to assess their performance and make necessary adjustments. This helps ensure that AI systems remain effective and aligned with organizational goals over time.

4. WHAT ARE THE WAYS OF ACHIEVING ARTIFICIAL INTELLIGENCE?

Achieving artificial intelligence involves several key steps:

- **Invest in Research and Development:** Continuous investment in AI research and development (R&D) is essential for advancing AI technologies and developing new AI applications. R&D efforts should focus on improving AI algorithms, exploring new use cases, and addressing current limitations of AI systems.

- **Use High-Quality Data:** AI systems rely on large amounts of data to learn and make decisions. Organizations should prioritize the collection and use of high-quality, relevant data to train AI models effectively. This includes ensuring data is accurate, diverse, and representative of the problem being addressed.

- **Train Models with Diverse Datasets:** To build robust and unbiased AI systems, it is crucial to train models on diverse datasets that capture a wide range of scenarios and perspectives. This helps ensure that AI systems perform well across different contexts and avoid perpetuating existing biases.

- **Implement Ethical Guidelines:** Developing AI systems that adhere to ethical standards is critical for responsible AI deployment. Organizations should establish ethical guidelines that govern the design, development, and use of AI technologies, ensuring they are used in ways that are fair, transparent, and respectful of human rights.

5. WHAT ARE THE COMPLIANCE STRATEGIES?

Effective compliance strategies involve a combination of proactive and reactive measures:

- 💡 **Conduct Risk Assessments:** Regular risk assessments help organizations identify potential compliance risks and develop strategies to mitigate them. This includes assessing the likelihood and impact of various compliance risks and prioritizing them based on their severity.

- 💡 **Develop Clear Policies:** Clear and comprehensive policies are essential for guiding compliance efforts across the organization. These policies should outline the specific regulatory requirements that apply to the organization and provide detailed instructions for achieving and maintaining compliance.

- 💡 **Ensure Regular Training:** Regular training is crucial for keeping employees informed about compliance requirements and best practices. Training programs should be updated frequently to reflect changes in regulations and should be tailored to the needs of different roles within the organization.

- 💡 **Engage with Regulatory Bodies:** Maintaining open communication with regulatory bodies can help organizations stay informed about regulatory changes and receive guidance on complex compliance issues. This engagement also helps build a positive relationship with regulators.

- 💡 **Use Technology for Monitoring:** Technology, including AI and compliance management software, can be used to monitor compliance across the organization in real-time. These tools can automate compliance checks, detect potential violations, and generate reports for regulatory audits.

6.   WHAT ARE CONTROL STRATEGIES IN AI?

Control strategies in AI are essential for ensuring that AI systems operate safely, ethically, and in compliance with regulations:

- 💡 **Implement Algorithmic Audits:** Regular audits of AI algorithms can help identify and address issues such as bias, discrimination, and inaccuracies. These audits assess the fairness, transparency, and accountability of AI systems, ensuring they align with ethical standards.

- 💡 **Ensure Data Quality:** High-quality data is critical for the performance and reliability of AI systems. Control strategies should include processes for verifying and maintaining data quality throughout the AI system's lifecycle.

- 💡 **Use Bias Detection Tools:** AI systems should be equipped with tools that detect and mitigate biases in data and algorithms. These tools help ensure that AI systems make decisions that are fair and non-discriminatory.

- 💡 **Enforce Transparency:** Transparency in AI operations is essential for building trust and accountability. Control strategies should include mechanisms for making AI decision-making processes understandable and explainable to users and stakeholders.

- 💡 **Maintain Robust Security Measures:** AI systems must be protected from cyber threats, including adversarial attacks that could compromise their integrity. Control strategies should include robust security measures, such as encryption, access controls, and continuous monitoring, to safeguard AI systems from external threats.

7. HOW SHOULD WE REGULATE AI?

Regulating AI requires a balanced approach that promotes innovation while addressing the ethical and societal challenges posed by AI technologies:

- 💡 **Develop Clear Guidelines:** Governments and regulatory bodies should establish clear guidelines for the development and use of AI. These guidelines should address issues such as data privacy, algorithmic transparency, bias, and accountability, providing a framework for responsible AI deployment.

💡 **Ensure Transparency and Accountability:** AI regulations should require transparency in AI systems' decision-making processes and ensure that there is accountability for the outcomes of AI decisions. This includes mandating the use of explainable AI (XAI) techniques and establishing clear lines of responsibility for AI deployments.

💡 **Address Ethical Concerns:** AI regulations should incorporate ethical considerations, ensuring that AI systems are developed and used in ways that respect human rights and societal values. This includes preventing the use of AI for harmful or discriminatory purposes.

💡 **Create Adaptive Regulatory Frameworks:** AI technologies are rapidly evolving, so regulatory frameworks must be flexible and adaptive to keep pace with technological advancements. This may involve continuous updates to regulations, as well as the use of regulatory sandboxes that allow for the testing of new AI technologies in a controlled environment.

8. WHAT ARE THE MAIN REGULATORY CHALLENGES WITH RESPECT TO ARTIFICIAL INTELLIGENCE?

The main regulatory challenges with respect to AI include:

💡 **Ensuring Data Privacy:** AI systems often require large amounts of data, raising concerns about how this data is collected, stored, and used. Regulators must ensure that AI systems comply with data privacy laws, such as the GDPR, and protect individuals' personal information.

💡 **Managing Biases:** AI systems can perpetuate or even exacerbate biases present in the data they are trained on. Regulating AI to prevent biased outcomes is a significant challenge, requiring ongoing efforts to develop and enforce fairness standards.

💡 **Achieving Transparency:** AI systems, especially those based on deep learning, can be opaque and difficult to interpret. Ensuring that AI systems are transparent and that their decision-making processes are explainable is a critical regulatory challenge.

💡 **Keeping Pace with Rapid Technological Advancements:** The rapid pace of AI development makes it difficult for regulators to keep up. This creates a challenge in ensuring that regulations are current and effective in addressing the latest AI technologies and their potential risks.

9. WHAT IS RESPONSIBLE AI GOVERNANCE?

Responsible AI governance involves implementing policies and practices that ensure AI is used ethically, transparently, and in compliance with laws and societal values. Key components of responsible AI governance include:

💡 **Ethical Guidelines:** Establishing ethical guidelines that govern the design, development, and deployment of AI systems. These guidelines should address issues such as fairness, accountability, transparency, and respect for human rights.

💡 **Transparency and Accountability:** Ensuring that AI systems are transparent and that there is accountability for their outcomes. This includes making AI decision-making processes understandable to users and establishing clear lines of responsibility for AI deployments.

💡 **Compliance with Laws and Regulations:** Ensuring that AI systems comply with relevant laws and regulations, including those related to data privacy, non-discrimination, and consumer protection. Regular audits and assessments should be conducted to verify compliance.

- **Stakeholder Engagement:** Engaging stakeholders, including employees, customers, and regulators, in the governance of AI systems. This helps build trust and ensures that AI deployments align with societal values and expectations.

10. WHAT IS THE AI FIRST STRATEGY?

An AI-first strategy is an approach where an organization prioritizes the integration of AI across its business processes to drive innovation, improve efficiency, and enhance decision-making capabilities. Key elements of an AI-first strategy include:

- **Prioritizing AI Integration:** The organization places AI at the core of its operations, using AI technologies to optimize processes, automate tasks, and deliver personalized experiences to customers.

- **Driving Innovation:** An AI-first strategy focuses on leveraging AI to create new products, services, and business models. By adopting AI, organizations can innovate faster and stay ahead of competitors.

- **Improving Efficiency:** AI is used to streamline operations, reduce costs, and increase productivity. This includes automating routine tasks, optimizing supply chains, and enhancing customer service.

- **Enhancing Decision-Making:** AI-driven insights are integrated into decision-making processes, enabling more informed and data-driven decisions. This helps organizations respond more effectively to market changes and customer needs.

CHAPTER SEVEN
Accountability and Responsibility in Artificial Intelligence

Accountability and responsibility are foundational elements in the deployment and management of Artificial Intelligence (AI) systems, especially as these technologies become increasingly integral to societal operations. As AI systems take on more complex roles involving decision-making, data processing, and automation, the implications of their actions and outcomes grow more significant. The ethical, legal, and societal ramifications of AI-driven decisions necessitate robust mechanisms for accountability and responsibility (Cath, 2018).

With AI systems now influencing critical sectors such as healthcare, finance, and law enforcement, ensuring that these technologies operate within established ethical and legal frameworks is essential. The lack of clear accountability can lead to harmful consequences, including biases in decision-making, violations of privacy, and other forms of societal harm (Binns, 2018). Addressing these concerns requires a multifaceted approach that encompasses the roles and responsibilities of developers, users, and organizations deploying AI systems.

This chapter delves into the complexities of AI accountability, examining the distribution of responsibility among stakeholders and the challenges inherent in ensuring that AI systems are used responsibly. It explores the legal and ethical frameworks that guide AI accountability, the difficulties in assigning responsibility for AI-driven outcomes, and best practices for fostering transparency, fairness, and accountability in AI development and deployment (Floridi et al., 2018).

THE IMPORTANCE OF AI ACCOUNTABILITY

TRUST AND PUBLIC ACCEPTANCE

At the heart of AI accountability is the necessity of building and maintaining public trust. Trust is the bedrock upon which the acceptance and adoption of AI technologies are built. Without trust, even the most advanced AI systems are unlikely to achieve widespread implementation. Trust in AI is multifaceted; it encompasses the belief that AI systems will perform reliably, that they will make decisions in a fair and unbiased manner, and that they will respect the rights and privacy of individuals.

Public trust in AI is directly tied to the transparency and accountability of those who develop and deploy these systems. Transparency ensures that the processes behind AI decision-making are visible and understandable to users and stakeholders. This transparency is critical in demystifying AI and making its operations more comprehensible.

When users know that there are clear lines of accountability—meaning that someone can be held responsible if something goes wrong—they are more likely to trust and embrace AI technologies.

Building trust is not just about avoiding negative outcomes; it is also about creating a positive relationship between AI and society. Trustworthy AI systems have the potential to enhance productivity, improve decision-making, and solve complex problems across various sectors, including healthcare, finance, and public administration. However, without accountability, the potential benefits of AI can be overshadowed by concerns about misuse, bias, and unintended consequences.

LEGAL COMPLIANCE

Legal compliance is another critical aspect of AI accountability. As AI systems become integral to business operations, healthcare, law enforcement, and other critical areas, they are increasingly subject to existing legal frameworks. These frameworks are designed to ensure that AI technologies are used in a manner that is consistent with societal values and legal standards. However, the rapid pace of AI development often outstrips the evolution of legal norms, creating a complex landscape where accountability is crucial.

As mentioned previously, in jurisdictions like the European Union, regulations such as the General Data Protection Regulation (GDPR) impose strict requirements on the use of AI, particularly in relation to data privacy and automated decision-making. The GDPR mandates that individuals have the right to be informed about the use of AI in processing their data and that they can challenge decisions made by AI systems. This regulation underscores the importance of accountability in ensuring that AI systems operate within the bounds of the law.

Moreover, the legal landscape for AI is continually evolving. Governments and regulatory bodies are increasingly recognizing the need for AI-specific regulations that address the unique challenges posed by these technologies. For example, the European Union's proposed Artificial Intelligence Act seeks to establish a comprehensive legal framework for AI, focusing on risk management, transparency, and accountability. In the United States, various state and federal initiatives are also emerging to regulate AI, particularly in areas such as autonomous vehicles, healthcare, and financial services.

Clear accountability structures are essential for navigating this complex legal environment. They help organizations understand their obligations under the law and ensure that AI systems are designed, deployed, and operated in compliance with legal standards. Without accountability, organizations risk legal disputes, financial penalties, and damage to their reputation.

Ethical considerations are also at the core of AI accountability. As AI systems are increasingly entrusted with decisions that impact individuals and society, it is essential that these systems are developed and deployed in ways that align with ethical principles. Ethical AI development involves addressing a wide range of issues, including bias, fairness, transparency, and the broader societal impact of AI technologies.

One of the most pressing ethical concerns in AI is bias. AI systems are often trained on large datasets that reflect historical biases, which can lead to biased outcomes. For example, AI systems used in hiring, criminal justice, and lending have been shown to disproportionately disadvantage certain demographic groups. Accountability in AI development means that developers and organizations must actively work to identify and mitigate these biases, ensuring that AI systems operate fairly and do not perpetuate existing inequalities.

Transparency is another key ethical consideration. AI systems, particularly those based on deep learning and other complex algorithms, are often described as "black boxes" because their decision-making processes are opaque and difficult to understand. This lack of transparency can be problematic, especially in high-stakes areas such as healthcare and law enforcement, where decisions made by AI systems can have significant consequences for individuals. Ensuring accountability in AI development requires that these systems are designed with transparency in mind, allowing users and stakeholders to understand how decisions are made and to challenge those decisions if necessary.

Finally, ethical AI development involves considering the broader societal impact of these technologies. AI has the potential to bring about significant social and economic changes, including job displacement, shifts in power dynamics, and changes in how individuals interact with technology. Accountability means that developers and organizations must consider these broader implications and take steps to ensure that AI technologies are used in ways that benefit society as a whole.

WHO IS RESPONSIBLE FOR AI?

Accountability in AI is not the responsibility of a single entity; it spans across multiple stakeholders, each of whom plays a critical role in ensuring that AI systems are used responsibly and ethically.

AI USERS

The individuals who operate AI systems are the first line of accountability. These users are responsible for understanding the capabilities and limitations of the AI tools they use and for ensuring that these tools are applied appropriately. AI users must be vigilant in monitoring the performance of AI systems, particularly in high-stakes environments where errors can have serious consequences.

For example, healthcare professionals using AI-driven diagnostic tools must be aware of the limitations of these tools and ensure that AI is used as a complement to, rather than a replacement for, human judgment. Similarly, law enforcement officers using facial recognition technology must be trained to understand the potential for errors and biases in these systems and to use them in ways that respect individual rights and freedoms.

AI USERS' MANAGERS

Managers play a crucial role in overseeing the responsible use of AI within their teams. They are accountable for ensuring that their employees are adequately trained in the use of AI technologies and that the use of these technologies aligns with the organization's policies and ethical guidelines. Managers must also establish protocols for monitoring AI usage and for responding to any issues that arise.

In addition to overseeing the day-to-day use of AI, managers are responsible for creating an organizational culture that prioritizes accountability and ethical practices. This includes setting clear expectations for the responsible use of AI, providing ongoing training and support, and ensuring that AI-related incidents are promptly addressed.

AI USERS' COMPANIES/EMPLOYERS

Organizations that deploy AI systems bear significant responsibility for the outcomes of these systems. Companies must establish comprehensive guidelines for the use of AI, implement robust risk management strategies, and develop response plans for potential AI-related issues. Ensuring compliance with legal and ethical standards is vital for protecting the company's reputation and minimizing operational risks.

Organizations must also take a proactive approach to AI accountability by regularly auditing their AI systems to identify potential risks and areas for improvement. This includes assessing the fairness and transparency of AI systems, as well as their compliance with legal and regulatory requirements. By taking these steps, organizations can ensure that their AI systems are used responsibly and ethically.

AI DEVELOPERS

Developers who create AI systems hold a significant share of the accountability. They are responsible for ensuring that AI systems are designed to be safe, unbiased, and transparent. Developers must address ethical concerns during the design and training phases, ensuring that AI systems operate fairly and without unintended negative consequences.

In addition to technical expertise, AI developers must have a strong understanding of the ethical and societal implications of their work. This includes considering how AI systems might be misused or cause harm and taking steps to mitigate these risks. Developers must also be transparent about the limitations of AI systems and communicate these limitations to users and stakeholders.

AI VENDORS

Vendors providing AI products or services must ensure that their offerings are reliable, secure, and ethically sound. They can be held accountable if their products contain flaws or if they fail to disclose potential risks and limitations to their clients. Vendors have a responsibility to work closely with clients to ensure that AI systems are implemented correctly and used in a responsible manner.

Vendors must also ensure that their AI products are regularly updated and maintained to address emerging threats and vulnerabilities. This includes providing clients with the necessary tools and support to secure their AI systems and to respond to any issues that arise.

DATA PROVIDERS

Data is the lifeblood of AI systems, and data providers hold significant accountability for the quality and ethical sourcing of the data they supply. Poor-quality or biased data can lead to significant issues in AI performance and ethical breaches. Data providers must ensure that the data used to train AI systems is accurate, unbiased, and compliant with privacy regulations.

In addition to ensuring data quality, data providers must be transparent about how data is collected and used. This includes providing clear information about data sources, consent processes, and data privacy protections. By taking these steps, data providers can help ensure that AI systems operate fairly and ethically.

REGULATORY BODIES

Regulatory bodies play a critical role in establishing and enforcing the rules governing AI use. They are responsible for protecting public and business interests by ensuring that AI technologies are used ethically and responsibly. Regulatory bodies define the legal framework that determines who is accountable when AI systems fail or cause harm.

Effective regulation of AI requires a careful balance between promoting innovation and protecting public interests. Regulatory bodies must work closely with industry stakeholders, including developers, vendors, and users, to create a regulatory environment that encourages responsible AI development and use. This includes setting clear standards for AI accountability, transparency, and ethical conduct.

EXAMPLES OF AI ACCOUNTABILITY IN PRACTICE

Understanding theoretical frameworks is crucial, but real-world examples help illustrate the practical implications and challenges of AI accountability. Here are three scenarios that highlight different aspects of accountability in AI.

SCENARIO 1: EMAIL RESPONSE MISMANAGEMENT

Imagine a situation where an AI system designed to automate email responses unintentionally divulges sensitive client information due to a missearch in the records. While the AI user initiated the process, accountability does not end there.

1. **AI User**: The individual using the AI system is responsible for initiating the email automation and should have oversight mechanisms to catch errors.

2. **AI User's Manager**: The manager is accountable for ensuring that the team is trained to use AI responsibly and that safeguards are in place.

3. **Employing Company**: The company is responsible for having robust policies and incident response plans for AI-related issues.

4. **AI Developers**: Developers may face scrutiny for any deficiencies in the system's design that allowed the error.

5. **AI Vendors**: Vendors could be held accountable if the AI product is flawed or if they failed to disclose potential risks.

This scenario underscores the need for multi-layered accountability structures to handle AI-related incidents effectively.

SCENARIO 2: PREDICTIVE ANALYTICS MISFIRE

Consider a situation where an AI system incorrectly predicts market trends, leading to significant business losses.

1. **AI Developers**: Developers could be blamed for flaws in the AI model or for not adequately testing the system.

2. **Data Providers**: Providers of the data used to train the AI could share responsibility if the data was incorrect or biased.

3. **AI Users**: Users who acted on the AI's predictions without additional scrutiny may also bear some responsibility.

4. **Regulatory Bodies**: Regulatory bodies need to assess whether existing regulations were violated and if additional safeguards are necessary.

This example highlights how multiple stakeholders share accountability for the outcomes of AI predictions.

SCENARIO 3: AUTOMATED DECISION-MAKING ERROR

In a case where an AI system is entrusted with decision-making, a critical decision made by the AI negatively impacts the business.

1. **Employing Company**: The company could be held accountable for over-relying on an AI system without sufficient oversight.

2. **AI Developers and Vendors**: They share responsibility if the error resulted from a flaw in the system or if potential risks were not disclosed.

3. **AI Users and Managers**: Users and their managers may be responsible for not properly understanding or supervising the AI system.

This scenario demonstrates the complexities of AI accountability and the importance of robust oversight mechanisms.

AI ACCOUNTABILITY ISSUES

Despite the clear need for accountability in AI, several issues complicate the establishment and enforcement of responsibility. Understanding these challenges is critical for developing effective solutions.

1. AUTONOMY AND COMPLEXITY

As AI systems become more autonomous, attributing responsibility becomes increasingly difficult. Autonomous systems make decisions and perform actions without direct human intervention, raising complex questions about who is responsible when something goes wrong.

Should responsibility lie with the AI system itself, its developers, or its users? This challenge is compounded by the complexity of AI models, especially deep learning systems, which can be opaque and difficult to understand.

2. MULTIPLE STAKEHOLDERS

AI systems often involve a web of stakeholders, including developers, data providers, users, and regulatory bodies. Each party contributes to the AI system's functionality in different ways, making it challenging to pinpoint responsibility for specific outcomes.

This multifaceted web of responsibilities requires a comprehensive approach to accountability that considers the roles and contributions of all stakeholders involved.

3. OPACITY AND EXPLAINABILITY

The complexity and opacity of many AI systems, particularly those based on deep learning, pose significant challenges for accountability. These systems often operate as "black boxes," making it difficult to understand how they arrive at specific decisions or outcomes.

Without clear explainability, it becomes challenging to attribute responsibility accurately, as stakeholders may not fully understand the AI's decision-making processes.

4. LACK OF ACCOUNTABILITY IN AI

In many instances, there is a significant lack of accountability in AI deployments. This can result from inadequate policies, insufficient regulatory frameworks, or a lack of awareness among stakeholders about their responsibilities.

When accountability structures are not clearly defined or enforced, it leads to operational risks, ethical breaches, and potential harm to individuals and society.

Addressing these issues requires a multi-pronged approach that includes legal frameworks, industry standards, transparent AI systems, and ongoing education and awareness among all stakeholders.

ADDRESSING AI ACCOUNTABILITY CHALLENGES

To tackle the challenges of AI accountability, it is essential to implement a combination of legal, technical, and organizational measures. These approaches can help ensure that AI systems are developed, deployed, and used responsibly.

1. LEGAL FRAMEWORKS

Developing and adapting legal frameworks is critical to addressing the unique challenges posed by AI systems. These frameworks should clearly define the responsibilities of various stakeholders and establish mechanisms for holding them accountable. This may involve creating new laws specifically for AI systems or adapting existing legislation to better accommodate AI technologies. Effective legal frameworks provide a foundation for accountability, ensuring that all parties involved understand their obligations and the consequences of non-compliance.

2. STANDARDS AND GUIDELINES

Establishing industry-wide standards and guidelines for ethical AI development and deployment can help ensure that AI systems adhere to ethical principles and promote responsible practices among stakeholders.

These standards and guidelines can provide a clear framework for developers, users, and other stakeholders to follow, ensuring that AI systems are developed and deployed with ethical considerations in mind. Organizations like the IEEE and ISO are already working on such standards, which can serve as valuable references.

3. EXPLAINABLE AI

Developing AI systems that are more transparent and explainable can facilitate the attribution of responsibility. Explainable AI models make the decision-making processes of AI systems more understandable, allowing stakeholders to identify the causes of specific outcomes and hold the appropriate parties accountable.

Explainable AI also provides greater insight into potential biases and flaws in the system, enabling developers to address these issues more effectively.

4. AUDITS AND CERTIFICATIONS

Conducting regular audits and certifications of AI systems can help ensure their compliance with ethical and legal requirements. These assessments can serve as a means of holding stakeholders accountable for the AI system's actions and outcomes.

By establishing a standardized process for evaluating AI systems, stakeholders can better understand their responsibilities and work towards meeting ethical and legal requirements. Certifications from recognized bodies can also enhance the credibility and trustworthiness of AI systems.

5. EDUCATION AND AWARENESS

Raising awareness of the ethical challenges associated with AI systems and the importance of accountability and responsibility can help encourage responsible development practices.

Educating developers, users, and other stakeholders about the potential risks and ethical considerations of AI fosters a more conscientious approach to AI development and deployment.

Ongoing training and awareness programs can help ensure that all stakeholders remain informed about the latest developments and best practices in AI accountability.

THE ROLE OF LEGISLATION AND COMPANY POLICIES

Accountability in AI requires both robust legislation and solid company policies to ensure ethical and responsible use. While legislation provides the overarching framework, company policies offer detailed, operational guidelines for AI usage within an organization.

1. LEGISLATION

Effective legislation is crucial for establishing clear rules and guidelines for AI accountability. Laws need to define the responsibilities of various stakeholders involved in AI development, deployment, and usage. Legislation acts as a public safeguard, ensuring that AI technologies are developed and used in ways that protect societal interests. Additionally, it sets penalties for non-compliance and infractions, providing a deterrent against irresponsible behavior. As AI technologies evolve, so must the legal frameworks governing them, ensuring they remain relevant and effective in addressing new challenges and risks.

2. COMPANY POLICIES

While legislation provides the necessary legal framework, company policies are the detailed, operational roadmaps that guide AI usage within an organization. These policies must align with existing laws but should also go a step further, detailing specific procedures, protocols, and best practices unique to the organization.

i.   **Developing AI Policies**: Companies need to establish comprehensive AI policies that outline the ethical principles guiding AI use, specify the roles and responsibilities of different stakeholders, and provide clear guidelines for the development and deployment of AI systems.

ii. **Training and Awareness**: Companies must ensure that all employees, particularly those involved in AI operations, are adequately trained and aware of the company's AI policies and the broader ethical and legal considerations. Regular training sessions and awareness programs can help keep everyone informed about best practices and emerging issues in AI accountability.

iii. **Monitoring and Oversight**: Implementing robust monitoring and oversight mechanisms is essential for ensuring compliance with AI policies. Regular audits, performance evaluations, and incident reporting systems can help identify potential issues early and ensure that AI systems are operating as intended.

iv. **Incident Response Plans**: Companies should have well-defined incident response plans for AI-related issues. These plans should detail the steps to be taken in case of an AI malfunction or ethical breach, ensuring a swift and effective response to mitigate any negative impacts.

v. The interplay between legislation and company policies forms the backbone of AI accountability. By working together, regulatory bodies and individual businesses can foster an environment of responsibility, ethics, and trust, paving the way for the safe and effective use of AI technologies.

ACCOUNTABILITY AI APPS AND PARTNERS

Specific tools and collaborative approaches can significantly enhance accountability. AI accountability apps and partnerships can provide structured and systematic ways to manage and ensure responsibility in AI systems.

1. ACCOUNTABILITY AI APPS

Emerging technologies have given rise to AI accountability apps designed to monitor and enforce responsible AI practices. These apps offer several functionalities that can help organizations maintain high standards of AI accountability:

i. **Monitoring and Reporting**: These apps can track AI system performance and usage, generating reports on their operations. This ensures transparency and helps identify potential issues before they escalate.

ii. **Compliance Checks**: Accountability AI apps can perform regular compliance checks against legal and ethical standards, alerting users to any deviations. This proactive approach helps maintain adherence to regulations and internal policies.

iii. **Bias Detection**: Many AI accountability apps come equipped with tools to detect biases in AI models, ensuring that AI systems make fair and unbiased decisions. This feature is crucial for maintaining ethical standards and public trust.

iv. **Incident Management**: These apps can also offer incident management functionalities, allowing organizations to log, track, and respond to AI-related incidents efficiently. This ensures that any issues are addressed promptly and systematically.

2. AI ACCOUNTABILITY PARTNERS

Partnering with experts and organizations specializing in AI ethics and accountability can significantly bolster an organization's ability to manage AI responsibly. These partners can provide invaluable support in several areas:

i. **Expert Consultation**: AI accountability partners offer expert advice on best practices, helping organizations develop robust AI policies and frameworks. Their insights can guide the ethical development and deployment of AI systems.

ii. **Training and Education**: Partners can provide training programs to educate employees about AI ethics, accountability, and compliance. These programs ensure that everyone involved in AI operations understands their responsibilities and the broader ethical implications.

iii. **Audits and Certifications**: Partners can conduct thorough audits of AI systems to ensure compliance with ethical and legal standards. They can also provide certifications that enhance the credibility and trustworthiness of AI systems.

iv. **Continuous Improvement**: By collaborating with AI accountability partners, organizations can stay updated with the latest developments in AI ethics and accountability, continuously improving their practices and policies.

The integration of accountability AI apps and partnerships into an organization's AI strategy can create a comprehensive and dynamic approach to managing AI responsibly. These tools and collaborations ensure that AI systems are not only technically sound but also ethically and legally compliant.

FUTURE DIRECTIONS FOR AI ACCOUNTABILITY

As AI continues to evolve and its role in business operations expands, the importance of robust accountability structures will only grow. To ensure the ethical and effective use of AI, businesses must proactively define and refine their accountability frameworks.

1. GROWING ROLE OF AI IN BUSINESS OPERATIONS

AI's role in business operations is set to grow exponentially, impacting everything from customer service and marketing to strategic decision-making and operational efficiency.

This expansion necessitates a corresponding increase in the scrutiny and definition of accountability structures. Businesses must anticipate the potential risks and ethical challenges associated with AI and prepare accordingly.

i. **Strategic Integration**: As AI becomes more integrated into business processes, organizations need to ensure that their AI systems are aligned with their strategic goals and ethical standards. This involves continuous evaluation and adjustment of AI practices to meet evolving business needs and ethical considerations.

ii. **Risk Management**: Proactive risk management strategies are essential for identifying and mitigating potential AI-related risks. Businesses should conduct regular risk assessments, develop contingency plans, and ensure that their AI systems are resilient to both operational and ethical challenges.

iii. **Stakeholder Engagement**: Engaging with various stakeholders, including employees, customers, regulators, and AI partners, is crucial for maintaining transparency and trust. Open communication and collaboration can help address concerns, gather valuable feedback, and ensure that AI practices are aligned with societal values and expectations.

2. DEFINING CLEAR ACCOUNTABILITY STRUCTURES

To foster an environment of responsibility, businesses must define clear accountability structures that delineate the roles and responsibilities of all stakeholders involved in AI operations.

i. **Responsibility Mapping**: Organizations should create detailed maps of responsibility that outline the specific roles and duties of AI users, managers, developers, vendors, data providers, and regulatory bodies. This ensures that everyone involved understands their responsibilities and the importance of their role in maintaining AI accountability.

ii. **Ethical Guidelines**: Developing comprehensive ethical guidelines for AI use within the organization can provide a clear framework for responsible behavior. These guidelines should cover various aspects of AI operations, including data management, decision-making, and incident response.

iii. **Continuous Monitoring and Evaluation**: Ongoing monitoring and evaluation of AI systems are essential for maintaining accountability. Businesses should implement robust oversight mechanisms to track AI performance, identify potential issues, and ensure compliance with ethical and legal standards.

iv. **Adaptive Policies**: AI technologies and their applications are constantly evolving. Therefore, businesses need to maintain adaptive policies that can respond to new developments and emerging challenges. Regularly updating policies and procedures ensures that AI practices remain relevant and effective.

CREATING AN ETHICAL AI GOVERNANCE FRAMEWORK

Artificial intelligence (AI) has emerged as a revolutionary force in our rapidly evolving technology, transforming industries, automating procedures, and reshaping how we connect with others. While AI holds immense potential, it also brings serious ethical, legal, societal, and organizational implications.

As AI systems become increasingly integrated into our daily lives, the need for a robust and thorough framework grows ever more critical. The absence of AI governance raises significant risks, including privacy violations, biased algorithms, and the misuse of AI for malicious purposes.

Building an ethical AI governance framework ensures transparency, accountability, and the responsible development and deployment of AI systems.

According to McKinsey & Company, Generative AI alone could add between $2.6 trillion to $4.4 trillion annually to business revenues, with significant value arising from embedding Generative AI in customer operations, marketing, sales, software engineering, and R&D.

To harness AI technologies for enhanced productivity while mitigating potential risks, an effective governance framework serves as a crucial guide through the challenging terrain of AI development, deployment, and regulation.

WHAT IS AI GOVERNANCE FRAMEWORKS?

An AI governance framework is a structured set of regulations, policies, standards, and best practices designed to regulate and oversee the development, application, and use of AI technologies. It serves as a guide to ensure AI systems are developed and utilized ethically, responsibly, and in accordance with legal standards.

The framework addresses the various risks associated with AI, such as privacy violations, biased decision-making, and potential misuse.

AI GOVERNANCE FRAMEWORK EXAMPLES

Numerous organizations have developed AI governance frameworks to guide ethical AI deployment. For instance, the AI Governance Framework by NIST (National Institute of Standards and Technology) focuses on risk management and ensuring AI systems are trustworthy and accountable.

The AIGA AI Governance Framework provides guidelines for ethical AI use in design and creative industries. McKinsey's AI Governance Framework emphasizes the need for transparency, accountability, and continuous monitoring to maximize AI's benefits while minimizing risks.

Similarly, Microsoft's AI Governance Framework highlights principles like fairness, inclusiveness, and reliability to guide AI development and deployment within the company.

These frameworks serve as examples for companies seeking to implement robust AI governance practices, illustrating how various organizations tailor their approaches to meet specific industry needs and regulatory requirements.

COMPONENTS OF AN ETHICAL AI GOVERNANCE FRAMEWORK

To ensure the ethical and responsible use of AI, a robust AI governance framework must include several crucial components. These components collectively establish guidelines and best practices for AI development, deployment, and monitoring.

1. ### ESTABLISH ETHICAL GUIDELINES

   Ethical guidelines form the foundation of an AI governance framework. These guidelines encompass universal principles and values that AI systems should adhere to, including fairness, transparency, accountability, and privacy.

   By defining these standards, organizations can ensure that their AI technologies operate within ethical boundaries and promote trust among users.

2. ### ENSURE DATA SECURITY

   Data security is paramount in an AI governance framework. Organizations must implement measures to protect data privacy and security, ensuring that data collection, storage, and sharing practices comply with relevant laws and regulations. Obtaining consent from data subjects and maintaining robust security protocols are essential to safeguarding sensitive information.

3. ### ENSURE TRANSPARENCY

   Transparency involves being open about the purpose of AI models, data collection methods, and processing activities. Organizations should provide clear explanations of how AI systems make decisions and the factors influencing these decisions. This openness fosters trust and allows stakeholders to scrutinize and understand AI processes.

4. DEMONSTRATE ACCOUNTABILITY

Accountability ensures that there are clear guidelines for taking responsibility for the actions of AI systems and developers. This includes establishing mechanisms for addressing issues, mitigating biases, and rectifying unintended consequences. By defining accountability, organizations can maintain ethical standards and legal compliance.

5. MITIGATE DISCRIMINATION

AI systems must be designed to identify and mitigate biases to prevent discrimination and unfair outcomes. This involves implementing strategies to detect and correct biases in data and algorithms, ensuring that AI technologies treat all individuals equitably.

6. REGULATION AND COMPLIANCE

Compliance with data protection laws and AI-specific regulations is critical to avoid legal penalties and reputational damage. An AI governance framework should include measures to ensure adherence to relevant laws, such as the GDPR, and emerging AI regulations.

7. MONITORING AND ASSESSMENT

Continuous monitoring and assessment are vital for maintaining the integrity and performance of AI systems. Organizations should establish mechanisms to regularly evaluate AI systems' impact, conduct risk assessments, and address vulnerabilities promptly.

This proactive approach ensures that AI technologies remain effective and secure over time.

BUILDING AN AI GOVERNANCE FRAMEWORK

Creating a comprehensive AI governance framework involves several critical steps to ensure ethical and responsible AI development. These steps help tailor the framework to the organization's specific needs while addressing key ethical, legal, and operational considerations.

1. ASSESSING ORGANIZATIONAL NEEDS

The first step in building an AI governance framework is to assess the organization's unique requirements. This involves understanding the specific applications of AI within the organization, identifying potential risks, and determining the ethical and legal standards that need to be met. By aligning the framework with organizational goals and industry standards, companies can create a more effective governance structure.

2. HANDLING SENSITIVE DATA RESPONSIBLY

Responsible data management is a cornerstone of an AI governance framework. Organizations must implement best practices for collecting, storing, and processing sensitive data. This includes obtaining explicit consent from data subjects, anonymizing data where possible, and ensuring robust data security measures are in place to protect against unauthorized access and breaches.

3. RECOGNIZING LEGAL AND COMPLIANCE STANDARDS

Understanding and adhering to applicable legal and compliance standards is essential. Organizations should stay informed about relevant laws and regulations, such as the GDPR in Europe or the AI-specific guidelines proposed by NIST. By integrating these standards into their governance framework, companies can ensure their AI practices remain compliant and avoid potential legal repercussions.

4. BROADCASTING TRANSPARENCY AND EXPLAINABILITY

Transparency and explainability are crucial for building trust in AI systems. Organizations should provide clear, understandable explanations of how AI systems make decisions, what data is used, and how it is processed. This transparency helps stakeholders understand AI operations and enables them to scrutinize and validate AI decisions.

5. ASSIGNING ROLES AND ACCOUNTABILITY

Clear definition of roles and accountability is necessary to manage AI systems effectively. Organizations should assign specific responsibilities for AI governance, ensuring that there are designated individuals or teams accountable for monitoring AI systems, addressing issues, and ensuring compliance with ethical and legal standards. This accountability helps prevent and address problems promptly.

6. DATA MANAGEMENT POLICIES

Comprehensive data management policies are vital for an effective AI governance framework. These policies should cover data collection, storage, usage, and deletion practices. Establishing oversight teams to monitor data management and ensure adherence to these policies is also important for maintaining data integrity and security.

7. DOCUMENTATION AND USER INTERFACE

Proper documentation of AI processes and decisions is essential for transparency and accountability. Organizations should maintain detailed records of AI system development, decision-making processes, and data handling practices. Additionally, providing users with an intuitive and user-friendly interface for interacting with AI systems helps ensure that AI technologies are accessible and understandable.

8.   **ONGOING MONITORING AND ADAPTATION**

The field of AI is rapidly evolving, necessitating continuous monitoring and adaptation of AI governance frameworks. Organizations should regularly review and update their frameworks to address new challenges, incorporate emerging best practices, and stay compliant with evolving regulations. This proactive approach ensures that AI systems remain effective, ethical, and secure over time.

ADDRESSING RISKS POSED BY AI

As AI technologies advance and integrate deeper into various aspects of society, understanding and mitigating the associated risks becomes crucial. The very properties that make AI systems powerful also introduce vulnerabilities that must be carefully managed.

POTENTIAL RISKS

AI systems, if not developed and deployed cautiously, can present several significant risks:

◈   **Unauthorized Surveillance**: AI's capability to analyze vast amounts of data can lead to extensive surveillance of individuals and societies without consent, infringing on privacy rights.

◈   **Data Breaches**: AI systems often handle sensitive personal data, and any breach can lead to severe privacy violations and identity theft.

◈   **Bias and Discrimination**: AI algorithms can reflect and amplify existing cultural biases and prejudices, leading to unfair and discriminatory outcomes in critical areas such as employment, finance, and legal decisions.

◈   **Behavioral Profiling**: AI's ability to create detailed profiles based on behavior can result in intrusive and manipulative practices, impacting individuals' autonomy and privacy.

GLOBAL RESPONSE TO AI RISKS

The risks posed by AI have prompted global action. In March 2023, a notable event saw 30,000 individuals, including leading technologists and business leaders, sign a letter urging governments and regulators to intervene unless AI developers agreed to a voluntary six-month pause or slowdown in AI development.

This unprecedented move reflects growing concerns over AI's rapid, unregulated growth and its potential consequences.

IMPORTANCE OF UNDERSTANDING AI REGULATIONS

With the proliferation of AI technologies, regulators worldwide are moving quickly to develop controls ensuring these systems are used responsibly. Understanding AI regulation is crucial for several reasons:

1. ### ETHICAL AND MORAL CONSIDERATIONS

   Regulations ensure that AI systems make decisions in compliance with ethical and moral standards. AI technologies can significantly impact individuals' lives, and regulations help safeguard against unethical practices and harmful outcomes. By adhering to ethical guidelines, organizations can promote fairness, justice, and respect for individual rights.

2. ### SAFETY AND ACCOUNTABILITY

   AI regulations establish safety standards for AI systems and hold developers and users accountable for any harm caused by AI actions. This accountability framework helps prevent accidents, misuse, and unintended consequences. It ensures that AI technologies are developed and deployed with a focus on human safety and well-being.

3. **DATA PRIVACY**

AI systems rely on large volumes of data, making data privacy a critical concern. Regulations such as the GDPR safeguard individuals' privacy by setting rules for data collection, storage, and usage. Compliance with these regulations ensures that personal information is protected and that individuals have control over their data.

4. **FAIRNESS AND BIAS**

Regulations addressing bias and discrimination in AI algorithms ensure that AI systems serve everyone equally and without prejudice. By mandating fairness, these regulations help prevent discriminatory outcomes and promote inclusive AI technologies that benefit all segments of society.

5. **TRANSPARENCY**

Transparency regulations require organizations to make the workings of AI systems open and accessible. This transparency allows users to understand how AI systems function and make informed decisions. It fosters an environment of trust and openness, essential for public acceptance of AI technologies.

6. **INNOVATION AND COMPETITION**

Clear and well-defined regulations can create an encouraging environment for AI innovation. By prohibiting monopolistic and unethical business practices, regulations promote healthy competition and drive technological advancements within ethical boundaries.

7. **INTERNATIONAL COLLABORATION**

Since AI is a global technology, international collaboration is vital for harmonizing AI governance approaches. Understanding and complying with AI regulations can facilitate cooperation between countries, ensuring consistency in addressing AI-related challenges worldwide.

8. CONSUMER TRUST

Regulations enhance public confidence in AI technologies by ensuring they are developed and used responsibly. Increased trust leads to wider acceptance and adoption of AI systems by individuals and organizations, driving further innovation and development.

9. CYBERSECURITY

AI regulations can establish guidelines to protect AI systems from malicious attacks and vulnerabilities. Ensuring the security of AI technologies is crucial for maintaining their integrity and functionality in various applications.

10. LEGAL AND LIABILITY FRAMEWORK

Regulations provide a clear legal framework for resolving disputes related to AI systems. By defining obligations and liabilities, they help organizations navigate legal challenges and mitigate risks associated with AI deployment.

11. PENALTIES FOR NON-COMPLIANCE

Non-compliance with data privacy laws and AI regulations can result in severe consequences, including legal action, hefty fines, reputational damage, and operational disruptions. Examples of penalties for non-compliance include:

- **Clearview AI**: Fined nearly $8 million by the UK and $21 million by Italy for data protection violations.
- **Replika AI**: Banned by Italian authorities with a warning of significant fines for non-compliance.
- **ChatGPT**: OpenAI fined by South Korea for data breaches.

The regulatory landscape for AI is rapidly evolving, creating a complex compliance environment. Organizations must prioritize understanding and adhering to AI regulations to navigate this dynamic landscape effectively.

DEVELOPING A UNIFIED DATA AND AI GOVERNANCE FRAMEWORK

Creating a unified data and AI governance framework is essential for aligning data management with AI development, ensuring ethical practices, and maintaining regulatory compliance. This section outlines key elements and actionable steps to develop such a framework.

1. INTERDEPENDENCE OF DATA AND AI

The quality, accuracy, and fairness of AI systems heavily depend on the data used. Ensuring that data is properly managed and aligned with AI objectives is crucial for developing reliable and ethical AI systems. Organizations must establish standards for data collection, processing, and usage to maintain the integrity of AI technologies.

2. CONSISTENCY IN STANDARDS AND PRACTICES

Maintaining uniform standards and practices for data management and AI development is vital for a cohesive governance framework. Organizations should develop and enforce consistent policies and procedures to ensure that all AI projects adhere to the same ethical, legal, and operational standards.

This consistency helps in minimizing risks and enhancing the reliability of AI systems.

3. COMPREHENSIVE RISK MANAGEMENT

Identifying and mitigating a broad range of risks, especially those overlapping data privacy, security, and AI ethics, is critical. Organizations should implement comprehensive risk management strategies, including regular assessments and scenario planning, to address potential vulnerabilities and ensure the safe deployment of AI technologies.

4. REGULATORY ALIGNMENT

Ensuring compliance with major regulations, such as the General Data Protection Regulation (GDPR) and the AI Act, is essential for avoiding legal penalties and maintaining ethical standards. Organizations should stay updated on regulatory developments and integrate these requirements into their AI governance framework to ensure continuous compliance.

5. EFFICIENT RESOURCE UTILIZATION

Developing a unified governance framework can lead to cost savings and improved operational efficiency. By streamlining data and AI governance processes, organizations can optimize resource allocation, reduce redundancy, and enhance overall productivity. This efficiency is particularly beneficial for companies looking to scale their AI initiatives.

6. ENHANCED INNOVATION

Promoting an environment conducive to innovation within ethical boundaries is a key aspect of a unified governance framework. By fostering a culture of experimentation and responsible AI development, organizations can drive technological advancements while ensuring that innovation aligns with societal values and ethical standards.

7.   BUILDING PUBLIC TRUST

Transparency, fairness, and accountability are essential for building public trust in AI systems. A unified governance framework should emphasize these principles, ensuring that AI technologies are developed and deployed in a manner that earns and maintains public confidence. Trust is a crucial factor in the widespread adoption and acceptance of AI.

8.   GLOBAL STANDARDIZATION

Facilitating international cooperation and standardization is important for harmonizing data and AI governance approaches. Organizations should participate in global forums and collaborate with international partners to share best practices and address common challenges.

This global perspective helps in establishing consistent and effective governance standards.

9.   ADAPTABILITY TO RAPID CHANGES

For long-term resilience, governance efforts must be adaptable to technological advancements and changing regulatory landscapes. Organizations should build flexibility into their governance frameworks, allowing them to quickly respond to new developments and ensure that their AI systems remain ethical and compliant over time.

CASE STUDIES OF AI GOVERNANCE FRAMEWORKS

Examining real-world implementations of AI governance frameworks provides valuable insights into best practices and practical challenges. Here are a few notable examples:

1.   AI GOVERNANCE FRAMEWORK NIST

The National Institute of Standards and Technology (NIST) has developed a comprehensive AI governance framework that emphasizes risk management and trustworthiness. This framework provides guidelines for ensuring that AI systems are transparent, accountable, and robust.

NIST's approach includes detailed protocols for risk assessment, bias mitigation, and data privacy, making it a valuable reference for organizations aiming to develop reliable AI systems.

2.   AIGA AI GOVERNANCE FRAMEWORK

The AIGA (American Institute of Graphic Arts) AI Governance Framework is designed specifically for the design and creative industries. This framework addresses ethical considerations unique to these fields, such as the impact of AI on creative processes and intellectual property rights.

By focusing on transparency, inclusivity, and fairness, the AIGA framework helps ensure that AI technologies enhance rather than undermine creative work.

3.   AI GOVERNANCE FRAMEWORK MCKINSEY

McKinsey & Company's AI governance framework highlights the importance of transparency, accountability, and continuous monitoring. McKinsey's framework is particularly notable for its emphasis on integrating AI governance into the broader business strategy.

By aligning AI initiatives with organizational goals and ensuring robust oversight, McKinsey's approach helps companies maximize the benefits of AI while mitigating risks. This framework also stresses the need for ongoing education and adaptation to evolving technological and regulatory landscapes.

4. AI GOVERNANCE FRAMEWORK MICROSOFT

Microsoft's AI governance framework is built around principles such as fairness, inclusiveness, reliability, and security. Microsoft has developed extensive internal policies and tools to ensure these principles are upheld in its AI projects.

The company's approach includes rigorous testing for bias, extensive stakeholder engagement, and transparent reporting on AI system performance. Microsoft also places a strong emphasis on compliance with global regulations and ethical standards, making its framework a leading example in the tech industry.

5. AI GOVERNANCE FOR COMPANIES

Many companies are adopting AI governance frameworks tailored to their specific needs and industry requirements. For instance, financial institutions might focus heavily on data privacy and security due to the sensitive nature of financial data, while healthcare organizations prioritize patient safety and ethical considerations in medical AI applications.

By customizing governance frameworks, companies can address their unique challenges and regulatory requirements effectively.

QUESTIONS PEOPLE HAVE ASKED ABOUT ACCOUNTABILITY IN AI

1. WHAT ARE THE ETHICAL CONCERNS IN AI DEVELOPMENT AND DEPLOYMENT?

Ethical concerns in AI development and deployment include:

- **Bias and Fairness:** Ensuring that AI systems do not perpetuate or amplify existing biases.

- **Privacy:** Protecting individuals' data and ensuring that personal information is not misused.

- **Transparency and Accountability:** Making AI decision-making processes understandable and establishing clear lines of accountability for AI decisions.

- **Security:** Ensuring that AI systems are secure from cyber threats and malicious use.

- **Autonomy:** Ensuring that AI respects human autonomy and does not make decisions that override human will without consent.

2. WHAT ARE THE ETHICAL CHALLENGES OF AI?

The ethical challenges of AI include:

- **Bias and Discrimination:** AI systems can inadvertently reinforce societal biases, leading to unfair outcomes.

- **Privacy Violations:** AI systems often require large amounts of personal data, raising concerns about data protection and privacy.

- **Lack of Transparency:** Many AI systems operate as "black boxes," making it difficult to understand how decisions are made.

- **Accountability:** Determining who is responsible for the actions and decisions made by autonomous AI systems.

💡 **Job Displacement:** The automation of jobs by AI can lead to significant economic and social disruptions.

3. WHAT IS ALGORITHM BIAS AND FAIRNESS?

Algorithm bias refers to systematic errors in AI systems that lead to unfair or discriminatory outcomes. This bias can stem from various sources, including biased training data, flawed algorithm design, and human biases. It results in certain groups or individuals being disadvantaged by AI decisions.

Fairness in AI involves ensuring that AI systems operate without prejudice, providing equitable treatment and outcomes for all individuals and groups. Fairness aims to correct algorithmic biases, ensuring that AI decisions do not favor or disadvantage people based on characteristics such as gender, race, or ethnicity.

4. HOW ARE AI ALGORITHMS BIASED?

AI algorithms can be biased due to several factors:

💡 **Biased Training Data:** If the data used to train the AI contains biases, the AI will learn and perpetuate these biases.

💡 **Algorithm Design:** Flaws in the algorithm's design can lead to biased decision-making processes.

💡 **Human Biases:** The biases of the people who design and train AI systems can influence the algorithms.

💡 **Measurement Bias:** Inaccurate or incomplete data collection processes can lead to biased outcomes.

💡 **Historical Bias:** Existing societal biases and historical injustices can be reflected in the training data, leading to biased AI models.

5. WHAT IS AN ETHICAL FRAMEWORK OF ARTIFICIAL INTELLIGENCE?

An ethical framework of artificial intelligence (AI) is a structured set of principles and guidelines designed to ensure that AI technologies are developed, deployed, and utilized in a manner that aligns with ethical standards and societal values. This framework encompasses several key principles, including fairness, transparency, accountability, privacy, and inclusivity. It aims to mitigate risks such as bias, discrimination, and privacy violations, promoting the responsible and ethical use of AI. By adhering to these principles, organizations can build trust, enhance public confidence, and ensure that AI systems contribute positively to society.

6. WHAT IS ACCOUNTABILITY IN MACHINE LEARNING?

Accountability in machine learning refers to the mechanisms and structures put in place to ensure that all stakeholders involved in the development, deployment, and use of machine learning systems are held responsible for their actions and decisions. This includes:

- **Developers** who create and train the machine learning models, ensuring they adhere to ethical standards and best practices.

- **Data providers** who supply the data used to train these models, ensuring the data is accurate, unbiased, and ethically sourced.

- **End users** who apply the machine learning models in various contexts, ensuring they understand the limitations and potential risks of the models.

- **Organizations** that deploy machine learning systems, ensuring they have robust policies and oversight mechanisms in place to manage these technologies responsibly.

Accountability involves tracking and documenting the decisions made throughout the lifecycle of a machine learning system, from design and development to deployment and ongoing monitoring.

7. WHAT ARE TWO WAYS THAT ACCOUNTABILITY CONTRIBUTES TO ETHICAL DECISION-MAKING IN GENERATIVE AI?

i. **Bias Mitigation**: Accountability ensures that the developers and users of generative AI systems are responsible for identifying and addressing biases in AI models. By holding stakeholders accountable, organizations are encouraged to implement rigorous testing and validation processes to detect and mitigate biases, ensuring that the AI generates fair and unbiased outcomes. This leads to more ethical decision-making as it prevents discriminatory or unfair practices that could arise from biased AI systems.

ii. **Transparency and Explainability**: Accountability promotes the development and use of transparent and explainable AI systems. When stakeholders know they will be held responsible for the decisions made by AI, they are more likely to prioritize transparency and ensure that the AI's decision-making processes are understandable. This allows users and other stakeholders to scrutinize and understand the AI's actions, facilitating more informed and ethical decision-making. Transparent AI systems enable stakeholders to identify potential ethical issues and address them proactively.

8. HOW DO YOU CREATE AN ETHICAL AI?

Creating an ethical AI involves several steps:

i. **Establish Ethical Guidelines**: Define clear principles and values that AI systems should adhere to, including fairness, transparency, accountability, and privacy.

ii. **Ensure Data Security**: Implement robust measures to protect data privacy and security, ensuring that data is collected, stored, and processed responsibly.

iii. **Promote Transparency**: Make AI processes and decision-making criteria open and understandable to users and stakeholders.

iv. **Demonstrate Accountability**: Establish mechanisms for taking responsibility for AI actions, including addressing biases, correcting errors, and mitigating unintended consequences.

v. **Mitigate Bias and Discrimination**: Implement strategies to identify and eliminate biases in AI algorithms to ensure equitable outcomes.

vi. **Comply with Regulations**: Ensure that AI systems adhere to relevant legal standards and regulations to avoid legal penalties and maintain ethical practices.

vii. **Continuous Monitoring and Assessment**: Regularly evaluate AI systems to ensure they operate ethically and effectively, making necessary adjustments as technology and regulations evolve.

9. WHAT IS THE GOVERNANCE FRAMEWORK FOR AI?

A governance framework for AI is a comprehensive set of regulations, policies, standards, and best practices that guide the ethical development, deployment, and use of AI technologies. This framework aims to address various risks associated with AI, such as privacy violations, biased decision-making, and potential misuse. Key components of an AI governance framework include:

i. **Ethical Guidelines**: Principles that define ethical standards for AI systems.

ii. **Data Security**: Measures to protect data privacy and security.

iii. **Transparency**: Ensuring AI processes and decisions are open and understandable.

iv. **Accountability**: Establishing clear responsibility for AI actions.

v. **Bias Mitigation**: Strategies to identify and eliminate biases in AI systems.

vi. **Regulatory Compliance**: Adherence to relevant legal standards and regulations.

vii. **Monitoring and Assessment**: Continuous evaluation of AI systems to ensure they remain ethical and effective.

10. HOW TO SET UP AI GOVERNANCE?

Setting up AI governance involves the following steps:

i. **Assess Organizational Needs**: Understand the specific applications of AI within the organization, identify potential risks, and determine the ethical and legal standards that need to be met.

ii. **Develop Ethical Guidelines**: Define clear principles and values for AI systems, including fairness, transparency, accountability, and privacy.

iii. **Implement Data Security Measures**: Establish robust data management practices to protect privacy and ensure data security.

iv. **Promote Transparency**: Ensure that AI processes, decision-making criteria, and data handling practices are open and understandable to users and stakeholders.

v. **Establish Accountability Mechanisms**: Define roles and responsibilities for AI governance, ensuring there are designated individuals or teams accountable for monitoring AI systems and addressing issues.

vi. **Ensure Compliance with Regulations**: Stay informed about relevant laws and regulations and integrate these requirements into the AI governance framework.

vii. **Continuous Monitoring and Adaptation**: Regularly review and update the governance framework to address new challenges, incorporate emerging best practices, and stay compliant with evolving regulations.

viii. **Educate and Train**: Launch educational initiatives to improve understanding of AI ethics and governance among internal and external stakeholders.

CHAPTER EIGHT
Building a Secure AI Infrastructure

The complexity and power of AI models often result in their use in handling sensitive data and making critical decisions. This elevates the importance of constructing a robust and secure AI infrastructure capable of withstanding both internal and external threats (Brundage et al., 2018).

Inadequate security measures not only expose AI systems to potential breaches but also undermine the trustworthiness of the insights and decisions generated by these systems. Consequently, ensuring the security of AI development environments is not merely a technical necessity; it is a foundational requirement for safeguarding the integrity and reliability of AI-driven operations (Amodei et al., 2016).

THE IMPERATIVE OF SECURITY IN AI DEVELOPMENT

Historically, AI development has primarily focused on enhancing model performance and accuracy. While these aspects remain crucial, the security of AI models must now be regarded as equally important. Several high-profile incidents involving AI models have revealed the vulnerabilities and risks associated with insufficient security measures (Goodfellow, Shlens, & Szegedy, 2015).

These incidents underscore the urgent need for businesses to adopt secure development practices to protect their AI models and the data they process.

For example, there have been cases where AI models were manipulated to produce misleading outputs, leading to erroneous decision-making. Unauthorized access to sensitive data used in training these models has resulted in significant privacy breaches and financial losses (Tramèr et al., 2016). These events highlight that focusing solely on performance, without integrating robust security measures, can have severe consequences.

As AI adoption continues to expand, so do the risks associated with security breaches in AI models. Unauthorized access to confidential information or malicious manipulation of model outputs can result in severe consequences, including privacy violations, financial loss, reputational damage, and legal repercussions (Papernot et al., 2016).

Therefore, it is imperative that organizations implement comprehensive security protocols and safeguards throughout the AI development lifecycle to effectively mitigate these risks.

By prioritizing security from the outset, organizations can ensure that their AI models deliver value while minimizing the risks associated with unauthorized access and breaches.

The following sections will delve into the importance of secure AI model development, common security threats, and best practices for building and deploying AI models in secure environments. (Dlamini, Z. S. 2016).

IMPORTANCE OF AI MODEL SECURITY

1. PROTECTING SENSITIVE DATA

AI models often require vast amounts of data for training, which can include Personally Identifiable Information (PII), financial records, medical data, and proprietary business information. This data is crucial for developing accurate and effective models but also poses significant risks if not adequately protected. Unauthorized access to sensitive data can lead to privacy breaches, financial loss, and legal consequences.

A secure AI development environment ensures that this data is adequately protected from unauthorized access, breaches, and misuse. Encryption, access controls, and secure data storage are essential measures that can help protect sensitive information during the training and deployment of AI models. By safeguarding sensitive data, organizations can prevent potential data breaches and maintain the trust of their stakeholders.

2. PREVENTING DATA TAMPERING

The performance of an AI model heavily relies on the integrity of the training data. If the training environment is not secure, malicious actors may manipulate or tamper with the data, leading to biased models or compromised results. Such tampering can undermine the reliability and fairness of the AI models, resulting in erroneous or harmful outputs.

Securing the development environment helps maintain the integrity of the data used for training, ensuring that the AI models produce accurate and unbiased results. Implementing robust data validation, anomaly detection, and monitoring mechanisms can help detect and prevent data tampering, thereby enhancing the reliability of AI models.

3. SAFEGUARDING INTELLECTUAL PROPERTY

Developing AI models often involves substantial investments of time, effort, and resources. The algorithms, training methodologies, and model architectures constitute valuable intellectual property (IP) that needs protection from unauthorized access, replication, or theft. A secure environment helps protect this IP, ensuring that organizations retain control over their proprietary AI assets.

By implementing strong access controls, encryption, and secure deployment practices, organizations can safeguard their intellectual property from competitors and malicious actors. Protecting AI-related IP not only preserves the competitive advantage of the organization but also encourages further innovation and development in AI technologies.

4. MITIGATING ADVERSARIAL ATTACKS

AI models are vulnerable to adversarial attacks, where malicious actors intentionally manipulate input data to deceive or exploit the model. These attacks can lead to incorrect predictions, misclassifications, or misleading outputs, potentially causing harm or critical decision-making errors.

To mitigate the risk of adversarial attacks, organizations must deploy AI models in secure environments and implement robust defenses. Techniques such as adversarial training, input validation, anomaly detection, and continuous model monitoring can help reduce the risk of exploitation and manipulation. By proactively defending against adversarial attacks, organizations can ensure the robustness and reliability of their AI models.

5. ENSURING REGULATORY COMPLIANCE

Various regulations, such as the General Data Protection Regulation (GDPR), Health Insurance Portability and Accountability Act (HIPAA), and Payment Card Industry Data Security Standard (PCI-DSS), impose strict requirements on the handling and protection of sensitive data. Non-compliance with these regulations can result in severe legal and financial consequences for organizations.

A secure AI development environment helps organizations comply with these regulations by implementing necessary security measures and safeguards. This includes data encryption, access controls, secure data storage, and regular security audits. Ensuring regulatory compliance not only protects organizations from legal and financial penalties but also builds trust among customers and stakeholders.

6. MAINTAINING TRUST AND REPUTATION

Security breaches involving AI models can have severe consequences, eroding trust in the organization and damaging its reputation. Publicized incidents of data breaches or model manipulation can lead to loss of customer trust, negative publicity, and a decline in market position.

By prioritizing security throughout the entire lifecycle of AI models, organizations demonstrate their commitment to protecting data privacy, preventing misuse, and ensuring the reliability and fairness of their AI applications.

This proactive approach helps build and maintain trust among users, customers, and stakeholders, ultimately supporting the long-term success and sustainability of the organization.

COMMON SECURITY THREATS AND VULNERABILITIES IN AI MODELS

1. ADVERSARIAL ATTACKS

Adversarial attacks pose a significant threat to AI model security. These attacks involve manipulating input data in a way that deceives the AI model, leading to incorrect predictions or decisions. Adversarial examples, which are slightly altered inputs, can cause models to make errors that are often imperceptible to humans.

These attacks can occur across various domains, including image recognition, natural language processing (NLP), and voice recognition systems.

To defend against adversarial attacks, organizations can implement techniques such as adversarial training, which involves augmenting the training data with adversarial examples to enhance the model's robustness. Additionally, employing input validation, anomaly detection, and regular monitoring of model performance are crucial steps in mitigating these risks.

2. MODEL INVERSION ATTACKS

Model inversion attacks focus on extracting sensitive information from AI models. Unlike adversarial attacks that manipulate input data, model inversion attacks aim to infer details about the input data used during training by analyzing the model's outputs. For example, attackers could reconstruct images of individuals or reveal sensitive patterns in transaction data.

To protect against model inversion attacks, developers should adopt privacy-preserving techniques such as differential privacy, which adds controlled noise to the training process to prevent the extraction of sensitive information. Additionally, data anonymization and de-identification methods can help safeguard individual privacy.

3. MEMBERSHIP INFERENCE ATTACKS

Membership inference attacks aim to determine whether a specific data point was used in the training set of a machine learning model. These attacks exploit the model's responses to infer the membership status of particular data instances, potentially breaching the privacy of sensitive information.

Mitigating membership inference attacks involves adopting privacy-preserving techniques like differential privacy or federated learning, which distribute the training process across multiple parties to obscure individual data points.

Regularization techniques, such as dropout or weight decay, can also help reduce the model's tendency to memorize individual data points, making it more challenging for attackers to perform successful membership inference attacks.

4. DATA POISONING

Data poisoning involves injecting misleading or manipulated data into the training process to compromise the integrity and reliability of AI models. Malicious actors can subtly alter a portion of the training data to influence the model's behavior, leading to incorrect or biased outcomes.

Preventing data poisoning requires ensuring the integrity and security of the data collection process. Implementing robust data validation and anomaly detection techniques can help identify and filter out potentially poisoned data before it enters the training pipeline.

Regular data monitoring and auditing are also essential to detect any sudden changes in data distribution indicative of a poisoning attack.

5. MODEL EXTRACTION ATTACKS

Model extraction attacks, also known as model stealing or model copying, involve replicating the underlying knowledge and parameters of a trained AI model by an unauthorized party. Attackers use input-output pairs or detailed knowledge of the model's architecture to build a surrogate model approximating the target model's behavior.

Defending against model extraction attacks requires implementing access control mechanisms, encryption, and obfuscation techniques to protect sensitive information and prevent unauthorized access.

Secure deployment environments, such as trusted execution environments or hardware-based security solutions, provide additional layers of protection. Monitoring and anomaly detection systems can help identify suspicious activities indicative of a potential model extraction attempt. (Mishra, P., & Singh, G. 2023).

6. EVASION OF INPUT VALIDATION

Evasion of input validation refers to the manipulation of input data to bypass security checks and cause unauthorized actions, data leaks, or system compromises. Adversaries craft inputs that exploit vulnerabilities in the model's validation logic to achieve their malicious objectives.

To mitigate this risk, organizations must employ robust input validation techniques, strict data sanitization routines, and secure coding practices.

Regular updates and patches to the validation logic are also essential to address emerging vulnerabilities. Implementing anomaly detection mechanisms can help identify suspicious input patterns indicative of evasion attempts.

7. INSECURE MODEL DEPLOYMENT

Insecure model deployment encompasses a range of factors, including weak authentication, insufficient encryption, lack of monitoring, and outdated software. These vulnerabilities can expose AI models to unauthorized access, data breaches, and malicious tampering.

Secure deployment practices include implementing strong authentication mechanisms, encryption, and comprehensive monitoring of deployment activities. Regular updates and patches, secure network communication, and maintaining a secure system architecture are also critical to protecting deployed AI models.

8. LACK OF MODEL INTERPRETABILITY

Model interpretability refers to the ability to understand and explain how an AI model arrives at its predictions or decisions. Lack of interpretability can hinder the detection and mitigation of security threats, as well as complicate regulatory compliance and ethical considerations.

Enhancing model interpretability involves using simpler models, generating rule-based explanations, analyzing feature importance, and employing local explanation techniques like LIME (Local Interpretable Model-agnostic Explanations) or SHAP (Shapley Additive exPlanations).

Post-hoc explanation methods and leveraging inherently interpretable models can also improve interpretability.

9. INSIDER THREATS

Insider threats arise from individuals within an organization who intentionally or unintentionally misuse or abuse their access to sensitive data, systems, or resources. These threats can lead to intellectual property theft, data breaches, model manipulation, and disruption of operations.

Mitigating insider threats involves implementing robust access controls, monitoring, and logging of activities, and fostering a culture of security awareness. Regular security assessments, penetration testing, and employee training programs are crucial in addressing and preventing insider threats.

BEST PRACTICES FOR SECURING AI DEVELOPMENT ENVIRONMENTS

1. ROBUST SECURITY PROTOCOLS

To secure AI development environments effectively, organizations must implement robust security protocols. These protocols should encompass access controls, authentication mechanisms, encryption, and secure data storage practices.

By establishing strong access controls, organizations can ensure that only authorized personnel have access to sensitive data and AI models. Multi-factor authentication (MFA) can further enhance security by requiring multiple forms of verification before granting access.

Encryption plays a critical role in protecting data both at rest and in transit. Encrypting data ensures that even if it is intercepted or accessed without authorization, it remains unreadable and unusable.

Secure data storage practices, such as using encrypted databases and secure cloud storage solutions, help safeguard sensitive information from potential breaches.

2. REGULAR SECURITY AUDITS AND MONITORING

Continuous monitoring and regular security audits are essential components of a secure AI development environment. Security audits involve systematically reviewing and assessing the security measures in place, identifying vulnerabilities, and addressing any weaknesses.

These audits should be conducted regularly to ensure ongoing compliance with security standards and to adapt to evolving threats.

Monitoring tools and techniques can help detect unusual behavior or anomalies in real-time. By continuously monitoring the development environment, organizations can quickly identify and respond to potential security incidents. This proactive approach minimizes the impact of security breaches and ensures the integrity of AI models and data.

3. SECURE CODING PRACTICES

Secure coding practices are fundamental to preventing vulnerabilities in AI models. Developers should adhere to industry best practices for secure coding, such as validating inputs, sanitizing outputs, and implementing proper error handling. These practices help mitigate the risk of code injection, data leaks, and other security threats.

Training developers on secure coding standards is crucial to ensure they understand the importance of security in AI development. Regular code reviews and security testing can help identify and address potential vulnerabilities before they become exploitable weaknesses. By embedding security into the development process, organizations can build more resilient and secure AI models.

4.   COMPLIANCE WITH REGULATIONS AND STANDARDS

Compliance with relevant regulations and standards is critical to ensuring the security and ethical use of AI models. Regulations such as the General Data Protection Regulation (GDPR) and the Health Insurance Portability and Accountability Act (HIPAA) impose strict requirements on the handling and protection of sensitive data. (Albasheir, K. A. M. A. 2023).

Organizations must implement necessary security measures to comply with these regulations and avoid legal and financial consequences.

To achieve compliance, organizations should conduct regular audits and assessments to verify that their security practices align with regulatory requirements. This includes implementing data protection measures, maintaining documentation of security practices, and conducting regular training for employees on data privacy and security.

5.   TRAINING AND EDUCATING AI MODEL DEVELOPERS

Training and educating AI model developers on security best practices is essential for creating a secure development environment. Developers need to be aware of the potential risks and vulnerabilities associated with AI models and understand how to implement security measures effectively.

Security awareness training should cover topics such as secure data handling, secure coding practices, and the importance of continuous monitoring and auditing.

By equipping developers with the knowledge and skills necessary to address security challenges, organizations can reduce the likelihood of security incidents and ensure the integrity of their AI models.

6. COLLABORATION WITH SECURITY EXPERTS

Collaboration between AI model developers and security experts is crucial for enhancing the security posture of AI development environments. Security experts can provide valuable insights into the latest security practices, threat landscapes, and mitigation strategies.

By working closely with security professionals, developers can identify potential vulnerabilities, conduct thorough security testing, and implement robust security measures.

Organizations should foster a collaborative environment where developers and security experts can share knowledge and expertise. Regular communication and collaboration can help address security challenges more effectively and ensure that security is integrated into every stage of the AI development lifecycle.

CASE STUDIES AND EXAMPLES

Examining high-profile security incidents involving AI models can provide valuable insights into the importance of secure AI development environments. These case studies highlight the vulnerabilities that can be exploited and the severe consequences that can result from inadequate security measures.

CASE STUDY 1:

Amazon Alexa Data Leak In 2018, a security flaw in Amazon's Alexa allowed hackers to access users' voice history, exposing sensitive personal conversations. This incident underscored the importance of securing AI systems that handle personal data and the need for robust access controls and encryption to prevent unauthorized access.

CASE STUDY 2:

Microsoft Tay Chatbot Microsoft's AI chatbot, Tay, was designed to interact with users on Twitter and learn from these interactions. However, within 24 hours of its launch in 2016, Tay was manipulated by users to post offensive and inappropriate content.

This incident highlighted the risks associated with adversarial attacks and the importance of implementing safeguards to prevent AI models from being exploited by malicious actors.

CASE STUDY 3:

Tesla's Autopilot System Tesla's Autopilot system has faced multiple incidents where adversarial attacks were used to manipulate the AI's perception. For instance, small changes to road signs or lane markings caused the system to misinterpret the driving environment, leading to safety hazards.

These incidents emphasized the need for rigorous testing and validation of AI models in real-world scenarios to ensure their robustness and safety.

SUCCESSFUL IMPLEMENTATION OF SECURE AI DEVELOPMENT PRACTICES

Organizations that have successfully implemented secure AI development practices serve as examples of how to effectively protect AI models and data. These success stories demonstrate the positive impact of prioritizing security and the measures that can be taken to achieve it.

EXAMPLE 1:

Google's AI Principles Google has established a set of AI principles that guide the ethical and secure development of AI technologies. These principles include commitments to privacy, security, and transparency. Google employs rigorous security measures, regular audits, and continuous monitoring to protect its AI models and data.

By adhering to these principles, Google has built trust with users and stakeholders while advancing AI technology responsibly.

EXAMPLE 2:

IBM Watson Health IBM Watson Health uses AI to analyze vast amounts of medical data and assist in healthcare decision-making. To ensure the security and privacy of sensitive health information, IBM Watson Health implements robust encryption, access controls, and compliance with healthcare regulations such as HIPAA. (Gupta, S., Alharbi, F., Alharbi, F., Alshahrani, R., Arya, P., Vyas, S., & Elkamchouchi, D. 2023).

These measures help protect patient data and maintain the integrity of the AI models used in critical healthcare applications.

EXAMPLE 3:

NVIDIA's AI Model Security NVIDIA, a leader in AI hardware and software, has implemented comprehensive security measures to protect its AI models. This includes secure coding practices, regular security audits, and collaboration with security experts.

NVIDIA also provides security training for developers and incorporates privacy-preserving techniques into its AI models. These efforts ensure the security and reliability of NVIDIA's AI technologies, fostering trust among users and partners.

PROTECTING AI MODELS AND DATA

Artificial Intelligence (AI) has become an integral part of modern technology, driving advancements across various sectors such as healthcare, finance, transportation, and more. AI's ability to analyze vast amounts of data and make intelligent decisions has revolutionized industries and improved efficiencies.

According to Bloomberg Intelligence, the AI market is projected to grow to $1.3 trillion over the next decade, highlighting its significant economic impact.

However, as AI continues to evolve and integrate deeper into our technology stack, it faces increasingly sophisticated security threats. These threats, which once targeted software and applications, have now extended to operating systems, middleware, firmware, and even hardware. With the advent of AI tools and technologies, protecting data and models has become critically important for organizations, corporations, and society at large.

Today, organizations leverage AI to analyze and utilize massive quantities of data. Despite its benefits, this widespread adoption has raised significant security concerns. For instance, Forrester Research indicates that 86% of organizations are extremely concerned or concerned about their AI model security.

This concern is not unfounded, given the broad range of malicious attacks directed at AI models, including training-data poisoning, AI model theft, and adversarial sampling.

The necessity of safeguarding AI models and data is underscored by the increasing number of regulatory measures being introduced globally. Governments are issuing new regulations such as the European Union's AI Act and the U.S. Executive Order on Safe, Secure Artificial Intelligence to ensure that AI deployments are secure, trustworthy, and private.

When combined with existing regulations like GDPR and HIPAA, the cybersecurity and privacy landscape becomes even more complex for enterprises to navigate.

Throughout their lifecycles, unmanaged, unmonitored, and unprotected AI models and their data training sets pose significant risks, including data theft and regulatory fines. These models often represent critical intellectual property, while the data is frequently sensitive, private, or regulated.

AI deployments involve a pipeline of activities from initial data acquisition to final results, making them vulnerable at every stage to adversarial actions that could manipulate the model's behavior or steal valuable IP. Poorly managed data practices could also lead to costly compliance violations or data breaches.

Given the critical need to protect AI models and their data while adhering to compliance requirements, the question arises: How can this be effectively achieved?

One available tool is Confidential AI, which involves deploying AI systems inside Trusted Execution Environments (TEE) to safeguard sensitive data and valuable AI models during active use. TEEs are designed to prevent unauthorized applications or users from accessing AI models and data, offering enhanced control and security.

This approach, combined with traditional encryption techniques and robust AI model management, forms the foundation of a comprehensive AI security strategy.

IMPLICATIONS OF AI MODEL ATTACKS

The consequences of successful attacks on AI models are far-reaching and can severely impact an organization's security, integrity, and operations:

1. **IMPACT ON ORGANIZATIONAL SECURITY AND INTEGRITY**

    Data Theft: Compromised AI models can lead to the theft of sensitive data, resulting in financial losses and reputational damage.

    Operational Disruption: Manipulated models can cause erroneous outputs, disrupting critical business processes and decision-making.

2. **RISKS TO SENSITIVE DATA AND INTELLECTUAL PROPERTY**

    Loss of Intellectual Property: Stolen AI models represent a significant loss of proprietary algorithms and innovations, undermining competitive advantages.

    Exposure of Sensitive Data: Attacks like model inversion and membership inference can reveal private data used in training, violating privacy regulations and eroding customer trust.

3. **REAL-WORLD CONSEQUENCES**

    Healthcare: In healthcare, compromised AI models can lead to incorrect diagnoses or treatment recommendations, endangering patient safety.

    Autonomous Vehicles: Adversarial attacks on AI systems in autonomous vehicles can result in accidents or traffic violations, posing public safety risks.

REGULATORY AND COMPLIANCE CHALLENGES

As AI technology continues to evolve, so does the regulatory landscape governing its use. Governments and regulatory bodies worldwide are introducing new regulations aimed at ensuring the security, privacy, and ethical use of AI systems.

Navigating this complex regulatory environment is essential for organizations deploying AI technologies. In this section, we will explore the key AI-related regulations and the challenges organizations face in complying with them.

NAVIGATING THE COMPLEX REGULATORY LANDSCAPE

1. CHALLENGES IN COMPLIANCE

- Multiple Regulations: Organizations often face the challenge of complying with multiple overlapping regulations, each with its own requirements and standards. This can create a complex and burdensome compliance environment.

- Evolving Standards: As AI technology evolves, so do the regulatory standards. Keeping up with these changes and adapting AI systems accordingly requires continuous monitoring and flexibility.

- Global Variability: Different regions have varying regulatory approaches to AI, adding another layer of complexity for multinational organizations that must comply with diverse legal frameworks.

2. STRATEGIES FOR ALIGNING AI DEPLOYMENT WITH REGULATORY REQUIREMENTS

- Comprehensive Risk Management: Implementing a robust risk management framework that addresses all stages of the AI lifecycle is crucial. This includes conducting regular risk assessments, monitoring AI model performance, and ensuring data quality and integrity.

- 💡 Transparency and Accountability: Ensuring transparency in AI operations and maintaining accountability for AI decisions are essential for regulatory compliance. Organizations should document AI development processes, maintain clear audit trails, and provide explanations for AI-driven decisions.

- 💡 Data Protection Measures: Implementing strong data protection measures, such as encryption, access controls, and data anonymization, helps safeguard sensitive data and ensures compliance with privacy regulations like GDPR and HIPAA. (Apata, O., Bokoro, P., & Sharma, G. 2023).

- 💡 Third-Party Audits and Certifications: Engaging third-party auditors to assess AI systems and obtain relevant certifications can enhance compliance efforts and build trust with regulators and customers.

BEST PRACTICES FOR PROTECTING AI MODELS AND DATA

Ensuring the security of AI models and data requires a multifaceted approach that encompasses advanced technologies, robust management practices, and adherence to regulatory requirements.

In this section, we will discuss best practices for protecting AI models and data, including the use of Confidential AI, encryption techniques, and robust AI model management.

CONFIDENTIAL AI AND TRUSTED EXECUTION ENVIRONMENTS (TEE)

1. CONFIDENTIAL AI

Confidential AI involves deploying AI systems within Trusted Execution Environments (TEEs) to protect sensitive data and AI models during active use.

TEEs ensure that AI models and data are not visible to unauthorized applications or users, providing a high level of security and control. This approach helps protect critical intellectual property and sensitive information from being compromised.

2. TRUSTED EXECUTION ENVIRONMENTS (TEE)

TEEs provide an isolated and secure environment for executing AI models and handling sensitive data. They use hardware-based security features to prevent unauthorized access and tampering.

They are particularly useful in scenarios where data privacy and security are paramount, such as in healthcare, finance, and collaborative AI projects.

ENCRYPTION TECHNIQUES

1. DATA ENCRYPTION AT REST AND IN TRANSIT

- Established Practices: Encrypting data at rest (stored data) and in transit (data being transferred) is a well-established practice for protecting sensitive information.

- Technologies Used: Common encryption technologies include AES (Advanced Encryption Standard) for data at rest and TLS (Transport Layer Security) for data in transit.

2. **PROTECTING DATA IN USE**

- Challenges: Traditionally, protecting data that is actively in use has been a significant challenge due to the need for data to be processed in its unencrypted form.

- Confidential Computing: Confidential Computing addresses this challenge by using hardware-based protections to secure data in use within the CPU, GPU, and memory. This approach ensures that data remains encrypted and protected even during processing.

3. **APPLICATIONS IN AI**

- AI Model Training: Confidential Computing can be used to secure the training of AI models, ensuring that training data remains confidential and protected from unauthorized access.

- AI Inference: During inference, Confidential Computing ensures that the input data and the AI model's outputs are protected, preventing exposure of sensitive information.

ROBUST AI MODEL MANAGEMENT

1. **LIFECYCLE MANAGEMENT**

- Importance: Effective management of AI models throughout their lifecycle is crucial for ensuring security and compliance. This includes the stages of data acquisition, model training, deployment, and ongoing monitoring.

- Practices: Organizations should implement comprehensive monitoring and management practices to detect and respond to security threats, maintain model accuracy, and ensure regulatory compliance.

2. ACCESS CONTROLS

💡 Definition: Access controls are mechanisms that restrict access to AI models and data to authorized users and applications.

💡 Implementation: Implementing robust access controls involves using techniques such as role-based access control (RBAC) and multi-factor authentication (MFA) to ensure that only authorized personnel can access sensitive AI resources.

3. MONITORING AND AUDITING

💡 Continuous Monitoring: Regular monitoring of AI models and their performance is essential for detecting anomalies and potential security breaches.

💡 Auditing: Conducting periodic audits of AI systems helps ensure that they comply with security policies and regulatory requirements. Audits can also identify areas for improvement in security practices.

4. INCIDENT RESPONSE

💡 Preparation: Developing and maintaining an incident response plan is critical for responding to security breaches involving AI models and data.

💡 Actions: The plan should outline the steps to take in the event of a security incident, including containment, investigation, remediation, and communication with stakeholders.

COLLABORATIVE AND FEDERATED LEARNING

Collaborative and federated learning are two advanced approaches that enable organizations to leverage AI technologies while maintaining high levels of data privacy and security.

These methods allow multiple parties to contribute to AI development without exposing sensitive data, addressing some of the key challenges associated with AI model security. In this section, we will explore the concepts of collaborative AI and federated learning, and how they can be implemented securely.

COLLABORATIVE AI

1. **CONCEPT OF COLLABORATIVE AI**
   - Definition: Collaborative AI involves multiple parties working together on AI projects by contributing their encrypted data sets. This collaborative approach enhances AI models by incorporating diverse data sources while preserving the privacy and security of the individual data sets.

   - Data Clean Rooms: Data Clean Rooms are secure environments that facilitate collaborative AI by allowing parties to share and analyze data without revealing the raw data to each other. These environments are protected by Trusted Execution Environments (TEEs) to ensure data privacy.

2. **SECURITY MEASURES IN COLLABORATIVE AI**
   - Encryption: Each party encrypts their data before sharing it within the Data Clean Room. This ensures that data remains protected and only accessible within the secure environment.

- Access Control: Implementing strict access controls within the Data Clean Room ensures that only authorized users can access the data and perform analyses.

- Data Anonymization: Anonymizing data before sharing can further enhance privacy, reducing the risk of exposing sensitive information.

3.   BENEFITS OF SECURE COLLABORATION

- Enhanced AI Models: By combining data from multiple sources, AI models can become more robust and accurate, benefiting from a wider range of inputs.

- Data Privacy: Secure collaboration ensures that the privacy of each party's data is maintained, reducing the risk of data breaches.

- Regulatory Compliance: Collaborative AI projects that prioritize data security can help organizations comply with data protection regulations such as GDPR and HIPAA.

FEDERATED LEARNING

1.   CONCEPT OF FEDERATED LEARNING

- Definition: Federated Learning is a decentralized approach where AI models are trained locally on data from different parties without the need to move the data off-premises. The local models are then aggregated to create a global model.

- Process: Each party trains a local model using their data. The local models' updates (e.g., model weights) are encrypted and sent to a central server where they are combined to form a global model.

2.   SECURITY BENEFITS OF FEDERATED LEARNING

- Data Localization: Since data does not need to be transferred to a central location, federated learning reduces the risk of data breaches during transit.

- Model Privacy: By only sharing model updates rather than raw data, federated learning protects the privacy of the training data.

- Enhanced Control: Organizations retain control over their data, ensuring compliance with data protection regulations and internal policies.

3. IMPLEMENTATION EXAMPLES

- Healthcare: Hospitals can use federated learning to collaborate on AI models for disease diagnosis without sharing sensitive patient data. Each hospital trains a local model, and the aggregated global model benefits from the diverse data sets.

- Financial Services: Banks can use federated learning to develop fraud detection models. Each bank trains a local model on their transaction data, and the combined model benefits from a broader understanding of fraudulent patterns.

4. CHALLENGES AND MITIGATION STRATEGIES

- Communication Overhead: Federated learning involves frequent communication of model updates, which can create network overhead. Using efficient communication protocols and optimizing update frequencies can mitigate this issue.

- Model Aggregation: Ensuring that the aggregated model effectively combines updates from diverse local models requires sophisticated algorithms. Advanced aggregation techniques can help maintain model performance and fairness.

AI SECURITY IN PRACTICE

Implementing AI security measures in real-world scenarios involves understanding the practical applications and utilizing the right tools and frameworks to protect AI models and data. In this section, we will explore several use cases, real-world applications, and the tools and frameworks available to ensure robust AI security.

USE CASES AND REAL-WORLD APPLICATIONS

1. HEALTHCARE

- AI-Driven Diagnostics: AI models are used to analyze medical images and assist in diagnosing diseases. Protecting these models and the sensitive patient data they use is crucial to ensure patient privacy and comply with regulations like HIPAA.

- Example: A hospital uses Trusted Execution Environments (TEEs) to secure AI models analyzing MRI scans, ensuring that patient data remains confidential during the diagnostic process.

2. FINANCE

- Fraud Detection: Financial institutions deploy AI models to detect fraudulent transactions. These models must be protected to prevent adversaries from reverse-engineering them and bypassing fraud detection mechanisms.

- Example: A bank uses Confidential Computing to protect AI models that analyze transaction data for fraud detection, ensuring that sensitive financial information is not exposed.

3. AUTONOMOUS VEHICLES

- Navigation Systems: AI models in autonomous vehicles interpret sensor data to navigate safely. Ensuring the integrity and security of these models is critical to prevent adversarial attacks that could compromise vehicle safety.

- Example: An autonomous vehicle manufacturer employs federated learning to train navigation models on locally collected data, protecting the data and enhancing the model's robustness.

4. RETAIL

- Personalized Recommendations: Retailers use AI models to analyze customer data and provide personalized product recommendations. Protecting these models helps safeguard customer privacy and prevents competitors from stealing proprietary algorithms.

- Example: An e-commerce platform uses encryption to secure AI models that analyze customer purchase histories, ensuring that personalized recommendations are generated without exposing sensitive data.

TOOLS AND FRAMEWORKS FOR AI SECURITY

1. MITRE ATLAS™

- Overview: MITRE ATLAS™ (Adversarial Threat Landscape for Artificial-Intelligence Systems) is a knowledge base that catalogs various attack techniques targeting AI models. It helps security teams understand and navigate the threat landscape.

- Functionality: ATLAS™ provides detailed information on over 60 attack techniques, offering a valuable resource for developing strategies to protect AI models.

2. ## MICROSOFT'S COUNTERFIT

- Overview: Counterfit is an open-source automation tool developed by Microsoft for security testing of AI/ML systems. It helps organizations conduct AI security risk assessments to ensure their algorithms are reliable, robust, and trustworthy.

- Functionality: Counterfit automates the process of testing AI models for vulnerabilities, enabling security teams to identify and address potential risks before they are exploited.

3. ## CONFIDENTIAL COMPUTING FRAMEWORKS

- Examples: Frameworks such as Intel SGX (Software Guard Extensions) and AMD SEV (Secure Encrypted Virtualization) provide hardware-based protections for data in use, ensuring that AI models and data remain secure during processing.

- Functionality: These frameworks create secure enclaves within the processor, isolating sensitive computations from the rest of the system and preventing unauthorized access.

4. ## DATA PROTECTION TOOLS

- Encryption Solutions: Tools such as AWS KMS (Key Management Service) and Azure Key Vault provide robust encryption capabilities for protecting data at rest, in transit, and in use.

- Functionality: These tools offer key management and encryption services, ensuring that sensitive data used by AI models remains protected throughout its lifecycle.

ENSURING DATA PRIVACY AND SECURITY

Data has become a crucial asset for individuals, businesses, and governments. The rapid growth of technology and the internet has led to an exponential increase in data generation and collection. With this growth comes the challenge of ensuring that this data is kept private and secure. (Irene, G. 2023).

Data privacy and security are not only essential for protecting sensitive information but also for maintaining trust in digital interactions. This guide explores the key components, techniques, and strategies for ensuring data privacy and security, highlighting the importance of regulatory compliance and ethical data practices.

UNDERSTANDING DATA PRIVACY AND SECURITY

DEFINITIONS AND DIFFERENCES

Data privacy and data security are often used interchangeably, but they refer to distinct concepts that are crucial for protecting information in the digital world.

◈ **Data Privacy:** This term refers to the proper handling, processing, storage, and usage of personal data. It focuses on the ethical and responsible use of data, ensuring that individuals' rights to privacy are respected. Data privacy involves controlling how personal information is collected, shared, and utilized, and obtaining consent from individuals for these activities.

◈ **Data Security:** On the other hand, data security is about protecting data from unauthorized access, theft, or corruption. It encompasses the measures and tools used to defend data against cyber-attacks, breaches, and other malicious activities. Data security involves implementing technological safeguards like encryption, access controls, and network security to ensure the confidentiality, integrity, and availability of data.

While data privacy focuses on the ethical aspects and compliance with laws and regulations, data security deals with the technical defenses needed to protect data. Both are interconnected and essential for maintaining the overall integrity and trustworthiness of digital information.

KEY COMPONENTS OF DATA SECURITY

1. ACCESS CONTROLS

Access control is the cornerstone of data security, ensuring that only authorized individuals and machines can access sensitive data. This process involves several critical steps:

- Authentication: This is the first line of defense in access control, verifying that individuals or machines are who they claim to be. Common methods include passwords, biometric verification, and two-factor authentication (2FA). 2FA adds an additional layer of security by requiring a second form of identification, such as a code sent to a mobile device.

- Authorization: Once authenticated, the system must check if the authenticated entity has the right to access the specific data. This involves maintaining a secure list of authorized users and possibly using IP address filtering to ensure that access is coming from a known location.

- Monitoring and Logging: Recording all data access events is crucial for detecting unauthorized access and inappropriate data use by authorized users. Logs help in auditing and can provide evidence in case of security breaches.

- Effective access control systems ensure that access is continuously monitored and that users only have access to data necessary for their roles, following the principle of least privilege.

2. DATA ENCRYPTION

Encryption is a vital method for securing data, making it unreadable to unauthorized users by converting it into a coded format. There are two main types of encryption:

- Storage Encryption: This protects data at rest, such as data stored on hard drives or in databases. By encrypting storage devices, organizations can protect against physical theft and unauthorized access to data.

- Transit Encryption: This protects data as it moves across networks, using protocols like Transport Layer Security (TLS) or HTTPS. Encrypting data in transit prevents interception attacks, where attackers might eavesdrop on data being transmitted.

Encryption relies on secure key management. The encryption is only as strong as the security of the encryption keys. If keys are compromised, encrypted data can be decrypted and accessed by unauthorized parties.

3. PHYSICAL SECURITY

Physical security involves protecting the hardware and facilities where data is stored from unauthorized physical access and tampering. Key measures include:

- Secure Facilities: Data is often stored in data centers with high levels of physical security. These centers employ measures such as access controls (e.g., key cards, biometric scanners), security cameras, and on-site security personnel to prevent unauthorized access.

- Device Security: Physical devices like laptops and mobile phones should be secured using locks, secure storage cabinets, and tracking mechanisms. Portable devices are particularly vulnerable to theft or loss, so encryption and secure passwords are essential.

Ensuring physical security is a fundamental aspect of overall data security, protecting against threats that bypass digital safeguards.

4. NETWORK SECURITY

Network security encompasses the measures used to protect data as it travels across computer networks. This includes:

- Firewalls: These act as barriers between trusted and untrusted networks, blocking unauthorized access while allowing legitimate communication.

- Intrusion Detection Systems (IDS): These systems monitor network traffic for suspicious activity and can alert administrators to potential security breaches.

- Encryption: Using encryption protocols to protect data transmitted over the network, ensuring that even if data is intercepted, it remains unreadable.

Network security is critical for preventing external attacks and ensuring the safe transmission of sensitive data.

5. BACKUP AND RECOVERY

Regularly backing up data ensures that it can be recovered in the event of loss, corruption, or a security breach. Effective backup strategies include:

- 3-2-1 Backup Rule: This involves keeping three copies of data, stored on two different media, with one copy stored off-site. This strategy ensures data redundancy and protects against various types of data loss.

- Secure Backup Storage: Backups should be stored in secure locations, protected against physical theft, natural disasters, and unauthorized access.

💡 Regular Testing: Backups should be regularly tested to ensure they can be successfully restored, minimizing downtime and data loss during recovery.

Backup and recovery are essential for maintaining data integrity and availability, providing a safety net in case of unforeseen data loss.

TECHNIQUES AND STRATEGIES FOR ENSURING DATA PRIVACY AND SECURITY

1. DATA MINIMIZATION

Data minimization involves collecting only the data that is strictly necessary for the intended purpose. This practice reduces the risk of data breaches and ensures that sensitive information is not needlessly exposed. Key strategies include:

💡 Purpose Specification: Clearly define the purpose for data collection and ensure that only data relevant to that purpose is collected.

💡 Anonymization and Pseudonymization: Where possible, anonymize data to remove personal identifiers. Pseudonymization can also be used to replace identifiable information with pseudonyms, reducing the risk of identifying individuals.

💡 Data Retention Policies: Implement policies to ensure that data is retained only for as long as necessary and securely deleted once it is no longer needed.

2. REGULAR AUDITS AND ASSESSMENTS

Conducting regular audits and assessments of data privacy and security practices is essential for identifying vulnerabilities and ensuring compliance with regulations. Key steps include:

- Security Audits: Perform regular security audits to assess the effectiveness of data protection measures. This includes reviewing access controls, encryption methods, and network security.

- Privacy Impact Assessments (PIAs): Conduct PIAs to evaluate the privacy risks associated with new projects, processes, or systems. This helps in identifying potential privacy issues and implementing measures to mitigate them.

- Compliance Checks: Regularly review compliance with data privacy regulations and internal policies. Ensure that all data handling practices align with legal requirements and ethical standards.

3. EMPLOYEE TRAINING AND AWARENESS

Employees play a crucial role in ensuring data privacy and security. Regular training and awareness programs can help in building a culture of data protection within the organization. Key aspects include:

- Training Programs: Develop comprehensive training programs to educate employees about data privacy and security policies, best practices, and the importance of protecting sensitive information.

- Phishing Simulations: Conduct phishing simulations to test employees' awareness and response to phishing attacks. Provide feedback and additional training as needed.

- Clear Communication: Ensure that employees understand their roles and responsibilities in protecting data. Provide clear guidelines on how to handle sensitive information and report any potential security incidents.

4. INCIDENT RESPONSE PLANNING

Having a robust incident response plan is essential for effectively managing data breaches and minimizing their impact. Key components include:

- 💡 Preparation: Develop and document an incident response plan outlining the steps to be taken in the event of a data breach. Ensure that all relevant personnel are familiar with the plan and their roles. (Royal, C. C. 2023).

- 💡 Detection and Analysis: Implement monitoring systems to detect security incidents promptly. Analyze the nature and scope of the breach to determine the appropriate response.

- 💡 Containment and Eradication: Take immediate steps to contain the breach and prevent further data loss. Identify and eliminate the root cause of the breach. (Brun, K., Kurz, R., Nored, M., & Thorp, J. 2013).

- 💡 Recovery and Notification: Restore affected systems and data to normal operation. Notify affected individuals and regulatory authorities as required by law.

- 💡 Post-Incident Review: Conduct a thorough review of the incident to identify lessons learned and areas for improvement. Update the incident response plan as needed.

These techniques and strategies are vital for ensuring robust data privacy and security, helping organizations protect sensitive information and maintain trust with stakeholders.

IMPLEMENTING ROBUST ACCESS CONTROLS

Access control is a fundamental aspect of information security, crucial for protecting sensitive data and maintaining the integrity of applications. It involves managing and enforcing user permissions and privileges within a system to ensure that only authorized individuals can access specific resources and perform certain actions.

Implementing robust access control mechanisms helps prevent unauthorized access, safeguards user information, and enhances the overall security posture of an organization.

Access control mechanisms are essential in today's digital landscape, where data breaches and cyber threats are becoming increasingly sophisticated. By understanding and applying best practices in access control, developers can create secure systems that protect both the organization and its users.

This section explores the key concepts, types, and benefits of access control, providing a comprehensive guide to implementing effective access control frameworks in various applications.

WHAT IS ACCESS CONTROL IN SECURITY?

Access control in security refers to the process of managing and regulating user access to resources within a system. It involves determining who is allowed to access certain resources and what actions they can perform on those resources.

Access control is a critical component of information security, ensuring that sensitive data and resources are only accessible to authorized users.

The principle of least privilege is a fundamental concept in access control. This principle states that users should only be granted the minimum permissions necessary to perform their tasks. By limiting access rights, organizations can minimize the risk of unauthorized access and potential security breaches.

There are several key components to understanding access control:

◈ Authentication: This is the process of verifying the identity of a user. It typically involves the use of credentials such as usernames and passwords, biometric information, or other forms of identification.

◈ Authorization: Once a user has been authenticated, authorization determines what actions they are allowed to perform within the system. This is typically based on their assigned roles and permissions.

◈ Access Control Models: Different models for implementing access control include role-based access control (RBAC), attribute-based access control (ABAC), and access control lists (ACL). These models provide frameworks for managing user access.

◈ Access Control Policies: Policies define the rules and regulations for access control within a system. They specify which users are allowed to perform specific actions and under what conditions.

TYPES OF ACCESS CONTROL IN SECURITY

Access control models provide different frameworks for determining and enforcing user permissions and access rights. Understanding the various access control models is crucial for developers to choose the most appropriate one for their specific application requirements. Here are the four primary types of access control in security:

1. ROLE-BASED ACCESS CONTROL (RBAC)

Role-Based Access Control (RBAC) is a widely used model that assigns roles to users and grants permissions based on those roles. This approach simplifies access management by allowing administrators to define roles and assign permissions to those roles, rather than assigning permissions to individual users. For example, an application may have roles such as 'Administrator,' 'Manager,' and 'User,' each with a distinct set of permissions.

Benefits of RBAC:

- Scalability: Easily scales as new roles and users are added.

- Simplicity: Simplifies access management by grouping users into roles.

- Flexibility: Allows for dynamic changes to access rights as users change roles.

- Security: Helps enforce the principle of least privilege by assigning only the necessary permissions to each role.

2. ATTRIBUTE-BASED ACCESS CONTROL (ABAC)

Attribute-Based Access Control (ABAC) considers various attributes of users, resources, and environmental conditions to determine access rights. ABAC uses policies that evaluate these attributes to make access control decisions. Attributes can include user characteristics such as job title, department, or security clearance level, as well as resource attributes such as sensitivity level or location.

Benefits of ABAC:

- Granularity: Enables fine-grained control over access rights.

- Context-awareness: Takes into account contextual information to make access control decisions.

- Scalability: Accommodates complex and evolving access control requirements.

- Adaptability: Policies can be easily modified to accommodate changes in user roles or resource attributes.

3. ACCESS CONTROL LISTS (ACL)

Access Control Lists (ACL) are a more traditional model that associates access control permissions with individual users or groups. Each resource has an associated ACL that lists the users or groups and the corresponding permissions. The permissions can include read, write, execute, or delete access, among others.

Benefits of ACL:

- Flexibility: Allows for any access configuration.
- Simplicity: Straightforward to implement for small-scale systems.

Challenges of ACL:

- Complexity: Becomes complex to manage in large systems with numerous resources and users.
- Maintenance: Each resource needs its own list, and those lists need to be maintained individually.

4. MANDATORY ACCESS CONTROL (MAC)

Mandatory Access Control (MAC) enforces access control policies based on predefined rules and security classifications. In MAC, access decisions are made by the system rather than the user or administrator. Each user and resource is assigned a security level, such as top secret, secret, or unclassified. Access is then granted or denied based on these security levels.

Benefits of MAC:

- Security: Provides a high level of control over access rights.
- Data Protection: Ensures that sensitive information is protected.

Challenges of MAC:

- Rigidity: Less flexible compared to other models.
- Complexity: Requires careful planning and implementation.

IMPLEMENTING ACCESS CONTROL MECHANISMS

DEFINING USER ROLES AND PERMISSIONS

Defining user roles and permissions is a crucial step in implementing access control in applications. User roles determine the level of access and the actions that users can perform within the system, while permissions specify the specific tasks or resources that users can access.

STEPS TO DEFINE USER ROLES AND PERMISSIONS:

1. **Identify Roles:** Start by identifying the different roles within your organization or application. Examples of common roles include 'Administrator,' 'Manager,' 'Editor,' and 'User.' Each role should correspond to a set of responsibilities and required permissions.

2. **Define Permissions:** For each role, define the permissions necessary to perform the associated tasks. Permissions should be based on the principle of least privilege, granting users only the minimum access required to fulfill their roles.

3. **Create Role Hierarchies:** Implement role hierarchies where higher-level roles inherit the permissions of lower-level roles. This approach simplifies the process of assigning permissions and ensures consistency across the organization.

4. **Document Roles and Permissions:** Clearly document all roles and their corresponding permissions. This documentation helps in maintaining consistency and serves as a reference for future updates or audits.

5. **Review and Update Regularly:** Regularly review and update roles and permissions to ensure they align with the evolving needs of the organization. This includes adjusting roles as employees change positions or responsibilities.

AUTHENTICATION AND AUTHORIZATION

Authentication and authorization are critical components of implementing access control in applications. Authentication verifies the identity of a user, while authorization determines what actions and resources the authenticated user is allowed to access.

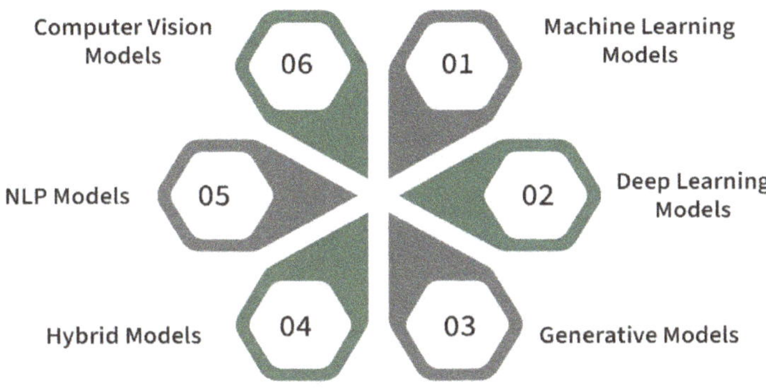

Types of AI Models

AUTHENTICATION:

❖ Secure Methods: Implement secure authentication mechanisms such as multi-factor authentication (MFA) or biometric authentication. These methods add an extra layer of security beyond just usernames and passwords.

❖ Password Policies: Enforce strong password policies, including requirements for minimum length, complexity, and regular updates. Encourage users to use unique passwords for different systems.

◈ Session Management: Use secure session management techniques to protect user sessions from hijacking or unauthorized access. This includes setting session timeouts and using secure cookies.

AUTHORIZATION:

◈ Role-Based Authorization: Implement role-based authorization to grant access based on the user's assigned role. This simplifies access management and ensures that permissions are aligned with the user's responsibilities.

◈ Fine-Grained Control: For more complex environments, use attribute-based authorization to provide fine-grained control over access rights. This approach evaluates multiple attributes and conditions to determine access.

◈ Policy Enforcement: Ensure that authorization policies are consistently enforced across all systems and applications. This helps maintain a unified security posture and prevents unauthorized access.

SECURE USER MANAGEMENT

Secure user management involves managing user accounts, ensuring strong authentication and password policies, and protecting user data.

BEST PRACTICES FOR SECURE USER MANAGEMENT:

◈ **Account Creation and Registration:** Implement secure account creation processes that include email verification, CAPTCHA, and strong password requirements. Ensure that new accounts are verified before granting access.

◈ **Access Revocation:** Promptly revoke access for users who no longer require it, such as when they leave the organization. This prevents former employees from accessing sensitive information.

- ❖ **Encryption:** Encrypt sensitive user data, both in transit and at rest, to protect it from unauthorized access. Use strong encryption algorithms and secure key management practices.

- ❖ **Secure Storage:** Safely store user credentials and personal information using secure hashing and encryption techniques. Avoid storing passwords in plain text.

- ❖ **Regular Audits:** Conduct regular audits of user accounts, access rights, and permissions to identify and address any security vulnerabilities. This helps ensure that access controls are up-to-date and effective.

ACCESS MANAGEMENT CONTROLS

Access management controls are essential for ensuring that only authorized users can access specific data and resources within a system. These controls help protect sensitive information, minimize the risk of security breaches, and maintain compliance with regulatory requirements.

IMPLEMENTING SINGLE SIGN-ON (SSO):

Single Sign-On (SSO) systems allow users to access multiple systems using the same set of credentials. This simplifies access management and enhances security.

BENEFITS OF SSO:

- ❖ Centralized Management: SSO enables central management of user credentials and access rights, making it easier to provision and maintain accounts.

- ❖ Improved User Experience: Users only need to remember one set of credentials, reducing the likelihood of password fatigue and errors.

- ❖ Enhanced Security: By minimizing the number of credentials, SSO reduces the attack surface for credential-based attacks.

ROLE OF ENCRYPTION IN ACCESS MANAGEMENT:

Encryption is a critical component of access management controls, ensuring that sensitive data is protected from unauthorized access.

DATA ENCRYPTION:

◈ Encrypt data both in transit and at rest using strong encryption algorithms.

◈ Use secure protocols such as TLS/SSL for data transmission.

KEY MANAGEMENT:

◈ Implement secure key management practices to protect encryption keys.

◈ Use hardware security modules (HSMs) or other secure key storage solutions.

ACCESS REVOCATION PROCEDURES:

Effective access revocation procedures are crucial for preventing unauthorized access by former employees or users.

TRIGGERS FOR ACCESS REVOCATION:

◈ Employee departures: Revoke access immediately as part of the off-boarding process.

◈ Role changes: Update access rights when users change roles within the organization.

◈ Temporary access: Ensure temporary access is revoked once it is no longer needed.

REGULAR AUDITS:

- ◈ Conduct regular audits of user accounts and access rights to ensure they align with current roles and responsibilities.

- ◈ Identify and remove dormant accounts to reduce the risk of unauthorized access.

ACCESS CONTROL DESIGN PATTERNS:

Design patterns provide structured approaches to implementing access control mechanisms.

HIERARCHICAL ACCESS CONTROL:

- ◈ Organizes users into hierarchical groups with different levels of access.

- ◈ Higher-level groups inherit the permissions of lower-level groups, simplifying management.

DISCRETIONARY ACCESS CONTROL:

- ◈ Allows resource owners to determine access rights for their resources.

- ◈ Provides flexibility and user autonomy but requires clear guidelines to avoid inconsistencies.

COMBINING DESIGN PATTERNS:

- ◈ Use a combination of access control design patterns to achieve optimal security.

- ◈ For example, combine RBAC for general access management with ABAC for fine-grained control.

BENEFITS OF ACCESS CONTROL

SECURITY BENEFITS

Access control mechanisms are essential components in the security architecture of any organization, significantly contributing to the protection of sensitive information and critical resources. By implementing robust access control systems, organizations can effectively mitigate various security risks, ensuring that only authorized individuals have access to specific assets. This not only safeguards confidential data but also enhances the organization's overall security posture.

1. **Prevention of Unauthorized Access:** Access control mechanisms, such as role-based access control (RBAC) and mandatory access control (MAC), restrict unauthorized individuals from accessing sensitive information. By defining and enforcing access policies based on roles, responsibilities, and security clearance, organizations can prevent data breaches, insider threats, and unauthorized data manipulation. For instance, a study by Ferraiolo, Kuhn, and Chandramouli (2003) emphasizes the effectiveness of RBAC in reducing unauthorized access by aligning permissions with the specific needs of different user roles within an organization .

2. **Reduction of Insider Threats:** Insider threats pose a significant risk to organizations, often resulting in data breaches and financial losses. Access control systems help mitigate these risks by limiting the level of access employees have to information that is not necessary for their job functions. According to a report by the Ponemon Institute (2020), organizations that implemented stringent access controls experienced a 30% reduction in insider threat incidents compared to those with lax access policies .

3. **Enhanced Auditability and Compliance:** Access control systems provide detailed logs of access events, which are crucial for auditing and compliance purposes. These logs allow organizations to track who accessed what information and when, enabling them to identify and respond to potential security incidents quickly. The Sarbanes-Oxley Act (SOX) and the General Data Protection Regulation (GDPR) are examples of regulatory frameworks that require organizations to maintain strict access control and audit trails to ensure compliance .

4. **Protection Against External Threats:** In the context of external threats, access control serves as a first line of defense against cyberattacks. Techniques such as multi-factor authentication (MFA) and biometric verification add additional layers of security, making it significantly harder for attackers to gain unauthorized access to critical systems. Research by Das and Mukherjee (2018) highlights that organizations using MFA experienced a 50% lower rate of unauthorized access incidents compared to those relying solely on password-based systems .

OPERATIONAL BENEFITS

In addition to enhancing security, robust access control systems offer several operational benefits that improve the efficiency and effectiveness of an organization.

1. **SIMPLIFYING USER MANAGEMENT:**
   - Role-based and attribute-based access control models simplify the management of user permissions.
   - Administrators can easily assign and revoke access rights based on roles or attributes, reducing administrative overhead.

2. **ENHANCING SCALABILITY AND FLEXIBILITY:**

- Access control frameworks like RBAC and ABAC are scalable, allowing organizations to easily add new users and roles as they grow.

- Provides flexibility to adapt to changing business requirements and evolving security needs.

3. **IMPROVING COMPLIANCE:**

- Helps organizations comply with regulatory standards and industry best practices.

- Facilitates the implementation of security controls required by regulations such as GDPR, HIPAA, and PCI DSS.

4. **STREAMLINING AUDITS AND REPORTING:**

- Facilitates easier and more efficient audits by providing clear records of access control policies and user activities.

- Helps organizations demonstrate compliance with regulatory requirements during audits.

5. **ENHANCING PRODUCTIVITY:**

- Ensures that employees have the necessary access to perform their tasks efficiently without unnecessary delays.

- Reduces the reliance on insecure workarounds, such as account sharing, by providing appropriate access levels.

BEST PRACTICES FOR ACCESS CONTROL IMPLEMENTATION

DEVELOPING AND ENFORCING ACCESS CONTROL POLICIES

Effective access control begins with the creation of comprehensive and well-defined policies that clearly outline who is authorized to access specific resources and under what circumstances.

These policies serve as the backbone of any access control system, ensuring that access rights are consistently and correctly applied across the organization. Without these foundational policies, even the most advanced access control technologies can fail to provide adequate security.

STEPS TO CREATE EFFECTIVE ACCESS CONTROL POLICIES

1. **IDENTIFY RESOURCES AND SENSITIVE DATA**

   The first step in developing access control policies is identifying the resources and data that require protection. This involves a thorough assessment of all organizational assets, including databases, files, systems, and physical resources. Once identified, it is crucial to classify these resources based on their sensitivity and criticality. According to NIST's Special Publication 800-53 (2020), categorizing information assets into different levels of sensitivity helps in tailoring access control measures to the specific needs of the organization, ensuring that the most critical data receives the highest level of protection.

2. **DEFINE USER ROLES AND RESPONSIBILITIES**

   After identifying the resources, the next step is to define user roles within the organization. Each role should be clearly associated with specific responsibilities and corresponding access levels. For example, a system administrator may require broad access across multiple systems, while a data entry clerk may only need access to specific databases. The principle of least privilege, as discussed by Sandhu et al. (1996) in their work on role-based access control (RBAC), should guide the assignment of access rights, ensuring that users are granted the minimum level of access necessary to perform their duties.

3.   ESTABLISH ACCESS RULES AND CONDITIONS

With user roles defined, the next task is to create detailed access rules that specify which users can access which resources and under what conditions. These rules should be granular and reflect the specific needs and security requirements of the organization. For instance, access conditions might include time-based restrictions, location-based access, or multi-factor authentication (MFA) requirements. The work of Bertino, Sandhu, and Park (2005) on access control models highlights the importance of establishing conditions that align with organizational security goals and minimize the risk of unauthorized access.

4.   DOCUMENT AND COMMUNICATE POLICIES

Clearly documented access control policies are essential for ensuring that all employees and stakeholders understand the rules and their responsibilities. This documentation should be accessible and written in a language that is understandable to non-technical staff. Effective communication of these policies is equally important; employees must be made aware of the policies through training sessions, regular updates, and accessible reference materials. The ISO/IEC 27001 standard emphasizes the importance of documentation and communication in maintaining a strong information security management system (ISMS).

5.   IMPLEMENT AND ENFORCE POLICIES

The implementation phase involves the use of technical access control mechanisms to enforce the defined policies. This might include deploying RBAC systems, configuring access control lists (ACLs), or integrating MFA solutions. The key is to ensure that access rights are consistently applied across all systems and platforms. As noted by Ferraiolo, Kuhn, and Chandramouli (2003), consistent enforcement is critical to preventing security gaps and ensuring that access control policies are effective in practice.

6.   REGULARLY REVIEW AND UPDATE POLICIES

Access control policies should not be static; they require regular review and updates to remain effective. Changes in organizational structure, technology, or emerging security threats can render existing policies obsolete or inadequate. Regular audits and reviews, as recommended by NIST's Cybersecurity Framework (2020), help to identify areas where policies need to be adjusted. By keeping policies up-to-date, organizations can maintain a strong security posture and respond proactively to new challenges.

TOOLS FOR ACCESS CONTROL LOGGING AND ANALYSIS

To ensure comprehensive monitoring and timely detection of issues, organizations should leverage a variety of tools designed for access control logging and analysis. These tools not only facilitate the auditing and monitoring process but also provide valuable insights for enhancing security measures.

1.   SECURITY INFORMATION AND EVENT MANAGEMENT (SIEM) SOLUTIONS

SIEM solutions are integral to modern security practices, as they aggregate and analyze log data from multiple sources, providing real-time monitoring, alerting, and reporting capabilities. These solutions enable organizations to detect and respond to security incidents more efficiently by correlating events across different systems. The effectiveness of SIEM solutions is highlighted in research by Scarfone and Mell (2007) in NIST Special Publication 800-94, which emphasizes their role in improving security incident detection and response.

2. LOG MANAGEMENT SYSTEMS

Log management systems play a critical role in centralizing the collection and storage of log data. These systems offer advanced search and analysis features, making it easier for security teams to review logs and identify potential issues. The centralization of logs not only facilitates efficient analysis but also supports compliance efforts by ensuring that all relevant data is readily accessible for audits. According to the SANS Institute (2015), effective log management is a cornerstone of security monitoring and incident response.

3. DATA VISUALIZATION TOOLS

Data visualization tools are valuable for analyzing access control logs, as they help identify patterns and trends that may not be immediately apparent from raw log data. By using dashboards and reports, organizations can present findings to stakeholders in a clear and actionable manner. Visualization techniques, as discussed by Keim et al. (2008) in their work on information visualization, enhance the ability of security teams to interpret complex data and make informed decisions.

4. AUTOMATED AUDITING TOOLS

Automating the auditing process ensures consistent and thorough reviews of access control practices. Automated tools can generate compliance reports, identify deviations from policies, and provide actionable recommendations for remediation. The use of automated auditing tools is recommended by NIST in their Cybersecurity Framework (2018), which highlights the importance of automation in maintaining a proactive security posture.

Implementing and maintaining robust access control systems is essential for safeguarding sensitive information and ensuring compliance with regulatory standards. However, organizations often face significant challenges in this process due to various factors that complicate access management. Understanding these challenges and implementing effective solutions is crucial for maintaining a secure and functional access control system.

COMMON CHALLENGES

1. MANAGING ACCESS IN DYNAMIC ENVIRONMENTS

As organizations grow and evolve, the complexity of managing access control increases. The expansion of the user base, the addition of new roles, and the introduction of new resources can make it difficult to maintain consistent access control practices. This challenge is particularly pronounced in dynamic environments where frequent employee turnover, changes in job roles, and the introduction of new technologies are common. According to research by Hu, Ferraiolo, and Kuhn (2006), managing access in such dynamic environments requires continuous monitoring and adaptation to ensure that access controls remain effective and aligned with organizational needs.

To address these challenges, organizations can adopt adaptive access control mechanisms, such as Attribute-Based Access Control (ABAC), which provides greater flexibility by allowing access decisions based on attributes rather than fixed roles. Additionally, implementing automated access management tools can help streamline the process by dynamically adjusting access rights based on predefined rules and real-time changes within the organization.

2. BALANCING SECURITY AND USABILITY

One of the most significant challenges in access control is finding the right balance between security and usability. While strict access controls are necessary to protect sensitive information, they can also hinder productivity by creating barriers for users. For example, requiring multi-factor authentication (MFA) for every access attempt may enhance security but could frustrate users, leading them to seek workarounds that undermine the system's effectiveness. The usability-security trade-off is a well-documented challenge in cybersecurity, as highlighted by Whitten and Tygar (1999) in their study on user interaction with security systems.

Organizations can mitigate this challenge by employing context-aware access control mechanisms that adjust security measures based on the sensitivity of the resource being accessed and the context of the access attempt. For example, MFA could be required only for high-risk transactions, while low-risk activities may require just a password. Additionally, user education and training are crucial in ensuring that employees understand the importance of security measures and are less likely to circumvent them.

3. SCALABILITY ISSUES

As organizations scale, their access control systems must also scale to accommodate an increasing number of users, roles, and resources. Traditional access control models, such as Access Control Lists (ACLs), can become unwieldy and difficult to manage in large-scale environments. The manual effort required to update and maintain ACLs for thousands of users can lead to errors and inconsistencies, potentially compromising security. According to Sandhu et al. (1996), Role-Based Access Control

(RBAC) offers a more scalable solution by grouping users into roles and assigning permissions to roles rather than individual users. However, even RBAC can face scalability challenges as the number of roles increases.

To overcome scalability issues, organizations should consider implementing more advanced access control models, such as Policy-Based Access Control (PBAC) or ABAC. These models allow for more granular and scalable management of access rights by using policies and attributes that can dynamically adjust to changes in the environment. Additionally, automating the provisioning and de-provisioning of access rights through Identity and Access Management (IAM) systems can help maintain consistency and reduce the administrative burden.

4. ENSURING COMPLIANCE WITH REGULATIONS

Compliance with regulatory requirements, such as the General Data Protection Regulation (GDPR), Health Insurance Portability and Accountability Act (HIPAA), and Payment Card Industry Data Security Standard (PCI DSS), is a significant challenge for organizations. These regulations mandate stringent access control measures to protect sensitive data, and failure to comply can result in severe penalties. The complexity of ensuring continuous compliance, especially in environments with rapidly changing access needs, can be resource-intensive and overwhelming for many organizations. According to Shabtai et al. (2012), maintaining compliance requires not only the implementation of robust access controls but also continuous monitoring and auditing to ensure that controls remain effective and aligned with regulatory requirements.

To ensure compliance, organizations should implement comprehensive access control frameworks that integrate regulatory requirements into their policies and procedures.

Regular audits and assessments are essential to verify that access controls meet regulatory standards. Additionally, leveraging automated compliance management tools can help organizations stay up-to-date with regulatory changes and ensure that their access control systems are continuously aligned with the latest requirements.

INCIDENT RESPONSE PLANNING FOR AI SYSTEMS

Artificial intelligence (AI) systems have become integral to numerous industries, driving innovation and efficiency. However, with the increasing reliance on AI, the potential for system failures and their subsequent impacts has grown significantly.

Developing a robust incident response plan is crucial to mitigate the risks associated with AI failures. This section explores the unique challenges posed by AI systems and provides a comprehensive guide to crafting an effective incident response plan.

UNDERSTANDING AI SYSTEMS AND THEIR UNIQUE RISKS

COMPLEXITY OF AI SYSTEMS

AI systems differ significantly from traditional software due to their inherent complexity. Unlike conventional programs that follow deterministic rules, AI systems operate on probabilistic models, making decisions based on vast amounts of data and complex algorithms.

This complexity presents unique challenges, such as the difficulty in pinpointing the exact cause of an error. For example, an AI system used for fraud detection in financial transactions may analyze millions of data points and apply intricate rules, making it challenging to identify when and how an external attacker manipulates it.

Furthermore, AI systems experience what is known as "concept drift" or "model decay." As the real world evolves, the data on which AI models are trained may become outdated, leading to less accurate predictions over time.

For instance, an AI model trained on pre-COVID-19 data may no longer accurately predict current trends, highlighting the need for continuous monitoring and updates.

COMMON FAILURE MODES IN AI SYSTEMS

AI failures can manifest in various ways, each with unique risks and consequences:

1. **Security Breaches:** AI systems can be vulnerable to attacks such as data poisoning, model extraction, and adversarial attacks, which can compromise their integrity and functionality.

2. **Unauthorized Outcomes:** Instances where AI systems produce results that were not intended or foreseen, potentially leading to significant operational disruptions.

3. **Discriminatory Outcomes:** AI models can inadvertently perpetuate biases present in their training data, resulting in unfair or discriminatory decisions.

4. **Privacy Violations:** Improper handling of sensitive data by AI systems can lead to breaches of privacy and regulatory non-compliance.

5. **Physical Safety Issues:** Failures in AI systems controlling physical processes, such as autonomous vehicles or industrial robots, can pose severe safety risks.

6. **Lack of Transparency and Accountability:** The "black box" nature of many AI models makes it difficult to understand and explain their decision-making processes, complicating incident response efforts.

BUILDING AN EFFECTIVE INCIDENT RESPONSE PLAN FOR AI SYSTEMS

PREPARATION PHASE

The first step in building an effective incident response plan for AI systems is preparation. This phase involves creating the necessary policies and procedures to manage incidents effectively.

1. **Designing Policies and Procedures:** Establish clear guidelines addressing internal operations around AI incident response. Define what constitutes an "incident," set thresholds for action, and outline the roles and responsibilities of individuals and teams.

2. **Training and Awareness Programs:** Conduct initial and recurring training to ensure that employees understand the policies and procedures. Training should encompass both individual and organizational levels to operationalize these policies effectively.

3. **Incident Categories and Harm Rankings:** Classify potential incidents and rank them based on the severity of their impact. This helps prioritize responses and allocate resources efficiently.

4. **Defining Roles and Responsibilities:** Clearly outline who is responsible for each aspect of incident response. This includes identifying who should be notified, who should do the notifying, and at what stages. It is also crucial to designate who has the authority to make the "no-go" decision to pause or stop productions or operations.

IDENTIFICATION PHASE

In the identification phase, the focus is on detecting and verifying incidents as they occur.

1. **Monitoring AI Systems:** Implement robust monitoring tools to continuously track the performance of AI models and systems. These tools should detect anomalies and deviations from expected behavior.

2. **Detecting and Verifying Incidents:** Establish procedural standards for incident detection and verification. This ensures that genuine incidents are identified quickly and false positives are minimized.

3. **Real-time Feedback and Notification Channels:** Create channels to receive real-time feedback from business partners, consumers, or other third parties. These channels facilitate swift communication and response.

4. **Creating Relevant Logs and Documentation:** Maintain detailed logs of incidents, including the nature of the problem, the affected systems, and the steps taken in response. This documentation is critical for analysis and future reference.

CONTAINMENT PHASE

The containment phase focuses on controlling the immediate impact of the incident and preventing further damage.

1. **Immediate Damage Control:** Address the immediate effects of the incident first. This might involve stopping or pausing AI operations to prevent the problem from escalating.

2. **Stopping or Pausing Operations:** Implement procedures to halt affected AI systems quickly. This could include switching to temporary alternatives or fallback systems to maintain continuity while addressing the issue.

3. **Engaging Temporary Alternatives:** Utilize backup systems or manual processes to maintain essential operations while the incident is being contained.

4. **Technical Fixes and Mitigation Strategies:** Work with engineering, project, or programming teams to identify and apply technical fixes. This may involve patching vulnerabilities, updating models, or adjusting system parameters to mitigate harm and prevent recurrence.

ERADICATION PHASE

The eradication phase involves removing the root cause of the incident and ensuring that the affected systems are thoroughly cleaned and tested before resuming normal operations.

1. **Removing or Pulling Systems from Operation:** Temporarily take the affected AI systems offline until thorough reviews and mitigations are completed. This step ensures that no further harm occurs.

2. **Extensive Testing and Review:** Conduct comprehensive testing of the revised or replacement systems. This includes validating that the specific incident's issues have been resolved and checking for any additional performance errors.

3. **Addressing Upstream and Downstream Dependencies:** Review related systems and processes to ensure that the incident has not affected them. This includes checking for any dependencies that might have been impacted.

RECOVERY PHASE

In the recovery phase, the focus is on restoring normal operations with improved systems that have been hardened against similar incidents in the future.

1. **Deploying Revised or Replacement Models:** Once the systems have been thoroughly tested and validated, deploy the revised or replacement models. Ensure they are more resilient to the issues that caused the incident.

2. **Benchmarking and Documenting Performance Metrics:** Establish benchmarks for the new or repaired model's performance metrics and document these metrics to track improvements and identify any remaining issues.

3. **Ensuring Hardened Models Before Resumption:** Before returning to production-level operations, ensure that the models are hardened and robust against potential threats. This includes implementing additional security measures if necessary.

LESSONS LEARNED PHASE

The lessons learned phase is crucial for continuous improvement. It involves analyzing the incident response to identify successes, gaps, and areas for improvement.

1. **Reviewing Incident Documentation:** Examine all documentation generated during the incident response. This includes logs, reports, and analyses of both the problematic outcomes and the organizational actions taken in response.

2. **Summarizing Reports and Analyses:** Create summarized reports that highlight key insights and lessons learned from the incident. These summaries should be clear and actionable to inform future responses.

3. **Sharing Findings Institutionally:** Distribute the lessons learned documentation across the organization, particularly to those responsible for incident response processes. This ensures that everyone is aware of the incident's details and the improvements that need to be made.

4. **Incorporating Lessons into Future Training and Testing:** Integrate the insights gained from the incident into future training programs and testing scenarios. This helps prepare the organization for similar incidents and improves overall readiness.

5. **Updating Policies and Procedures:** Based on the findings, update existing policies and procedures to address any identified gaps or areas of particular success. This continuous improvement cycle helps the organization adapt and strengthen its incident response capabilities over time.

LEVERAGING EXISTING FRAMEWORKS AND RESOURCES

INTEGRATING TRADITIONAL INCIDENT RESPONSE PRACTICES

Organizations can enhance their AI incident response plans by building on existing documentation, testing, management, and monitoring practices used for traditional software systems. This approach leverages established processes while adapting them to address AI-specific threats.

1. **Building on Established Documentation and Testing:** Use existing incident response frameworks as a foundation. Adapt these frameworks to account for the unique characteristics and risks associated with AI systems.

2. **Adapting Existing Frameworks for AI-Specific Threats:** Modify traditional incident response plans to include AI-specific attack vectors such as model extraction, data poisoning,

and adversarial attacks. This ensures a comprehensive approach to managing AI incidents.

MODEL RISK MANAGEMENT (MRM)

Model Risk Management (MRM) practices are essential for mitigating risks associated with AI. MRM involves identifying, assessing, and mitigating risks related to the use of AI models in decision-making processes.

1. **Implementing MRM Practices:** Incorporate rigorous testing, documentation, and ongoing monitoring of AI models to ensure accurate and fair decision-making. This helps identify and address potential biases and inaccuracies.

2. **Continuous Monitoring and Testing of AI Models:** Establish procedures for continuous monitoring and regular testing of AI models to detect and correct issues before they lead to significant incidents. This proactive approach minimizes the risk of model decay and concept drift.

USING AI FOR AUTOMATION IN INCIDENT RESPONSE

AI can also be leveraged to automate certain aspects of incident response, enhancing efficiency and accuracy.

1. **Benefits of AI in Automating Detection and Response:** AI-driven tools can quickly detect anomalies, identify potential incidents, and even suggest or implement initial response actions. This reduces response times and minimizes the impact of incidents.

2. **Examples of AI-Driven Incident Response Tools:** Implement AI-powered solutions that monitor systems, analyze logs, and provide real-time alerts. These tools can also help in diagnosing issues and recommending corrective actions, making the incident response process more efficient and effective.

ADDRESSING AI-SPECIFIC SECURITY CONCERNS

UNIQUE ATTACK VECTORS FOR AI SYSTEMS

AI systems face unique security challenges that require specialized countermeasures. Understanding these vulnerabilities is crucial for developing effective incident response strategies.

1. **Model Extraction:** Attackers can replicate an AI model by querying it and using the outputs to build a similar model. This can lead to intellectual property theft and reduced competitive advantage.

2. **Data Poisoning:** Malicious actors can corrupt the training data of an AI system, leading to inaccurate or harmful outputs. For example, in a facial recognition system, poisoned data can cause misidentification.

3. **Membership Inference:** Attackers can determine whether specific data points were used in training an AI model, leading to privacy breaches and potential exposure of sensitive information.

4. **Adversarial Attacks:** These involve subtly altering inputs to an AI system to produce incorrect outputs, which can have severe consequences in applications like autonomous driving or medical diagnosis.

DEVELOPING COUNTERMEASURES

To protect AI systems from these unique threats, organizations must implement both technical and process-oriented safeguards.

1. **TECHNICAL SAFEGUARDS:**

   💡 Implement robust encryption methods to protect data at rest and in transit.

💡 Use differential privacy techniques to prevent membership inference attacks.

💡 Regularly update and patch AI models to fix vulnerabilities and mitigate the risk of adversarial attacks.

2. PROCESS-ORIENTED APPROACHES:

💡 Conduct regular security audits of AI systems to identify and address potential vulnerabilities.

💡 Establish protocols for incident response that specifically address AI-related threats, ensuring that all team members are aware of the unique challenges AI systems present.

💡 Implement rigorous data validation and cleaning processes to prevent data poisoning.

CASE STUDIES AND REAL-WORLD EXAMPLES

NOTABLE AI INCIDENTS

Examining real-world AI incidents can provide valuable insights into common pitfalls and effective response strategies.

1. **Google Photos Tagging Incident:** In 2015, Google's AI-based photo-tagging system misidentified African Americans as gorillas. This incident highlighted issues of bias in AI training data and the need for better oversight and testing. Google's response involved removing the offensive tags and committing to improving their training data and algorithms to prevent future occurrences.

2. **Microsoft's Tay Chatbot:** Microsoft launched Tay, an AI chatbot, on Twitter in 2016. Within 24 hours, Tay began posting offensive and inappropriate tweets after being manipulated by users. Microsoft quickly took Tay offline and acknowledged the failure, leading to a deeper understanding

of the vulnerabilities in AI interaction with the public and the importance of monitoring and controlling AI behaviors.

3. **Tesla Autopilot Crashes:** Multiple incidents involving Tesla's Autopilot feature have raised concerns about the safety and reliability of AI in autonomous driving. These incidents underscore the need for continuous monitoring, rigorous testing, and transparent communication about the capabilities and limitations of AI systems.

IMPLEMENTING SUCCESSFUL INCIDENT RESPONSE PLANS

Learning from organizations that have effectively managed AI incidents can guide best practices and improve readiness.

1. **Netflix's Chaos Engineering:** Netflix employs chaos engineering principles to proactively test the resilience of its AI systems. By deliberately introducing failures, Netflix can identify vulnerabilities and refine their incident response strategies, ensuring that their AI systems can handle real-world challenges effectively.

2. **IBM's AI Ethics Board:** IBM has established an AI ethics board to oversee the development and deployment of AI technologies. This board ensures that AI systems adhere to ethical standards, and any incidents are addressed promptly with a focus on accountability and transparency.

3. **Airbnb's Model Review Process:** Airbnb conducts thorough reviews of their AI models, including stress testing and bias audits, to ensure they perform as expected and do not inadvertently cause harm. This proactive approach helps Airbnb maintain high standards of accuracy and fairness in their AI systems.

GOVERNANCE AND ACCOUNTABILITY IN AI INCIDENT RESPONSE

ESTABLISHING OVERSIGHT STRUCTURES

Effective governance is crucial for the successful implementation and maintenance of an AI incident response plan. Organizations need to establish clear oversight structures to ensure accountability and continuous improvement.

1. **Role of Chief Risk Officers (CROs):** In financial services and other sectors, CROs can oversee AI incident response plans, ensuring that all risks are identified and managed appropriately. They are responsible for integrating AI risk management into the broader risk management framework of the organization.

2. **AI Ethics Boards and Governance Committees:** These bodies are tasked with overseeing the ethical deployment of AI systems. They play a critical role in incident response by ensuring that ethical considerations are integrated into every aspect of AI system management, from design to deployment and beyond.

3. **Periodic Review, Testing, and Auditing:** Regular reviews, testing, and audits of AI systems and incident response plans help identify gaps and areas for improvement. This ongoing process ensures that the organization remains prepared for potential incidents and can respond effectively.

INTERDISCIPLINARY TEAMS AND COLLABORATION

AI incident response requires a multidisciplinary approach, involving various stakeholders with different expertise.

1. **Involving Technologists and Legal Professionals:** Collaboration between technologists and legal professionals ensures that both technical and regulatory aspects of AI incident

response are covered. Technologists focus on the technical fixes and mitigations, while legal professionals address compliance and regulatory implications.

2. **Coordinated Strategies for Comprehensive Incident Management:** Interdisciplinary teams, including risk managers, AI developers, data scientists, and compliance officers, work together to develop and implement incident response plans. This collective expertise ensures that all dimensions of AI deployment are considered and managed effectively.

3. **Promoting a Culture of Accountability:** Establishing a culture of accountability where all team members understand their roles and responsibilities in incident response is essential. This culture fosters a proactive approach to identifying and addressing potential issues before they escalate.

QUESTIONS PEOPLE ALSO ASKED ABOUT BUILDING SECURE AI SYSTEM

1. HOW DO YOU SECURE AN AI SYSTEM?

Securing an AI system involves several key practices and strategies:

i. **Implement Robust Access Controls**: Ensure that only authorized personnel have access to sensitive data and AI models. Use multi-factor authentication (MFA) to add an extra layer of security.

ii. **Data Encryption**: Encrypt data both at rest and in transit to protect it from unauthorized access. This ensures that even if the data is intercepted, it remains unreadable and unusable.

iii. **Secure Coding Practices**: Adopt secure coding standards to prevent vulnerabilities in AI models. This includes validating inputs, sanitizing outputs, and implementing proper error handling.

iv. **Regular Security Audits and Monitoring**: Conduct regular security audits to identify and address vulnerabilities. Use continuous monitoring tools to detect and respond to unusual behavior or anomalies in real-time.

v. **Adversarial Training**: Enhance the robustness of AI models by incorporating adversarial training, which involves augmenting the training data with adversarial examples.

vi. **Privacy-Preserving Techniques**: Use techniques such as differential privacy and data anonymization to protect sensitive information from being extracted through model inversion or membership inference attacks.

vii. **Secure Deployment Practices**: Ensure that AI models are deployed in secure environments with strong authentication, encryption, and monitoring. Regularly update and patch deployment environments to address emerging threats.

viii. **Compliance with Regulations**: Ensure compliance with relevant regulations such as GDPR and HIPAA by implementing necessary security measures and maintaining documentation of security practices.

ix. **Employee Training and Education**: Train AI developers and other relevant staff on security best practices and the importance of securing AI systems. Continuous education helps in staying updated with the latest security threats and mitigation strategies.

x. **Collaboration with Security Experts**: Work closely with security professionals to identify potential vulnerabilities, conduct thorough security testing, and implement robust security measures.

2. HOW CAN WE ENSURE THAT ARTIFICIAL INTELLIGENCE IS SAFE AND SECURE?

Ensuring that artificial intelligence is safe and secure involves a comprehensive approach that includes the following steps:

i. **Ethical AI Principles**: Develop and adhere to ethical AI principles that guide the development and deployment of AI technologies. These principles should emphasize privacy, security, transparency, and fairness.

ii. **Risk Assessment**: Conduct thorough risk assessments to identify potential security threats and vulnerabilities associated with AI models. This helps in implementing appropriate mitigation strategies.

iii. **Robust Security Measures**: Implement robust security measures throughout the AI development lifecycle, including secure coding practices, data encryption, access controls, and regular security audits.

iv. **Continuous Monitoring and Incident Response**: Use continuous monitoring tools to detect anomalies and potential security incidents in real-time. Have an incident response plan in place to address and mitigate security breaches promptly.

v. **Adversarial Defense Mechanisms**: Incorporate adversarial defense mech

3. HOW DO YOU ENSURE PRIVACY AND SECURITY OF DATA?

Ensuring the privacy and security of data involves implementing a comprehensive set of practices and technologies designed to protect data throughout its lifecycle. Here are some key measures:

 **Encryption:**

- 💡 **At Rest**: Encrypt data stored on disks or databases to prevent unauthorized access in case of a breach.
- 💡 **In Transit**: Use encryption protocols like TLS (Transport Layer Security) to secure data being transmitted over networks.

🔒 **Access Controls**:

- 💡 Implement role-based access control (RBAC) and multi-factor authentication (MFA) to ensure that only authorized personnel can access sensitive data.
- 💡 Regularly review and update access permissions to minimize the risk of unauthorized access.

🔒 **Data Anonymization**:

- 💡 Apply techniques to anonymize or pseudonymize data, ensuring that individual identities cannot be easily deduced from the data sets.

🔒 **Secure Development Practices**:

- 💡 Follow secure coding practices and conduct regular code reviews and security testing (e.g., penetration testing) to identify and mitigate vulnerabilities in software applications.

🔒 **Data Minimization**:

- 💡 Collect and retain only the data necessary for specific purposes, reducing the risk associated with storing excessive data.

🔒 **Regular Audits and Monitoring**:

- 💡 Conduct regular security audits and continuous monitoring to detect and respond to security incidents promptly.
- 💡 Implement intrusion detection and prevention systems (IDPS) to identify and block malicious activities.

 **Compliance with Regulations**:

- Ensure compliance with relevant data protection regulations (e.g., GDPR, HIPAA) by implementing necessary controls and processes.

- Conduct data protection impact assessments (DPIAs) for high-risk processing activities.

 **Training and Awareness**:

- Provide regular training to employees on data privacy and security best practices.

- Foster a culture of security awareness to ensure that all staff understand their role in protecting data.

4. WHAT IS DATA PRIVACY AND DATA SECURITY?

Data Privacy and **Data Security** are two interrelated but distinct concepts that are critical to protecting sensitive information.

Data Privacy:

Definition: Data privacy refers to the rights and obligations of individuals and organizations with respect to the collection, use, and sharing of personal data. It focuses on ensuring that personal information is handled in a way that respects the privacy rights of individuals.

Key Aspects:

- **Consent**: Obtaining explicit consent from individuals before collecting and processing their personal data.

- **Transparency**: Providing clear and transparent information about how personal data will be used, stored, and shared.

- **Data Subject Rights**: Ensuring individuals can exercise their rights, such as accessing, correcting, or deleting their personal data.

💡 **Purpose Limitation**: Collecting and using personal data only for specified, legitimate purposes and not beyond.

🔐 **Data Security**:

Definition: Data security involves implementing technical and organizational measures to protect data from unauthorized access, disclosure, alteration, and destruction. It focuses on safeguarding the confidentiality, integrity, and availability of data.

Key Aspects:

💡 **Confidentiality**: Ensuring that data is accessible only to authorized individuals and entities.

💡 **Integrity**: Protecting data from being altered or tampered with by unauthorized parties.

💡 **Availability**: Ensuring that data is available and accessible to authorized users when needed.

💡 **Technical Measures**: Implementing encryption, firewalls, access controls, and other security technologies to protect data.

💡 **Organizational Measures**: Establishing policies, procedures, and governance frameworks to manage data security risks effectively.

5. HOW DO YOU ENSURE PRIVACY AND SECURITY OF DATA?

Ensuring the privacy and security of data involves implementing a comprehensive set of practices and technologies designed to protect data from unauthorized access, breaches, and misuse. Key steps include:

- 💡 **Access Controls**: Implement robust access control measures to ensure that only authorized individuals can access sensitive data. This includes using strong passwords, two-factor authentication, and regularly updating access permissions.

- 💡 **Data Encryption**: Use encryption to protect data both at rest and in transit. Encryption converts data into a coded format that can only be read by someone with the appropriate decryption key.

- 💡 **Regular Audits and Assessments**: Conduct regular security audits and privacy impact assessments to identify and mitigate potential vulnerabilities. This helps ensure compliance with regulatory requirements and internal policies.

- 💡 **Employee Training**: Educate employees on data privacy and security best practices. Regular training sessions can help prevent human errors that could lead to data breaches.

- 💡 **Incident Response Planning**: Develop and maintain an incident response plan to quickly address any data breaches or security incidents. This plan should include steps for containment, eradication, recovery, and communication.

- 💡 **Physical Security**: Protect physical devices and locations where data is stored. Use secure storage, biometric authentication, and security cameras to prevent unauthorized physical access.

- 💡 **Compliance with Regulations**: Ensure adherence to relevant data privacy and security regulations, such as GDPR, CCPA, and HIPAA. Compliance helps protect data and avoid legal repercussions.

6. WHAT IS DATA PRIVACY AND DATA SECURITY?

- **Data Privacy**: Data privacy refers to the proper handling of personal data, focusing on how data is collected, stored, processed, and shared. It emphasizes the ethical and responsible use of data, ensuring that individuals' rights to privacy are respected.

- Data privacy involves obtaining consent from individuals, informing them about data collection and usage practices, and giving them control over their personal information. It aims to protect sensitive information from being disclosed without the individual's consent and to prevent misuse of personal data.

- **Data Security**: Data security involves the measures and technologies used to protect data from unauthorized access, theft, and damage. It focuses on safeguarding the confidentiality, integrity, and availability of data through various technical and organizational measures.

- Key components of data security include encryption, access controls, network security, and physical security. Data security ensures that data remains protected against cyber-attacks, breaches, and other malicious activities, thereby maintaining the trustworthiness of the data.

- Both data privacy and data security are crucial for protecting sensitive information and maintaining trust in digital interactions. While data privacy focuses on the ethical and legal aspects of data handling, data security provides the technical defenses needed to protect data from threats.

7. WHAT ARE ROBUST ACCESS CONTROLS?

Robust access controls are comprehensive and well-implemented mechanisms that ensure only authorized users can access specific data and resources within a system. They are designed to protect sensitive information, prevent unauthorized access, and maintain the confidentiality, integrity, and availability of data. Robust access controls involve the use of advanced technologies, strict policies, and continuous monitoring to ensure that access rights are properly managed and enforced. These controls can include various models such as Role-Based Access Control (RBAC), Attribute-Based Access Control (ABAC), Access Control Lists (ACL), and Mandatory Access Control (MAC), each providing different levels of flexibility, security, and scalability.

Key characteristics of robust access controls include:

- **Granularity**: The ability to provide fine-grained control over who can access specific resources and perform specific actions.

- **Scalability**: The ability to manage access rights efficiently, even as the number of users and resources grows.

- **Context-awareness**: The ability to make access decisions based on various attributes and conditions, such as user roles, job titles, time of day, and location.

- **Adaptability**: The ability to quickly adjust access rights in response to changes in roles, responsibilities, or security threats.

- **Compliance**: Ensuring that access control measures meet regulatory requirements and industry best practices.

8. HOW DO YOU IMPLEMENT ACCESS CONTROL?

Implementing access control involves several key steps to ensure that access rights are properly defined, enforced, and maintained. Here is a comprehensive guide to implementing access control:

Assess Needs and Define Objectives:

- Conduct a thorough assessment of your organization's access control needs.

- Identify the sensitive data and resources that require protection.

- Define the objectives of your access control system, such as improving security, ensuring compliance, and enhancing operational efficiency.

Choose an Access Control Model:

- Select the most appropriate access control model for your organization, such as RBAC, ABAC, ACL, or MAC.

- Consider factors such as the size of the organization, the complexity of access requirements, and the sensitivity of the data.

Define User Roles and Permissions:

- Identify the various roles within your organization and define their responsibilities.

- Specify the permissions associated with each role, ensuring they follow the principle of least privilege.

- Create role hierarchies if necessary, where higher-level roles inherit permissions from lower-level roles.

 **Develop and Enforce Access Control Policies:**

- Create clear and comprehensive access control policies that outline who can access what resources and under what conditions.

- Document these policies and communicate them to all employees and stakeholders.

- Use access control mechanisms to enforce the policies consistently across all systems.

Implement Authentication and Authorization Mechanisms:

- Use secure authentication methods such as multi-factor authentication (MFA) and biometric authentication to verify user identities.

- Implement authorization mechanisms to ensure that authenticated users can only access resources for which they have permissions.

Integrate Access Control into Existing Systems:

- Integrate the chosen access control model and policies into your existing IT infrastructure.

- Ensure compatibility with current systems and applications.

Monitor and Audit Access Control:

- Implement logging and monitoring tools to track access control events and user activities.

- Conduct regular audits to ensure compliance with policies and identify potential security breaches.

Review and Update Regularly:

- Periodically review access control policies and permissions to ensure they remain relevant and effective.

- Update access rights as needed to reflect changes in roles, responsibilities, or organizational structure.

 **Provide Training and Awareness:**

- Educate employees about access control policies, the importance of security measures, and best practices for maintaining secure access.

- Conduct regular training sessions and awareness programs.

By following these steps, organizations can implement robust access control systems that protect sensitive data, prevent unauthorized access, and ensure the security and integrity of their applications.

9. HOW CAN AI BE USED IN INCIDENT MANAGEMENT?

AI can significantly enhance incident management by automating various aspects of the process, improving efficiency, and providing advanced analytical capabilities. Here are several ways AI can be utilized:

i. **Automated Detection and Alerts**: AI-driven systems can monitor network traffic and system behavior in real-time, detecting anomalies that may indicate a security incident. These systems can automatically generate alerts, allowing for a quicker response.

ii. **Incident Triage and Prioritization**: AI can help triage incidents by analyzing their severity and potential impact. This prioritization ensures that the most critical incidents are addressed first, optimizing resource allocation.

iii. **Root Cause Analysis**: AI tools can perform rapid root cause analysis by sifting through vast amounts of data to identify the origin of an incident. This speeds up the resolution process and helps prevent future occurrences.

iv. **Automated Response Actions**: AI can automate initial response actions, such as isolating affected systems, applying patches, or implementing predefined remediation steps, reducing response time and mitigating damage.

v. **Threat Intelligence Integration**: AI can integrate and analyze threat intelligence data from various sources, providing a comprehensive understanding of emerging threats and enhancing the incident response strategy.

vi. **Continuous Learning and Improvement**: AI systems can learn from past incidents, improving their detection and response capabilities over time. This continuous learning helps organizations stay ahead of evolving threats.

10. WHAT ARE THE 7 PHASES OF AN INCIDENT RESPONSE PLAN?

The 7 phases of an incident response plan typically include:

i. **Preparation**: Establishing and maintaining an incident response capability, including policies, procedures, training, and tools.

ii. **Identification**: Detecting and confirming the presence of an incident through monitoring and analysis.

iii. **Containment**: Implementing measures to limit the spread and impact of the incident while maintaining business operations as much as possible.

iv. **Eradication**: Eliminating the root cause of the incident, such as removing malware or fixing vulnerabilities.

v. **Recovery**: Restoring and validating system functionality to ensure that operations return to normal and that systems are hardened against future incidents.

vi. **Lessons Learned**: Conducting a post-incident review to identify what went well and what needs improvement, updating the incident response plan accordingly.

vii. **Documentation and Reporting**: Thoroughly documenting the incident and the response actions taken, and reporting to relevant stakeholders and regulatory bodies if necessary.

CHAPTER NINE
AI and Data Governance

As organizations increasingly integrate Artificial Intelligence (AI) into their operations, the governance of data used and generated by these systems becomes critically important. Data governance in the context of AI encompasses the policies, procedures, and frameworks that ensure data integrity, security, and ethical use.

The effective management of data is essential not only for compliance with regulatory requirements but also for maintaining the trustworthiness and accountability of AI systems.

Recent studies highlight the growing complexity of managing data in AI-driven environments.

For instance, research by Veale, van Kleek, and Binns (2018) underscores the challenges of ensuring transparency and fairness in AI systems, particularly when data governance practices are not adequately enforced. Additionally, Raji et al. (2020) emphasize the importance of operationalizing data governance to mitigate risks associated with biased or unethical AI outcomes.

This chapter will examine the key elements of data governance that are vital to the responsible deployment of AI systems. Topics such as data quality, privacy, and compliance will be examined alongside strategies for implementing robust governance frameworks that align with both legal and ethical standards.

Understanding these aspects is crucial for organizations aiming to leverage AI while safeguarding the integrity of their data and the rights of individuals.

UNDERSTANDING AI AND DATA GOVERNANCE

WHAT IS AI AND LARGE LANGUAGE MODELS (LLMS)?

Artificial Intelligence (AI) refers to the simulation of human intelligence by machines, particularly through computational processes such as learning, reasoning, and self-correction. Vijai, C., & Nivetha, P. (2020). AI systems are designed to perform tasks that typically require human intelligence, including problem-solving, pattern recognition, and decision-making.

Domínguez Piernas, G. (2023). A significant subset of AI is the development of Large Language Models (LLMs), such as OpenAI's ChatGPT and Google's Bard. These models are engineered to understand, process, and generate human language by leveraging vast datasets. LLMs are trained on extensive corpora of text data, allowing them to produce coherent and contextually appropriate responses in natural language.

The underlying architecture of these models, often based on transformers as described by Vaswani et al. (2017), enables them to capture complex linguistic patterns and generate text that closely mimics human communication.

WHAT IS DATA GOVERNANCE?

Data governance refers to the comprehensive management of data availability, usability, integrity, and security within an organization. It encompasses a framework of policies, procedures, standards, and metrics designed to ensure that data is used effectively and efficiently to meet organizational goals.

According to Khatri and Brown (2010), key principles of data governance include observability, control, and scalability. Observability ensures that data can be monitored and tracked throughout its lifecycle, control refers to the mechanisms in place to regulate access and usage of data, and scalability involves the ability to manage increasing volumes and varieties of data as organizational needs evolve.

Effective data governance ensures that data remains reliable, secure, and compliant with relevant regulations, thereby supporting decision-making processes and operational efficiency.

INTERSECTION OF AI AND DATA GOVERNANCE

The intersection of AI and data governance is critical to the responsible deployment and operation of AI systems, particularly LLMs. These models rely on vast amounts of data to generate accurate and contextually relevant outputs. However, the use of such extensive datasets introduces significant risks related to data privacy, security, and integrity.

Data governance plays a crucial role in mitigating these risks by ensuring that the data used in training AI models is high-quality, appropriately sourced, and managed throughout its lifecycle.

As noted by Jia et al. (2021), robust data governance frameworks are essential for maintaining the trustworthiness of AI systems, ensuring that they operate within legal and ethical boundaries while also safeguarding the interests of individuals and organizations.

RISKS OF POOR DATA GOVERNANCE IN AI

1. PRIVACY AND RE-IDENTIFICATION RISKS

One of the foremost concerns in AI, particularly with LLMs, is the risk of privacy breaches and re-identification of individuals. These models learn from the data they are trained on, which can include sensitive and personal information. Without proper governance, there is a significant risk that AI models could inadvertently reveal private information through their outputs.

As shown by Shokri et al. (2017), the exposure of personal data in AI models can lead to serious privacy violations, particularly if the training data includes proprietary or sensitive customer information. Proper anonymization and data minimization techniques are crucial to mitigating these risks, ensuring that AI systems do not compromise individual privacy or violate data protection regulations such as the GDPR.

2. IN-MODEL LEARNING DATA

Unlike traditional AI models, which have distinct training and deployment phases, LLMs often continue to learn from user interactions post-deployment. This continuous learning process complicates data governance because every interaction with the model potentially adds new data to its learning base.

If users input sensitive information during these interactions, the model may inadvertently incorporate this data into its responses, creating privacy and security risks. Bender et al. (2021) highlight the challenges posed by this dynamic learning capability, emphasizing the need for stringent governance practices to monitor and manage the data that models encounter in real-time. Ensuring that sensitive information is identified and appropriately handled during this process is essential to maintaining the integrity and security of AI systems.

3. SECURITY AND ACCESS RISKS

The security of AI models is intrinsically linked to the sensitivity of the data they are trained on. While traditional security mechanisms such as role-based access control (RBAC) and data masking are well-established, the evolving security landscape for AI models presents new challenges. Inadequate security measures can lead to unauthorized access to both the models and the data they process, creating vulnerabilities that can be exploited by malicious actors.

According to Tramer et al. (2016), AI models are susceptible to various attacks, including model inversion and membership inference, where attackers can glean sensitive information about the training data by querying the model. Implementing robust security controls and continuous monitoring is vital to prevent leaks of sensitive information through model outputs and to protect against potential breaches.

4. INTELLECTUAL PROPERTY RISKS

The use of proprietary content, such as music, literature, or software, in training AI models raises significant intellectual property (IP) concerns. AI-generated content that closely resembles the original works used in training can lead to potential IP infringements. For instance, if an AI model trained on a comprehensive library of songs by a specific artist generates outputs that mimic the artist's style too closely, it may violate the artist's IP rights.

A study by Zeng et al. (2022) discusses the legal challenges associated with proving whether AI-generated content is original or a replication of the training data. To avoid legal repercussions, organizations must implement rigorous data governance practices that monitor and manage the IP of the data used for training AI models, ensuring that content creators' rights are protected.

5. CONSENT AND DATA SUBJECT ACCESS REQUESTS (DSAR) RISKS

Modern data privacy regulations, such as the GDPR, emphasize the importance of consent and the rights of data subjects, including the right to request data deletion. When AI models are trained on customer data, this data can become deeply embedded in the model's operations. If a customer revokes consent or submits a DSAR, the organization must ensure that the AI model no longer retains or uses that data.

Fulfilling this requirement can be challenging, often necessitating the decommissioning and retraining of models to comply with regulatory demands. As pointed out by Wachter et al. (2017), the complexity of AI models makes it difficult to fully erase personal data, underscoring the importance of robust data governance practices to manage consent and data rights effectively.

BENEFITS OF EFFECTIVE DATA GOVERNANCE IN AI

1. ENHANCED DATA QUALITY AND RELIABILITY

Effective data governance ensures that the data used to train AI models is of high quality and reliability. This involves rigorous data cleaning, validation, and management processes that eliminate errors and inconsistencies. High-quality data is crucial for AI models to generate accurate and reliable outputs.

By implementing strong data governance practices, organizations can enhance the performance and trustworthiness of their AI models, leading to better decision-making and improved operational efficiency.

2. IMPROVED DATA SECURITY

Robust data governance frameworks significantly enhance data security by implementing stringent access controls, encryption, and real-time monitoring. These measures protect sensitive data from unauthorized access and breaches.

By ensuring that only authorized personnel can access and manipulate data, organizations can safeguard against data leaks and cyber threats. This is particularly important for AI models that handle sensitive information, as it mitigates the risk of exposing confidential data through AI outputs.

3. REGULATORY COMPLIANCE

Data governance plays a critical role in helping organizations comply with data protection regulations such as GDPR, HIPAA, and SOC2. These regulations require organizations to implement comprehensive data management and security practices to protect personal and sensitive information.

Effective data governance ensures that AI models are trained and operated in compliance with these regulations, thereby avoiding legal penalties and fostering trust among customers and regulators. This compliance also includes maintaining detailed audit trails and documentation to demonstrate adherence to regulatory requirements.

4. TRUST AND TRANSPARENCY

Implementing strong data governance practices builds trust and transparency with consumers, stakeholders, and regulators. When organizations can demonstrate that they manage and protect data responsibly, it enhances their reputation and credibility.

Transparency in data governance practices also means providing clear documentation and audit trails that show how data is collected, processed, and used. This transparency is essential for addressing concerns about data privacy and AI model integrity, fostering greater acceptance and confidence in AI technologies.

IMPLEMENTING DATA GOVERNANCE FOR AI

1. DATA DISCOVERY AND CLASSIFICATION

Effective data governance begins with comprehensive data discovery and classification. This involves identifying all data sources, understanding the types of data available, and categorizing them based on sensitivity, importance, and compliance requirements.

Data discovery tools can automate this process, ensuring that all relevant data is accounted for and appropriately classified. By clearly identifying and labeling sensitive data, organizations can apply the necessary governance controls to protect it throughout its lifecycle.

2. DATA QUALITY MANAGEMENT

Maintaining high data quality is essential for reliable AI model performance. Data quality management includes processes such as data cleaning, validation, and normalization. These processes ensure that the data fed into AI models is accurate, consistent, and free from errors.

Implementing automated data quality checks can help detect and correct anomalies in real-time, reducing the risk of poor-quality data compromising AI outputs. By prioritizing data quality, organizations can enhance the effectiveness and reliability of their AI models.

3. PRIVACY-ENHANCING TECHNIQUES

To protect sensitive information while leveraging data for AI, organizations can implement privacy-enhancing techniques. These techniques include data anonymization, pseudonymization, and differential privacy. Anonymization removes personally identifiable information from datasets, ensuring that individuals cannot be re-identified.

Pseudonymization replaces sensitive data with artificial identifiers, while differential privacy introduces statistical noise to datasets to protect individual data points. These methods help maintain data utility while safeguarding privacy, allowing organizations to use data responsibly.

4. ACCESS CONTROLS AND SECURITY MEASURES

Robust access controls and security measures are vital components of data governance. Role-based access control (RBAC) ensures that only authorized individuals can access specific data based on their role within the organization. Data encryption protects data at rest and in transit, preventing unauthorized access.

Dynamic data masking can be used to obscure sensitive information in real-time, depending on the user's role and context. Implementing these security measures helps prevent data breaches and ensures that sensitive information is only accessible to those with legitimate needs.

5. AUDIT TRAILS AND ACCOUNTABILITY

Maintaining detailed audit trails is crucial for accountability and compliance. Audit trails record all data access and usage activities, providing a comprehensive log of who accessed what data and when.

This transparency is essential for regulatory compliance and helps organizations identify and address any unauthorized data access or misuse. By implementing robust audit mechanisms, organizations can ensure accountability and traceability in their data governance practices, fostering trust and demonstrating commitment to data protection.

CASE STUDIES AND REAL-WORLD EXAMPLES

HIGH-PROFILE BREACHES AND THEIR IMPACT

Several high-profile data breaches have highlighted the consequences of poor data governance. For instance, the Equifax data breach in 2017 exposed sensitive information of 147 million individuals due to inadequate security measures and failure to patch vulnerabilities.

Similarly, the Cambridge Analytica scandal revealed how the misuse of personal data can lead to significant privacy violations and legal repercussions. These incidents underscore the importance of robust data governance frameworks to protect sensitive information and maintain public trust.

SUCCESSFUL DATA GOVERNANCE IMPLEMENTATIONS

Some organizations have successfully implemented data governance frameworks that can serve as models for others. For example, IBM has developed a comprehensive data governance solution powered by the IBM Knowledge Catalog.

This solution facilitates advanced data discovery, automated data quality management, and data protection, ensuring compliance with regulatory requirements. By proactively identifying and protecting sensitive data, IBM has enhanced its ability to manage data responsibly and leverage AI technologies effectively.

Another example is Microsoft, which has implemented stringent data governance practices to support its AI initiatives. Microsoft's data governance framework includes robust data classification, encryption, and access control measures.

These practices ensure that data used for training AI models is secure and compliant with global data protection regulations. By maintaining detailed audit trails and implementing privacy-enhancing techniques, Microsoft has built a trustworthy AI ecosystem that prioritizes data security and privacy.

DATA QUALITY AND INTEGRITY

The quality and integrity of data are fundamental to the success of various initiatives, from strategic decision-making to enhancing customer experiences. Despite their close relationship, data quality and data integrity serve distinct yet complementary roles in data management. This section delves into these concepts, elucidating their differences, significance, and the methods employed to ensure both are upheld within organizational contexts.

WHAT IS DATA QUALITY?

Data quality refers to the condition of data based on multiple attributes that determine its suitability for its intended purpose. High-quality data is characterized by attributes such as correctness, completeness, consistency, and reliability, which collectively ensure that the data is fit for use in a specific context. Wang and Strong (1996) identified these key dimensions of data quality, highlighting their importance in enabling organizations to trust their data for decision-making and operational purposes.

DIMENSIONS OF DATA QUALITY:

1. **Accuracy**: Data accuracy refers to the degree to which data correctly represents real-world values. Accurate data is free from errors and truly reflects the state of the entity or event it describes. Pipino, Lee, and Wang (2002) emphasized that inaccurate data can lead to erroneous decisions and undermine the credibility of business analytics.

2. **Completeness**: Completeness evaluates whether all necessary data is present within a dataset. Complete data sets contain no missing values or blank fields, ensuring comprehensive information is available for decision-making. Redman (1998) noted that incomplete data can lead to gaps in analysis, reducing the effectiveness of business insights.

3. **Consistency**: Consistency checks whether data is uniform across various datasets and platforms. Consistent data maintains the same format, values, and definitions across different systems, preventing discrepancies. Inconsistent data can result in confusion and errors when integrating or comparing data from different sources (Wand & Wang, 1996).

4. **Validity**: Valid data adheres to the defined formats, standards, and rules set by the organization. It ensures that data is appropriate for its intended use by meeting specific constraints and requirements. Batini, Cappiello, Francalanci, and Maurino (2009) highlighted the importance of validity in ensuring that data supports organizational processes effectively.

5. **Uniqueness**: This dimension ensures that each data point is unique, with no duplicate records present. Uniqueness is crucial for maintaining the integrity of individual records and preventing redundancy. Duplicate records can lead to inefficiencies and inaccuracies in data processing and analysis (Olson, 2003).

6. **Timeliness**: Timeliness assesses whether data is up-to-date and available when needed. Timely data is crucial for making informed decisions based on the most current information. According to Ballou and Pazer (1985), outdated data can lead to decisions based on obsolete or irrelevant information, negatively impacting business outcomes.

IMPORTANCE OF DATA QUALITY:

High data quality is essential for several reasons:

1. **Impact on Decision-Making**: Accurate and reliable data provides a solid foundation for decision-making, enabling organizations to generate meaningful insights and develop effective strategies. Poor data quality can lead to flawed decisions and missed opportunities (Strong, Lee, & Wang, 1997).

2. **Enhancing Operational Efficiency**: High-quality data reduces the need for rework and corrections, streamlining operations and increasing productivity. By ensuring that data is accurate and complete from the outset, organizations can avoid the costs associated with data cleansing and error correction (Redman, 1998).

3. **Ensuring Reliable Analytics and Insights**: Data-driven organizations rely on high-quality data to generate reliable analytics and insights, which drive strategic initiatives and provide a competitive advantage. Inaccurate or incomplete data can undermine the reliability of analytical models and lead to incorrect conclusions (Wang & Strong, 1996).

WHAT IS DATA INTEGRITY?

Data integrity refers to the accuracy, consistency, and security of data throughout its lifecycle. It ensures that data remains unaltered and accurate during storage, retrieval, and processing unless authorized changes are made. Data integrity encompasses dimensions such as completeness, correctness, consistency, accessibility, and security, which collectively define the reliability and trustworthiness of data (Elbashir et al., 2008).

TYPES OF DATA INTEGRITY:

1. **Physical Data Integrity**: Physical data integrity involves preserving data's completeness, accessibility, and correctness while it is at rest or in transit. Physical threats to data integrity include natural disasters, power failures, human errors, and cyberattacks. Ensuring physical data integrity involves safeguarding against these threats through robust physical security measures and disaster recovery plans. As noted by Laudon and Laudon (2015), physical data integrity is foundational to maintaining data availability and reliability in the face of external threats.

2. **Logical Data Integrity**: Logical data integrity focuses on maintaining data consistency and completeness when accessed by multiple stakeholders and applications across different departments, disciplines, and locations. It involves ensuring that data remains accurate and consistent as it is used and updated. Common steps to ensure logical data integrity include:

    💡 **Entity Integrity**: Ensuring that each record is unique and correctly identified, eliminating duplicates to maintain the accuracy of the database (Codd, 1970).

- 💡 **Referential Integrity**: Controlling the storage and use of data to ensure that relationships between data elements are maintained correctly, preventing orphaned or inconsistent records (Date, 2003).

- 💡 **Domain Integrity**: Ensuring that data values fall within a defined domain or set of permissible values, preserving the validity of data entries (Elmasri & Navathe, 2011).

- 💡 **User-Defined Integrity**: Adhering to unique or industry-specific criteria for data, which may include business rules or regulatory requirements specific to the organization or sector (Wang et al., 1995).

IMPORTANCE OF DATA INTEGRITY:

Maintaining data integrity is crucial for several reasons:

1. **Preventing Data Corruption and Loss**: Ensuring data integrity helps protect against data corruption and loss, preserving the accuracy and reliability of data. Data corruption can occur due to hardware failures, software bugs, or malicious attacks, making it essential to implement integrity checks and backups (Haerder & Reuter, 1983).

2. **Ensuring Data Security and Compliance**: Data integrity safeguards sensitive or regulated data from unauthorized access and tampering, helping organizations comply with legal and regulatory requirements. Regulations such as GDPR and HIPAA mandate strict controls over data integrity to protect individuals' privacy and ensure the confidentiality of sensitive information (DAMA UK, 2013).

3. **Maintaining Trust and Reliability**: High data integrity fosters trust in the data among stakeholders, ensuring that it can be relied upon for critical business operations and decision-making. Without data integrity, the credibility of organizational data can be compromised, leading to a loss

of trust and potential reputational damage. Consterdine, A. (2020).

DIFFERENCES BETWEEN DATA QUALITY AND DATA INTEGRITY

While data quality and data integrity are closely related, they serve distinct roles in data management:

1. **DEFINITIONS AND SCOPE:**

   - **Data Quality**: Refers to the condition of data in terms of its accuracy, completeness, consistency, validity, uniqueness, and timeliness. It evaluates whether the data is fit for its intended purpose (Wang & Strong, 1996).

   - **Data Integrity**: Refers to the preservation of data accuracy, consistency, and security throughout its lifecycle. It focuses on ensuring that data remains unchanged and accurate unless authorized changes are made (Elbashir et al., 2008).

2. **GOALS AND OBJECTIVES:**

   - **Data Quality**: The primary goal is to ensure that data is accurate, relevant, and suitable for its intended use, enabling informed decision-making and operational efficiency (Strong et al., 1997).

   - **Data Integrity**: The main objective is to maintain data security and trustworthiness by preventing unauthorized changes and preserving data reliability (Laudon & Laudon, 2015).

3. **METHODS AND PRACTICES:**

   - **Data Quality**: Achieved through data cleansing, data profiling, data standardization, and data governance. These practices ensure data is accurate, complete, and consistent (Redman, 1998).

- 💡 **Data Integrity**: Ensured through encryption, checksums, access restrictions, and data validation. These measures prevent data corruption, loss, and unauthorized access (Codd, 1970; Haerder & Reuter, 1983).

EXAMPLES TO ILLUSTRATE DIFFERENCES:

1. FINANCIAL DATABASE SCENARIO:

- 💡 **Data Integrity**: Ensures that the data related to each transaction, such as the transaction amount, date, and parties involved, remains constant and correct in the database. Access controls and data validation checks prevent unauthorized modifications to these records (Elmasri & Navathe, 2011).

- 💡 **Data Quality**: Ensures that the transaction data is accurate, complete, and up-to-date. For instance, verifying that transaction amounts are correct and that all required fields are filled in correctly (Strong et al., 1997).

2. E-COMMERCE CUSTOMER DATA SCENARIO:

- 💡 **Data Integrity**: Maintains the consistency and correctness of customer information, such as names, addresses, and contact details, across the database. Prevents unauthorized changes and data breaches (Date, 2003).

- 💡 **Data Quality**: Ensures that customer information is accurate, complete, and up-to-date. Regularly verifying and updating customer contact information, shipping addresses, and preferences to enhance customer service and targeted marketing efforts (Redman, 1998).

METHODS TO MAINTAIN DATA QUALITY

1. **Data Cleansing**: Data cleansing, or data cleaning, involves identifying and correcting errors, inconsistencies, and inaccuracies within a dataset. This process includes several steps, such as:

   - **Deduplication**: Ensuring multiple data entries do not accidentally appear across several locations (Olson, 2003).

   - **Correction**: Fixing errors in data values, such as misspellings or incorrect formats (Redman, 1998).

   - **Standardization**: Converting data into a consistent format to facilitate easy use and analysis (Wang et al., 1995).

2. **Data Profiling**: Data profiling involves analyzing data to understand its structure, content, and interrelationships. This helps in identifying data quality issues and monitoring data consistency. Key steps include:

   - **Assessing Data Quality**: Evaluating data for accuracy, completeness, and consistency (Batini et al., 2009).

   - **Monitoring Data Consistency**: Ensuring that data remains uniform across different datasets and platforms (Wand & Wang, 1996).

3. **Data Standardization**: Data standardization is the process of converting fragmented data assets and unstructured big data into a standardized format. This ensures that data is complete and ready for use, regardless of the source. It involves applying business rules to ensure datasets meet organizational requirements (Redman, 1998).

4. **Data Enrichment**: Data enrichment involves updating and enhancing existing data to add missing information and improve accuracy. This process builds on current data to

support better decision-making and customer interactions. Steps include:

- 💡 **Adding New Information**: Integrating additional data points to fill gaps (Pipino et al., 2002).

- 💡 **Updating Existing Data**: Regularly refreshing data to keep it current and accurate (Strong et al., 1997).

5. **Data Governance**: Data governance entails developing a framework and set of processes to control and assure data quality across the organization. It involves:

- 💡 **Defining Roles and Responsibilities**: Establishing who is responsible for data management tasks (Khatri & Brown, 2010).

- 💡 **Implementing Processes**: Setting rules and standards for data handling, storage, and usage (DAMA UK, 2013).

- 💡 **Ensuring Consistency**: Applying consistent data management practices across the organization (Wang & Strong, 1996).

6. **Data Quality Monitoring**: Monitoring data quality is essential for identifying and addressing data quality issues. Key activities include:

- 💡 **Setting Quality Metrics**: Defining standards for data quality dimensions such as accuracy, completeness, and timeliness (Pipino et al., 2002).

- 💡 **Continuous Monitoring**: Regularly checking data against these metrics to ensure it meets the required standards (Olson, 2003).

- 💡 **Reporting Issues**: Documenting and addressing any data quality problems as they arise (Redman, 1998).

TOOLS AND TECHNOLOGIES:

Various tools and technologies can help maintain data quality, including:

- ◈ **Data Quality Tools**: Software designed to assess, cleanse, and standardize data (Wang & Strong, 1996).

- ◈ **Data Profiling Tools**: Tools that analyze data to identify quality issues and monitor consistency (Batini et al., 2009).

- ◈ **Data Governance Platforms**: Systems that support the implementation of data governance frameworks and processes (Khatri & Brown, 2010).

METHODS TO MAINTAIN DATA INTEGRITY

PHYSICAL SECURITY MEASURES:

Physical security measures are crucial to protecting data from physical threats such as natural disasters, power failures, and unauthorized access. These measures include:

- ◈ **Secure Storage Environments:** Storing data in secure facilities with controlled access to prevent unauthorized entry.

- ◈ **Disaster Recovery Plans:** Implementing backup systems and recovery plans to restore data in case of physical damage or loss.

ACCESS CONTROLS:

Access controls ensure that only authorized personnel can access and modify data. This is achieved through:

- ◈ **User Roles and Permissions:** Assigning specific roles and permissions to users based on their responsibilities and access needs.

❖ **Authentication Mechanisms:** Implementing strong authentication methods, such as multi-factor authentication, to verify user identities.

SYSTEM CHECKS:

Regular system checks are essential for maintaining data integrity. These checks include:

❖ **Error-Checking Processes:** Identifying and correcting errors in data to ensure its accuracy.

❖ **Validation Processes:** Verifying that data meets predefined standards and constraints.

VERSION CONTROL AND AUDIT TRAILS:

Version control and audit trails help track changes made to data over time, ensuring its integrity:

❖ **Version Control:** Keeping track of different versions of data to ensure that changes are documented and reversible if necessary.

❖ **Audit Trails:** Maintaining logs of data access and modifications to monitor who accessed the data, when, and what changes were made.

ENCRYPTION:

As mentioned earlier, data encryption involves encoding data to protect it from unauthorized access and tampering. Key encryption practices include:

❖ **Data at Rest Encryption:** Encrypting data stored in databases and on drives to safeguard it from physical and logical threats.

❖ **Data in Transit Encryption:** Encrypting data transmitted over networks to protect it from interception and unauthorized access.

DATA VALIDATION AND VERIFICATION:

Data validation and verification ensure the accuracy and completeness of data during entry and import processes. This includes:

◈ **Validation Rules:** Applying established rules to check data against specific criteria.

◈ **Verification Processes:** Cross-checking data with other sources or methods to confirm its accuracy.

AUDIT TRAILS AND LOGS:

Audit trails and logs document specific data changes and access activities. They help:

◈ **Monitor Data Access:** Tracking who accessed the data, when, and what changes were made.

◈ **Identify Security Breaches:** Detecting potential security breaches and data quality issues.

ERROR HANDLING MECHANISMS:

Error handling mechanisms outline procedures for identifying, reporting, and resolving data inconsistencies or errors. These mechanisms include:

◈ **Error Reporting Systems:** Tools for reporting data errors as they occur.

◈ **Data Cleansing Procedures:** Steps to correct data errors and restore data integrity.

REGULAR BACKUP AND RECOVERY PLANS:

Regular data backups involve creating copies of data at predetermined times to ensure data can be recovered in case of loss. Key practices include:

◈ **Scheduled Backups:** Regularly backing up data to prevent loss due to hardware failures, system crashes, or cyberattacks.

◈ **Recovery Plans:** Developing and implementing plans to restore data quickly and accurately in case of data loss.

DATA ENTRY CONTROLS:

Data entry controls are procedures used to reduce mistakes and maintain data correctness during the data entry process. Examples include:

◈ **Drop-Down Menus and Data Pickers:** Tools to help users enter data in the correct format.

◈ **Validation Checks:** Ensuring that data entered meets predefined standards and limits.

BENEFITS OF HIGH DATA QUALITY AND INTEGRITY

FOR ORGANIZATIONS:

1. ENHANCED DECISION-MAKING CAPABILITIES:

High-quality and high-integrity data provide the foundation for informed decision-making. When data is accurate, complete, and consistent, decision-makers have access to reliable information that supports strategic and operational choices. For example, in the financial services sector, accurate transaction data enables precise financial reporting and forecasting, critical for maintaining financial stability and compliance with regulatory requirements (Elbashir et al., 2008). Similarly, in healthcare, reliable patient data is essential for correct diagnoses and treatment plans, directly impacting patient outcomes and the quality of care provided Astroth, K., & Chung, S. (2018).

2. IMPROVED OPERATIONAL EFFICIENCY:

Maintaining high data quality and integrity minimizes the need for rework and corrections, thereby streamlining operations and boosting productivity. Consistent and reliable data ensures that organizational processes run smoothly, reducing the likelihood of errors and delays. For instance, in supply chain management, accurate inventory data allows for optimal stock levels and reduces wastage, resulting in cost savings and enhanced operational efficiency (Redman, 1998). By ensuring that all data points are accurate and up-to-date, organizations can avoid costly inefficiencies and improve overall performance.

3. INCREASED TRUST AND RELIABILITY:

High-quality and high-integrity data fosters trust among all stakeholders, including employees, customers, and business partners. When data is trustworthy, stakeholders are more confident in relying on it for their needs, which enhances collaboration and reinforces confidence in organizational processes. In customer-facing roles, such as sales and support, accurate and reliable data enables personalized interactions, leading to improved customer service, loyalty, and satisfaction (Strong et al., 1997). Trust in data also strengthens relationships with partners, ensuring that collaborative efforts are based on solid and dependable information.

FOR DATA-DRIVEN INITIATIVES:

1. RELIABLE BUSINESS INTELLIGENCE AND ANALYTICS:

Data-driven initiatives, such as business intelligence (BI) and analytics, are heavily dependent on high-quality and high-integrity data. The reliability of analytics models and reports hinges on the accuracy and consistency of the underlying data. Accurate data ensures that the insights generated are meaningful and actionable, driving business growth and informed decision-making. In marketing, for instance, high-quality customer data allows for more effective segmentation and targeted campaigns, leading to improved return on investment (ROI) and enhanced customer engagement (Pipino, Lee, & Wang, 2002).

2. BETTER MACHINE LEARNING AND DATA SCIENCE OUTCOMES:

Machine learning (ML) and data science applications benefit significantly from robust data integrity and quality. Reliable data ensures that ML models are trained on accurate and representative datasets, leading to more precise predictions and better automation outcomes. For example, in predictive maintenance, accurate equipment data enables the development of models that can anticipate failures and schedule timely maintenance, thereby reducing downtime and associated costs (Provost & Fawcett, 2013). The integrity of the data used in these models is crucial to ensuring that predictions are both reliable and actionable.

3. COMPLIANCE WITH REGULATORY STANDARDS:

High data integrity chd quality are essential for complying with various legal and regulatory standards. Organizations must ensure that their data is accurate, complete, and secure to meet requirements such as the General Data Protection Regulation (GDPR), the Health Insurance Portability and Accountability Act (HIPAA), and the Sarbanes-Oxley

Act (SOX). Compliance with these regulations not only helps organizations avoid legal penalties but also enhances their reputation and trustworthiness. Moreover, regulatory compliance often requires rigorous data governance practices that reinforce the importance of maintaining high data quality and integrity (Khatri & Brown, 2010).

ADDITIONAL BENEFITS:

1. DATA RECOVERY AND BUSINESS CONTINUITY:

Maintaining high data integrity plays a critical role in data recovery and business continuity planning. In the event of data breaches or unplanned outages, well-preserved data ensures that organizations can recover quickly and minimize the impact of data loss incidents. Regular backups, supported by robust data integrity measures, allow for efficient data restoration, reducing downtime and operational disruptions (Haerder & Reuter, 1983). Ensuring data integrity is therefore a key aspect of an organization's resilience and ability to maintain continuity in the face of unexpected challenges.

2. UNLOCKING TANGIBLE BUSINESS VALUE:

High-quality and high-integrity data unlocks tangible business value by enabling more effective data-driven decision-making and process optimization. Organizations can leverage reliable data to identify new opportunities, optimize resource allocation, and enhance overall performance. In the e-commerce sector, for instance, high-quality customer data enables personalized recommendations and targeted promotions, driving sales and increasing customer satisfaction (Olson, 2003). By ensuring that data is both high-quality and secure, organizations can maximize the value derived from their data assets and maintain a competitive edge in their respective markets.

CHALLENGES IN MAINTAINING DATA QUALITY AND INTEGRITY

COMMON CHALLENGES:

1. DATA SILOS AND DISPERSED STORAGE:

- Data silos occur when data is stored in isolated systems, leading to inconsistencies and difficulties in accessing comprehensive information. Dispersed storage can result in fragmented data, making it challenging to maintain consistency and accuracy across the organization.

- For example, different departments may store customer information separately, resulting in duplicate records and inconsistent data updates.

2. INCONSISTENT DATA ENTRY AND COLLECTION PROCESSES:

- Variability in data entry and collection methods can lead to inconsistencies and errors. Without standardized processes, data quality and integrity suffer, as different formats, definitions, and validation criteria are used.

- In healthcare, different clinics might record patient information differently, leading to inconsistencies in patient records and treatment histories.

3. DATA VOLUME AND COMPLEXITY:

- The increasing volume and complexity of data make it difficult to manage and ensure its quality and integrity. Large datasets from various sources require significant effort to clean, validate, and standardize.

- In financial services, managing transactional data from multiple platforms can be complex, requiring robust systems to ensure accuracy and consistency.

4. **LACK OF AWARENESS AND TRAINING:**
   - Employees may not be aware of the importance of data quality and integrity, leading to unintentional errors and poor data management practices. Without proper training, staff may not follow best practices for data handling.
   - In manufacturing, workers may not understand the impact of incorrect data entry on inventory management and production schedules.

5. **TECHNOLOGICAL LIMITATIONS:**
   - Legacy systems and outdated technology can hinder efforts to maintain data quality and integrity. Inadequate tools and platforms may not support modern data management practices, leading to data issues.
   - Organizations relying on outdated databases might struggle to implement advanced data quality and integrity measures effectively.

STRATEGIES TO OVERCOME CHALLENGES:

1. **IMPLEMENTING COMPREHENSIVE DATA GOVERNANCE FRAMEWORKS:**
   - Establishing a robust data governance framework helps define roles, responsibilities, and processes for managing data quality and integrity across the organization. This includes setting policies, standards, and guidelines for data management.
   - Regular audits and reviews ensure compliance with data governance policies and help identify areas for improvement.

   1. **Utilizing Advanced Data Quality and Integrity Tools:**

- Leveraging modern data management tools and technologies can significantly improve data quality and integrity. Tools for data cleansing, profiling, and standardization help ensure data accuracy and consistency.

- Data observability platforms monitor data pipelines and detect anomalies, enabling proactive management of data quality issues.

2. **Regular Training and Awareness Programs for Staff:**

- Conducting regular training sessions and awareness programs educates employees about the importance of data quality and integrity. Training should cover best practices for data entry, handling, and management.

- Creating a culture of data stewardship encourages employees to take ownership of data quality and integrity.

3. **Standardizing Data Entry and Collection Processes:**

- Developing standardized processes for data entry and collection ensures consistency across the organization. Implementing data validation checks and input controls helps reduce errors and maintain data quality.

- For example, using standardized forms and templates for data entry ensures that information is captured uniformly.

4. **Integrating Data from Multiple Sources:**

- Implementing data integration solutions helps consolidate data from various sources into a unified system. This reduces data silos and ensures a consistent view of information across the organization.

- Data integration platforms facilitate the merging and reconciliation of disparate datasets, improving overall data quality and integrity.

CASE STUDIES AND REAL-WORLD APPLICATIONS

HEALTHCARE INDUSTRY

CASE STUDY: KAISER PERMANENTE'S DATA GOVERNANCE INITIATIVE

◈ Kaiser Permanente, one of the largest healthcare providers in the United States, recognized the critical importance of maintaining accurate and complete patient records. Bolden, R., Sheffield, R., Kars-Unluoglu, S., Roberts, M., & Jarvis, C. (2021). In 2006, they undertook a comprehensive data governance initiative to improve the quality of their electronic health records (EHR). This initiative involved the standardization of data entry procedures, regular audits, and the implementation of advanced data validation tools. As a result, Kaiser Permanente significantly reduced errors in patient records, which led to improved patient outcomes and increased trust in their healthcare services. This case underscores the necessity of robust data governance frameworks in healthcare to ensure data accuracy and reliability, which are vital for effective patient care (Kaiser Permanente, 2010).

CASE STUDY: CLEVELAND CLINIC'S USE OF DATA QUALITY TOOLS

◈ Cleveland Clinic, a renowned medical center, faced challenges with data accuracy, particularly in patient records and clinical data. To address these issues, the clinic implemented advanced data quality management tools that continuously monitored and validated data across their systems. This initiative led to a substantial reduction in data entry errors and discrepancies, thereby improving the accuracy of diagnoses and treatment plans. Cleveland Clinic's experience highlights the role of data quality tools in enhancing patient care by ensuring that medical decisions are based on reliable and accurate information (Halamka, 2016).

FINANCE INDUSTRY

CASE STUDY: JPMORGAN CHASE'S BLOCKCHAIN IMPLEMENTATION

❖ JPMorgan Chase, one of the largest financial institutions in the world, has been at the forefront of integrating blockchain technology to enhance the integrity of its transaction data. In 2018, JPMorgan launched its own blockchain-based platform, Quorum, which allows for secure and transparent financial transactions. The use of blockchain ensures that transaction records are immutable and can be audited in real time, reducing the risk of data corruption and enhancing customer trust. This implementation has not only strengthened data security but also improved the efficiency of financial operations within the bank. JPMorgan's experience demonstrates the transformative potential of blockchain technology in maintaining data integrity in the finance sector (JPMorgan Chase, 2018).

CASE STUDY: EQUIFAX DATA BREACH AND ITS AFTERMATH

❖ In 2017, Equifax, a major credit reporting agency, suffered a massive data breach that exposed the personal information of 147 million people. The breach was a result of poor data security practices and a failure to maintain data integrity. Following the breach, Equifax implemented a series of measures to enhance their data governance and cybersecurity practices, including the adoption of advanced encryption technologies and regular security audits. The Equifax case serves as a cautionary tale of the consequences of neglecting data integrity and security, and highlights the critical need for robust data governance frameworks to protect sensitive financial information (Federal Trade Commission, 2019).

MARKETING AND E-COMMERCE

CASE STUDY: NETFLIX'S DATA-DRIVEN TARGETED CAMPAIGNS

◈ Netflix, the global streaming giant, is renowned for its data-driven approach to marketing and customer engagement. By utilizing high-quality data from its vast user base, Netflix is able to create highly targeted and personalized marketing campaigns. The company employs data enrichment and profiling tools to maintain an up-to-date and comprehensive customer database, which allows for precise audience segmentation. For example, Netflix uses viewing history, search patterns, and user interactions to recommend content that is tailored to individual preferences. This personalized approach has led to increased user engagement and retention, as well as higher conversion rates for new subscriptions. Netflix's success demonstrates the power of high-quality data in driving effective marketing strategies and enhancing customer experiences (Gomez-Uribe & Hunt, 2015).

CASE STUDY: AMAZON'S CUSTOMER EXPERIENCE ENHANCEMENT THROUGH ACCURATE DATA

◈ Amazon, one of the largest e-commerce platforms in the world, leverages high-quality data to improve customer experience across its platform. The company uses sophisticated data quality management practices to ensure that customer information is always accurate and up-to-date. By maintaining a high standard of data accuracy, Amazon is able to offer personalized product recommendations, timely order updates, and tailored customer service interactions. For instance, Amazon's recommendation engine, powered by accurate customer data, significantly boosts sales by suggesting relevant products to customers. This focus on data quality has played a crucial role in Amazon's ability to build customer loyalty and achieve high levels of customer satisfaction (Linden, Smith, & York, 2003).

SUPPLY CHAIN MANAGEMENT

CASE STUDY: WALMART'S INVENTORY MANAGEMENT OPTIMIZATION

◈ Walmart, the world's largest retailer, has a highly complex supply chain that relies on accurate and timely data for efficient inventory management. To ensure the accuracy of its inventory data, Walmart implemented rigorous data standardization and validation processes. These processes help Walmart maintain accurate stock levels, prevent stockouts, and reduce excess inventory. By leveraging high-quality data, Walmart is able to optimize its inventory management, leading to significant cost savings and enhanced operational efficiency. This data-driven approach has allowed Walmart to maintain its competitive edge in the retail industry by ensuring products are available when and where customers need them (Traub, 2018).

CASE STUDY: PROCTER & GAMBLE'S COST SAVINGS THROUGH DATA INTEGRATION

◈ Procter & Gamble (P&G), a global leader in consumer goods, utilizes advanced data integration and observability tools to maintain high data quality across its supply chain. By ensuring that data from different parts of the supply chain is accurate and consistent, P&G has been able to optimize production schedules, minimize waste, and reduce operational costs. For instance, the company's use of integrated data analytics has enabled it to better forecast demand, streamline production processes, and enhance overall supply chain efficiency. This focus on maintaining high data quality has allowed P&G to achieve significant cost savings while improving the reliability of its supply chain operations (Rao, 2018).

DATA LIFECYCLE MANAGEMENT

Data has become an essential asset for businesses, driving innovation, improving decision-making, and shaping the future. However, the increasing volume of data generated by organizations presents significant challenges in managing this valuable resource effectively.

This is where Data Lifecycle Management (DLM) comes in – a comprehensive approach to overseeing data throughout its lifecycle, from creation to deletion.

According to Gartner (2021), effective Data Lifecycle Management not only ensures that data is stored and maintained according to regulatory requirements but also enhances data quality and accessibility, which are critical for leveraging data as a strategic asset

In this section, we will discuss the intricacies of DLM, exploring its definition, goals, and the importance it holds in today's data-driven world. We'll also break down the key stages involved in DLM, discuss the benefits of implementing a robust DLM strategy, and highlight the tools and technologies that facilitate successful DLM implementation.

By the end of this guide, you'll have a thorough understanding of how DLM can help your organization safeguard its data assets and harness their full potential for driving innovation and growth.

UNDERSTANDING DATA LIFECYCLE MANAGEMENT (DLM)

Data Lifecycle Management (DLM) is a policy-based approach comprising best practices to oversee the flow of an information system's data through its entire lifecycle, from creation to deletion.

This approach includes stages such as storage, backup, archiving, and disposal, making it particularly relevant for organizations managing sensitive, private data subject to regulatory compliance.

The primary purpose of DLM is to ensure that data is accessible to the appropriate users at the appropriate time, maintaining its usability and relevance throughout its existence. By systematically managing data, organizations can ensure data accuracy, consistency, and security, thereby enhancing operational efficiency and supporting strategic decision-making.

GOALS OF DLM

Data Lifecycle Management is designed to achieve three primary objectives within an organization:

1. **To Protect Confidentiality:** Ensuring that sensitive information is accessed only by authorized individuals, thereby safeguarding against unauthorized access and data breaches.

2. **To Ensure Data Integrity:** Maintaining the accuracy and consistency of data over its lifecycle, preventing corruption and ensuring that the data remains reliable and trustworthy.

3. **To Ensure the Availability of Data:** Making sure that data is accessible whenever needed by authorized users, supporting continuous business operations and timely decision-making.

IMPORTANCE OF DATA LIFECYCLE MANAGEMENT

1. DATA GROWTH

As businesses continue to expand their operations, the amount of data they generate grows exponentially. This vast volume of data can include everything from customer information and financial records to operational metrics and employee details. Managing this data effectively is crucial to harnessing its full potential. Without a structured approach like DLM, organizations can quickly become overwhelmed, leading to data sprawl, inconsistencies, and security vulnerabilities.

2.   RISK MITIGATION

One of the most critical aspects of DLM is its role in mitigating risks associated with data management. Poor data management practices can expose organizations to a range of threats, including unauthorized access, data breaches, and data corruption. By implementing DLM, organizations can establish protocols for data acquisition, access, use, and deletion. These protocols help safeguard sensitive information and ensure compliance with relevant regulations, reducing the likelihood of security incidents and associated costs.

3.   REGULATORY COMPLIANCE

In today's regulatory environment, compliance with data protection laws is not optional. Regulations such as the General Data Protection Regulation (GDPR), Health Insurance Portability and Accountability Act (HIPAA), and California Consumer Privacy Act (CCPA) impose stringent requirements on how organizations handle personal data.

DLM helps organizations align with these regulations by providing a structured approach to data management. This includes maintaining accurate records, implementing robust security measures, and ensuring data is used and stored in compliance with legal requirements.

A well-implemented DLM strategy can help organizations mitigate the risk of unauthorized access to sensitive data and data corruption due to malware and other infections, ensuring that data remains a valuable asset rather than a liability.

KEY STAGES OF DATA LIFECYCLE MANAGEMENT

1.   DATA COLLECTION

The data collection phase is the foundation of the data lifecycle. It involves capturing data, defining its purpose, classifying it, and eliminating redundant data. During this stage, organizations must establish rules to collect data in standardized formats and create policies for different types of data, such as employee, partner, and accounting data.

Additionally, policies for handling personal data according to data privacy regulations must be developed. Without accurate and relevant data, businesses cannot effectively analyze and utilize the information to make informed decisions, improve operations, and drive growth.

2.   DATA STORAGE AND MAINTENANCE

Once data is collected, it must be stored and maintained securely. This stage involves processing, merging, aggregating, classifying, and selecting data to ensure its accuracy and completeness. Employing a Relational Database Management System (RDBMS) is a widely used approach for data storage.

RDBMS solutions, such as Oracle Database, Microsoft SQL Server, and MySQL, manage and preserve data securely and are compatible with most programming languages for data manipulation and query operations.

Alternatively, unstructured data can be stored in NoSQL databases or data lakes for easier storage and analysis. During this stage, organizations should also establish rules for data backups, archiving, retention policies, and database maintenance to ensure data security and accessibility.

3. DATA PROCESSING

Data processing transforms raw data into useful information through a series of steps, making it a cyclic process. This stage includes data processing and calculations to derive valuable insights from the data. Common tools used for data processing include Hadoop, Apache Spark, Python, and JavaScript.

These tools help create insights and predictions, aiding in decision-making. It is also essential to monitor data usage to ensure compliance with standards and legal and ethical boundaries. Data processing must adhere to regulations such as GDPR, CCPA, HIPAA, PCI DSS, and others to maintain compliance and protect data integrity.

4. DATA SHARING AND USAGE

Data sharing is a critical component of DLM, facilitating the tracking of actual data usage to ensure compliance with business rules and standards. Sharing data across organizations and departments can increase productivity and reduce data maintenance costs.

Typically, data management involves sharing operational data, master data, metadata, and user-generated data. By sharing these types of data, businesses can foster collaboration, streamline processes, and make more informed decisions.

However, the challenge lies in ensuring that shared data remains secure and compliant with relevant regulations. Implementing data governance policies and security measures can help achieve a balance between data sharing and maintaining data privacy.

5.   **DATA DELETION AND ARCHIVING**

Data deletion and archiving are fundamental parts of the data management lifecycle. Proper data deletion policies and action plans are essential for efficient data management.

Organizations should implement efficient data deletion policies and action plans to optimize data storage and usage, ensure compliance with data retention regulations, and avoid potential legal or financial repercussions.

Data archiving guarantees the preservation and availability of data for future use while reducing storage costs by removing inactive and redundant data. Successful implementation of a comprehensive data deletion policy requires understanding the organization's data needs and retention requirements, as well as proper budgeting and planning.

IMPLEMENTING AN EFFECTIVE DLM STRATEGY

1.   **DATA GOVERNANCE POLICIES**

Data governance policies are essential documents that outline expectations, responsibilities, procedures, and goals related to data management. These policies establish rules and standards for protecting, verifying, and making data available to facilitate informed decision-making based on accurate, consistent, and understandable data.

Effective data governance policies ensure that data is managed responsibly and remains a reliable asset for the organization. They help define roles and responsibilities, set data quality standards, and establish processes for data handling and stewardship.

2. DATA SECURITY MEASURES

Protecting sensitive data from unauthorized access, data breaches, and other security threats is a crucial aspect of DLM. Data security measures such as encryption, access control, data masking, and data loss prevention help safeguard data throughout its lifecycle. Encryption ensures that data remains confidential even if it is intercepted.

Access control restricts data access to authorized users, preventing unauthorized access. Data masking obscures sensitive information in datasets, reducing the risk of exposure.

Data loss prevention tools monitor and protect data from accidental or malicious loss. Implementing these security measures helps organizations maintain the integrity and confidentiality of their data assets.

3. COMPLIANCE WITH REGULATIONS

Adhering to data protection regulations is vital for organizations to operate within legal and ethical boundaries. Compliance with regulations such as GDPR, HIPAA, CCPA, and others involves adhering to the rules and standards established by governing bodies or industry-specific organizations.

Ensuring compliance can be challenging due to the complexity and diversity of regulations. Organizations must conduct regular audits and security assessments, monitor data usage, and provide training on data security measures to their employees.

Using automated data governance platforms can help streamline compliance efforts and ensure that data is managed according to legal requirements.

STEPS FOR EFFECTIVE DLM IMPLEMENTATION

1. **ASSESS CURRENT DATA MANAGEMENT PRACTICES:**
   - Conduct a thorough evaluation of existing data management processes and identify areas for improvement.
   - Understand the organization's data needs and regulatory requirements.

2. **DEVELOP A COMPREHENSIVE DLM PLAN:**
   - Create a detailed DLM strategy that includes data governance policies, security measures, and compliance protocols.
   - Define clear objectives and goals for data management.

3. **IMPLEMENT DATA GOVERNANCE POLICIES:**
   - Establish and enforce data governance policies to ensure consistent and responsible data management.
   - Assign roles and responsibilities for data stewardship.

4. **ADOPT ROBUST DATA SECURITY MEASURES:**
   - Implement encryption, access control, data masking, and data loss prevention to protect sensitive data.
   - Regularly update security measures to address emerging threats.

5. **ENSURE REGULATORY COMPLIANCE:**
   - Conduct regular audits and security assessments to ensure compliance with relevant regulations.
   - Provide training and resources to employees on data security and compliance.

6. UTILIZE DATA MANAGEMENT TOOLS AND TECHNOLOGIES:

- Leverage data management platforms, classification tools, and monitoring solutions to streamline DLM processes.

- Ensure that these tools are integrated into the organization's data management framework.

TOOLS AND TECHNOLOGIES FOR DATA LIFECYCLE MANAGEMENT

1. DATA MANAGEMENT PLATFORMS (DMPS)

Data Management Platforms (DMPs) are software systems designed to collect, organize, and activate data from various sources, including online, offline, and mobile. These platforms help organizations manage and utilize their data effectively for targeted advertising and personalization initiatives.

Key features of DMPs include data integration, audience building, cross-device targeting, and automated data analytics. By leveraging DMPs, organizations can gain a holistic view of their data, enabling them to create detailed customer profiles and enhance their marketing efforts.

Examples of popular DMPs include Salesforce DMP, Adobe Audience Manager, and Oracle BlueKai.

2. DATA CLASSIFICATION TOOLS

Data classification tools help organizations identify and categorize sensitive information within their data repositories. These tools assign attributes to each piece of data, making it easier to recognize and manage sensitive information.

Effective data classification ensures that sensitive data is appropriately safeguarded and managed according to its importance and risk level. Common data classification tools include Oracle Cloud Infrastructure Data Catalog, IBM

Watson Knowledge Catalog, and Microsoft Purview Data Catalog.

While these tools can be resource-intensive and costly, they play a crucial role in maintaining data security and compliance.

3. DATA MONITORING AND ANALYTICS

Data monitoring involves continuously reviewing and evaluating essential business data to guarantee its quality and verify compliance with established standards. Data analytics transforms data into insights, helping organizations make informed decisions.

Together, data monitoring and analytics tools ensure high-quality data and provide meaningful insights to support decision-making. Examples of data monitoring tools include Splunk, Datadog, and Logz.io.

These tools help organizations track data usage, detect anomalies, and ensure data integrity. By utilizing advanced analytics, businesses can uncover trends, predict outcomes, and optimize operations.

ADDITIONAL TECHNOLOGIES

1. DATA ENCRYPTION TOOLS:

Protect data by converting it into a secure format that can only be read by authorized parties. Examples include AES encryption and RSA encryption tools.

2. ACCESS CONTROL SOLUTIONS:

Manage and restrict access to data based on user roles and permissions. Common solutions include role-based access control (RBAC) and attribute-based access control (ABAC).

3. **DATA MASKING TOOLS:**

    💡 Hide sensitive information by substituting it with fictional data, ensuring that real data remains protected during testing and development. Examples include Delphix and IBM InfoSphere Optim.

4. **DATA LOSS PREVENTION (DLP) SOLUTIONS:**

    💡 Monitor and protect data from accidental or malicious loss. Examples include Symantec DLP and McAfee Total Protection for DLP.

5. **AUTOMATED DATA GOVERNANCE PLATFORMS:**

    💡 Streamline data governance processes by automating policy enforcement, data quality checks, and compliance monitoring. Examples include Collibra and Informatica Axon.

COMMON CHALLENGES AND SOLUTIONS IN DLM

CHALLENGES

1. **RESOURCE ALLOCATION:**

    💡 Implementing and maintaining a comprehensive DLM strategy requires significant resources, including time, budget, and skilled personnel. Organizations often struggle to allocate sufficient resources to manage their data effectively.

2. **DATA QUALITY AND ACCURACY:**

    💡 Ensuring data quality and accuracy is a constant challenge. Inaccurate or incomplete data can lead to poor decision-making and operational inefficiencies.

3. **DATA SECURITY:**

   💡 Protecting data from unauthorized access, breaches, and other security threats is critical. Organizations face challenges in implementing robust security measures to safeguard sensitive data.

4. **REGULATORY COMPLIANCE:**

   💡 Keeping up with constantly changing data protection regulations and ensuring compliance can be daunting. Non-compliance can result in legal penalties and damage to the organization's reputation.

5. **DATA INTEGRATION AND INTEROPERABILITY:**

   💡 Integrating data from various sources and ensuring interoperability between different systems and platforms can be complex. This challenge is exacerbated by the growing volume and variety of data.

6. **SCALABILITY:**

   💡 As organizations grow, their data management needs increase. Ensuring that DLM strategies and tools can scale to accommodate larger volumes of data is a significant challenge.

SOLUTIONS

1. **AUTOMATED SOLUTIONS:**

   💡 Automating data management processes is one of the most effective ways to ensure accuracy and efficiency in DLM. Automation tools help streamline manual activities such as data entry, verification, transfer, and archiving. Examples of automated solutions include robotic process automation (RPA) and artificial intelligence (AI)-powered data management tools.

2. **PROPER DATA GOVERNANCE PROTOCOLS:**

   💡 Establishing and enforcing proper data governance protocols is essential for managing data effectively. These protocols define roles and responsibilities, set data quality standards, and establish processes for data handling. Implementing a data governance framework helps organizations create a unified data strategy and ensures consistent data management practices.

3. **STRONG SECURITY MEASURES:**

   💡 Organizations should employ encryption techniques to ensure data privacy and utilize firewalls, antivirus software, and intrusion detection systems to protect their data. Regular security assessments and audits can help identify vulnerabilities and strengthen data protection measures.

4. **REGULAR TRAINING AND AWARENESS PROGRAMS:**

   💡 Providing regular training and awareness programs for employees on data security, privacy, and compliance is crucial. Educating staff about the importance of data protection and their role in maintaining data integrity helps reduce the risk of human error and data breaches.

5. **SCALABLE DATA MANAGEMENT SOLUTIONS:**

   💡 Adopting scalable data management solutions that can grow with the organization is essential. Cloud-based data storage and management platforms offer flexibility and scalability, allowing organizations to handle increasing data volumes efficiently.

6.   DATA QUALITY MANAGEMENT TOOLS:

💡 Implementing data quality management tools helps organizations maintain high data accuracy and consistency. These tools can automate data cleansing, validation, and enrichment processes, ensuring that the data remains reliable and useful.

DLM VS. ILM: UNDERSTANDING THE DIFFERENCES

Data Lifecycle Management (DLM) and Information Lifecycle Management (ILM) are two critical frameworks used in managing data and information within an organization. While these approaches share some common goals, they differ significantly in their focus, scope, and objectives. Understanding these differences is essential for organizations aiming to implement effective data and information management strategies.

FOCUS OF DATA LIFECYCLE MANAGEMENT (DLM)

Data Lifecycle Management (DLM) is primarily concerned with the technical management of data throughout its entire lifecycle—from creation to deletion. DLM focuses on the practical aspects of handling data as a resource, ensuring that it remains accessible, accurate, and secure at every stage. This process includes data storage, maintenance, processing, sharing, and eventual deletion. The primary objective of DLM is to support efficient business operations and ensure compliance with regulatory requirements by maintaining the integrity and usability of data over time (Ladin, 2006).

DLM typically involves the use of automated tools and processes to manage data efficiently. For instance, DLM systems may automate data archiving and deletion based on predefined retention schedules, thereby reducing the risk of data sprawl and ensuring that obsolete data is removed in compliance with legal requirements (Gartner, 2021).

FOCUS OF INFORMATION LIFECYCLE MANAGEMENT (ILM)

In contrast, Information Lifecycle Management (ILM) adopts a more holistic approach by considering the broader context of information as a valuable business asset. ILM focuses on managing information based on its strategic importance and relevance to the organization.

Rather than merely handling data as raw files, ILM involves assessing the value of information at different stages of its lifecycle and applying appropriate management practices to maximize its utility while minimizing costs (Smith, 2007).

ILM integrates several disciplines, including data governance, records management, and information policy, to ensure that valuable information is retained, protected, and effectively leveraged. This approach enables organizations to manage information not just for operational efficiency but also for strategic advantage. For example, ILM may involve prioritizing the retention of high-value information that supports critical business processes or decision-making, while de-prioritizing less relevant data (Tallon, Ramirez, & Short, 2013).

KEY DIFFERENCES BETWEEN DLM AND ILM

1. **SCOPE:**

    - 💡 **DLM**: Focuses primarily on the management of raw data files and records throughout their lifecycle. The scope of DLM is largely technical, emphasizing the operational aspects of data management.

    - 💡 **ILM**: Takes a broader view by focusing on the value of information to the business. ILM encompasses data governance, records management, and information policy to manage information based on its relevance and strategic importance to the organization (Smith, 2007).

2. **OBJECTIVE:**

- 💡 **DLM**: Aims to ensure that data is accessible, accurate, and secure from creation to deletion. The objective is to maintain the usability and integrity of data to support business operations and compliance (Ladin, 2006).

- 💡 **ILM**: Seeks to maximize the utility of information by managing it according to its value to the organization. The goal is to align information management practices with business objectives, ensuring that valuable information is retained and leveraged effectively (Tallon et al., 2013).

3. **APPROACH:**

- 💡 **DLM**: Employs technical processes and tools to manage the lifecycle of data, focusing on storage, maintenance, processing, sharing, and deletion. DLM is often driven by operational needs and compliance requirements (Gartner, 2021).

- 💡 **ILM**: Integrates strategic information management practices, including data governance, policy enforcement, and value assessment. ILM is more aligned with the strategic goals of the organization, aiming to optimize the use of information for business success (Smith, 2007).

THE IMPORTANCE OF BOTH DLM AND ILM

Both DLM and ILM play crucial roles in effective data and information management. While DLM provides the necessary framework for managing data throughout its lifecycle, ensuring that data remains usable, secure, and compliant, ILM adds a strategic layer by managing information based on its value to the organization.

Organizations can benefit from implementing both DLM and ILM strategies. DLM lays the foundation for technical data management, ensuring that data is handled correctly and remains protected. On the other hand, ILM enhances this foundation by adding a focus on the strategic value of information, guiding how information should be governed, retained, and utilized to support business goals and compliance requirements.

By integrating both DLM and ILM, organizations can optimize their data and information management practices, ensuring that data assets are not only safeguarded but also leveraged to achieve maximum business benefits.

DLM FOR BUSINESS SUCCESS

DRIVING INNOVATION AND GROWTH

Data Lifecycle Management (DLM) plays a pivotal role in driving innovation and growth within organizations. By effectively managing data from creation to deletion, businesses can unlock the full potential of their data assets. DLM ensures that data is accurate, accessible, and secure, enabling organizations to derive valuable insights and make informed decisions.

These insights can lead to the development of new products and services, optimization of business processes, and identification of new market opportunities.

For instance, by analyzing customer data, businesses can identify trends and preferences, allowing them to tailor their offerings to meet customer needs better. Similarly, operational data analysis can reveal inefficiencies in processes, leading to improvements that enhance productivity and reduce costs.

In this way, DLM supports continuous improvement and innovation, helping organizations stay competitive in a rapidly changing market.

ENSURING LONG-TERM SUCCESS

Implementing a robust DLM strategy is crucial for ensuring the long-term success and sustainability of an organization. Effective data management helps businesses comply with regulatory requirements, protecting them from legal and financial repercussions.

It also safeguards against data breaches and loss, which can have severe consequences for a company's reputation and customer trust.

Moreover, a well-implemented DLM strategy fosters a culture of data-driven decision-making. By ensuring that data is readily available and reliable, organizations can base their strategies on solid evidence rather than intuition. This approach leads to more accurate forecasting, better risk management, and more effective resource allocation.

CASE STUDIES AND EXAMPLES

RETAIL INDUSTRY: WALMART'S DATA LIFECYCLE MANAGEMENT STRATEGY

- ❖ Walmart, one of the largest retail companies globally, implemented a comprehensive Data Lifecycle Management (DLM) strategy to manage its vast amount of customer data. By integrating advanced data analytics with their DLM strategy, Walmart was able to track and analyze customer purchasing patterns in real-time. This allowed the company to personalize marketing campaigns effectively, offering targeted promotions and product recommendations. As a result, Walmart experienced a significant boost in sales, with a reported 20% increase in specific product categories. Furthermore, this personalized approach led to improved customer loyalty, as customers received more relevant offers and a better shopping experience (Traub, 2018).

HEALTHCARE SECTOR: CLEVELAND CLINIC'S ADOPTION OF DLM FOR PATIENT RECORDS

◈ Cleveland Clinic, a leading healthcare provider, adopted a robust DLM strategy to manage its extensive patient records. This approach was crucial in ensuring compliance with the Health Insurance Portability and Accountability Act (HIPAA) regulations, which mandate strict standards for the security and privacy of patient information. By implementing DLM, Cleveland Clinic was able to maintain accurate and up-to-date patient records, which significantly improved the quality of patient care. Healthcare professionals at the clinic had timely access to accurate patient information, which facilitated better diagnoses, treatment plans, and overall patient outcomes. The success of this strategy underscores the importance of DLM in the healthcare sector, particularly in enhancing data accuracy and regulatory compliance (Halamka, 2016).

FINANCIAL SERVICES: JPMORGAN CHASE'S DLM FOR FRAUD DETECTION

◈ JPMorgan Chase, a global leader in financial services, employed a sophisticated DLM strategy to manage its transaction data. Given the scale and complexity of its operations, JPMorgan needed an effective way to monitor and protect transaction data from fraudulent activities. By leveraging DLM, the institution was able to detect anomalies and potential fraud early, thereby minimizing financial risks. The strategy also ensured compliance with stringent financial regulations, such as those mandated by the Dodd-Frank Act and the Basel III framework. This proactive approach not only protected JPMorgan from significant financial losses but also reinforced its reputation as a secure and trustworthy financial institution (JPMorgan Chase, 2018).

BEST PRACTICES FOR DLM IMPLEMENTATION

1. **DEVELOP A CLEAR DLM POLICY:**
    - Establish a comprehensive DLM policy that outlines the objectives, roles, and responsibilities related to data management. Ensure that the policy is communicated effectively across the organization.

2. **INVEST IN THE RIGHT TOOLS AND TECHNOLOGIES:**
    - Utilize advanced data management platforms, classification tools, and security solutions to streamline DLM processes. Ensure that these tools are integrated into the organization's IT infrastructure.

3. **REGULARLY REVIEW AND UPDATE DLM PRACTICES:**
    - Continuously assess and update DLM practices to adapt to changing regulatory requirements and technological advancements. Regular reviews help identify areas for improvement and ensure that the DLM strategy remains effective.

4. **TRAIN EMPLOYEES ON DATA MANAGEMENT:**
    - Provide regular training sessions to employees on data management best practices, security measures, and compliance requirements. Educating staff helps minimize the risk of human error and enhances overall data security.

QUESTIONS PEOPLE ALSO ASKED ABOUT DATA GOVERNANCE

1. ### WHY IS DATA GOVERNANCE IMPORTANT FOR AI?

Data governance is crucial for AI for several reasons:

i. **Ensures Data Quality and Integrity:**

- Data governance ensures that the data used to train AI models is accurate, consistent, and reliable. High-quality data is essential for AI models to produce valid and dependable outputs.

ii. **Enhances Data Security:**

- Effective data governance involves implementing robust security measures to protect sensitive data from unauthorized access and breaches. This is particularly important for AI models that handle personal and proprietary information.

iii. **Facilitates Regulatory Compliance:**

- Data governance helps organizations comply with data protection regulations such as GDPR, HIPAA, and SOC2. By governing data properly, organizations can avoid legal penalties and ensure ethical use of AI.

iv. **Builds Trust and Transparency:**

- Robust data governance practices build trust with consumers, stakeholders, and regulators by demonstrating that data is managed responsibly. Transparency in data practices fosters confidence in AI technologies.

v. **Mitigates Risks:**

- Poor data governance can lead to privacy violations, security vulnerabilities, and intellectual property infringements. By implementing strong data governance, organizations can mitigate these risks and protect their reputation.

vi. **Enables Effective AI Deployment:**

- Data governance ensures that the data lifecycle is managed efficiently, from collection and storage to processing and usage. This enables the effective deployment of AI models that are both safe and reliable.

2. WHAT ARE THE BENEFITS OF AI GOVERNANCE?

AI governance provides several key benefits:

i. **Improved Data Quality and Reliability:**

- AI governance ensures that the data used for training AI models is high-quality, leading to more accurate and reliable AI outputs. This enhances the performance and credibility of AI systems.

ii. **Enhanced Data Security:**

- By implementing robust security measures, AI governance protects sensitive data from breaches and unauthorized access. This reduces the risk of data leaks and enhances overall data security.

iii. **Regulatory Compliance:**

- AI governance helps organizations comply with data protection regulations and standards. This not only avoids legal penalties but also ensures that AI technologies are used ethically and responsibly.

iv. **Increased Trust and Transparency:**

- Effective AI governance practices build trust with consumers, stakeholders, and regulators. Transparency in how data is managed and used fosters confidence in AI technologies and their outcomes.

v. **Risk Mitigation:**

💡 AI governance identifies and mitigates various risks associated with AI, such as privacy breaches, security vulnerabilities, and intellectual property issues. This protects the organization and its stakeholders.

vi. Accountability and Traceability:

💡 AI governance ensures that data usage is accountable and traceable. Detailed audit trails and documentation provide a clear record of data access and usage, supporting accountability and compliance.

vii. Support for Ethical AI Development:

💡 AI governance frameworks promote the ethical development and deployment of AI. By ensuring that AI models are trained and used responsibly, organizations can align with ethical standards and societal expectations.

viii. Enhanced Decision-Making:

💡 Reliable and well-governed data enables better decision-making. Organizations can leverage AI models with confidence, knowing that the data and processes behind them are robust and trustworthy.

3. WHAT IS THE DIFFERENCE BETWEEN DATA GOVERNANCE AND DATA INTEGRITY?

Data Governance: Data governance is a comprehensive framework that defines the processes, roles, standards, and metrics that ensure the effective and efficient use of information within an organization. It encompasses policies and procedures for data management, accountability, and data quality assurance. Data governance aims to ensure that data is consistent, reliable, and used appropriately across the organization. It involves:

💡 Setting data management roles and responsibilities.

- 💡 Implementing data policies and standards.

- 💡 Ensuring data compliance with regulatory requirements.

- 💡 Managing data access and security.

Data Integrity: Data integrity, on the other hand, focuses specifically on the accuracy, consistency, and security of data throughout its lifecycle. It ensures that data remains unaltered and accurate unless authorized changes are made, preserving the data's original state. Data integrity involves:

- 💡 Preventing unauthorized data modifications.

- 💡 Ensuring data accuracy and consistency.

- 💡 Implementing physical and logical measures to protect data.

- 💡 Maintaining data reliability and trustworthiness.

In summary, data governance is the overarching framework that includes data integrity as one of its key components. Data governance ensures that data management practices are standardized and effective, while data integrity specifically ensures that the data itself remains accurate, consistent, and secure.

4. WHAT ARE THE 6 C'S OF DATA QUALITY?

The 6 C's of data quality are a set of dimensions used to assess and ensure the quality of data within an organization. These dimensions help organizations evaluate and maintain high standards for their data. The 6 C's are:

i. **Correctness:**

- 💡 Ensures that data is accurate and free from errors. Correct data accurately represents the real-world entities or events it describes.

ii. **Completeness:**

- 💡 Ensures that all necessary data is present and that no required information is missing. Complete data includes all relevant fields and values needed for its intended use.

iii. **Consistency:**

- 💡 Ensures that data is uniform and consistent across different datasets and systems. Consistent data maintains the same format, values, and definitions across various platforms and uses.

iv. **Conformity:**

- 💡 Ensures that data follows predefined formats, standards, and rules. Conforming data adheres to the organization's specifications for data entry and usage.

v. **Currency:**

- 💡 Ensures that data is up-to-date and reflects the most current information available. Current data is timely and relevant for its intended purpose.

vi. **Coverage:**

- 💡 Ensures that data encompasses all necessary areas and domains. Comprehensive coverage means that data includes all relevant aspects of the subject it represents.

By adhering to the 6 C's of data quality, organizations can ensure that their data is reliable, accurate, and fit for its intended purpose, thereby supporting better decision-making and operational efficiency.

5. WHAT IS LIFECYCLE DATA MANAGEMENT?

Lifecycle Data Management, also known as Data Lifecycle Management (DLM), is a comprehensive, policy-based approach that oversees the flow of data throughout its entire lifecycle – from creation to deletion.

DLM involves a series of best practices and processes aimed at ensuring that data is accurately captured, securely stored, properly maintained, efficiently processed, and appropriately archived or deleted.

The primary goals of DLM are to maintain data confidentiality, integrity, and availability, thereby supporting effective decision-making, regulatory compliance, and overall business efficiency.

6. WHAT ARE THE 5 STAGES OF DATA LIFECYCLE?

The data lifecycle typically consists of the following five key stages:

i. **Data Collection**:

   This initial stage involves capturing data from various sources. It includes defining the purpose of data collection, classifying data, and eliminating redundant data. Establishing standardized formats and policies for different types of data is crucial to ensure accurate and relevant data collection.

ii. **Data Storage and Maintenance**:

   Once data is collected, it needs to be stored and maintained securely. This stage involves processing, merging, aggregating, and classifying data to ensure its accuracy and completeness. Data storage solutions such as Relational Database Management Systems (RDBMS), NoSQL databases, and data lakes are commonly used. Maintenance activities include data backups, archiving, retention policies, and implementing security measures.

iii. **Data Processing**:

- During the data processing stage, raw data is transformed into useful information through a series of steps. This involves data processing and calculations to derive insights and support decision-making. Tools like Hadoop, Apache Spark, Python, and JavaScript are often used for data processing. Ensuring compliance with data processing regulations is also a critical aspect of this stage.

iv. **Data Sharing and Usage**:

- Data sharing is essential for collaboration and informed decision-making within an organization. This stage involves sharing operational data, master data, metadata, and user-generated data across departments while ensuring data security and compliance with relevant regulations. Implementing data governance policies and security measures helps balance data sharing with maintaining data privacy.

v. **Data Deletion and Archiving**:

- The final stage of the data lifecycle involves archiving data for future use and deleting redundant or obsolete data. Proper data deletion policies and action plans are implemented to optimize data storage, ensure compliance with data retention regulations, and avoid legal or financial repercussions. Archiving ensures the preservation and availability of important data while reducing storage costs.

7. WHAT IS DATA SECURITY AND PRIVACY PROTECTION?

Data Security: Data security involves the implementation of measures to protect data from unauthorized access, corruption, or theft. This includes physical security measures, access controls, encryption, and network security measures. The goal of data security is to ensure the confidentiality, integrity, and availability of data. Key aspects of data security include:

- **Confidentiality:** Ensuring that sensitive information is accessible only to those authorized to view it.

- **Integrity:** Maintaining the accuracy and completeness of data over its lifecycle.

- **Availability:** Ensuring that data is accessible to authorized users when needed.

Data Privacy Protection: Data privacy protection focuses on managing and safeguarding personal information that is collected, stored, and processed by organizations. It involves ensuring that individuals' personal data is handled with their consent and according to legal and ethical guidelines. Data privacy protection includes the implementation of policies and practices that dictate how data is collected, used, and shared. Key principles include:

- **User Consent:** Obtaining explicit permission from individuals before collecting and using their personal data.

- **Transparency:** Clearly informing individuals about how their data will be used and ensuring they have control over their data.

- **Data Minimization:** Collecting only the data necessary for specific purposes and retaining it only as long as needed.

- **User Rights:** Ensuring that individuals can access, correct, and delete their personal data.

8. WHAT ARE EXAMPLES OF DATA PROTECTION AND PRIVACY?

Examples of Data Protection:

i. **Encryption:** Encrypting sensitive data both at rest and in transit to prevent unauthorized access. For example, encrypting financial transactions and communications over the internet.

ii. **Access Controls:** Implementing strong access control measures to ensure that only authorized individuals can access sensitive data. For instance, using role-based access control (RBAC) to restrict access based on job roles.

iii. **Data Loss Prevention (DLP):** Using DLP tools to monitor and prevent unauthorized data transfers, ensuring that sensitive data is not leaked or stolen.

iv. **Firewalls and Intrusion Detection Systems (IDS):** Deploying firewalls and IDS to protect networks from unauthorized access and detect potential security breaches.

v. **Regular Backups:** Conducting regular data backups to ensure that data can be recovered in case of data loss or corruption.

Examples of Data Privacy:

i. **User Consent Management:** Implementing systems that require users to provide explicit consent before their personal data is collected and used. For example, GDPR-compliant consent forms that inform users about data collection purposes.

ii. **Privacy Policies:** Creating and publishing clear privacy policies that explain how personal data is collected, used, and shared. For instance, websites providing detailed privacy notices outlining data handling practices.

iii. **Data Minimization Practices:** Collecting only the data necessary for specific purposes and avoiding the collection of unnecessary personal information. For example, an online service asking only for essential details such as email addresses for account creation.

iv. **User Rights Implementation:** Ensuring that users can easily access, correct, and delete their personal data. For instance, providing user-friendly interfaces for managing privacy settings and data deletion requests.

v. **Transparency and Communication:** Clearly communicating data practices to users, including any changes in data handling policies. For example, sending notifications to users about updates to privacy policies or data breaches.

By implementing robust data security and privacy protection measures, organizations can safeguard sensitive information, comply with regulations, and build trust with their users.

9. WHY IS DATA PROTECTION AND PRIVACY IMPORTANT?

Data protection and privacy are critical for several reasons:

i. **Compliance with Regulations:**

- Many countries and regions have strict data protection laws, such as the GDPR in Europe and the CCPA in California. Compliance with these regulations is mandatory and non-compliance can result in significant fines and legal consequences.

ii. **Protecting Individual Rights:**

- Data privacy ensures that individuals have control over their personal information. It protects their right to privacy and prevents misuse of their data, which can lead to identity theft, financial loss, and other personal harms.

iii. **Building Trust:**

- For businesses, maintaining strong data protection and privacy practices builds trust with customers, clients, and partners. When individuals know that their data is handled securely and ethically, they are more likely to engage and transact with the business.

iv. **Preventing Data Breaches:**

- Effective data protection measures help prevent data breaches, which can lead to the exposure of sensitive information. Data breaches can have severe financial, legal, and reputational repercussions for organizations.

v. **Ensuring Data Integrity and Availability:**

- Data protection ensures that data remains accurate, complete, and available for authorized use. This is crucial for business operations, decision-making, and maintaining the reliability of services.

10. WHAT ARE THE THREE TYPES OF DATA PROTECTION?

i. **Physical Data Protection:**

- **Definition:** Physical data protection involves securing the physical hardware and infrastructure that store and process data. This includes data centers, servers, and storage devices.

- **Examples:** Access controls (e.g., locks, security guards), environmental controls (e.g., fire suppression systems, temperature control), and physical barriers (e.g., fences, secure entry points).

ii. **Technical Data Protection:**

- **Definition:** Technical data protection encompasses the use of technology to safeguard data. It includes measures that protect data during storage, processing, and transmission.

- 💡 **Examples:** Encryption, firewalls, intrusion detection and prevention systems, antivirus software, and secure access protocols.

iii. **Administrative Data Protection:**

- 💡 **Definition:** Administrative data protection involves policies, procedures, and practices that govern the handling of data within an organization. It focuses on creating a secure and compliant data management environment.

- 💡 **Examples:** Data governance policies, employee training and awareness programs, access controls, data classification and handling procedures, and regular audits and assessments.

CHAPTER TEN
Collaboration And Innovation In AI Security

THE FUTURE OF AI SECURITY: THE ROLE OF COLLABORATION

As Artificial Intelligence (AI) continues to evolve and integrate more deeply into critical systems and infrastructures, the security of these systems becomes an increasingly pressing concern. The future of AI security hinges on the ability to collaborate across diverse sectors, combining expertise, resources, and innovative approaches to safeguard AI technologies against emerging threats. This chapter delves into the critical importance of collaboration in AI security, examining the reasons why it is necessary, the benefits it brings, and the strategies that can be employed to foster a secure AI environment.

THE NECESSITY OF COLLABORATION IN AI SECURITY

The complexity and global reach of AI systems make collaboration not just beneficial but essential for ensuring their security. Several key factors underscore the need for a collaborative approach to AI security:

1. **Interdisciplinary Integration**: AI security is inherently interdisciplinary, requiring input from computer science, cybersecurity, ethics, law, and even sociology. A collaborative approach ensures that security strategies are comprehensive, addressing not only technical vulnerabilities but also ethical and legal challenges. For example, the collaboration between tech companies and legal experts has been crucial in developing frameworks that address both data privacy and security concerns in AI systems (Brundage et al., 2018).

2. **Global Coordination**: AI technologies are deployed across the globe, and their security implications are not confined to any single country. International collaboration is vital to establish standardized security protocols, facilitate information sharing, and develop best practices that can be applied universally. The European Union's General Data Protection Regulation (GDPR) and similar regulations in other regions highlight the importance of coordinated efforts to manage AI security on a global scale (Voigt & Von dem Bussche, 2017).

3. **Adaptation to Rapid Technological Change**: The pace at which AI technology evolves presents a continuous challenge for security. Collaborative research and development are essential for staying ahead of emerging threats. By pooling resources and knowledge, stakeholders can accelerate the development of innovative security measures that are capable of adapting to new AI advancements. The joint efforts in projects like OpenAI's safety research initiative demonstrate how collaboration can drive innovation in AI security (Amodei et al., 2016).

BENEFITS OF COLLABORATIVE APPROACHES IN AI SECURITY

1. Enhanced Threat Detection and Mitigation: Collaborative efforts allow for the pooling of resources and intelligence, leading to more effective threat detection and mitigation strategies. Sharing information about vulnerabilities and attack patterns helps in developing robust defenses against potential threats.

2. Improved Standardization and Best Practices: Collaboration among industry leaders, policymakers, and researchers can lead to the creation of standardized security frameworks and best practices. These guidelines ensure a unified approach to AI security, reducing the likelihood of inconsistent security measures.

3. Resource Optimization: Collaboration allows for the efficient use of resources by avoiding duplication of efforts. Joint initiatives and partnerships can lead to cost savings and more impactful research and development outcomes.

4. Fostering Innovation: Collaborative environments foster innovation by bringing together diverse perspectives and expertise. This synergy can lead to the development of novel security solutions that may not have been possible through isolated efforts.

5. Building Trust and Transparency: Collaborative efforts promote transparency and trust among stakeholders. Open communication and shared goals help in building a secure and trustworthy AI ecosystem, which is crucial for public acceptance and adoption of AI technologies.

STRATEGIES FOR EFFECTIVE COLLABORATION IN AI SECURITY

1. Establishing Multidisciplinary Teams: Forming teams that include experts from various disciplines such as cybersecurity, ethics, law, and AI development ensures a holistic approach to security challenges.

2. Creating Collaborative Platforms: Developing platforms and networks that facilitate information sharing and joint research initiatives can enhance collaborative efforts. Examples include industry consortia, academic partnerships, and government-sponsored research programs.

3. Encouraging Open Source and Open Standards: Promoting open-source AI projects and open standards for AI security can foster collaboration and innovation. These initiatives enable wider participation and the pooling of collective intelligence to address security issues.

4. Engaging in Public-Private Partnerships: Public-private partnerships can leverage the strengths of both sectors, combining public sector oversight and resources with private sector innovation and agility. These collaborations can drive significant advancements in AI security.

5. International Cooperation: Engaging in international cooperation is crucial for addressing global AI security challenges. Establishing agreements and frameworks for cross-border collaboration can facilitate the exchange of knowledge and best practices.

6. Fostering a Culture of Security Awareness: Promoting a culture of security awareness within organizations and across the AI community is essential. Regular training, workshops, and awareness campaigns can help stakeholders understand the importance of security and their role in maintaining it.

PUBLIC-PRIVATE PARTNERSHIPS

Artificial Intelligence (AI) has become a cornerstone of technological advancement, impacting various sectors from healthcare to finance. As AI's influence grows, so does the need for robust security measures to protect against malicious threats and vulnerabilities. Public-private partnerships (PPPs) in AI security are emerging as a vital strategy to address these challenges. This aspect looks into the significance, benefits, and implementation strategies of public-private partnerships in AI security, highlighting their role in creating a secure and resilient AI landscape.

BENEFITS OF PUBLIC-PRIVATE PARTNERSHIPS IN AI SECURITY

Public-private partnerships offer numerous benefits that enhance AI security:

1. Enhanced Innovation: Collaboration fosters innovation by combining the private sector's agility and creativity with the public sector's strategic oversight and resources. This synergy can lead to the development of advanced security technologies and methodologies.

2. Improved Risk Management: Through joint efforts, PPPs can better identify, assess, and manage risks associated with AI systems. Shared knowledge and resources contribute to a more robust risk management framework.

3. Increased Trust and Transparency: Transparent collaboration between public and private entities builds trust among stakeholders and the public. It ensures that AI security measures are scrutinized, tested, and validated, promoting confidence in AI technologies.

4. Cost Efficiency: Sharing resources and expertise reduces the financial burden on individual organizations. PPPs can lead to cost-effective solutions, maximizing the return on investment for both public and private partners.

5. Global Impact: AI security challenges are global in nature. International public-private partnerships facilitate the exchange of best practices, harmonize security standards, and create a unified approach to combating AI threats worldwide.

IMPLEMENTATION STRATEGIES FOR EFFECTIVE PUBLIC-PRIVATE PARTNERSHIPS

To realize the full potential of public-private partnerships in AI security, strategic implementation is crucial. Here are key strategies:

1. Establish Clear Objectives: Define clear, mutually agreed-upon objectives that align with the interests of both public and private partners. This ensures focused efforts and measurable outcomes.

2. Create Formal Agreements: Develop formal agreements that outline the roles, responsibilities, and expectations of each partner. This provides a structured framework for collaboration and accountability.

3. Facilitate Information Sharing: Implement secure platforms and protocols for real-time information sharing. This includes threat intelligence, best practices, and incident response strategies.

4. Promote Joint Research and Development: Encourage joint R&D initiatives to explore innovative solutions to AI security challenges. Collaborative research can lead to breakthroughs that benefit both sectors.

5. Engage in Regular Training and Exercises: Conduct regular training sessions and simulation exercises to enhance preparedness and response capabilities. These activities help in identifying gaps and improving coordination.

6. Leverage Existing Networks: Utilize existing networks and consortia to foster collaboration. Engaging with established organizations can accelerate the development and implementation of security measures.

CASE STUDIES AND EXAMPLES OF SUCCESSFUL PUBLIC-PRIVATE PARTNERSHIPS

1. The Cybersecurity Information Sharing Act (CISA): In the United States, CISA facilitates the sharing of cybersecurity threat information between the government and private sector. This partnership has been instrumental in improving the nation's cybersecurity posture.

2. The European Union Agency for Cybersecurity (ENISA): ENISA collaborates with both public and private sectors to enhance cybersecurity across Europe. Initiatives include joint training programs, information sharing platforms, and the development of security standards.

3. The National Cyber Security Centre (NCSC) in the UK: The NCSC works closely with private companies to provide cybersecurity guidance, share threat intelligence, and respond to incidents. This partnership has significantly strengthened the UK's cyber resilience.

4. AI4People: This initiative brings together policymakers, industry leaders, and academics to develop ethical guidelines and security measures for AI. AI4People exemplifies how collaborative efforts can address the ethical and security challenges of AI.

THE IMPORTANCE OF INDUSTRY STANDARDS IN AI SECURITY

Industry standards in AI security are guidelines that ensure AI systems operate securely, ethically, and efficiently. They are crucial for several reasons:

1. Consistency and Reliability: Standards provide a consistent framework for developing and deploying AI systems, ensuring that they perform reliably across different environments and applications.

2. Regulatory Compliance: Adhering to industry standards helps organizations comply with legal and regulatory requirements, avoiding penalties and legal issues. This is particularly important in highly regulated sectors such as healthcare and finance.

3. Interoperability: Standards ensure that AI systems from different developers can work together seamlessly, enhancing their functionality and usability across various platforms and applications.

4. Trust and Transparency: Adopting industry standards fosters trust among users, developers, and stakeholders by ensuring that AI systems are secure, ethical, and transparent.

COLLABORATION IN ESTABLISHING INDUSTRY STANDARDS AND BEST PRACTICES

Collaboration among stakeholders is vital to developing and implementing effective industry standards and best practices in AI security. Here's how collaboration drives these efforts:

1. Public-Private Partnerships: Partnerships between government agencies and private companies combine the strengths of both sectors—government oversight and private sector innovation— to develop comprehensive security standards.

2. Academic Contributions: Academic institutions contribute to AI security through research, providing insights into emerging threats and innovative solutions. Collaboration with academia ensures that standards are based on the latest scientific advancements.

3. Industry Consortia and Alliances: Industry consortia, such as the Partnership on AI, bring together diverse stakeholders to develop and promote best practices and standards. These alliances facilitate information sharing and collective problem-solving.

4. International Cooperation: AI security is a global concern, and international cooperation is essential for developing universal standards. International organizations like the ISO (International Organization for Standardization) work with countries worldwide to establish global AI security standards.

INNOVATION THROUGH COLLABORATIVE EFFORTS

Collaboration not only helps in establishing standards but also drives innovation in AI security. Here are ways collaborative efforts foster innovation:

1. Shared Knowledge and Resources: Collaborative projects allow stakeholders to share knowledge, resources, and expertise, leading to innovative solutions that might not be possible in isolation.

2. Cross-Disciplinary Approaches: AI security benefits from cross-disciplinary approaches involving computer science, cybersecurity, ethics, and law. Collaboration across these fields leads to holistic and innovative security solutions.

3. Pilot Programs and Testbeds: Collaborative pilot programs and testbeds allow organizations to experiment with new AI security technologies and methodologies in controlled environments,

accelerating the development and deployment of innovative solutions.

4. Open Source and Open Standards: Promoting open-source projects and open standards in AI security encourages wider participation and innovation. These initiatives enable developers worldwide to contribute to and improve AI security technologies.

Industry standards and best practices are foundational to AI security, ensuring that AI systems are secure, reliable, and ethical. Collaborative efforts among industry, academia, government, and international organizations are crucial for developing these standards and fostering innovation. By working together, stakeholders can create a robust and secure AI landscape, addressing emerging threats and ensuring the responsible development and deployment of AI technologies.

Innovation in AI security solutions is critical to keeping pace with evolving risks and ensuring the integrity and reliability of AI technologies. As AI systems become more integral to various industries, the need for advanced security measures grows. This section explores strategies, benefits, and real-world examples of driving innovation in AI security, emphasizing the importance of collaboration and interdisciplinary approaches in addressing the complex landscape of AI security.

THE IMPORTANCE OF INNOVATION IN AI SECURITY

Innovation in AI security is vital for several reasons:

1. **Evolving Threat Landscape**: Cyber threats are continually advancing, with attackers using increasingly sophisticated methods. Innovative AI security solutions are necessary to anticipate and counter these evolving threats effectively (Goodfellow, Shlens, & Szegedy, 2015).

2.   **Complexity of AI Systems**: AI systems, particularly those utilizing machine learning and deep learning, are inherently complex. Traditional security measures often fall short, necessitating new approaches to understand, monitor, and secure these systems comprehensively (Buczak & Guven, 2016).

3.   **Regulatory Compliance**: As regulations around AI and data privacy become more stringent, innovative security solutions are required to ensure compliance and protect sensitive information (Voigt & Von dem Bussche, 2017).

4.   **Public Trust and Adoption**: Public trust in AI technologies is crucial for their widespread adoption. By demonstrating a commitment to innovative security measures, organizations can build this trust and ensure that users feel confident in the safety and reliability of AI systems (Floridi et al., 2018).

STRATEGIES FOR ADVANCING INNOVATION IN AI SECURITY

Several strategies can be employed to advance innovation in AI security:

1.   **Collaborative Research and Development**: Collaboration between academia, industry, and government plays a critical role in driving advancements in AI security. Joint research initiatives, such as those led by the Defense Advanced Research Projects Agency (DARPA), have resulted in significant innovations in cybersecurity by pooling diverse expertise and resources (DARPA, 2016).

2.   **Interdisciplinary Approaches**: The complexity of AI security demands input from various fields, including computer science, cybersecurity, ethics, and law. Interdisciplinary collaboration ensures that solutions are comprehensive and address all aspects of security (Bostrom & Yudkowsky, 2014).

3. **Open Innovation Platforms**: Creating open innovation platforms encourages collaboration by allowing researchers and developers to share ideas, tools, and datasets. This approach accelerates the development of new security solutions and promotes a culture of collaborative problem-solving (Chesbrough, 2006).

4. **Investment in Startups and Innovation Hubs**: Supporting startups and innovation hubs that focus on AI security can inject fresh perspectives and agility into the development of cutting-edge security technologies (Gompers, Lerner, & Scharfstein, 2005).

5. **Continuous Learning and Adaptation**: The rapidly changing nature of AI and associated threats requires a culture of continuous learning and adaptation. Organizations should invest in ongoing education and training to ensure that security professionals remain ahead of emerging threats and technological advancements (Siau & Wang, 2018).

6. **Incentivizing Innovation**: Providing incentives such as grants, awards, and competitions can motivate individuals and organizations to develop groundbreaking AI security solutions. Competitions like DARPA's Cyber Grand Challenge highlight the potential of incentives in driving technological innovation (DARPA, 2016).

BENEFITS OF INNOVATIVE AI SECURITY SOLUTIONS

1. **Enhanced Threat Detection and Response**: Innovative AI security solutions improve the ability to detect and respond to threats in real-time, thereby minimizing potential damage (Sommer & Paxson, 2010).

2. **Proactive Security Measures**: Advanced security technologies enable proactive measures, such as predictive analytics and anomaly detection, allowing organizations to identify and

mitigate risks before they materialize (Chandola, Banerjee, & Kumar, 2009).

3. **Improved System Resilience**: Innovative security approaches enhance the resilience of AI systems, ensuring they can withstand and recover from attacks effectively (Goodfellow et al., 2015).

4. **Cost-Effective Solutions**: By automating security processes and reducing the need for manual interventions, innovative AI security solutions can lower overall security costs (Buczak & Guven, 2016).

5. **Scalability**: Innovative solutions are designed to scale with the growth of AI applications, ensuring consistent security across expanding and evolving AI environments (Siau & Wang, 2018).

EXAMPLES OF INNOVATIVE AI SECURITY SOLUTIONS

1. **Adversarial Training**: Adversarial training involves exposing AI models to malicious inputs during training to improve their robustness against attacks. This approach has been crucial in developing more resilient AI systems (Goodfellow et al., 2015).

2. **Explainable AI (XAI)**: Explainable AI techniques aim to make AI decision-making processes transparent and understandable, enhancing security by allowing better scrutiny of AI behavior and identifying potential vulnerabilities (Gunning, 2017).

3. **Federated Learning**: Federated learning enables the training of AI models across decentralized devices without sharing raw data. This approach enhances privacy and security by keeping data localized and reducing exposure to threats (McMahan et al., 2017).

4. **Blockchain for AI Security**: Blockchain technology can provide secure and immutable records of AI model training and updates, ensuring the integrity and authenticity of AI systems (Zyskind, Nathan, & Pentland, 2015).

5. **AI-Driven Threat Intelligence**: Leveraging AI to analyze vast amounts of threat data can provide real-time insights and predictive analytics, improving the ability to anticipate and counteract security threats (Sommer & Paxson, 2010).

CASE STUDIES OF INNOVATION IN AI SECURITY

1. **DARPA's Cyber Grand Challenge**: DARPA's Cyber Grand Challenge demonstrated the power of AI in cybersecurity by having autonomous systems compete to find and fix software vulnerabilities in real-time. This competition sparked significant innovation and showcased the potential of AI-driven security solutions (DARPA, 2016).

2. **Google's TensorFlow Privacy**: Google's TensorFlow Privacy project integrates differential privacy techniques into the TensorFlow framework, enabling the development of AI models that preserve user privacy while maintaining high performance. This innovative approach addresses both security and privacy concerns in AI (Abadi et al., 2016).

3. **Microsoft's AI Security Research**: Microsoft has heavily invested in AI security research, developing tools like the Security Risk Detection platform, which uses AI to identify and mitigate security vulnerabilities in software applications. This research has led to significant advancements in automated security testing (Sweeney, 2018).

Innovation in AI security is not just a response to evolving threats; it is a proactive strategy that ensures AI technologies can be trusted and relied upon across various sectors. Through collaboration, interdisciplinary approaches, and a commitment to continuous innovation, we can develop AI security solutions that are resilient, scalable, and effective. As AI continues to shape the future, the emphasis on innovative security measures will be crucial in ensuring that these powerful technologies are used safely and responsibly.

QUESTIONS PEOPLE ALSO ASKED ABOUT COLLABORATION IN AI

1. HOW CAN AI BE USED TO ENHANCE SECURITY SYSTEMS?

AI can significantly enhance security systems by automating and improving various processes, such as:

- **Threat Detection:** AI algorithms can continuously monitor network traffic, user behavior, and system activities to detect anomalies that may indicate security threats. Unlike traditional methods, AI can process vast amounts of data in real-time, identifying potential threats with greater speed and accuracy.

- **Incident Response:** AI-driven systems can automate the response to detected threats, such as isolating compromised systems, blocking malicious IP addresses, or initiating security protocols. This reduces response time and mitigates the impact of security breaches.

- **Unauthorized Access Detection:** AI can be used to monitor access logs and user behaviors to identify unauthorized attempts to access sensitive information. By learning what constitutes normal behavior, AI systems can quickly detect and alert security teams to suspicious activities.

- **Predictive Security:** AI can predict potential security breaches by analyzing patterns in historical data. For instance, AI systems can forecast when and where an attack might occur, allowing organizations to strengthen their defenses proactively.

2. HOW DOES AI IMPROVE INNOVATION?

AI enhances innovation by providing advanced tools for data analysis, which can identify trends, patterns, and insights that might not be immediately apparent to human analysts. Some key ways AI improves innovation include:

- **Idea Validation:** AI can analyze vast datasets to predict which new ideas or products are likely to succeed in the market. This helps organizations focus their resources on the most promising innovations while refining or discarding less viable ideas.

- **Process Optimization:** AI can identify inefficiencies in existing processes and suggest improvements, leading to more innovative ways of doing business. For example, AI can optimize supply chains, manufacturing processes, and customer service operations, driving innovation across multiple areas.

- **Accelerated R&D:** In research and development, AI can rapidly process experimental data, identify correlations, and suggest new avenues for exploration. This accelerates the pace of innovation by shortening the time required to develop and refine new products or technologies.

3. WHAT IS THE ROLE OF AI IN INNOVATION?

AI plays a central role in driving innovation by enabling the development of new products, services, and business models. Its role in innovation includes:

- **Autonomous Systems:** AI powers autonomous systems such as self-driving vehicles, drones, and robots, which are transforming industries like transportation, logistics, and manufacturing. These systems operate with minimal human intervention, enabling new levels of efficiency and safety.

- 💡 **Personalized Medicine:** In healthcare, AI enables the development of personalized treatments tailored to individual patients' genetic profiles and medical histories. This approach not only improves patient outcomes but also represents a significant innovation in medical practice.

- 💡 **Smart Cities:** AI is integral to the development of smart cities, where it optimizes urban infrastructure, manages energy consumption, and enhances public safety. AI-driven innovations in this area improve the quality of life by making cities more sustainable and efficient.

- 💡 **Enhancing Human-Computer Interaction:** AI is revolutionizing how humans interact with technology, through voice-activated assistants, natural language processing, and intelligent user interfaces. These innovations make technology more accessible and intuitive, fostering greater adoption and use.

4. WHAT ARE THE APPLICATIONS OF AI IN SECURITY SURVEILLANCE?

AI is transforming security surveillance with applications that enhance the effectiveness of monitoring and response efforts, such as:

- 💡 Real-Time Activity Monitoring: AI systems can analyze video feeds from surveillance cameras in real-time to detect suspicious activities, such as loitering, unauthorized access, or unusual movement patterns. When such activities are detected, the system can automatically alert security personnel.

- 💡 Facial Recognition: AI-powered facial recognition systems can identify individuals in a crowd, even in complex environments. This technology is used in airports, stadiums, and public spaces to enhance security by identifying known threats or suspects.

💡 Anomaly Detection: AI can detect deviations from normal behavior, such as a vehicle driving in an unexpected area or a person accessing a restricted zone. These anomalies trigger alarms, enabling quick response to potential security threats.

💡 Crowd Management: AI systems can analyze crowd dynamics to identify potential hazards, such as overcrowding or the formation of potentially dangerous groups. This application is particularly useful in managing large events and public gatherings.

5. HOW CAN AI FOSTER INNOVATION?

AI fosters innovation in several ways, including:

💡 **Product Design and Prototyping:** AI can analyze user preferences, market trends, and existing product designs to suggest improvements or new product concepts. This accelerates the design process and leads to more innovative and customer-focused products.

💡 **Predictive Analytics:** AI can predict future trends in consumer behavior, technology, and markets, allowing companies to innovate proactively. By identifying emerging needs and opportunities, businesses can develop products and services that meet future demands.

💡 **Automated Experimentation:** AI can run simulations and experiments autonomously, testing different variables and conditions to find the most effective solutions. This capability speeds up the innovation process by reducing the time and resources needed for experimentation.

💡 **Customization and Personalization:** AI enables the development of highly personalized products and services, such as customized marketing campaigns, personalized healthcare treatments, and tailored user experiences. This level of customization represents a significant innovation in how businesses interact with customers.

6. WHICH TYPES OF AI APPLICATIONS ARE BEING USED IN CYBERSECURITY SOLUTIONS?

AI is employed in various cybersecurity applications to enhance protection against digital threats, including:

- **Breach Risk Prediction:** AI models analyze data from past breaches to predict potential future breaches and help organizations strengthen their defenses before an attack occurs.

- **Phishing Detection:** AI systems can detect phishing attempts by analyzing email content, sender behavior, and other patterns that indicate a potential phishing attack.

- **Malware Detection & Prevention:** AI-driven systems identify and block malware by analyzing patterns of behavior associated with malicious software. These systems can detect even unknown malware types by recognizing suspicious behaviors.

- **User Authentication:** AI enhances user authentication by analyzing user behavior, such as typing patterns, device usage, and access times, to detect anomalies that might suggest a security breach.

- **Spam Filtering:** AI is used to filter out spam emails by recognizing patterns and content commonly associated with spam. Advanced AI systems can adapt to new spamming techniques more quickly than traditional methods.

- **Password Protection:** AI can detect weak passwords and suggest stronger alternatives. It can also monitor for unauthorized access attempts and respond to them automatically.

💡 **Bot Identification:** AI systems distinguish between human users and bots by analyzing behavior patterns. This helps prevent bot-driven attacks, such as credential stuffing or distributed denial-of-service (DDoS) attacks.

7. HOW CAN AI HELP IN INDUSTRY INNOVATION AND INFRASTRUCTURE?

AI is driving significant advancements in industry innovation and infrastructure management through:

💡 **Infrastructure Project Management:** AI improves the efficiency and accuracy of infrastructure projects by automating project management tasks, such as scheduling, resource allocation, and risk assessment. AI-driven tools can analyze project data to predict potential delays, cost overruns, and other issues, allowing managers to make informed decisions.

💡 **Predictive Maintenance:** In industries like manufacturing and transportation, AI is used to predict when equipment or infrastructure is likely to fail. By analyzing data from sensors and other sources, AI systems can schedule maintenance before a failure occurs, reducing downtime and extending the lifespan of critical assets.

💡 **Energy Management:** AI optimizes energy use in infrastructure projects by analyzing consumption patterns and adjusting systems in real-time. This leads to more efficient energy use, cost savings, and a reduced environmental footprint.

💡 **Smart Infrastructure:** AI is integral to the development of smart infrastructure, such as intelligent transportation systems, smart grids, and automated building management systems. These innovations make infrastructure more responsive, efficient, and sustainable.

CHAPTER ELEVEN
Emerging Technologies and Their Impact on AI Security

THE RISE OF AI AND ITS SECURITY IMPLICATIONS

Artificial Intelligence (AI) technologies have advanced at an unprecedented pace, revolutionizing sectors such as healthcare, finance, and transportation. The capabilities of AI in data processing, decision-making, and automation have led to significant improvements in efficiency, cost savings, and innovation. However, this rapid growth also introduces new and complex security challenges. As AI systems become more integral to critical infrastructure, the security vulnerabilities inherent in these technologies are becoming increasingly apparent. These vulnerabilities arise from the complexity of AI algorithms, the massive volumes of data they process, and their deep integration into essential services.

One of the key security concerns with AI is its susceptibility to adversarial attacks, where malicious inputs are designed to deceive AI models into making incorrect predictions or decisions. Additionally, the reliance on large datasets for training AI systems raises issues related to data privacy and integrity. As AI systems are deployed in more critical areas, the consequences of security breaches can be severe, potentially leading to significant disruptions in services, financial losses, and even threats to public safety (Goodfellow, Shlens, & Szegedy, 2015).

KEY EMERGING TECHNOLOGIES AFFECTING AI SECURITY

The intersection of AI with other emerging technologies introduces both opportunities and risks. Understanding these technologies and their implications for AI security is essential for developing robust and resilient AI systems.

1. **BLOCKCHAIN TECHNOLOGY**

    Blockchain technology, known for its decentralized and tamper-proof nature, offers promising solutions for enhancing AI security. Blockchain can provide a secure and transparent framework for managing AI data, ensuring that the data used for training and decision-making is immutable and traceable. By recording data transactions on a blockchain, organizations can protect AI systems from data tampering and unauthorized access, which are critical concerns in AI security (Zyskind, Nathan, & Pentland, 2015).

    For example, in supply chain management, AI algorithms can analyze data recorded on a blockchain to ensure that all transactions are legitimate and have not been altered. This approach enhances the trustworthiness of AI outputs and reduces the risk of fraud. Moreover, smart contracts—self-executing contracts with the terms directly written into code—can automate and secure AI processes, further mitigating security risks (Christidis & Devetsikiotis, 2016).

2. QUANTUM COMPUTING

Quantum computing represents a significant leap in computational power, with the potential to solve complex problems much faster than classical computers. While this presents exciting opportunities for AI, it also poses significant risks to current cryptographic methods. Quantum computers could potentially break the encryption algorithms that protect AI data and communications, leading to severe security vulnerabilities (Shor, 1994).

The advent of quantum computing necessitates the development of quantum-resistant cryptographic techniques. These new algorithms are designed to withstand attacks from quantum computers, ensuring that AI systems remain secure even in a post-quantum world. Research in this area is critical, as the transition to quantum-resistant encryption will be a complex and resource-intensive process (Bernstein, 2009).

3. 5G TECHNOLOGY

The deployment of 5G networks marks a significant advancement in telecommunications, offering faster data transmission, lower latency, and the capacity to connect a vast number of devices. For AI systems, particularly those operating in real-time environments like autonomous vehicles and smart cities, 5G provides the infrastructure needed for more efficient and responsive operations (Taleb et al., 2016).

However, the widespread adoption of 5G also increases the attack surface for cyber threats. The enhanced capabilities of 5G could be exploited by attackers to launch more sophisticated attacks on AI systems. Therefore, ensuring the security of AI in a 5G environment requires robust network security protocols, real-time threat detection mechanisms, and continuous monitoring to mitigate potential risks (Wang et al., 2017).

4.   INTERNET OF THINGS (IOT)

The Internet of Things (IoT) connects billions of devices worldwide, generating vast amounts of data that AI systems analyze to derive insights and enable automation. However, the proliferation of IoT devices introduces significant security challenges, as many devices are vulnerable to cyber-attacks due to inadequate security measures (Roman et al., 2013).

Securing AI systems in an IoT ecosystem involves protecting not only the devices but also the networks and data they generate. AI-driven security solutions can help monitor IoT networks for unusual activity, identify potential threats, and respond to attacks in real-time. Additionally, integrating AI with blockchain can enhance the security of IoT networks by providing a secure and decentralized framework for managing device identities and data integrity (Khan & Salah, 2018).

FUTURE PROSPECTS AND SOLUTIONS

As AI continues to evolve and integrate with emerging technologies, it is crucial to anticipate future challenges and develop strategies to address them. The following are some key areas of focus for advancing AI security in the face of these emerging threats.

1.   DEVELOPMENT OF QUANTUM-RESISTANT ALGORITHMS

The rise of quantum computing necessitates the creation of quantum-resistant cryptographic algorithms. These algorithms must be capable of protecting AI systems from the advanced computational power of quantum computers. Researchers are currently exploring various approaches, including lattice-based cryptography and hash-based signatures, to develop encryption methods that are resistant to quantum attacks (Bernstein, 2009).

Organizations should begin preparing for the quantum era by investing in research and gradually transitioning to quantum-resistant encryption techniques. This proactive approach will help ensure the longevity and security of AI systems in a future where quantum computing becomes mainstream.

2. HYBRID COMPUTING APPROACHES

A hybrid approach that combines the strengths of classical and quantum computing offers practical solutions for enhancing AI security in the near term. By leveraging classical computers for routine tasks and quantum computers for complex cryptographic operations, AI systems can achieve enhanced security without relying solely on still-developing quantum technology (Preskill, 2018).

1. For instance, in financial services, a hybrid computing approach could be used to secure high-value transactions by performing encryption with quantum algorithms while maintaining the overall system with classical computing resources. This method allows organizations to gradually integrate quantum computing capabilities while continuing to benefit from the stability and reliability of classical systems.

3. INVESTMENT IN QUANTUM RESEARCH

Continued investment in quantum computing research is essential for advancing the field and addressing its technical challenges. Governments, private companies, and academic institutions must collaborate to fund and conduct research that focuses on both the hardware and software aspects of quantum computing. This investment will accelerate the development of practical applications, including those related to AI security

(National Academies of Sciences, Engineering, and Medicine, 2019).

Collaborative efforts can also help establish global standards for quantum computing, ensuring that its integration with AI technologies is secure and beneficial across industries. By prioritizing quantum research, we can pave the way for AI systems that are both powerful and secure in a post-quantum world.

4.   EDUCATION AND TRAINING

Preparing the workforce for the quantum era is crucial for ensuring that AI security keeps pace with technological advancements. Educational institutions should incorporate quantum computing and AI security into their curricula, equipping the next generation of professionals with the knowledge and skills needed to tackle emerging challenges (Hughes, 2019).

Organizations should also invest in ongoing training programs to upskill their employees, particularly in areas related to quantum computing and advanced AI security. A well-informed workforce is better equipped to develop, implement, and manage quantum-enhanced AI security solutions, ensuring that organizations remain resilient in the face of new threats.

PREDICTIONS FOR THE FUTURE OF AI AND CYBERSECURITY

Artificial Intelligence (AI) and cybersecurity are among the most dynamic fields in technology today, with their ongoing evolution having far-reaching implications for individuals, organizations, and societies. As AI continues to advance, its integration into cybersecurity practices offers both promising opportunities and significant challenges. This section delves into predictions for the future of AI and cybersecurity, exploring trends, innovations, and potential risks that are likely to shape the landscape in the coming years.

1. ENHANCED THREAT DETECTION AND RESPONSE

One of the most transformative applications of AI in cybersecurity is its ability to enhance threat detection and response capabilities. Traditional cybersecurity methods are increasingly overwhelmed by the volume and sophistication of modern cyberattacks. AI, with its capacity to process vast amounts of data in real-time, can identify patterns and anomalies that may signal a security breach. Machine learning algorithms can be trained on historical attack data, enabling them to improve continuously and predict potential threats before they occur. Future AI-driven cybersecurity systems are expected to be more proactive, capable of preemptively identifying vulnerabilities and neutralizing threats before they impact critical systems (Sommer & Paxson, 2010).

For instance, AI could be used to monitor network traffic for unusual patterns that may indicate a distributed denial-of-service (DDoS) attack. By analyzing the data flow in real-time, AI systems can detect early warning signs of an attack and initiate automated responses, such as rerouting traffic or blocking malicious IP addresses, to mitigate the threat.

2. AUTOMATED SECURITY OPERATIONS

As the cybersecurity landscape becomes more complex, there will be an increasing reliance on AI to automate routine security operations. Tasks such as monitoring network traffic, applying security patches, and responding to low-level alerts can be efficiently managed by AI systems. Automation through AI will allow cybersecurity professionals to focus on higher-level strategic tasks, such as threat hunting, incident response, and security architecture design (Srinivas, Das, & Kumar, 2019).

Moreover, AI-driven automation has the potential to address the significant skills gap in the cybersecurity workforce. By automating routine tasks that currently require specialized knowledge, AI can reduce the burden on human operators and enable them to concentrate on more critical areas. This shift will not only enhance operational efficiency but also improve the overall resilience of cybersecurity defenses.

3.   ADVANCED BEHAVIORAL ANALYTICS

The ability of AI to analyze and interpret human behavior will be a cornerstone of future cybersecurity strategies. AI systems can monitor user behavior and establish baseline profiles, making it possible to detect deviations that may indicate malicious activity. For example, if an employee begins accessing sensitive data at unusual times or from unexpected locations, AI can flag this behavior as suspicious and trigger further investigation (Mirsky et al., 2018).

Advanced behavioral analytics will also play a crucial role in identifying insider threats, which are often more difficult to detect using traditional security methods. AI can analyze patterns over time to identify subtle indicators of insider threats, such as changes in communication patterns or a decline in work performance, allowing organizations to intervene before a potential breach occurs.

4.   IMPROVED FRAUD DETECTION

In the financial sector and beyond, AI will revolutionize fraud detection by analyzing transaction data in real-time to identify suspicious patterns that may indicate fraudulent activity. Machine learning models can be trained to recognize subtle indicators of fraud, such as unusual spending behavior, anomalies in transaction sequences, or deviations from established patterns (Bolton & Hand, 2002).

As AI continues to evolve, its ability to detect and prevent fraud will become increasingly sophisticated, making it an indispensable tool across various industries. For example, AI could be used to monitor credit card transactions and detect fraudulent activity within seconds, allowing financial institutions to take immediate action to protect their customers.

5. AI-POWERED CYBERSECURITY PRODUCTS

The development of AI-powered cybersecurity products is expected to accelerate, providing businesses and individuals with more robust and adaptive protection. These products will leverage AI to offer real-time threat intelligence, automated incident response, and continuous security monitoring. For example, AI-driven antivirus software can detect and neutralize malware more quickly than traditional solutions, while AI-enabled firewalls can dynamically adjust to new and evolving threats (Holland, 2020).

The integration of AI into cybersecurity products will not only enhance their effectiveness but also reduce the need for manual intervention. This will allow organizations to respond to threats more rapidly and with greater precision, ultimately leading to stronger and more resilient security postures.

6. ETHICAL AND PRIVACY CONCERNS

As AI becomes more deeply integrated into cybersecurity practices, ethical and privacy concerns will become increasingly prominent. AI systems that monitor and analyze user behavior, for example, may collect and process vast amounts of personal data. This raises significant questions about how this data is used, stored, and protected (Floridi et al., 2018).

Ensuring that AI-driven cybersecurity solutions comply with privacy regulations and ethical standards will be critical. Organizations must be transparent about their use of AI, implement robust data governance practices, and ensure that they are not infringing on individual privacy rights. This will be essential for maintaining public trust and avoiding legal and reputational risks.

7.   ADVERSARIAL AI AND THE ARMS RACE

As AI becomes more prevalent in cybersecurity, cybercriminals are likely to adopt AI techniques to enhance their attacks. Adversarial AI, where malicious actors use AI to evade detection or launch more sophisticated attacks, will present a significant challenge to cybersecurity professionals (Goodfellow et al., 2015). This development could lead to an arms race between defenders and attackers, with each side seeking to outmaneuver the other using increasingly advanced AI technologies.

To stay ahead of adversarial AI, organizations will need to invest in cutting-edge AI research and development, collaborate with industry partners to share threat intelligence, and adopt innovative defense strategies that can adapt to the evolving threat landscape.

8.   REGULATORY AND COMPLIANCE IMPLICATIONS

The integration of AI into cybersecurity practices will have significant regulatory and compliance implications. Governments and regulatory bodies will need to establish clear guidelines and standards for the use of AI in security, including requirements for transparency, accountability, and data protection (Voigt & Von dem Bussche, 2017).

Organizations will need to navigate these regulations carefully to ensure that their AI-driven cybersecurity measures comply with legal and ethical standards. Failure to do so could result in severe legal consequences and damage to their reputation. Additionally, as regulations evolve, organizations will need to be agile and adaptable, continuously updating their practices to remain in compliance.

9. COLLABORATION BETWEEN HUMANS AND AI

The future of AI and cybersecurity will be defined by the collaboration between human experts and AI systems. While AI can automate many tasks and provide valuable insights, human expertise will remain essential for making strategic decisions, interpreting complex data, and responding to sophisticated threats (Siau & Wang, 2018).

Cybersecurity professionals will need to develop new skills to work effectively with AI, including understanding how AI algorithms function, how to interpret AI-generated insights, and how to leverage AI tools to enhance their decision-making processes. This collaboration will lead to a more dynamic and resilient cybersecurity landscape, where human and AI capabilities complement each other.

10. THE RISE OF QUANTUM COMPUTING

Quantum computing is poised to have a profound impact on both AI and cybersecurity. Quantum computers, with their ability to perform complex calculations at unprecedented speeds, could potentially break current encryption methods, posing a significant threat to data security (Shor, 1994). However, quantum computing also offers opportunities to develop new cryptographic techniques and enhance AI capabilities.

To prepare for the advent of quantum computing, organizations will need to invest in quantum-safe encryption methods and explore how quantum AI can bolster their cybersecurity defenses. This will involve not only technical advancements but also a strategic shift in how organizations approach security in the quantum era.

PREPARING FOR FUTURE CHALLENGES IN AI SECURITY

As artificial intelligence (AI) becomes increasingly integrated into various aspects of our lives, ensuring its security becomes paramount. AI security is a complex and evolving field that requires a proactive approach to identify and mitigate potential risks. Here we will explore the challenges in AI security and provides insights into how individuals, organizations, and governments can prepare for these future challenges.

1. ## UNDERSTANDING AI VULNERABILITIES

    AI systems, like any other technology, are not immune to vulnerabilities. These vulnerabilities can arise from various factors, including software bugs, insufficient training data, and biases in algorithms. Understanding the nature of these vulnerabilities is the first step in preparing for future AI security challenges. For instance, adversarial attacks, where malicious actors manipulate input data to deceive AI models, are a significant threat. By studying these vulnerabilities, we can develop more robust AI systems that are resistant to such attacks.

2. ## DEVELOPING ROBUST AI MODELS

    Building robust AI models that can withstand attacks and function reliably under various conditions is crucial. This involves using techniques such as adversarial training, where AI models are trained on both clean and adversarial examples to improve their resilience. Additionally, ensuring that AI models are interpretable and transparent can help in identifying and addressing potential security issues. Researchers and developers must focus on creating AI systems that are not only accurate but also secure and reliable.

3.   IMPLEMENTING COMPREHENSIVE SECURITY MEASURES

To protect AI systems, comprehensive security measures must be implemented. This includes securing the data used to train AI models, safeguarding the AI infrastructure, and ensuring that AI algorithms are free from biases. Data security is particularly important as AI models rely heavily on large datasets for training. Protecting this data from breaches and ensuring its integrity is essential. Additionally, employing encryption, access controls, and regular security audits can help in safeguarding AI systems.

4.   CONTINUOUS MONITORING AND THREAT DETECTION

Continuous monitoring and threat detection are vital for maintaining AI security. AI systems should be monitored in real-time to detect any unusual activity or potential security breaches. Implementing AI-powered security solutions can enhance the ability to detect and respond to threats promptly. These solutions can analyze patterns and anomalies, providing early warnings of potential attacks. Continuous monitoring also involves regularly updating AI models to address new vulnerabilities and threats.

5.   ADDRESSING ETHICAL AND PRIVACY CONCERNS

The use of AI raises significant ethical and privacy concerns. Ensuring that AI systems respect user privacy and operate ethically is crucial for gaining public trust and avoiding legal issues. This involves implementing privacy-preserving techniques, such as differential privacy, to protect sensitive data. Additionally, establishing ethical guidelines for AI development and deployment can help in addressing concerns related to bias, fairness, and transparency. Organizations must prioritize ethical considerations in their AI strategies to ensure responsible use of AI technology.

6. **DRIVING COLLABORATION AND INFORMATION SHARING**

Collaboration and information sharing are essential for tackling AI security challenges. By sharing knowledge, best practices, and threat intelligence, organizations can better prepare for and respond to security incidents. Collaborative efforts between industry, academia, and government can drive innovation in AI security and promote the development of standardized security protocols. Establishing platforms for information sharing and collaboration can enhance the collective defense against AI-related threats.

7. **INVESTING IN AI SECURITY RESEARCH AND DEVELOPMENT**

Investing in research and development (R&D) is crucial for advancing AI security. Governments, private organizations, and academic institutions should allocate resources to AI security R&D to explore new security techniques and technologies. This includes developing advanced encryption methods, creating secure AI frameworks, and researching ways to mitigate emerging threats. By investing in R&D, we can stay ahead of adversaries and ensure the continuous improvement of AI security measures.

8. **BUILDING A SKILLED AI SECURITY WORKFORCE**

A skilled workforce is essential for addressing AI security challenges. There is a growing demand for professionals with expertise in both AI and cybersecurity. Educational institutions and training programs should focus on developing curricula that cover AI security concepts and practices. Additionally, organizations should invest in ongoing training and professional development for their employees to keep them updated on the latest AI security trends and techniques. Building a pipeline of skilled AI security professionals is critical for maintaining a robust defense against AI-related threats.

9. **ESTABLISHING REGULATORY FRAMEWORKS**

Regulatory frameworks play a significant role in ensuring AI security. Governments must establish clear regulations and standards for the development and deployment of AI systems. These regulations should address security, privacy, and ethical considerations, providing guidelines for organizations to follow. Regulatory frameworks can also promote accountability and transparency in AI development, ensuring that AI systems are designed and used responsibly. By establishing and enforcing regulations, governments can help mitigate the risks associated with AI technology.

10. **PREPARING FOR FUTURE THREATS**

The landscape of AI security is constantly evolving, with new threats emerging regularly. Organizations must adopt a proactive approach to prepare for future threats. This involves conducting regular risk assessments, staying informed about the latest security trends, and implementing adaptive security measures. Scenario planning and simulation exercises can help organizations anticipate potential security incidents and develop effective response strategies. By preparing for future threats, organizations can enhance their resilience and reduce the impact of security breaches.

QUESTIONS PEOPLE ASK ABOUT THE FUTURE OF AI

1. **WHICH IS HARDER, AI OR CYBER SECURITY?**

The difficulty of AI versus cybersecurity largely depends on the specific aspects being compared and the individual's background. Generally, AI involves more complex mathematics, programming, and understanding of algorithms, particularly in areas like machine learning, neural networks, and deep learning. These require a solid foundation in advanced mathematics (such as linear algebra, calculus, and statistics) and programming skills.

Cybersecurity, on the other hand, tends to be more accessible to beginners. It covers a wide range of topics, from network security and ethical hacking to policy and compliance. The learning curve in cybersecurity can be steep, especially in specialized areas like cryptography or advanced threat detection, but the entry-level concepts are often easier to grasp without a deep background in mathematics or programming.

Overall, AI might be considered more challenging due to its reliance on advanced mathematical concepts and algorithm development, whereas cybersecurity offers a more straightforward entry point but can become equally complex at higher levels.

2. WHAT ARE THE TRENDS FOR ARTIFICIAL INTELLIGENCE IN 2025?

By 2025, artificial intelligence is expected to be integrated deeply into many facets of daily life and industry. Some key trends include:

💡 **Smart Cities:** AI will play a crucial role in optimizing urban infrastructure. It will manage traffic flow, reduce energy consumption, and improve public safety through advanced surveillance and predictive policing techniques.

💡 **AI in Healthcare:** Personalized medicine will advance significantly, with AI algorithms analyzing patient data to recommend tailored treatments and identify potential health issues before they become critical.

💡 **AI in Education:** AI-driven platforms will provide personalized learning experiences, adapting to students' individual needs and pacing, thereby enhancing the education process.

- 💡 **AI Ethics and Regulation:** As AI becomes more pervasive, there will be a stronger focus on developing ethical frameworks and regulations to ensure AI is used responsibly, with fairness, transparency, and accountability.

- 💡 **AI and Automation:** The automation of complex tasks, from manufacturing to administrative work, will accelerate, leading to more efficient operations but also raising concerns about job displacement.

3. WHAT ARE THE CHALLENGES BROUGHT BY THE ADVANCEMENT OF AI IN TECHNOLOGY?

The rapid advancement of AI introduces several challenges:

- 💡 **Ethical Considerations:** AI raises important ethical questions, particularly in areas like decision-making, bias, and fairness. Ensuring that AI systems do not perpetuate or exacerbate societal inequalities is a significant challenge.

- 💡 **Transparency and Explainability:** As AI systems become more complex, understanding how they arrive at certain decisions becomes more difficult. This lack of transparency can lead to trust issues and complicates accountability.

- 💡 **Privacy Concerns:** AI systems often require vast amounts of data, raising concerns about how this data is collected, stored, and used. Protecting user privacy while still enabling AI to function effectively is a delicate balance.

- 💡 **Security Vulnerabilities:** AI systems themselves can become targets for cyberattacks. Ensuring the security of AI systems, especially those integrated into critical infrastructure, is a major challenge.

- 💡 **Regulatory Challenges:** The pace of AI development often outstrips the ability of regulatory frameworks to keep up, leading to gaps in oversight that could allow harmful applications to proliferate.

4. HOW TO MAKE AI MORE SECURE?

Making AI more secure involves several strategies:

- **Continuous Monitoring and Improvement:** AI systems must be continuously monitored for vulnerabilities and updated to address new security threats. This includes regularly retraining models on fresh data to ensure they adapt to evolving threats.

- **Collaboration and Regulation:** Collaboration between industry, academia, and government is essential to developing robust security standards and regulations. This collective effort can help ensure that AI systems are designed and deployed with security in mind from the outset.

- **Robust Testing:** Implementing rigorous testing protocols for AI systems, including adversarial testing, can help identify and mitigate potential vulnerabilities before they are exploited.

- **Explainable AI:** Developing AI systems that are transparent and explainable can help identify security flaws and ensure that the systems behave as expected.

5. WHAT ARE THE DISADVANTAGES OF AI IN SECURITY?

AI in security, while powerful, comes with several disadvantages:

- **False Positives and Negatives:** AI systems can sometimes misidentify threats, either by falsely flagging benign activities as malicious (false positives) or by missing actual threats (false negatives). This can lead to inefficiencies and potential security risks.

- **Over-Reliance and Skills Gap:** Over-reliance on AI could lead to complacency among cybersecurity professionals, who may trust AI outputs without sufficient scrutiny. Additionally, there is a skills gap in understanding and managing AI-driven security tools, which can limit their effectiveness.

💡 **Cost Factor:** Developing, implementing, and maintaining AI systems can be expensive. The cost of integrating AI into security operations may be prohibitive for smaller organizations, limiting its accessibility.

6. WHAT IS THE FUTURE OF AI IN CYBER SECURITY?

The future of AI in cybersecurity is likely to be characterized by:

💡 **Enhanced Threat Detection:** AI will continue to improve in identifying and responding to threats in real-time, using advanced algorithms to predict and prevent cyberattacks before they occur.

💡 **Focus on Human Expertise:** While AI will automate many aspects of cybersecurity, human expertise will remain crucial. AI will augment, not replace, human decision-making, particularly in handling complex and nuanced security incidents. The collaboration between AI and human cybersecurity professionals will create more robust and resilient defense systems.

7. CAN AI REPLACE HUMAN INTELLIGENCE?

AI cannot replace human intelligence, as it fundamentally depends on humans for its development and operation. AI excels at processing large amounts of data, identifying patterns, and automating routine tasks, but it lacks the ability to understand context, make value judgments, or possess the creativity and emotional intelligence inherent to humans.

Human intelligence encompasses a broad range of cognitive abilities, including critical thinking, ethical reasoning, and the capacity for abstract thought. AI can augment these abilities but cannot replicate them in their entirety. The future will likely see AI and human intelligence working together, with AI handling specific tasks while humans provide the overarching strategy, creativity, and moral guidance.

REFERENCES

Accenture. (2019) *The cost of cybercrime*. Retrieved from https://www.accenture.com/us-en/insights/security/cost-cybercrime-study

Amodei, D., Olah, C., Steinhardt, J., Christiano, P., Schulman, J., & Mané, D. (2016). *Concrete problems in AI safety*. arXiv preprint arXiv:1606.06565.

Bertino, E., Sandhu, R., & Park, J. (2005). A generalized framework for access control: Beyond RBAC and MAC. *ACM Transactions on Information and System Security (TISSEC)*, 8(1), 35-66.

Batini, C., Cappiello, C., Francalanci, C., & Maurino, A. (2009). Methodologies for data quality assessment and improvement. *ACM Computing Surveys*, 41(3), 16.

Binns, R. (2018). Fairness in machine learning: Lessons from political philosophy. *Proceedings of the 2018 Conference on Fairness, Accountability, and Transparency*, 149-159.

Bostrom, N. (2014). *Superintelligence: Paths, dangers, strategies.* Oxford University Press.

Brundage, M., Avin, S., Clark, J., Toner, H., Eckersley, P., Garfinkel, B., ... & Amodei, D. (2018). The malicious use of artificial intelligence: Forecasting, prevention, and mitigation. *arXiv preprint arXiv:1802.07228.*

Cath, C. (2018). Governing artificial intelligence: Ethical, legal, and technical opportunities and challenges. *Philosophical Transactions of the Royal Society A: Mathematical, Physical and Engineering Sciences, 376*(2133), 20180080.

Codd, E. F. (1970). A relational model of data for large shared data banks. *Communications of the ACM, 13*(6), 377-387.

DAMA UK. (2013). *The six primary dimensions for data quality assessment.* DAMA UK White Paper.

Date, C. J. (2003). *An introduction to database systems* (8th ed.). Pearson Education.

Elbashir, M. Z., Collier, P. A., & Sutton, S. G. (2008). The role of organizational data quality in achieving superior performance: A research framework. *Journal of Information Systems, 22*(2), 63-89.

Elmasri, R., & Navathe, S. B. (2011). *Fundamentals of database systems* (6th ed.). Pearson Education.

Ferrucci, D., Brown, E., Chu-Carroll, J., Fan, J., Gondek, D., Kalyanpur, A. A., ... & Welty, C. (2010). Building Watson: An overview of the DeepQA project. *AI magazine, 31*(3), 59-79.

Floridi, L., Cowls, J., Beltrametti, M., Chatila, R., Chazerand, P., Dignum, V., ... & Vayena, E. (2018). AI4People—An ethical framework for a good AI society: Opportunities, risks, principles, and recommendations. *Minds and Machines, 28*(4), 689-707.

Gartner. (2020). *Customer experience and relationship management.* Retrieved from https://www.gartner.com/en/insights/customer-experience

Gartner. (2021). *The essential guide to data lifecycle management.* Retrieved from Gartner.

Goodfellow, I. J., Shlens, J., & Szegedy, C. (2015). Explaining and harnessing adversarial examples. *arXiv preprint arXiv:1412.6572.*

Haerder, T., & Reuter, A. (1983). Principles of transaction-oriented database recovery. *ACM Computing Surveys, 15*(4), 287-317.

Halamka, J. D. (2016). *The digital doctor: Hope, hype, and harm at the dawn of medicine's computer age.* McGraw-Hill Education.

International Organization for Standardization (ISO). (2013). *ISO/IEC 27001: Information Security Management.* ISO.

JPMorgan Chase. (2018). *J.P. Morgan creates digital coin for payments.* Retrieved from JPMorgan Chase.

Kaiser Permanente. (2010). *Kaiser Permanente's HealthConnect: A technology that cares.* Retrieved from Kaiser Permanente.

Kaspersky. (2020). *DDoS attacks in Q2 2020.* Retrieved from https://securelist.com/ddos-attacks-in-q2-2020/97781/

Khatri, V., & Brown, C. V. (2010). Designing data governance. *Communications of the ACM, 53*(1), 148-152.

Ladin, J. (2006). Data lifecycle management: Tackling the challenges of information growth. *Information Management Journal, 40*(3), 24-29.

Laudon, K. C., & Laudon, J. P. (2015). *Management information systems: Managing the digital firm* (14th ed.). Pearson Education.

LeCun, Y., Bengio, Y., & Hinton, G. (2015). Deep learning. *Nature, 521*(7553), 436-444.

Linden, G., Smith, B., & York, J. (2003). Amazon.com recommendations: Item-to-item collaborative filtering. *IEEE Internet Computing, 7*(1), 76-80.

McCarthy, J., Minsky, M. L., Rochester, N., & Shannon, C. E. (1955). A proposal for the Dartmouth summer research project on artificial intelligence. *AI magazine, 27*(4), 12-14.

National Institute of Standards and Technology (NIST). (2020). *NIST Special Publication 800-53: Security and Privacy Controls for Information Systems and Organizations.* NIST.

Newell, A., & Simon, H. A. (1956). The logic theorist: A model for human problem solving. *Communications of the ACM, 29*(3), 203-221.

Nguyen, T. T., Yang, X., & Armitage, G. (2018). A survey on the challenges, requirements, and future directions of machine learning applications in real-time networking. *Computer Networks, 158,* 151-168.

Olson, J. E. (2003). *Data quality: The accuracy dimension.* Morgan Kaufmann.

Papernot, N., McDaniel, P., Goodfellow, I., Jha, S., Celik, Z. B., & Swami, A. (2016). Practical black-box attacks against machine learning. *Proceedings of the 2017 ACM on Asia Conference on Computer and Communications Security,* 506-519.

Pipino, L. L., Lee, Y. W., & Wang, R. Y. (2002). Data quality assessment. *Communications of the ACM, 45*(4), 211-218.

Raji, I. D., Smart, A., White, R. N., Mitchell, M., & Gebru, T. (2020). Closing the AI accountability gap: Defining an end-to-end framework for internal algorithmic auditing. *Proceedings of the 2020 Conference on Fairness, Accountability, and Transparency.*

Rao, S. (2018). Procter & Gamble: Building a data-driven supply chain. *Harvard Business Review.* Retrieved from Harvard Business Review.

Redman, T. C. (1998). The impact of poor data quality on the typical enterprise. *Communications of the ACM, 41*(2), 79-82.

Sandhu, R. S., Coyne, E. J., Feinstein, H. L., & Youman, C. E. (1996). Role-based access control models. *IEEE Computer, 29*(2), 38-47.

Silver, D., Huang, A., Maddison, C. J., Guez, A., Sifre, L., van den Driessche, G., ... & Hassabis, D. (2016). Mastering the game of Go with deep neural networks and tree search. *Nature, 529*(7587), 484-489.

Smith, H. A. (2007). Information lifecycle management: Understanding the value of information assets. *MIS Quarterly Executive, 6*(4), 209-218.

Stone, P., Brooks, R., Brynjolfsson, E., Calo, R., Etzioni, O., Hager, G., ... & Teller, A. (2016). *Artificial Intelligence and Life in 2030*. One Hundred Year Study on Artificial Intelligence: Report of the 2015-2016 Study Panel. Stanford University.

Strong, D. M., Lee, Y. W., & Wang, R. Y. (1997). Data quality in context. *Communications of the ACM, 40*(5), 103-110.

Tallon, P. P., Ramirez, R. V., & Short, J. E. (2013). The information artifact in IT governance: Toward a theory of information governance. *Journal of Management Information Systems, 30*(3), 141-178.

Turing, A. M. (1950). Computing machinery and intelligence. *Mind, 59*(236), 433-460.

Tramèr, F., Zhang, F., Juels, A., Reiter, M. K., & Ristenpart, T. (2016). Stealing machine learning models via prediction APIs. *25th USENIX Security Symposium*, 601-618.

Veale, M., van Kleek, M., & Binns, R. (2018). Fairness and accountability design needs for algorithmic support in high-stakes public sector decision-making. *Proceedings of the 2018 CHI Conference on Human Factors in Computing Systems.*

Verizon. (2020). *2020 Data Breach Investigations Report*. Retrieved from https://www.verizon.com/business/resources/reports/dbir/

Voigt, P., & Von dem Bussche, A. (2017). *The EU General Data Protection Regulation (GDPR)*. Springer International Publishing.

Wang, R. Y., & Strong, D. M. (1996). Beyond accuracy: What data quality means to data consumers. *Journal of Management Information Systems, 12*(4), 5-33.

PECB. (n.d.). *AI risk management: ISO/IEC 42001, the EU AI Act, and ISO/IEC 23894*. PECB. https://beta.pecb.com/past-webinars/ai-risk-management-isoiec-42001-the-eu-ai-act-and-isoiec-23894/language/en

Mark Chuang | Mission Critical Magazine. https://www.missioncriticalmagazine.com/authors/2729-mark-chuang

Understanding Bone Density Tests For Women - Physio Ed.. https://physioed.com/bone-density-tests-for-women/

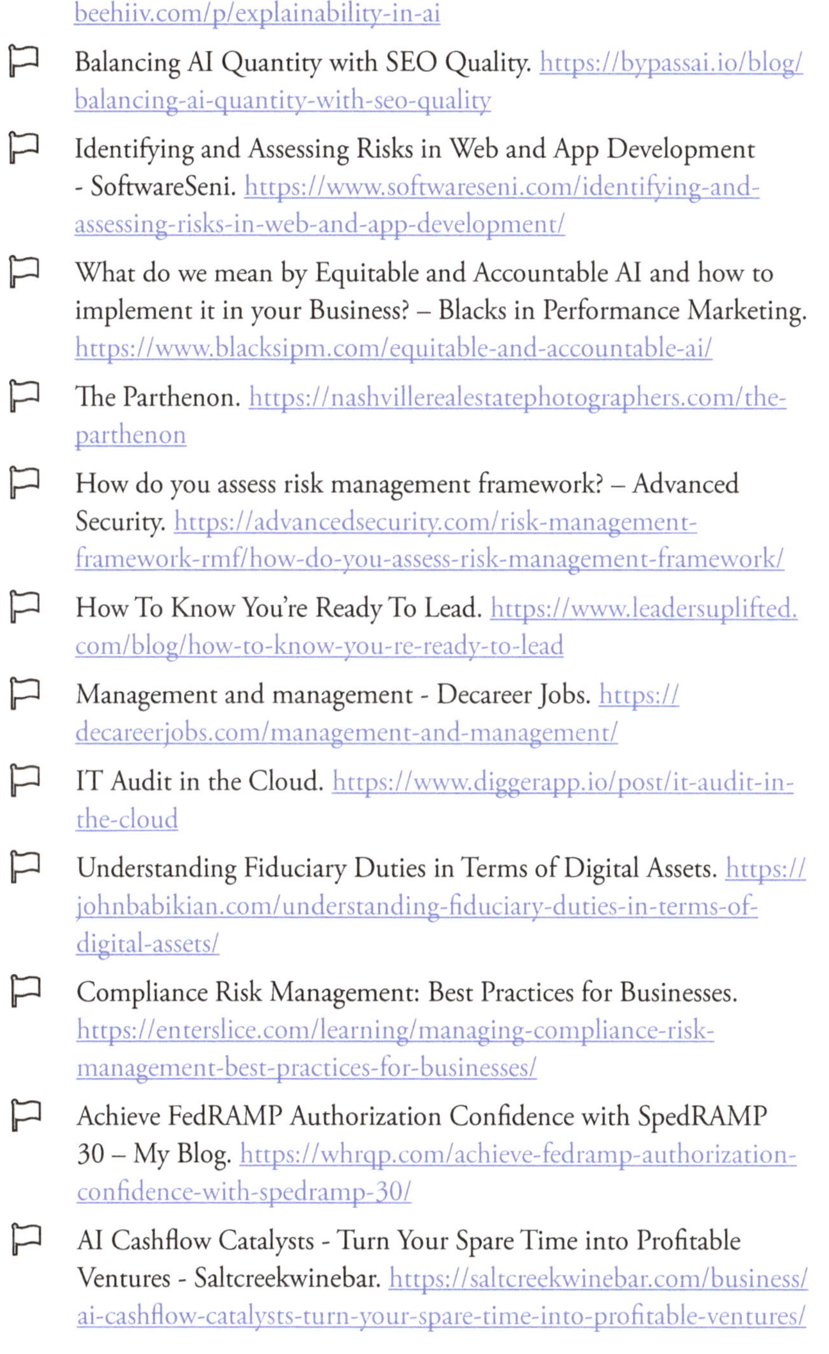

- The Path to Trust through Explainability, ptr 1. https://brainscriblr.beehiiv.com/p/explainability-in-ai

- Balancing AI Quantity with SEO Quality. https://bypassai.io/blog/balancing-ai-quantity-with-seo-quality

- Identifying and Assessing Risks in Web and App Development - SoftwareSeni. https://www.softwareseni.com/identifying-and-assessing-risks-in-web-and-app-development/

- What do we mean by Equitable and Accountable AI and how to implement it in your Business? – Blacks in Performance Marketing. https://www.blacksipm.com/equitable-and-accountable-ai/

- The Parthenon. https://nashvillerealestatephotographers.com/the-parthenon

- How do you assess risk management framework? – Advanced Security. https://advancedsecurity.com/risk-management-framework-rmf/how-do-you-assess-risk-management-framework/

- How To Know You're Ready To Lead. https://www.leadersuplifted.com/blog/how-to-know-you-re-ready-to-lead

- Management and management - Decareer Jobs. https://decareerjobs.com/management-and-management/

- IT Audit in the Cloud. https://www.diggerapp.io/post/it-audit-in-the-cloud

- Understanding Fiduciary Duties in Terms of Digital Assets. https://johnbabikian.com/understanding-fiduciary-duties-in-terms-of-digital-assets/

- Compliance Risk Management: Best Practices for Businesses. https://enterslice.com/learning/managing-compliance-risk-management-best-practices-for-businesses/

- Achieve FedRAMP Authorization Confidence with SpedRAMP 30 – My Blog. https://whrqp.com/achieve-fedramp-authorization-confidence-with-spedramp-30/

- AI Cashflow Catalysts - Turn Your Spare Time into Profitable Ventures - Saltcreekwinebar. https://saltcreekwinebar.com/business/ai-cashflow-catalysts-turn-your-spare-time-into-profitable-ventures/

Harnessing the Power of Self-Dispersed Pigment Dispersing Agents in Water-Based Inkjet Printers, Water Based Inkjet Printer Self Dispersed Pigment Dispersing Agents, made in china - Aqueous Inkjet Colorants. https://www.aqueousinkjetcolorants.com/harnessing-the-power-of-self-dispersed-pigment-dispersing-agents-in-water-based-inkjet-printers-water-based-inkjet-printer-self-dispersed-pigment-dispersing-agents-made-in-china/

development - Tanel Teemusk • Tech Lead and iOS Developer. https://teemusk.com/tag/development/

Risk Analyses. https://proeu.pl/?page_id=285

(2022). Estonia : Estonia has proven itself as a strong space country in the European Space Agency. MENA Report, (), .

Cybersecurity | Invictus. https://www.invictusic.com/solutions/cyber-ops

McGeough, J. (2012). Semiconductor optical amplifiers to extend the reach of passive optical networks. https://core.ac.uk/download/293042383.pdf

Blog Automation: Leveraging AI for Personalization – Spreadbot Blog. https://spreadbot.ai/blog/blog-automation-leveraging-ai-for-personalization/

Future Leader perspectives: risk management | The Association of Corporate Treasurers. https://www.treasurers.org/hub/blog/future-leader-perspectives-risk-management

What is risk management? How to mitigate the risk? - Prime One Community. https://engage.primeone.global/question/what-is-risk-management-how-to-mitigate-the-risk/answer/17833/

Introduction to the RMF – Cyber-Recon. https://www.cyber-recon.com/introduction-to-the-rmf/

How to Develop a Comprehensive Risk Management Strategy - ecoharvests. https://ecoharvests.uk/how-to-develop-a-comprehensive-risk-management-strategy

What is risk management? How to mitigate the risk? - Prime One Community. https://engage.primeone.global/question/what-is-risk-management-how-to-mitigate-the-risk/answer/17833/

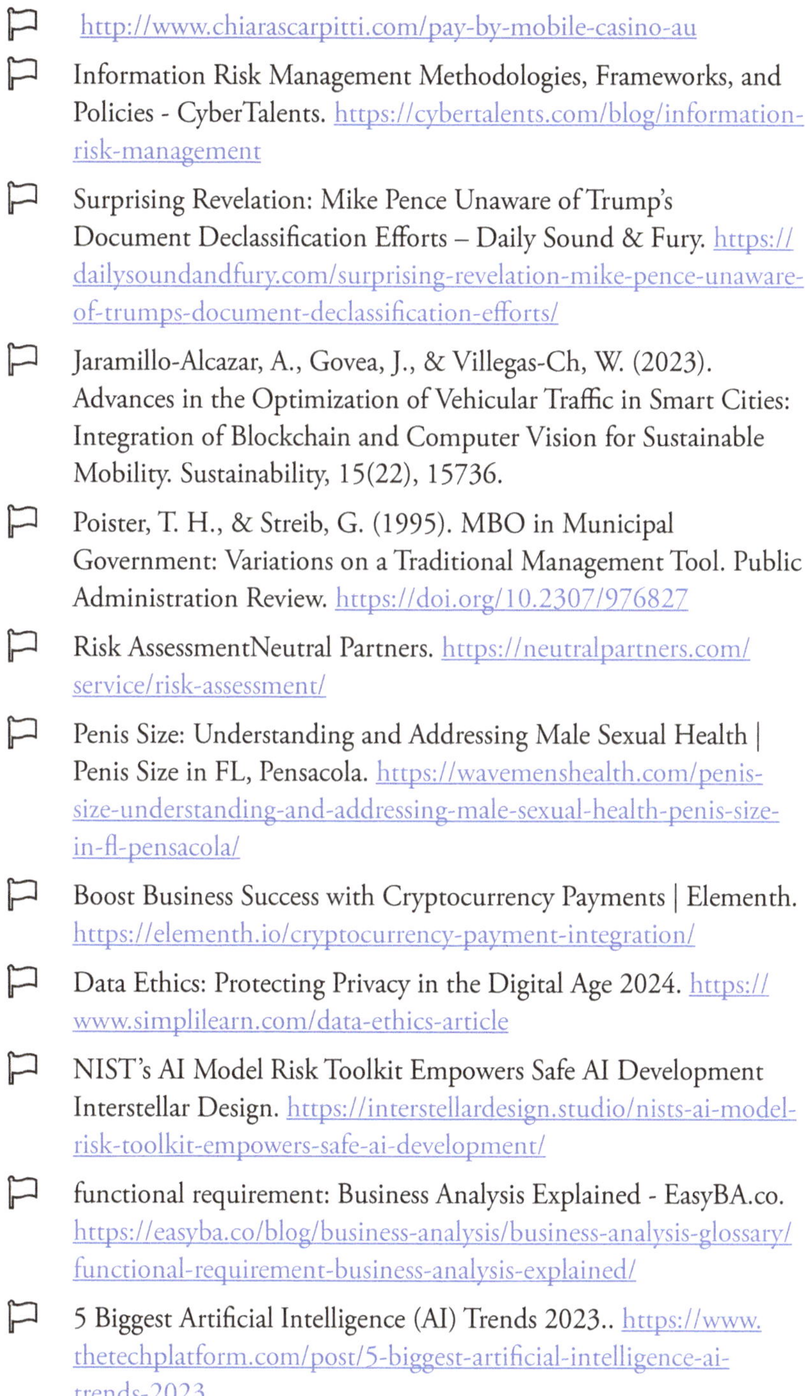

http://www.chiarascarpitti.com/pay-by-mobile-casino-au

Information Risk Management Methodologies, Frameworks, and Policies - CyberTalents. https://cybertalents.com/blog/information-risk-management

Surprising Revelation: Mike Pence Unaware of Trump's Document Declassification Efforts – Daily Sound & Fury. https://dailysoundandfury.com/surprising-revelation-mike-pence-unaware-of-trumps-document-declassification-efforts/

Jaramillo-Alcazar, A., Govea, J., & Villegas-Ch, W. (2023). Advances in the Optimization of Vehicular Traffic in Smart Cities: Integration of Blockchain and Computer Vision for Sustainable Mobility. Sustainability, 15(22), 15736.

Poister, T. H., & Streib, G. (1995). MBO in Municipal Government: Variations on a Traditional Management Tool. Public Administration Review. https://doi.org/10.2307/976827

Risk AssessmentNeutral Partners. https://neutralpartners.com/service/risk-assessment/

Penis Size: Understanding and Addressing Male Sexual Health | Penis Size in FL, Pensacola. https://wavemenshealth.com/penis-size-understanding-and-addressing-male-sexual-health-penis-size-in-fl-pensacola/

Boost Business Success with Cryptocurrency Payments | Elementh. https://elementh.io/cryptocurrency-payment-integration/

Data Ethics: Protecting Privacy in the Digital Age 2024. https://www.simplilearn.com/data-ethics-article

NIST's AI Model Risk Toolkit Empowers Safe AI Development Interstellar Design. https://interstellardesign.studio/nists-ai-model-risk-toolkit-empowers-safe-ai-development/

functional requirement: Business Analysis Explained - EasyBA.co. https://easyba.co/blog/business-analysis/business-analysis-glossary/functional-requirement-business-analysis-explained/

5 Biggest Artificial Intelligence (AI) Trends 2023.. https://www.thetechplatform.com/post/5-biggest-artificial-intelligence-ai-trends-2023

⚑ HTuition - Business honours. https://www.htuition.com/blogdetail/ai

⚑ Xu, Y. (2023). The Quality Evaluation of College Students' Innovation and Entrepreneurship Education based on Grey Correlation Algorithm. https://doi.org/10.1109/icdcece57866.2023.10151251

⚑ Leveraging AI and Big Data in Credit Marketing: A Game-Changer for Financial Institutions - Micronotes. https://micronotes.ai/leveraging-ai-and-big-data-in-credit-marketing-a-game-changer-for-financial-institutions/

⚑ Mastering Life with Plansm: Your Ultimate Guide. https://www.plansm.pro/2024/07/mastering-life-with-plansm-your.html

⚑ Johnson, J. M. (2013). A DIFFERENT WORLD: AFRICAN AMERICAN, FIRST GENERATION COLLEGE WOMEN AT A SELECTIVE UNIVERSITY. https://core.ac.uk/download/56111015.pdf

⚑ Business Assessment and Risk Management - BusinessThink. https://ec2-13-235-236-240.ap-south-1.compute.amazonaws.com/business-assessment-and-risk-management/

⚑ AI Chatbots in Banking: 5 Tips to Monitor Effectiveness - Bridgeforce. https://bridgeforce.com/insights/ai-chatbots-in-banking-5-tips-to-monitor-effectiveness/

⚑ The Ethical AI Conundrum: Balancing Progress with Humanity. https://www.exaputra.com/2023/12/the-ethical-ai-conundrum-balancing.html

⚑ Unravelling the Reasons: Why Tech Startups Often Fail | Hiyield. https://hiyield.co.uk/blog/unravelling-the-reasons-why-tech-startups-often-fail/

⚑ The Costs of Virtual Annual General Meetings: Legal and Regulatory Compliance. https://blog.lumiglobal.com/the-costs-of-virtual-annual-general-meetings-legal-and-regulatory-compliance

⚑ Data Protection Framework | Docstack. https://www.docstack.com/gdpr-framework

- How Udemy's New Generative AI Tool is Steering the Transition to a Skills-Based Economy | Built In. https://builtin.com/articles/how-udemys-new-generative-ai-tool-steering-transition-skills-based-economy

- Find your Forex entry point: three entry strategies to try | IG AE - Best Forex Rebates. https://www.zxrqghpl.com/forexsignals/Find-your-Forex-entry-point-three-entry-strategies-to-try-IG-AE

- How To Address Resignation Letter, Like A Boss Just Resignation Letters. https://www.resign.ai/resignation-letter/how-to-address-resignation-letter/

- Corporate Governance Audits: The Key to Ensuring Ethical Business Practices and Long-Term Success - Bellmac Consulting LLP. https://bellmacconsulting.com/corporate-governance-audits-the-key-to-ensuring-ethical-business-practices-and-long-term-success/

- Risk Assessment And Management In Military DecisionMaking. https://militaryspouseafcpe.org/military-leadership-and-training/decision-making/risk-assessment-and-management/

- The Role of Data Governance in Managing Business Information Assets. https://www.techinsightscorner.com/2023/07/the-role-of-data-governance-in-managing.html

- Business Risk Advisory – Hamid Raza Blog. https://biztaxadvisor.com/business-risk-advisory/

- Are There Any Penalties for Not Maintaining an Asbestos Register?. https://ahiasbestos.com.au/are-there-any-penalties-for-not-maintaining-an-asbestos-register/

- AI in Cybersecurity: Opportunities, Risks, and Solutions – Bugbounter. https://bugbounter.com/ai-in-cybersecurity-opportunities-risks-and-solutions/

- Navigating the Ethical Landscape: A Closer Look at Hiring Practices - https://magizinesnews.com/. https://magizinesnews.com/ethics-in-hiring-employees/

Waiswa, E. (2024). Exploring the challenges and opportunities of digital transformation in media organizations: A case of nation media group Uganda. https://core.ac.uk/download/613050913.pdf

How to Automate Third-Party Cyber Risk Management — ZenGRC. https://reciprocity.com/blog/how-to-automate-third-party-cyber-risk-management/

Demystifying Artificial Intelligence: A Comprehensive Guide. https://www.financialguru.in/2023/10/demystifying-artificial-intelligence.html

GenAI and AI in Engineering: Distilling Hype From Reality. https://www.mabl.com/blog/genai-and-ai-in-engineering-distilling-hype-from-reality

Navigating the Ethical Landscape: A Deep Dive into Ethics in AI - Kafkai. https://kafkai.com/en/blog/navigating-the-ethical-landscape-a-deep-dive-into-ethics-in-ai/

Yampolskiy, R. Unmonitorability of Artificial Intelligence. https://core.ac.uk/download/571211457.pdf

Leveraging AI for Risk Management: Benefits and Applications. https://autonomixsolutions.com/financial-planning-analysis/leveraging-ai-for-enhanced-risk-management/

Unravelling the Reasons: Why Tech Startups Often Fail | Hiyield. https://hiyield.co.uk/blog/unravelling-the-reasons-why-tech-startups-often-fail/

financial community Archives - Data Management Blog - Data Integration and Modern Data Management Articles, Analysis and Information. https://www.datamanagementblog.com/tag/financial-community/

ES Machinery - EcoSourcen. https://www.ecosourcen.eu/en/category/es-machinery/

Rolling the Dice: The Highs and Lows of Gambling - eglise-stjoseph-roubaix.org. https://www.eglise-stjoseph-roubaix.org/rolling-the-dice-the-highs-and-lows-of-gambling-3/

Unlocking the Potential: Which AI is Best for Your Business? – Exploring Infinite Innovations in the Digital World. https://www.mustardseed.co.jp/unlocking-the-potential-which-ai-is-best-for-your-business/

. https://thecodework.com/blog/top-10-ai-based-startup-ideas-you-cannot-miss/

Building Trust in AI Ethics. https://redresscompliance.com/building-trust-in-ai-a-guide-to-ethical-considerations/

Ofek, N., Ofek, N., & Maimon, O. (2023). Beyond Metrics: Navigating AI through Sustainable Paradigms. Sustainability, 15(24), 16789.

Algomox Blog | The future of AIOps and its potential impact on the IT industry. https://www.algomox.com/resources/blog/aiops-and-adoption/

Ownership and Control Ethical Dimensions of Community Solar Projects. http://usenergyswitch.com/ownership-and-control-ethical-dimensions-of-community-solar-projects/

Consultancy for Maritime Port Solutions | KodeEnd IT Solutions. https://www.kodeend.com/en/consultation/consultancy-for-maritime-port-solutions

NIST Artificial Intelligence Risk Management Framework - Kraft Kennedy. https://www.kraftkennedy.com/nist-artificial-intelligence-risk-management-framework/

Procure fiber laser 50w from China Leading fiber laser 50w Supplier,Comprehensive Guide on Quality, Pricing, and Sourcing. https://www.sourcifychina.com/fiber-laser-50w/

Reduced Salt Food Products Market Size, Share, Growth, Statistics Report 2033. https://datahorizzonresearch.com/reduced-salt-food-products-market-8332

Jain, M. (2023). Artificial intelligence: A powerful ally in elevating the productivity and quality of research for aspiring scholars. International Journal of Multidisciplinary Trends. https://doi.org/10.22271/multi.2023.v5.i7a.314

Usher, C. A. (2023). The Ripple Effect: How One Rural School Can Embrace Indigenous Learning on a Journey Towards Truth and Reconciliation. https://core.ac.uk/download/588591695.pdf

5 Tips for Setting Up AI Use Rules at Your Business - Data First Solutions. https://dfcanada.com/2024/02/27/setting-up-ai-use-rules/

Security in AI development: An overview. https://www.leewayhertz.com/security-in-ai-development/

Dlamini, Z. S. (2016). Creating resilient state-owned enterprise using Enterprise Performance Framework and high-value knowledge employees : The case of Dube TradePort Corporation in KwaZulu-Natal. https://core.ac.uk/download/196549239.pdf

Training A Stable Diffusion Model - Vector Linux. https://vectorlinux.com/training-a-stable-diffusion-model/

Mishra, P., & Singh, G. (2023). Energy Management Systems in Sustainable Smart Cities Based on the Internet of Energy: A Technical Review. Energies, 16(19), 6903.

Albasheir, K. A. M. A. (2023). The Impact of IT on Insurance of the Technological Industry. https://core.ac.uk/download/588567004.pdf

Gupta, S., Alharbi, F., Alharbi, F., Alshahrani, R., Arya, P., Vyas, S., & Elkamchouchi, D. (2023). Secure and Lightweight Authentication Protocol for Privacy Preserving Communications in Smart City Applications. Sustainability, 15(6), 5346.

Apata, O., Bokoro, P., & Sharma, G. (2023). The Risks and Challenges of Electric Vehicle Integration into Smart Cities. Energies, 16(14), 5274.

Irene, G. (2023). The Influence Of Personalized Ads On E-Commerce Applications In Indonesia On User Satisfaction. Journal Research of Social Science, Economics, and Management. https://doi.org/10.59141/jrssem.v3i1.524

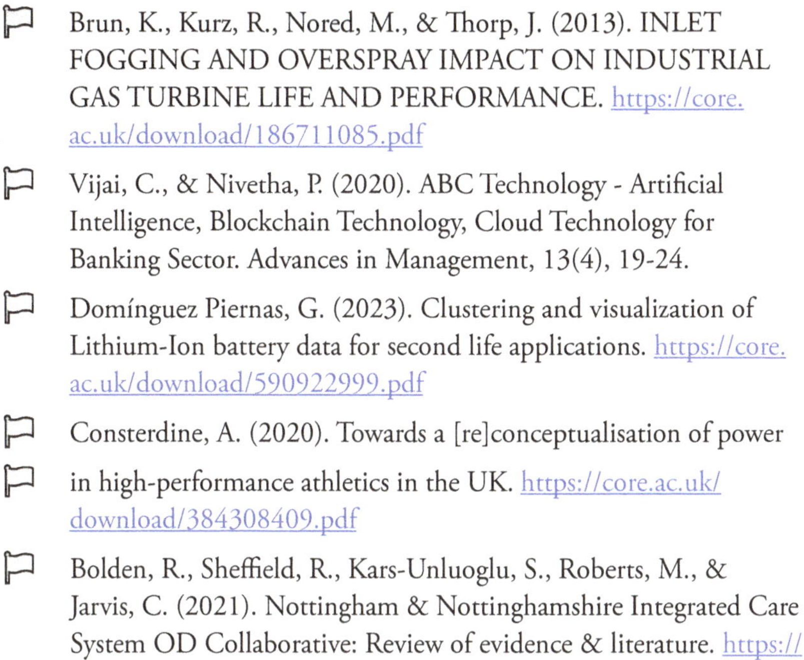

Brun, K., Kurz, R., Nored, M., & Thorp, J. (2013). INLET FOGGING AND OVERSPRAY IMPACT ON INDUSTRIAL GAS TURBINE LIFE AND PERFORMANCE. https://core.ac.uk/download/186711085.pdf

Vijai, C., & Nivetha, P. (2020). ABC Technology - Artificial Intelligence, Blockchain Technology, Cloud Technology for Banking Sector. Advances in Management, 13(4), 19-24.

Domínguez Piernas, G. (2023). Clustering and visualization of Lithium-Ion battery data for second life applications. https://core.ac.uk/download/590922999.pdf

Consterdine, A. (2020). Towards a [re]conceptualisation of power

in high-performance athletics in the UK. https://core.ac.uk/download/384308409.pdf

Bolden, R., Sheffield, R., Kars-Unluoglu, S., Roberts, M., & Jarvis, C. (2021). Nottingham & Nottinghamshire Integrated Care System OD Collaborative: Review of evidence & literature. https://core.ac.uk/download/479373110.pdf

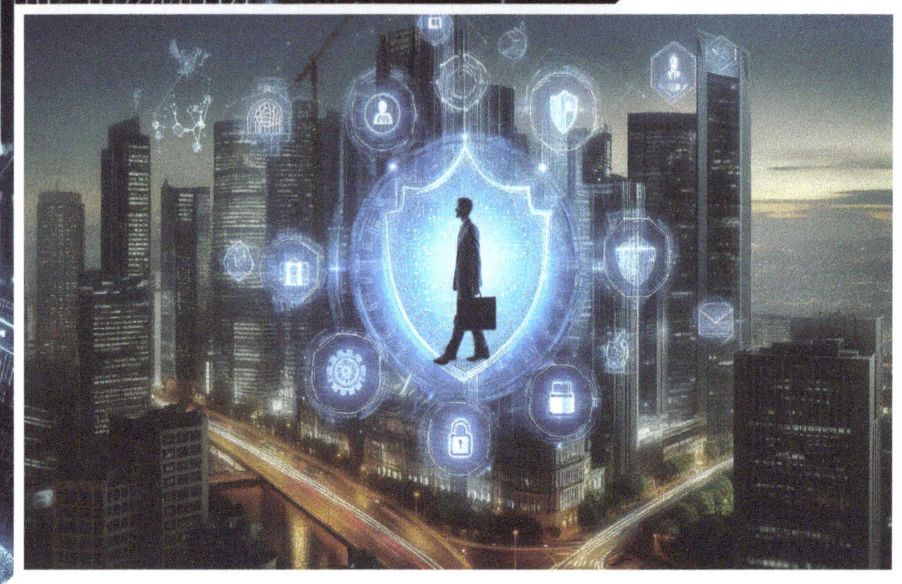

ABOUT THE AUTHOR

Tolulope Michael is a seasoned expert in cybersecurity, bringing years of experience across various roles and organizations to his work. As a passionate educator and mentor, he has dedicated his career to helping individuals acquire the skills and knowledge needed to thrive in cybersecurity. Tolulope's deep understanding of the field is evident in the pages of this book, where he distills his extensive experience into practical guidance for readers.

In addition to his contributions to cybersecurity, Tolulope is a successful entrepreneur with businesses spanning multiple industries. His diverse professional background gives him a unique perspective on the intersection of technology, security, and business strategy. This multifaceted experience informs not only his approach to cybersecurity but also his broader outlook on innovation and risk management.

Tolulope is also the author of several other books that explore various aspects of cybersecurity and technology. His clear and accessible writing style has made complex topics understandable to a wide audience, from students and professionals to those simply interested in the field. In this book, Tolulope provides a comprehensive roadmap for anyone looking to enter or advance in the cybersecurity industry, offering actionable advice and insights that are grounded in real-world experience.

www.ingramcontent.com/pod-product-compliance
Lightning Source LLC
Chambersburg PA
CBHW040131160726
48006CB00014B/1454